SOUTHERN
PROVISIONS

SOUTHERN PROVISIONS

*The Creation & Revival
of a Cuisine*

DAVID S. SHIELDS

The University of Chicago Press
Chicago and London

DAVID S. SHIELDS is the McClintock Professor of Southern Letters at the University of South Carolina and chairman of the Carolina Gold Rice Foundation. His other books include *Still: American Silent Motion Picture Photography*, also published by the University of Chicago Press.

The University of Chicago Press, Chicago 60637
The University of Chicago Press, Ltd., London
© 2015 by The University of Chicago
All rights reserved. Published 2015.
Printed in the United States of America

24 23 22 21 20 19 18 17 16 15   1 2 3 4 5

ISBN-13: 978-0-226-14111-4 (cloth)
ISBN-13: 978-0-226-14125-1 (e-book)
DOI: 10.7208/chicago/9780226141251.001.0001

The interior illustrations are by Lauren Nassef.

Library of Congress Cataloging-in-Publication Data
Shields, David S., 1951– author.
Southern provisions: the creation and revival of a cuisine /
David S. Shields.
pages cm
Includes bibliographical references and index.
ISBN 978-0-226-14111-4 (cloth: alkaline paper)—
ISBN 0-226-14111-X (cloth: alkaline paper)—
ISBN 978-0-226-14125-1 (e-book)—
ISBN 0-226-14125-X (e-book)
1. Cooking, American—Southern style—History. 2. Gastronomy—
Southern States—History. 3. Cooking—Southern States—
History. I. Title.
TX633.S55 2015
641.5975—dc23
2014034899

♾ This paper meets the requirements of ANSI/NISO Z39.48-1992
(Permanence of Paper)

For Glenn Roberts

CONTENTS

PREFACE

Southern food, like Italian food, is a universally recognized category; yet to a southerner, like an Italian, it doesn't much look like a single category in terms of understanding what he or she eats on a regular basis. What matters is the *region* within the South—Tidewater, Lowcountry, Appalachian, Gulf Coast, Louisiana, Bluegrass, or Texas. While all of these regions may share some ingredients and foodways, each has evolved distinctive foods and practices that have become enduring signatures of local identity. Cookbooks have long recognized these regions of the South, offering recipes somehow characteristic of the cooking of the various places. Yet how these places came to be separate modes of southern cuisine and what agricultural, horticultural, and culinary histories enabled their emergence have rarely been addressed adequately. Only Louisiana among the different regions has nourished a community of historians that elucidates its legacies. Until recently, most places have been content to know their food heritage through culinary folklore.

That changed in 1999, when John Egerton convened the Southern Foodways Alliance (SFA) to document and celebrate the diverse cultures at play in southern food. In the past fifteen years, the SFA (of which I am a member) has undertaken a heroic effort to call attention to the distinctive qualities of southern cuisines through film, oral history, and events featuring significant practitioners of regional foodways. Since 1999, the SFA has celebrated vernacular cookery (whether home cooking, artisanal production of products, or local eateries), highlighting stories told by the growers, harvesters, processors, cooks, and consumers. It has also greatly concerned itself with matters of social justice in the region.

What the SFA has *not* undertaken is any large-scale history of any locale. It has not engaged with the extensive written record treating fields, gardens, and cookhouses from colonial times to the present, and it has not explored in any systematic way the profession of cookery or considered the greatest creations of these professional masters. This book is an experiment in bringing all of these back into our understanding of what the heritage of southern food entails, and to see what it means in the effort to improve the quality of what we eat hereabouts.

Egerton's ideal was to celebrate "the now"; historical understanding gives rise to other sentiments. In the Lowcountry of South Carolina, for example, it has inspired distress that the signature rice dishes found in its cookbooks could not be adequately enjoyed because the rice that inspired them — Carolina Gold rice — was no longer grown, and the delicious rice-birds that fed on the old rice fields cannot now be roasted because habitat destruction has endangered them.

History happens quickly now. Traditional practices of planting, processing, and cooking are supplanted by industrial agriculture and fast food. Old presumptions about food quality — for instance, that local soil and local water inflect taste — are pushed aside by agronomic directives, such as the notion that *anything* can be grown *anywhere* with the proper genetic adjustment and chemical supplementation, or the public's willingness to pass on taste if food is cheap. In one sense, the SFA felt the pressure of these historical forces, and its projects of celebration work to instill sufficient mystique in certain things so that people will not permit them to disappear; to do so would be to surrender identity and embrace a kind of cosmopolitan anonymity.

Yet for anyone touched by historical consciousness, there is a sense that these efforts are holding actions. Other groups have been moved to be more active in their securing of agricultural and culinary heritage. Slow Food USA's Ark of Taste, for example, enlists a network of farmers, breeders, chefs, and consumers to intervene to save and promote endangered foods. As chair of the Ark of Taste's southeastern regional nominating committee as this book goes to press, I am tasked with directing the effort to locate the imperiled plants, animals, and products, and to initiate steps to restore their place in regional foodways.

But this is not enough. Much has already been lost, not just plants and animals, but also knowledge. In some regions of the South, the loss has reduced what once was a cuisine to simply local cooking. Such was the case in the Lowcountry, that region of the south Atlantic coast of North America that ranges from Wilmington, North Carolina, to the St. Johns River region in Florida. We can still read the old recipes and tally vanished ingredients: benne, guinea squash, tanya, Carolina-African peanuts, Carolina Gold rice, rice peas, sturgeon, American chestnuts. Those ingredients are only the most conspicuous. But a quick thumbing through of nineteenth-century seed catalogs or nursery bulletins will confront a reader with *hundreds* of varieties extolled for taste, conformation, and utility that no longer appear in any garden source, not even the Seed Savers Exchange. Amnesia has so cleansed cultural memory that we don't even know what the cuisines *were*, or how the planting shaped the larder that supplied those cuisines. That is, you can't bring *back* a cuisine if you don't know *what* it was that you are restoring.

This book did not come into being as some academic exercise documenting a past state of affairs for the pleasure of knowing a greatness now gone. Rather, it began as a piecemeal series of studies attempting to supply information needed to reconstitute the Carolina Rice Kitchen and its associated foodways in the Lowcountry. It began in 2004, as one of the initiatives of the Carolina Gold Rice Foundation, the network of scientists, farmers, and cultural historians called into existence by Dr. Merle Shepard of Clemson University. Bringing back Carolina Gold rice, the staple of the regional cuisine, was the first order of business; but since rice existed as the central node in a complex of other cultivars and foods, the foundation also felt compelled to understand the bigger picture. Supplying that knowledge was my task. And putting that knowledge in the hands of growers and chefs was my charge and the genesis of the research undergirding the chapters that follow. Early pieces of writing from this book have circulated in manuscript form since 2006, first among the rice cognoscenti, then among local chefs.

The reconstruction of Lowcountry cuisine particularly, and southern cuisine generally (one cannot study a regional cuisine in isolation from a consideration of the general language of culinary practice in a nation or cultural community), took place in conversation with the research and growing insights of Glenn Roberts, president of the Carolina Gold Rice

Foundation and CEO of Anson Mills. He sent me into the microfilm bunker of Thomas Cooper Library at the University of South Carolina to read old agricultural journals, newspapers, and magazines. Roberts also introduced me to the southern chefs who in the past decade have led the public crusade to recover the great tastes of the South. Sean Brock, in particular, was avid for the knowledge we were attempting to recover. As Roberts and other growers brought ingredients back into cultivation, Brock took them up and experimented in making the next manifestation of southern cuisine. He also spoke to his fellow chefs and shared the tastes of the recovered ingredients so they, too, understood the effort under way and the culinary possibilities it enabled. Many of them became part of the manuscript network reading the backstory of grains, plants, and fruits.

Some who learned of our historical explorations and the extensive program of culinary reconsolidation were nervous, however. They realized that a kind of nostalgia for "old times there" infected a contingent of white southerners. Yet our desire was not to reenact an antebellum world of elite feasts. Nor was it the wish of the chefs who spearheaded the renovation of southern cuisine during the last decade. The greatest traditional food-stuffs of the region were created as much by African Americans and Native Americans as by Anglo-Americans, a point made by the late culinary historian Karen Hess more than a decade ago. The heyday of Lowcountry cuisine, research would show, took place during the Reconstruction era, not in colonial or antebellum times. And *taste* was the justification for all of our revivals, not some notion of historical appositeness.

What people did with the *most* tasty and resonant things that we restored was their own concern—they could redo regional classics or create new dishes from the most evocative traditional flavors. Indeed, though we did the culinary research that could enable the *former*, we inclined toward the *latter*.

Certain of my botanist friends have also been skeptical of our concern with landraces and heirloom plants, suspecting us of an "anything old is better" prejudice. We have reasons for our preferences. Most of the vegetables and plants that appeared and quickly vanished in old seed catalogs did so for good reason. But those cultivars that enjoyed a long popularity did so because of taste, productivity, and seasonability. The primacy of taste is important, for since the 1890s, when monoculture gave rise to mass decimation of fields of watermelons, asparagus, wheat, and corn, pest and disease resistance became paramount among the concerns of plant breeders, followed by transportability, then size, then productivity. Taste has become an increasingly subordinate concern for plant breeders and agricultural geneticists; it remains the prime concern here.

The pages that follow supply the rationales for why certain things have been essential to Lowcountry cuisine and should be included in any version of the cuisine going forward. They also explain how these things were marketed locally, regionally, and nationally. Finally, they tell how food was processed and prepared in light of southern, American, and European cooking techniques.

Until today this knowledge has been the private preserve of the growers (Nat Bradford, Steven Chase, Campbell Coxe, Ben and Kristen DuBard, Kenneth DuBard, Thom Duncan, John and Wendy Eleazer, Jimmy Hagood, Hal Hanvey, James Helms, Max L. Hill III, Ted Hopkins, Joe and Amanda Jones, Ethan Kaufman, James Kibler, Aziz Mustafa, Matthew Raiford, Sharon Ray, Landon K. Thorne, Madison Turnblad, and Dr. Brian Ward), food advocates (Nathalie Dupree, John T. Edge, Dr. Marcie Cohen Ferris, Rien Fertel, Damon Lee Fowler, Dr. Bernard Herman, Kate Krauss, Megan Larmer, Ronni Lundy, Colleen Minton, Dr. Jane Przybysz, Hanna Raskin, Jamie Simpson Ross, Marion Sullivan, John Martin Taylor, Poppy Tooker, Janette Wesley, Liz Williams), and chefs (Hugh Acheson, Sean Brock, Tyler Brown, Michael Carmel, Ashley Christensen, Marc Collins, Mike Davis, Paul Fehribach, Travis Grimes, Linton Hopkins, Jeremiah Langhorne, Mike Latta, Joseph Lenn, Travis Milton, Forrest Parker, Matthew Raiford, April McGreger, Bill Smith, and Nathan Thurston). Now most of the material is in your hands. What I have withheld—studies of chestnuts, pecans, watermelons, peaches, rye, sweet potatoes, collards, and okra—will be published shortly in other venues or already appear in my American Heritage Vegetables website at the University of South Carolina: http://lichen.csd.sc.edu/vegetable/.

Columbia, South Carolina
June 2013

ACKNOWLEDGMENTS

Conversations with several persons influenced the arguments that appear in the pages that follow. Foremost among these have been debates with my colleagues in the Carolina Gold Rice Foundation: Dr. Merle Shepard of Clemson University, Charles Duel, Dr. Richard Porcher, Max E. Hill, Glenn Roberts, Campbell Coxe, Dr. Richard Schulze, and Mack Rhodes. The circle of persons who organized the 2003 Conference on the Cuisines of the Lowcountry and Caribbean has been instrumental in shaping my understanding of the region: Marion Sullivan, Nathalie Dupree, Robert J. Lukey, and Jeffrey Pilcher. At the University of South Carolina, I have benefited from the support of my department chairs, Steve Lynn and Bill Rivers, Dean Mary Ann Fitzpatrick, and Provost Michael Amiridis, whose funding initiative permitted the construction of the American Heritage Vegetables website. My colleagues Catherine Keyser, Scott Trafton, and Paula Feldman have stimulated me with their observations and interest. Biologists John Nelson, Joe Jones, and Steve Kresovich have been reliable resources for several years. The university's first lady, Patricia Moore-Pastides, has been a forceful advocate of local sourcing of food and healthy eating. My student and collaborator in the creation of the American Heritage Vegetables website, Stephen Spratt, deserves particular thanks for his insights into the history of the nourishment of the soil.

My initial awareness of Lowcountry cuisines was shaped in the 1980s and '90s with John Martin Taylor. Since that time, I've benefited by my exchanges with Damon Lee Fowler, Marcie Cohen Ferris, Jessica Harris, Jane Lear, Molly O'Neill, Karen Hall, Ted Lee, and Dan Barber. Yet my deepest and most wide-ranging explorations of food studies and historiography have been with my profoundest friend, Bernard L. Herman, the champion of traditional eastern shore foodways.

John T. Edge and his colleagues at the Southern Foodways Alliance have done more than any other entity to raise consciousness about the agricultural and kitchen legacies of the region.

The growers, chefs, and food advocates who contributed to this work receive recognition in the preface and at places in the course of the book.

Finally, a word of commendation for my family: my wife, Lucinda, and my son, Marcus, had to endure *many* an experimental meal using old southern ingredients. Their pleasurable and enthusiastic responses have done much to convince me of the rightness of reviving these traditional tastes.

* * *

An earlier version of chapter 14 first appeared under the title "Of Strife and Sweetness: The Civil War and the Rise of Sorghum," in *Repast: Quarterly Publication of the Culinary Historians of Ann Arbor* 27, no. 3 (Summer 2011); and an earlier version of chapter 15 was first published in *Gastronomica* 10, no. 4 (Winter 2010). I thank the editors of the journals for allowing me to rehearse the ideas contained in these two chapters first in their pages.

ONE   *Rebooting a Cuisine*

"I want to bring back Carolina Gold rice. I want there to be authentic Lowcountry cuisine again. Not the local branch of southern cooking incorporated." That was Glenn Roberts in 2003 during the waning hours of a conference in Charleston exploring "The Cuisines of the Lowcountry and the Caribbean."

When Jeffrey Pilcher, Nathalie Dupree, Marion Sullivan, Robert Lukey, and I brainstormed this meeting into shape over 2002, we paid scant attention to the word *cuisine*.[1] I'm sure we all thought that it meant something like "a repertoire of refined dishes that inspired respect among the broad public interested in food." We probably chose "cuisines" rather than "foodways" or "cookery" for the title because its associations with artistry would give it more splendor in the eyes of the two institutions—the College of Charleston and Johnson & Wales University—footing the administrative costs of the event. Our foremost concern was to bring three communities of people into conversation: culinary historians, chefs, and provisioners (i.e., farmers and fishermen) who produced the food cooked along the southern Atlantic coast and in the West Indies. Theorizing cuisine operated as a pretext.

Glenn Roberts numbered among the producers. The CEO of Anson Mills, he presided over the American company most deeply involved with growing, processing, and selling landrace grains to chefs.[2] I knew him only by reputation. He grew and milled the most ancient and storied grains on the planet—antique strains of wheat, oats, spelt, rye, barley, faro, and corn—so that culinary professionals could make use of the deepest traditional flavor chords in cookery: porridges, breads, and alcoholic beverages. Given Roberts's fascination with grains, expanding the scope of cultivars to include Carolina's famous rice showed intellectual consistency. Yet I had always pegged him as a preservationist rather than a restorationist. He asked me, point-blank, whether I wished to participate in the effort to restore authentic Lowcountry cuisine.

Roberts pronounced *cuisine* with a peculiar inflection, suggesting that it was something that was and could be but that in 2003 did not exist in this part of the South. I knew in a crude way what he meant. Rice had been the glory of the southern coastal table, yet rice had not been commercially cultivated in the region since a hurricane breached the dykes and salted the soil of Carolina's last commercial plantation in 1911. (Isolated planters on the Combahee River kept local stocks going until the Great Depression, and several families grew it for personal use until World War II, yet Carolina Gold rice disappeared on local grocers' shelves in 1912.)

When Louisa Stoney and a network Charleston's *grandes dames* gathered their *Carolina Rice Cook Book* in 1901, the vast majority of ingredients were locally sourced.[3] When John Martin Taylor compiled his *Hoppin' John's Lowcountry Cooking* in 1992,[4] the local unavailability of traditional ingredients and a forgetfulness about the region's foodways gave the volume a shock value, recalling the greatness of a tradition while alerting readers to its tenuous hold on the eating habits of the people.

Glenn Roberts had grown up tasting the remnants of the rice kitchen, his mother having mastered in her girlhood the art of Geechee black skillet cooking. In his younger days, Roberts worked on oyster boats, labored in fields, and cooked in Charleston restaurants, so when he turned to growing grain in the 1990s, he had a peculiar perspective on what he wished for: he knew he wanted to taste the terroir of the Lowcountry in the food.[5] Because conventional agriculture had saturated the fields of coastal Carolina with pesticides, herbicides, and chemical fertilizers, he knew he had to restore the soil as well as restore Carolina Gold, and other crops, into cultivation.

I told Roberts that I would help, blurting the promise before understanding the dimensions of what he proposed. Having witnessed the resurgence in Creole cooking in New Orleans and the efflorescence of Cajun cooking in the 1980s, and having read John Folse's pioneering histories of Louisiana's culinary traditions, I entertained romantic visions of lost foodways being restored and local communities being revitalized. My default opinions resembled those of an increasing body of persons, that fast food was aesthetically impoverished, that grocery preparations (snacks, cereals, and spreads) had sugared and salted themselves to a brutal lowest common denominator of taste, and that industrial agriculture was insuring indifferent produce by masking local qualities of soil with chemical supplementations. When I said "yes," I didn't realize that good intentions are a kind of stupidity in the absence of an attuned intuition of the problems at hand. When Roberts asked whether I would like to restore a cuisine, my thoughts gravitated toward the payoffs on the consumption end of things: no insta-grits made of GMO corn in my shrimp and grits; no farm-raised South American tiger shrimp. In short, something *we all knew around here* would be improved.

It never occurred to me that the losses in Lowcountry food had been so great that *we all don't know jack* about the splendor that was, even with the aid of historical savants such as "Hoppin' John" Taylor. Nor did I realize that traditional cuisines cannot be understood simply by reading old cookbooks; you can't simply re-create recipes and—voilà! Roberts, being a grower and miller, had fronted the problem: cuisines had to be understood from the production side, from the farming, not just the cooking or eating. If the ingredients are mediocre, there will be no revelation on the tongue. There is only one pathway to understanding how the old planters created rice that excited the gastronomes of Paris—the path leading into the dustiest, least-used stacks in the archive, those holding century-and-a-half-old agricultural journals, the most neglected body of early American writings.

In retrospect, I understand why Roberts approached me and not some chef with a penchant for antiquarian study or some champion of southern cooking. While interested in culinary history, it was not my interest but my *method* that drew Roberts. He must've known at the time that I create histories of subjects that have not been explored; that I write "total histories" using only primary sources, finding, reading, and analyzing every extant source of information.[6] He needed someone who could navigate the dusty archive of American farming, a scholar who could reconstruct how cuisine came to be from the ground up. He found me in 2003.

At first, questions tugged in too many directions. When renovating a cuisine, what is it, exactly, that is being restored? An aesthetic of plant breeding? A farming system? A set of kitchen practices? A gastronomic philosophy? We decided not to exclude questions at the outset, but to pursue anything that might serve the goals of bringing back soil, restoring cultivars, and renovating traditional modes of food processing. The understandings being sought had to speak to a practice of growing and kitchen creation. We should not, we all agreed, approach cuisine as an ideal, a theoretical construction, or a utopian possibility.

Our starting point was a working definition of that word I had used so inattentively in the title of the conference: *cuisine*. What is a cuisine? How does it differ from diet, cookery, or food? Some traditions of reflection on these questions were helpful. Jean-François Revel's insistence in *Culture and Cuisine* that cuisines are regional, not national, because of the enduring distinctiveness of local ingredients, meshed with the agricultural preoccupations of our project.[7] Sidney Mintz usefully observed that a population "eats that cuisine with sufficient frequency to consider themselves experts on it. They all believe, and care that they believe, that they know what it consists of, how it is made, and how it should taste. In short, a genuine cuisine has common social roots."[8] The important point here is consciousness. Cuisine becomes a signature of community and, as such, becomes a source of pride, a focus of debate, and a means of projecting an identity in other places to other people.

There is, of course, a commercial dimension to this. If a locale becomes famous for its butter (as northern New York did in the nineteenth century) or cod (as New England did in the eighteenth century), a premium is paid in the market *for* those items *from* those places. The self-consciousness about ingredients gives rise to an artistry in their handling, a sense of tact from long experience of taste, and a desire among both household and professional cooks to satisfy the popular demand for dishes by improving their taste and harmonizing their accompaniments at the table.

One hallmark of the maturity of a locale's culinary artistry is its discretion when incorporating non-local ingredients with the products of a region's field, forest, and waters. Towns and cities with their markets and groceries invariably served as places where the melding of the world's commodities with a region's produce took place. Cuisines have two faces: a cosmopolitan face, prepared by *professional* cooks; and a common face, prepared by *household* cooks. In the modern world, a cuisine is at least bimodal in constitution, with an urbane style and a country vernacular style. At times, these stylistic differences become so pronounced that they described two distinct foodways—the difference between Creole and Cajun food and their disparate histories, for example. More frequently, an urban center creates its style elaborating the bounty of the surrounding countryside—the case of Baltimore and the Tidewater comes to mind.

With a picture of cuisine in hand, Roberts and I debated how to proceed in our understanding. In 2004 the Carolina Gold Rice Foundation was formed with the express purpose of advancing the cultivation of landrace grains and insuring the repatriation of Carolina Gold.[9] Dr. Merle Shepard of Clemson University (head of the Clemson Coastal Experimental Station at Charleston), Dr. Richard Schulze (who planted the first late twentieth-century crops of Carolina Gold on his wetlands near Savannah), Campbell Coxe (the most experienced commercial rice farmer in the Carolinas), Max E. Hill (historian and planter), and Mack Rhodes and Charles Duell (whose Middleton Place showcased the historical importance of rice on the Lowcountry landscape) formed the original nucleus of the enterprise.

It took two and a half years before we knew enough to reformulate our concept of cuisine and historically contextualize the Carolina Rice Kitchen well enough to map our starting point for the work of replenishment—a reboot of Lowcountry cuisine. The key insights were as follows: The *enduring distinctiveness of local ingredients* arose from very distinct sets of historical circumstances and a confluence of English, French Huguenot, West African, and Native American foodways. What is grown where, when, and for what occurred for very particular reasons. A soil crisis in the early nineteenth century particularly shaped the Lowcountry cuisine that would come, distinguishing *it* from food produced and prepared elsewhere.

The landraces of rice, wheat, oats, rye, and corn that were brought into agriculture in the coastal Southeast were, during the eighteenth century, planted as cash crops, those same fields being replanted season after season, refreshed only with manuring until the early nineteenth century. Then the boom in long staple Sea Island cotton, a very "exhausting" plant, pushed Lowcountry soil into crisis. (A similar crisis related to tobacco culture and soil erosion because of faulty plowing methods afflicted Maryland, Virginia, and North Carolina.) The soil crisis led to the depopulation of agricultural lands as enterprising sons went westward seeking newly cleared land, causing a decline in production, followed by rising farm debt and social distress. The South began to echo with lamentations and warnings proclaimed by a generation of agrarian prophets—John Taylor of Caroline County in Virginia, George W. Jeffreys of North Carolina, Nicholas Herbemont of South Carolina, and Thomas Spalding of Georgia.[10] Their message: Unless the soil is saved; unless crop rotations that build nutrition in soil be instituted; unless agriculture be diversified—then the long-cultivated portions of the South will become a wasteland. In response to the crisis in the 1820s, planters formed associations; they published agricultural journals to exchange information; they read; they planted new crops and employed new techniques of plowing and tilling; they rotated, intercropped, and fallowed fields. The age of experiment began in American agriculture with a vengeance.[11]

The *Southern Agriculturist* magazine (founded 1828) operated as the engine of changes in the Lowcountry. In its pages, a host of planter-contributors published rotations they had developed for rice, theories of geoponics (soil nourishment), alternatives to monoculture, and descriptions of the world of horticultural options. Just as Judge Jesse Buel in Albany, New York, systematized the northern dairy farm into a self-reliant entity with livestock, pastures, fields, orchard, garden, and dairy interacting for optimum benefit, southern experimentalists conceived of the model plantation. A generation of literate rice planters—Robert F. W. Allston, J. Bryan, Calvin Emmons, James Ferguson, William Hunter, Roswell King, Charles Munnerlyn, Thomas Pinckney, and Hugh Rose—

contributed to the conversation, overseen by William Washington, chair of the Committee on Experiments of the South Carolina Agricultural Society. Regularizing the crop rotations, diversifying cultivars, and rationalizing plantation operations gave rise to the distinctive set of ingredients that coalesced into what came to be called the Carolina Rice Kitchen, the cuisine of the Lowcountry.

Now, in order to reconstruct the food production of the Lowcountry, one needs a picture of how the plantations and farms worked internally with respect to local markets, in connection with regional markets, and in terms of commodity trade. One has to know how the field crops, kitchen garden, flower and herb garden, livestock pen, dairy, and kitchen cooperated. Within the matrix of uses, any plant or animal that could be employed in multiple ways would be more widely raised in a locality and more often cycled into cultivation. The sweet potato, for instance, performed many tasks on the plantation: It served as winter feed for livestock, its leaves as fodder; it formed one of the staple foods for slaves; it sold well as a local-market commodity for the home table; and its allelopathic (growth-inhibiting chemistry) made it useful in weed suppression.[12] Our first understandings of locality came by tracing the multiple transits of individual plants through farms, markets, kitchens, and seed brokerages.

After the 1840s, when experiments stabilized into conventions on Lowcountry plantations, certain items became fixtures in the fields. Besides the sweet potato, one found benne (low-oil West African sesame), corn, colewort/kale/collards, field peas, peanuts, and, late in the 1850s, sorghum. Each one of these plant types would undergo intensive breeding trials, creating new varieties that (a) performed more good for the soil and welfare of the rotation's other crops; (b) attracted more purchasers at the market; (c) tasted better to the breeder or his livestock; (d) grew more productively than other varieties; and (e) proved more resistant to drought, disease, and infestation than other varieties.

From 1800 to the Civil War, the number of vegetables, the varieties of a given vegetable, the number of fruit trees, the number of ornamental flowers, and the numbers of cattle, pigs, sheep, goat, and fowl breeds all multiplied prodigiously in the United States, in general, and the Lowcountry, in particular. The seedsman, the orchardist, the livestock breeder, the horticulturist—experimentalists who maintained model farms, nurseries, and breeding herds—became fixtures of the agricultural scene and drove innovation. One such figure was J. V. Jones of Burke County, Georgia, a breeder of field peas in the 1840s and '50s. In the colonial era, field peas (cowpeas) grew in the garden patches of African slaves, along with okra, benne, watermelon, and guinea squash. Like those other West African plants, their cultivation was taken up by white planters. At first, they grew field peas as fodder for livestock because it inspired great desire among hogs, cattle, and horses. (Hence the popular name *cowpea*.) Early in the nineteenth century, growers noticed that it improved soils strained by "exhausting plants." With applications as a green manure, a table pea, and livestock feed, the field pea inspired experiments in breeding with the ends of making it less chalky tasting, more productive, and less prone to mildew when being dried to pea hay. Jones reported on his trials. He grew every sort of pea he could obtain, crossing varieties in the hopes of breeding a pea with superior traits.

1. Blue Pea, hardy and prolific. A crop of this pea can be matured in less than 60 days from date of planting the seed. Valuable.
2. Lady, matures with No. 1. Not so prolific and hardy. A delicious table pea.
3. Rice, most valuable table variety known, and should be grown universally wherever the pea can make a habitation.
4. Relief, another valuable table kind, with brown pods.
5. Flint Crowder, very profitable.
6. Flesh, very profitable.
7. Sugar, very profitable.
8. Grey, very profitable. More so than 5, 6, 7. [Tory Pea]
9. Early Spotted, brown hulls or pods.
10. Early Locust, brown hulls, valuable.
11. Late Locust, purple hulls, not profitable.
12. Black Eyes, valuable for stock.
13. Early Black Spotted, matures with nos. 1, 2, and 3.
14. Goat, so called, I presume, from its spots. Very valuable, and a hard kind to shell.
15. Small Black, very valuable, lies on the field all winter with the power of reproduction.

16. Large Black Crowder, the largest pea known, and produces great and luxuriant vines. A splendid variety.
17. Brown Spotted, equal to nos. 6, 7, 8 and 14.
18. Claret Spotted, equal to nos. 6, 7, 8 and 14.
19. Large Spotted, equal to nos. 6, 7, 8 and 14.
20. Jones Little Claret Crowder. It is my opinion a greater quantity in pounds and bushels can be grown per acre of this pea, than any other grain with the knowledge of man. Matures with nos. 1, 2, 3, 9 and 13, and one of the most valuable.
21. Jones Black Hull, prolific and profitable.
22. Jones Yellow Hay, valuable for hay only.
23. Jones no. 1, new and very valuable; originated in the last 2 years.
24. Chickasaw, its value is as yet unknown. Ignorance has abused it.
25. Shinney or Java, this is the Prince of Peas.[13]

The list dramatizes the complex of qualities that bear on the judgments of plant breeders—flavor, profitability, feed potential, processability, ability to self-seed, productivity, and utility as hay. And it suggests the genius of agriculture in the age of experiment—the creation of a myriad of tastes and uses.

At this juncture, we confront a problem of culinary history. If one writes the history of taste as it is usually written, using the cookbook authors and chefs as the spokespersons for developments, one will not register the multiple taste options that pea breeders created. Recipes with gnomic reticence call for field peas (or cowpeas). One would not know, for example, that the Shinney pea, the large white lady pea, or the small white rice pea would be most suitable for this or that dish. It is only in the agricultural literature that we learn that the Sea Island red pea was the traditional pea used in rice stews, or that the red Tory pea with molasses and a ham hock made a dish rivaling Boston baked beans.

Growers drove taste innovation in American grains, legumes, and vegetables during the age of experiment. And their views about texture, quality, and application were expressed in seed catalogs, agricultural journals, and horticultural handbooks. If one wishes to understand what was distinctive about regional cookery in the United States, the cookbook supplies but a partial apprehension at best. New England's plenitude of squashes, to take another example, is best comprehended by reading James J. H. Gregory's *Squashes: How to Grow Them* (1867), not Mrs. N. Orr's *De Witt's Connecticut Cook Book, and Housekeeper's Assistant* (1871). In the pages of the 1869 annual report of the Massachusetts Board of Agriculture, we encounter the expert observation, "As a general rule, the Turban and Hubbard are too grainy in texture to enter the structure of that grand Yankee luxury, a squash pie. For this the Marrow [autumnal marrow squash] excels, and this, I hold, is now the proper sphere of this squash; it is now a pie squash."[14] No cookbook contains so trenchant an assessment, and when the marrow squash receives mention, it suggests it is a milder-flavored alternative to the pumpkin pie.[15]

Wendell Berry's maxim that "eating is an agricultural act" finds support in nineteenth-century agricultural letters. The aesthetics of planting, breeding, and eating formed a whole sense of the ends of agriculture. No cookbook would tell you why a farmer chose a clay pea to intercrop with white flint corn, or a lady pea, or a black Crowder, but a reader of the agricultural press would know that the clay pea would be plowed under with the corn to fertilize a field (a practice on some rice fields every fourth year), that the lady pea would be harvested for human consumption, and that the black Crowder would be cut for cattle feed. Only reading a pea savant like J. V. Jones would one know that a black-eyed pea was regarded as "valuable for stock" but too common tasting to recommend it for the supper table.

When the question that guides one's reading is which pea or peas should be planted today to build the nitrogen level of the soil and complement the grains and vegetables of Lowcountry cuisines, the multiplicity of varieties suggests an answer. That J. V. Jones grew at least four of his own creations, as well as twenty-one other reputable types, indicates that one should grow *several* sorts of field peas, with each sort targeted to a desired end. The instincts of southern seed savers such as Dr. David Bradshaw, Bill Best, and John Coykendall were correct—to preserve the richness of southern pea culture, one had to keep multiple strains of cowpea viable. Glenn Roberts and the Carolina Gold Rice Foundation have concentrated on two categories of peas—those favored in rice dishes and those known for soil replenishment. The culinary peas are the Sea Island red pea, known for traditional dishes such as reezy peezy, red pea soup, and red pea gravy; and the rice pea, cooked as an edible pod pea, for most hoppin' John recipes and for the most refined version of field peas with butter. For soil building, iron and clay peas have been a mainstay of warm-zone agriculture since the second half of the nineteenth century.

It should be clear by this juncture that this inquiry differs from the projects most frequently encountered in food history. Here, the value of a cultivar or dish does not reside in its being a heritage marker, a survival from an originating culture previous to its uses in southern planting and cooking. The Native American origins of a Chickasaw plum, the African origins of okra, the Swedish origins of the rutabaga don't much matter for our purposes. This is not to discount the worth of the sort of etiological food genealogies that Gary Nabhan performs with the foods of Native peoples,[16] that Karen Hess performed with the cooking of Jewish conversos, or that Jessica Harris and others perform in their explorations of the food of the African diaspora,[17] but the hallmark of the experimental age was change in what was grown—importation, alteration, ramification, improvement, and repurposing. The parched and boiled peanuts/pindars of West Africa were used for oil production and peanut butter. Sorghum, or imphee grass, employed in beer brewing and making flat breads in West Africa and Natal became in the hands of American experimentalists a sugar-producing plant. That said, the expropriations and experimental transformations did not entirely supplant traditional uses. The work of agronomist George Washington Carver at the Tuskegee Agricultural Experiment Station commands particular notice because it combines its novel recommendations for industrial and commercial uses of plants as lubricants, blacking, and toothpaste, with a thoroughgoing recovery of the repertoire of Deep South African American sweet potato, cowpea, and peanut cookery in an effort to present the maximum utility of the ingredients.[18]

While part of this study *does* depend on the work that Joyce E. Chaplin and Max Edelson have published on the engagement of southern planters with science, it departs from the literature concerned with agricultural reform in the South.[19] Because this exploration proceeds from the *factum brutum* of an achieved regional cuisine produced as the result of agricultural innovations, market evolutions, and kitchen creativity, it stands somewhat at odds with that literature, arguing the ineffectuality of agricultural reform. Works in this tradition—Charles G. Steffen's "In Search of the Good Overseer" or William M. Mathew's *Edmund Ruffin and the Crisis of Slavery in the Old South*—argue that what passed for innovation in farming was a charade, and that soil restoration and crop diversification were fitful at best.[20] When a forkful of hominy made from the white flint corn perfected in the 1830s on the Sea Islands melts on one's tongue, there is little doubting that something splendid has been achieved.

The sorts of experiments that produced white flint corn, the rice pea, and the long-grain form of Carolina Gold rice did not cease with the Civil War. Indeed, with the armistice, the scope and intensity of experimentation increased as the economies of the coast rearranged from staple production to truck farming. The reliance on agricultural improvement would culminate in the formation of the network of agricultural experimental stations in the wake of the Hatch Act of 1886. One finding of our research has been that the fullness of Lowcountry agriculture and the efflorescence of Lowcountry cuisine came about during the Reconstruction era, and its heyday continued into the second decade of the twentieth century.

The Lowcountry was in no way exceptional in its embrace of experiments and improvement or insular in its view of what should be grown. In the 1830s, when Carolina horticulturists read about the success that northern growers had with Russian strains of rhubarb, several persons attempted with modest success to grow it in kitchen gardens. Readers of Alexander von Humboldt's accounts of the commodities of South America experimented with Peruvian quinoa in grain rotations. Because agricultural letters and print mediated the conversations of the experimentalists, and because regional journals reprinted extensively from other journals from other places, a curiosity about the best variety of vegetables, fruits, and berries grown anywhere regularly led many to secure seed from northern brokers (only the Landreth Seed Company of Pennsylvania maintained staff in the Lowcountry), or seedsmen in England, France, and Germany. Planters regularly sought new sweet potato varieties from Central and South America, new citrus fruit from Asia, and melons wherever they might be had.

Because of the cosmopolitan sourcing of things grown, the idea of a regional agriculture growing organically out of the indigenous productions of a geographically delimited zone becomes questionable. (The case of the harvest of game animals and fish is different.) There is, of course, a kind of provocative poetry to reminding persons, as Gary Nabhan has done, that portions of the Southeast once regarded the American chestnut as a staple and food mapping an area as "Chestnut Nation,"[21] yet it has little resonance for a population that has never tasted an American chestnut in their lifetime. Rather, region makes sense only as a geography mapped by consciousness—by a community's attestation in naming, argumentation, and sometimes attempts at legal delimitation of a place.

We can see the inflection of territory with consciousness in the history of the name "Lowcountry." It emerges as "low country" in the work of early nineteenth-century geographers and geologists who were attempting to characterize the topography of the states and territories of the young nation. In 1812 Jedidiah Morse uses "low country" in the *American Universal Gazetteer* to designate the coastal mainland of North Carolina, South Carolina, and Georgia. Originally, the Sea Islands were viewed as a separate topography. "The sea coast," he writes, "is bordered with a fine chain of islands, between which and the shore there is a very convenient navigation. The main land is naturally divided into the Lower and Upper country. The low country extends 80 or 100 miles from the coast, and is covered with extensive forests of pitch pine, called pine barrens, interspersed with swamps and marshes of rich soil."[22] Geologist Elisha Mitchell took up the characterization in his 1828 article, "On the Character and Origin of the Low Country of North Carolina," defining the region east of the Pee Dee River to the Atlantic coast by a stratigraphy of sand and clay layers as the low country.[23] Within a generation, the designation had entered into the usage of the population as a way of characterizing a distinctive way of growing practiced on coastal lands. Wilmot Gibbs, a wheat farmer in Chester County in the South Carolina midlands, observed in a report to the US Patent Office: "The sweet potatoes do better, much better on sandy soil, and though not to be compared in quantity and quality with the lowcountry sweet potatoes, yet yield a fair crop."[24] Two words became one word. And when culture—agriculture—inflected the understanding of region, the boundaries of the map altered. The northern boundary of rice growing and the northern range of the cabbage palmetto were just north of Wilmington, North Carolina. The northern bound of USDA Plant Hardiness Zone 8 in the Cape Fear River drainage became the cultural terminus of the Lowcountry. Agriculturally, the farming on the Sea

Islands differed little from that on the mainland, so they became assimilated into the cultural Lowcountry. And since the Sea Islands extended to Amelia Island, Florida, the Lowcountry extended into east Florida. What remained indistinct and subject to debate was the interior bound of the Lowcountry. Was the St. Johns River region in Florida assimilated into it, or not? Did it end where tidal flow became negligible upriver on the major coastal estuaries? Perceptual regions that do not evolve into legislated territories, such as the French wine regions, should be treated with a recognition of their mutable shape.

Cuisines are regional to the extent that the ingredients the region supplies to the kitchen are distinctive, not seen as a signature of another place. Consequently, Lowcountry cuisine must be understood comparatively, contrasting its features with those of other perceived styles, such as "southern cooking" or "tidewater cuisine" or "New Orleans Creole cooking" or "American school cooking" or "cosmopolitan hotel gastronomy." The comparisons will take place, however, acknowledging that all of these styles share a deep grammar. A common store of ancient landrace grains (wheat, spelt, rye, barley, oats, corn, rice, millet, faro), the oil seeds and fruits (sesame, sunflower, rapeseed, linseed, olive), the livestock, the root vegetables, the fruit trees, the garden vegetables, the nuts, the berries, the game, and the fowls—all these supply a broad canvas against which the novel syncretisms and breeders' creations emerge. It is easy to overstate the peculiarity of a region's farming or food.

One of the hallmarks of the age of experiment was openness to new plants from other parts of the world. There was nothing of the culinary purism that drove the expulsion of "ignoble grapes" from France in the 1930s. Nor was there the kind of nationalist food security fixation that drives the current Plant Protection and Quarantine (PPQ) protocols of the USDA. In that era, before crop monocultures made vast stretches of American countryside an uninterrupted banquet for viruses, disease organisms, and insect pests, nightmares of continental pestilence did not roil agronomists. The desire to plant a healthier, tastier, more productive sweet potato had planters working their connections in the West Indies and South America for new varieties. Periodically, an imported variety—a cross between old cultivated varieties, a cross between a traditional and an imported variety, or a sport of an old or new variety—proved something so splendid that it became a classic, a brand, a market variety, a seed catalog–illustrated plant. Examples of these include the Carolina African peanut, the Bradford watermelon, the Georgia pumpkin yam, the Hanson lettuce, Sea Island white flint corn, the Virginia peanut, the Carolina Long Gold rice, the Charleston Wakefield cabbage, and the Dancy tangerine. That something from a foreign clime might be acculturated, becoming central to an American regional cuisine, was more usual than not.

With the rise of the commercial seedsmen, naming of vegetable varieties became chaotic. Northern breeders rebranded the popular white-fleshed Hayman sweet potato, first brought from the West Indies into North Carolina in 1854, as the "Southern Queen sweet potato" in the hope of securing the big southern market, or as the "West Indian White." Whether a seedsman tweaked a strain or not, it appeared in the catalogs as new and improved. Only with the aid of the skeptical field-trial reporters working the experimental stations of the 1890s can one see that the number of horticultural and pomological novelties named as being available for purchase substantially *exceeds* the number of varieties that *actually exist*.

Numbers of plant varieties enjoyed sufficient following to resist the yearly tide of "new and improved" alternatives. They survived over decades, supported by devotees or retained by experimental stations and commercial breeders as breeding stock. Of Jones's list of cowpeas, for instance, the blue, the lady, the rice, the flint Crowder, the claret, the small black, the black-eyed, and Shinney peas still exist in twenty-first-century fields, and two remain in commercial cultivation: the lady and the Crowder.

In order to bring back the surviving old varieties important in traditional Lowcountry cuisine yet no longer commercially farmed, Dr. Merle Shepard, Glenn Roberts, or I sought them in germplasm banks and through the networks of growers and seed savers. Some important items seem irrevocably lost: the Neunan's strawberry and the Hoffman seedling strawberry, both massively cultivated during the truck-farming era in the decades following the Civil War. The Ravenscroft watermelon has perished. Because of the premium placed on taste in nineteenth-century plant and fruit breeding, we believed the repatriation of old strains to be important. Yet we by no means believed that skill at plant breeding suddenly ceased in 1900. Rather, the aesthetics of breeding changed so that cold tolerance, productivity, quick maturity, disease resistance, transportability, and slow decay often trumped taste in the list of desiderata. The recent revelation that the commercial tomato's roundness and redness was genetically accomplished at the expense of certain of the alleles governing *taste* quality is only the most conspicuous instance of the subordination of flavor in recent breeding aesthetics.

We have reversed the priority—asserting the primacy of *taste* over other qualities in a plant. We cherish plants that in the eyes of industrial farmers may seem inefficient, underproductive, or vulnerable to disease and depredation because they offer more to the kitchen, to the tongue, and to the imagination. The simple fact that a plant is heirloom does not make it pertinent for our purposes. It had to have had traction agriculturally *and* culinarily. It had to retain its vaunted flavor. Glenn Roberts sought with particular avidity the old landrace grains because their flavors provided the fundamental notes comprising the harmonics of Western food, both bread and alcohol. The more ancient, the better. I sought benne, peanuts, sieva beans, asparagus, peppers, squashes, and root vegetables. Our conviction has been—and is—that the quality of the ingredients will determine the vitality of Lowcountry cuisine.

While the repertoire of dishes created in Lowcountry cuisine interested us greatly, and while we studied the half-dozen nineteenth-century cookbooks, the several dozen manuscript recipe collections, and the newspaper recipe literature with the greatest attention, we realized that our project was not the culinary equivalent of Civil War reenactment, a kind of temporary evacuation of the present for some vision of the past. Rather, we wanted to revive the ingredients that had made *that* food so memorable and make the tastes available again, so the best cooks of *this* moment could combine them to invoke or invent a cooking rich with this place. Roberts was too marked by his Californian youth, me by formative years in Japan, Shepard by his long engagement with Asian food culture, Campbell Coxe with his late twentieth-century business mentality, to yearn for some antebellum never-never land of big house banqueting. What *did* move us, however, was the taste of rice. We all could savor the faint hazelnut delicacy, the luxurious melting wholesomeness of Carolina Gold. And we all wondered at those tales of Charleston hotel chefs of the Reconstruction era who could identify which stretch of which river where a plate of gold rice had been nourished. They could, they claimed, *taste* the water and the soil in the rice.

The quality of ingredients depends upon the quality of the soil, and this book is not, to my regret, a recovery of the lost art of soil building. Though we have unearthed, with the aid of Dr. Stephen Spratt, a substantial body of information about crop rotations and their effects, and though certain of these traditional rotations have been followed in growing rice, benne, corn, beans, wheat, oats, et cetera, we can't point to a particular method of treating soil that we could attest as having been sufficient and sustainable in its fertility in all cases.[25] While individual planters hit upon soil-building solutions for their complex of holdings, particularly in the Sea Islands and in the Pee Dee River basin, these were often vast operations employing swamp muck, rather than dung, as a manure. Even planter-savants, such as John Couper and Thomas Spalding, felt they had not optimized the growing potential of their lands. Planters who farmed land that had suffered fertility decline and were bringing it back to viability often felt dissatisfaction because its productivity could not match the newly cleared lands in Alabama, Louisiana, Texas, and Mississippi. Lowcountry planters were undersold by producers to the west. Hence, coastal planters heeded the promises of the great advocates of manure—Edmund Ruffin's call to crush fossilized limestone and spread calcareous manures on fields, or Alexander von Humboldt's scientific case for Peruvian guano—as the answer to amplifying yield per acre. Those who could afford it became guano addicts. Slowly, southern planters became habituated to the idea that in order to yield a field needed some sort of chemical supplementation. It was then a short step to industrially produced chemical fertilizers.

What we now know to be irrefutably true, after a decade of Glenn Roberts's field work, is that grain and vegetables grown in soil that has never been subjected to the chemical supplementations of conventional agriculture, or that has been raised in fields cleansed of the chemicals by repeated organic grow-outs, possess greater depth and distinct local inflections of flavor. Tongues taste terroir. This is a truth confirmed by the work of other cuisine restorationists in other areas—I think particularly of Dan Barber's work at Stone Barns Center in northern New York and John Coykendall's work in Tennessee.

Our conviction that enhancing the quality of flavors a region produces as the goal of our agricultural work gives our efforts a clarity of purpose that enables sure decision making at the local level. We realize, of course, the human and animal health benefits from consuming food free of toxins and chemical additives. We know that the preservation of the soil and the treatment of water resources in a non-exploitative way constitute a kind of virtue. But without the aesthetic focus on flavor, the ethical treatment of resources will hardly succeed. When pleasure coincides with virtue, the prospect of an enduring change in the production and treatment of food takes on solidity.

Since its organization a decade ago, the Carolina Gold Rice Foundation has published material on rice culture and the cultivation of landrace grains. By 2010 it became apparent that the information we had gleaned and the practical experience we had gained in plant repatriations had reached a threshold permitting a more public presentation of our historical sense of this regional cuisine, its original conditions of production, and observations on its preparation. After substantial conversation about the shape of this study with Roberts, Shepard, Bernard L. Herman, John T. Edge, Nathalie Dupree, Sean Brock, Linton Hopkins, Jim Kibler, and Marcie Cohen Ferris, I determined that it should not resort to the conventional chronological, academic organization of the subject, nor should it rely on the specialized languages of botany, agronomy, or nutrition. My desire in writing *Southern Provisions* was to treat the subject so that a reader could trace the connections between plants, plantations, growers, seed brokers, markets, vendors, cooks, and consumers. The focus of attention had to alter, following the transit of food from field to market, from garden to table. The entire landscape of the Lowcountry had to be included, from the Wilmington peanut patches to the truck farms of the Charleston Neck, from the cane fields of the Georgia Sea Islands to the citrus groves of Amelia Island, Florida. For comparison's sake, there had to be moments when attention turned to food of the South generally, to the West Indies, and to the United States more generally.

In current books charting alternatives to conventional agriculture, there has been a strong and understandable tendency to announce crisis. This was also the common tactic of writers at the beginning of the age of experimentation in the 1810s and '20s. Yet here, curiosity and pleasure, the quest to understand a rich world of taste, direct our inquiry more than fear and trepidation.

Because we are renovating a cuisine, we begin with an account of what that cuisine was and what institutions shaped it. So this book reverses the order of "farm to table"—we must know the traditional table to know what to restore to the farm. The chapters that follow explore three subjects in three sections: cooking, selling, and planting. What results is a history of the rise of both southern and Lowcountry cuisines that speaks to the current effort by chefs and cooks throughout America to know the most enduring culinary expressions of these regions. Chapters 2 through 7 reveal how regional understandings of taste and culinary performance emerged in the American South and in the Lowcountry, particularly in the antebellum period. They document how professional cooks shaped the standards of taste that elevated cookery to cuisine in three locales (New Orleans, the Tidewater, and the Lowcountry) and in a distinct set of venues (the hotel saloon, the restaurant, the confectioner's shop, and the catered banquet in a civic space). Chapters 8 through 11 examine the role of food markets in focusing demand for ingredients and enabling producers and preparers to come into conversation. In a series of capsule histories, chapters 12 through 17 show how the key ingredients of Lowcountry cuisine—rice, sugarcane, sorghum, benne and cottonseed oil, peanuts, and citrus—emerged, and what role they played in commerce and consumption. As a coda, the final chapter returns us to the present day to reconsider some of the problems of recovering field and kitchen heritage, while considering the case history of the 2011 reintroduction of Sea Island white flint corn in cultivation.

PART ONE

Cooking in the South

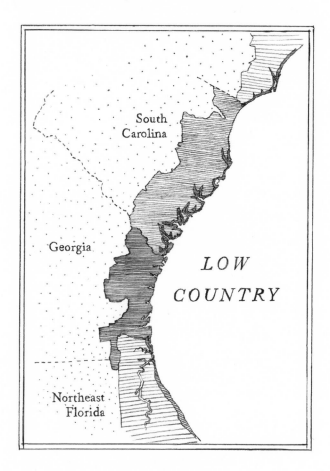

South
Carolina

Georgia

LOW
COUNTRY

Northeast
Florida

TWO · *The South and the Institutions of American Food*

If you talk about southern food, you have to say something about "the South." There is a problem presuming that southern food has long been an integral body of time-honored ingredients, cooking techniques, dishes, and foodways. There is also a problem supposing that there existed a common cookery confessed of old by Texans and Kentuckians, Marylanders and Floridians, and recognized by visitors from other regions. The problem is, in part, historical. "The South," as a cultural identity, is of relatively recent vintage. To speak of southern food before there is a conscious south risks incoherence.

But when did "the South" begin? When did people over the region begin confessing a regional identity? Historians wrangle over the nativity. Did it emerge unannounced and unnamed in the US Constitutional Convention, when Maryland and the states below voted as a block on all provisions reflecting on slavery? Was it "the South" that declared common cause in the press and public meetings denouncing the 1828 "Tariff of Abominations"? Was it the nation that materialized with the chartering of the Confederacy? Whichever moment of nativity one chooses, one encounters the paradox that "the South" was an imagined community that valued the sovereignty of its constituent states over the potency of its corporate being. States' rights was weak ground upon which to erect a common culture.

Food gives a familiar face to the primacy of the local over the regional, the states over the nation. "Carolina rice," "Carolina peanut," "Carolina bean," "Virginia ham," "Louisiana sugar," "New Orleans molasses," "Florida oranges," "Georgia yam." All of these characteristic brands—and more—emerged before the first appearance of the phrase "southern cooking" in print in 1860 and "southern food" in 1861.[1] "Southern-fried" would not debut until 1870. Search the newspaper ads and customs manifests of pre-1860 America, and you will find a solitary "southern" ingredient listing: namely, "southern hams," a designation found exclusively in northern city papers from 1800 onward. Southern papers listed the state of origin of the hams—or a provenance from the Fulton Market in New York.

If the marketers and servers of food lacked southern consciousness before 1860, the producers of food had it to spare. Agriculturists had taken up the geographic/cultural region in the 1820s. In 1851 the *Soil of the South*, a periodical launched in Columbus, Georgia, announced in its title one ground of regional interest: the soil—particularly the soil exhausted by intensive cultivation of staple crops such as cotton, tobacco, corn, rice, and sugarcane—created an anxiety among farmers not restricted to locality or contained by state bounds. Since the publication of the first works of soil apocalyptic—*Arator* (1814) by John Taylor of Caroline County, Virginia, and *A Series of Essays on Agriculture and Rural Affairs* (1819) by George Jeffreys of North Carolina—literate planters strove to remedy soil exhaustion and erosion by exchanging information about fallowing, crop rotation, restorative plantings, winter cover crops, and "horizontal plowing." By 1820 the age of experiment had been shocked into existence, and the desperate curiosity of cultivators about ways to counter soil degradation made them readers and correspondents with farmers in other places. In 1828 the *Southern Agriculturist* began publication in Charleston, the first of a number of farming journals that materialized the region's anxieties in its contents. It was sectional as well as regional.

Sectionalism, the spirit of division that arose in the second quarter of the nineteenth century in the United States, expressed the diverging political economies of the industrializing North and the slave states. The passage

by the US Congress of the Tariff of 1828—the "Tariff of Abominations"—
proved a catalytic moment. A tax upon cheap imported goods intended to
protect northern industries and fund internal improvements, it threatened
the English importation of cotton and forced the slave states to pay more
for goods that they imported. The English market for cotton seemed about
to evaporate, threatening a general collapse of a major regional cash crop.[2]
The *Southern Agriculturist* came into print to envision a path forward in
case the disaster occurred, publishing experiments in cane planting, grape
growing, and the reformation of rice planting.[3] Vice President John C.
Calhoun sought a state-based constitutional remedy (nullification), but
the political effect of the tariff was to create a sectional political identity
that mapped onto the regional agricultural interest. For the first time, persons confessed an allegiance to "the South" as a cultural, particularly agricultural, *and* political interest. For this reason, one encounters historians
who claim that "the South"—in the character we now recognize—came
into existence in 1828.

Was there a south before "the South"? Yes—but it was not a confessed
community; rather, it was an imposed political category. The Lords of
Trade in Whitehall in London created the Southern Customs District
early in the eighteenth century, policing and taxing British American external trade from Pennsylvania to Barbados. These colonies all had staple
economies, agricultural monocultures employing slave labor that produced
one of the commodities enumerated in the Acts of Trade and Navigation. This shared political economy in no way fostered a sense among
these entities of common interest or cause. Indeed, each viewed its neighbors as economic rivals vying for advantage with the merchants of the
metropole. Virginia promoted the interests of Virginia, not Maryland,
though both grew tobacco. South Carolina disparaged Georgia's commodities while touting its own. The sugar islands—Barbados, Jamaica,
Saint Kitts, Grenada, Dominica—jostled each other for commercial and
political advantage. Perhaps a negative community existed, for staple colonies only viewed other staple colonies as threats. This separatism survived
the American Revolution, shaping convictions of state autonomy.

And what of "the South" that people avowed after 1828? It was a vapor-
ous thing. The shared creed of "states' rights" gave the South the contra-
dictory tensions found in entities such as the "Libertarian Party." The old

jealousies between states proved so strong that commonsensical projects in regional improvement—such as road laying, railway expansion, or canal construction—faltered. Few expended much energy on imagining "being southern"—that is, asserting regional commonalities, recalling common history, or envisioning a shared future. Only William Gilmore Simms could be called a strong southern nationalist among public intellectuals before the Civil War. Visitors to the region from abroad and from parts north did more searching work perceiving regional manners, practices, beliefs, and ambitions. One resident group that *did* firmly grasp the common regional identity was the experimental agricultural community. Corresponding with local and even northern journals, they reported on innovations and problems of farming and gardening "at the south." Some northern journals—the *Genesee Farmer*, for instance—reserved space for regular contributions treating southern agriculture. Before "southern food" became fixed as a thing in print in 1861, the produce of southern orchards, gardens, and fields had long been recognized as "southern."

I hew to the chronology above in this history of southern food, presenting southern food's development in light of the region's own cultural consolidation from the 1820s through Reconstruction. I am consequently not greatly concerned in these pages with those narratives that dominate the telling of colonial food history: the stories of the Columbian exchange; the forced diaspora of African foodways and plant material occasioned by slavery; the transportation of Europe's livestock—the horse, cow, pig, sheep, and goat—into the Western Hemisphere; the importation of Europe's landrace grains and garden vegetables in the Americas; the appropriation of Native corn, squash, and beans and their cultivation methods into settler agriculture; the rise of staple monocultures in North America and the West Indies. Those histories have been capably told and serve as preconditions for the developments explored here. But in most particulars, the story I tell concerns other matters.

Some differences: colonial farmers learned their craft by rote imitation and planted crops believing the soil's vitality to be inexhaustible, provided they manured and fallowed their fields periodically; in the age of experiment, the degradation of soil quality forced farmers to read about farming, form associations, rotate crops, and discover restorative cultivars to maintain soil quality. During the colonial era, the free forage of hogs and livestock deprived farmers of the use of manure and created problems in animal management, particularly in terms of hogs ravaging fields; in the nineteenth century, the penning and fencing of animals forced farmers to devise feeding regimens, cultivate grasses and root crops, grains and vetches, for year-round sustenance, and made animal power and manure immediately available. During the eighteenth century, no system existed in America for the improvement and maintenance of seed. During the nineteenth century, professional seedsmen sold and traded seed trans-atlantically, often vending their product through grocery stores, supplying most of the garden vegetables and driving innovation in plant breeding.

What about cooking? In the eighteenth century, cooks prepared meals hearthside, with the approximate temperature control provided by thick-bodied cast-iron Carron wares (skillets, Dutch ovens, spiders); in the 1820s, with wood/coal cookstoves; and in the 1850s, the gas stove pro-vided fine-tuned temperature control, permitting the creation at low tem-perature of delicate sauces and enabling the reliable baking of cakes and breads at home without a brick oven. In the colonial era, yeast, with its long maturation time, governed the baking process; in the nineteenth century, new chemical leavens gave rise to the quick breads, inaugurating the biscuit age. While the colonial era saw the primacy of the household cook (whether the mistress of the household or a servant cook) in setting the standard of good eating, in the nineteenth century, the professional caterer served as the standard-bearer of fine cuisine. In the colonial era, the institutions of public entertainment and dining were the inn, tavern, and coffeehouse; the nineteenth century saw the rise of the hotel, the res-taurant, and the confectioner's shop as the temples of taste. In the colonial era, one was trained in kitchen craft by practical emulation of an accom-plished cook; the manuscript recipe collection was the commonest refer-ence. The nineteenth century saw the rise of the cooking school and the institution of the cookbook as an authoritative guide to kitchen practice. Cookbooks and magazine cooking instruction alerted readers about inno-vations in practice and asserted a cosmopolitan standard, against which local practices had to be judged.

Markets changed, too. As historian John Lauritz Larson and his fol-lowers have shown,[4] a market revolution occurred, overthrowing colo-nial dependency upon transatlantic goods by growing a robust domestic production and trade system. Improvement of roads, the construction of railways, and the rationalization of coastal shipping, particularly after the introduction of steam-packet vessels, gave rise to an efficiently networked scheme of national, regional, and local markets for meat, fish, and produce, as well as a parallel system of grocers dealing in dry goods, prepared foods, seed, alcoholic beverages, tea, coffee, sugar, and salt.

The southern food encountered here will be approached in light of the history of nineteenth-century developments sketched above. Yet in no way can southern food claim a distinct and organic character on the basis of these developments. Growers, marketers, and food preparers in the southern states embraced all of the innovations of plant breeding, selling, baking, and cooking that transformed practice throughout the United States and Europe. Participation in this restless course of innovation kept agricultural and kitchen practices evolving in the South. But what distinguished southern food depended upon a complex of other matters cultural, climactic, and economic.

Here I construct the tale of how and when the South *and* the Lowcountry became edibly distinctive. I will try to tell it without resorting to the type of characters that historians have constructed to stand in for various sorts of "voiceless" common folk: the farm family eating hog and hominy in the hill country; the subsistence farmer risking pellagra by depending too greatly upon his corn patch; or the slave woman stirring the kettle of greens at a hearth fire in the quarters. As a historian trained in the 1970s, when concern intensified for including the common people, the disadvantaged, and the intentionally excluded in narratives of what was, I initially subscribed to the notion that the written record presented the worldviews and interests of an articulate power elite. My work with historical archaeologists in Williamsburg in the 1970s doubly reinforced this article of faith. But thirty years of archival work in written records has convinced me that this article of faith does not hold water. Having reconstructed from various written sources the complex foodways surrounding West African and southern benne, the fruit-preservation techniques of mountain squatters in Tennessee, and the nut-curing processes of several southeastern Native Nations from print sources—matters not recorded in the WPA slave testimonies, in Appalachian oral history, or the tribal traditions of the Catawba and Creek peoples—I decided in this book to make a demonstration of just how much information on the emergence of this food heretofore unknown can be gleaned from published historical sources. I don't demean the value of oral history—but here I offer a complementary testimony that supplies a great amount of information shedding light on this region's food and foodways.

I've been particularly moved to include evidence from people whose contributions to the growing, harvesting, marketing, and cooking of food earned them names in their lifetimes. These were persons who bred and popularized the plants, organized the markets, created the dishes, and erected the institutions (hotels, restaurants, confectioner's shops, expositions) that projected to the public a face for food that would be recognized as regional. These names may not have passed down to posterity, but they registered in the writings, institutions, and objects that survive from the nineteenth century. These people were not nameless and voiceless. These people were not all, or even mostly, elite Anglo-Americans.

Whom will we meet? Sally Seymour, a free black pastry cook who founded a cooking dynasty in antebellum Charleston and whose own kitchen slaves would eventually introduce French artistry to the great town houses of that city. A West Point–trained engineer, Francis L. Dancy, whose love of citrus would give rise to the tangerine. South Carolina governor James Henry Hammond, disgraced because of sexual relations with underage nieces, who rehabilitated his political career by promoting the growth and processing of a cold-tolerant relative of sugarcane, South African imphee grass, or "sorghum." A plump Alsatian woman who emigrated to Louisiana and rose to the pinnacle of the male-dominated cooking profession in New Orleans, Madame Eugène. A black ex-Confederate gunrunner, Charles C. Leslie, who organized newly freed African Americans into the most efficient fishing fleet on the East Coast, and who became a celebrity in the world of scientific ichthyology for his knowledge of Atlantic fishes. John Michel, a lawyer and floriculturist, whose experiments with artichokes, strawberries, and rare potatoes galvanized his fellow horticultural enthusiasts into competitions that improved the produce quality in Charleston's famous market. A Falstaffian Revolutionary War guerrilla leader who introduced gold rice to the Carolinas after the Civil War had disrupted seed supply for traditional white rice—Hezekiah Mayham. Nat Fuller, a black butcher turned restaurateur, who staged the first mixed-race "miscegenation dinner" in Charleston in 1865 at his restaurant, the Bachelor's Retreat, and who founded a dynasty of African American cooks who would eventually preside over the city's hotel kitchens from Reconstruction to the Gilded Age. And a trio of sibling savants—the Summers—Thomas, a European-trained soil chemist; William, a crippled pomologist; and Adam, an adventurous livestock and vegetable breeder who wrote humorous magazine sketches as a hobby. And dozens more.

These are not the familiar names that have appeared repeatedly in the books that chronicle the rise of America's regional foodways. What are the familiar names? The botanists from John White of Roanoke to George Washington Carver of Tuskegee who documented the flora and fauna of the region. The trio of president planters—George Washington, Thomas Jefferson, and James Madison—who thought deeply and wrote profoundly about the need to reform American agriculture. The trio of literary mothers of southern cookery, the antebellum cookbook authors: Mary Randolph, author of *The Virginia House-wife*; Lettice Bryan, author of *The Kentucky Housewife*; and Sarah Rutledge, author of *The Carolina Housewife*. I have discussed the legacies of all of these significant figures in articles and public lectures over the past decade, but here they will play subsidiary rather than leading roles.

Yet certain things must be said about the trinity of founding cooking manuals here at the outset of our story. One cannot help but notice the pre-southern orientation of the titles—the reader invoked in the title is a housewife of a state, not of the South. Those familiar with early cookbooks will notice that the ordering of sections—soup, beef, veal, mutton, venison, pork, et cetera—follows the English template. The soup section contains the most American array of dishes and ingredients of any in the books; of the forty-one preparations in Randolph's volume, seven have no precedents in European manuals: Butter Bean Soup, Cat Fish Soup, Corn Soup, Field Pea Soup, Ochra Soup, and Squirrel Soup. The chief ingredient, not the mode of preparation, supplied the novelty. The least novel section of the books? The meat recipes are nearly entirely traditional.

In *The Kentucky Housewife,* the fish recipes surprise because of the number of saltwater creatures named—shad, halibut, sea bass, sturgeon, salmon, flounder, mackerel, rockfish—as well as lobsters, oysters, and crabs. Live portage of seafood up the Mississippi and Ohio Rivers to Louisville made seafood available in the northern section of the state from Evansville to Louisville. The thirteen venison recipes suggest the enduring importance of the wild harvest of game in the state in the antebellum period.

The Virginia House-wife is noteworthy for its regional vegetables, its collection of fritter recipes, and the extent of its poultry and wildfowl offerings. *The Carolina Housewife* dramatizes the importance of breakfast, beginning the collection with morning quick breads. The placement of fish and shellfish before beef and veal also conveyed the different emphasis of Lowcountry cuisine, as did the number of rice recipes in the entrée and baking sections (a matter that Karen Hess explored exhaustively).

All three books exploited the boom in American sugar production, including sections on preserves and homemade liquors—both indices of cheap sugar (see chapter 13 on sugarcane below). All three presume the possession of a cookstove with sufficient temperature control to perform the sauces and cakes. All recognize the imperative to supply pickled versions of garden vegetables when they are out of season. Yet the matter that most needs recognition is that despite the English heritage of all three authors, the cooking aesthetics of the collections have been inflected by *French* kitchen practices.[5]

Culinary historian Susan Pinkard identified the distinguishing characteristics of modern French cuisine in her 2008 book *A Revolution in Taste*. As codified in Nicolas de Bonnefons's classic *Les délices de la campagne* (1655), French cuisine sought refinement and delicacy by featuring the natural taste of the chief ingredient framed by complementary sauces, usually employing herbs—not spices—as in early modern European cookery. The new delicacy lavished attention on vegetables and fruits, exploring their qualities and affinities. While Enlightenment English dieticians embraced features of the new French style, some aspects provoked resistance. Hannah Glasse, the matriarch of bluestocking cookbook authors, denounced the sauces—the time-consuming roux and emulsions—for their demands upon the common cook and their expense. Indeed, an English cult of meat and pudding simplicity arose, denouncing ragouts and fricassees while exalting the rare roast beef of Britain.

Yet in the three founding regional cookbooks, one finds the French aesthetic firmly in place: the interest in vegetables, the sauces, the puff pastry, and the confectionery. It is against the background of dishes cooked simply and featuring their chief ingredient that the African American stews and composite dishes stand out as a distinct supplement to household cooking.

When we calculate the influence of French cuisine on American cookery, the tendency is to argue that the post–Civil War ascendency of chef Charles Ranhofer of Delmonico's restaurant in New York inaugurated an era when French *haute cuisine* became the measure of professional cooking in the country. Its temples were the hotel and restaurant, not the household. In the South, its bastion was New Orleans, and the most potent combination of French technique and American ingredients took place in Louisiana, as chronicled in the trio of founding Creole cookbooks: *The Creole Cookery Book* (1885), *La Cuisine Creole* (1885), and *The Picayune Creole Cook Book* (1901).

Let me begin here by charting how the influence of French cuisine became ubiquitous *throughout the South in the antebellum period*, with the French aesthetic influencing the cooking of the Chesapeake, the Lowcountry, and the Gulf Coast with equal directness, and how restaurants, hotels, and clubs drove the refinement of local approaches to ingredients. In the chapters that follow, I provide detailed histories of the rise of the profession of catering in New Orleans and Charleston, supplying a summary view of the hotels, restaurants, and chefs. I then take signature meals from the Chesapeake, the Lowcountry, and from the Old Southwest to suggest the breadth of performance in professional cooking. Though these initial chapters concentrate on a few major centers (and a minor one), every southern city from the 1830s through the 1870s boasted at least one standard-bearing Gallic eatery that handled local ingredients and the finest imported groceries with delicacy and savor. These would influence even those dining places that pursued the alternate aesthetic: the Anglo beef, game, oysters, and alcoholic spirits model of entertainment.

Let us take a whirlwind tour of the finest early restaurants in the antebellum South. Baltimore stood as the northernmost bastion of French treatment of southern ingredients, famous for its club cuisine as well as its restaurants. Hooke's Parisian Restaurant, located on the corner of Gay and Lombard Streets, introduced continental decorum to the city in the 1840s, enabling women and men to dine together in public in a setting undisturbed by saloon boisterousness.[6] It offered an alternative to the venison and oyster restaurants, such as the Rainbow House, Mrs. Cloud's restaurant, and Moody's. The contest of styles reached a climax in the 1850s, with the emergence of two great restaurants epitomizing the paths of southern cuisine. The high temple of meat in the Monument City was Charles Haffcke's restaurant at No. 5 Fourth Street. "Gamester and caterer," Haffcke periodically advertised his offerings of the premier cuts from the greatest butchers in New York and Baltimore, for instance: "the finest portions of the magnificent beef just slaughtered by Jacob Rice of this city."[7] French refinement "à la Paris" could be had at F. Lagroue's French Restaurant on North Charles. Lagroue's greatest contribution to the region's cookery took place, however, in his formulation of the menu for the "Maryland Feast," the finest achievement of American club cuisine in the antebellum period. Because this meal became a benchmark of both American and southern fine dining, I have devoted a separate chapter to exploring Lagroue's masterwork.

Maryland's capital, the colonial city of Annapolis, also had its venue for Gallic fine dining in the antebellum period in the mid-nineteenth century, J. Bonnafous's French Hotel and Restaurant on Main Street opposite the city hotel. Though it indicated a willingness to serve breakfast and supper at the convenience of the customer, it specified its regular dinner seating at the hours 2:30 to 4:00 p.m. in the afternoon.[8] Its status as the city's standard of fine dining was supplanted by Black's on State House Circle, an establishment also on the European plan.

The nation's capital had a community of French chefs and confectioners active in the antebellum period. The dean of these culinarians was Joseph Boulanger, who had come to Washington, DC, as steward of Ambassador Sir Charles Vaughan of Great Britain. He stayed, became the White House chef under president Andrew Jackson, and afterward opened the American and French Restaurant on Pennsylvania Avenue across from Gadsby's National Hotel. He served the city until his death in the early years of the Civil War.[9] Louis Galabran came to Washington, DC, in the mid-1830s setting up a restaurant, the European House, on the corner of Thirteenth and Pennsylvania Avenue. It became a fixture of conviviality in the city.[10] His chief rival, John Prevaux, opened the Franco-American restaurant on Sixth Street. It angled for a congressional clientele and became a favorite resort of the European diplomatic corps.[11] Charles Gautier could be consider Galabran's successor, becoming the city's high-end caterer after Galabran's death in 1847. His La Ville de Paris confectionery store on the corner of Eleventh and Pennsylvania blossomed into a restaurant, grocery, and wine-importation empire. Gautier's Saloon erected in 1853 was for its time the most splendid purpose-built restaurant in Washington, DC.[12] Gautier served every significant national figure in politics, the military, and the theater during the 1850s.

The restaurant scene in Richmond, Virginia, was dominated by the dining rooms of its hotels—the Spottswood, the Monumental, the Powhatan, the Ballard House, and the St. Charles. Because these institutions followed the New York/Boston model of hotel cuisine that emphasized proteins, particularly game—wildfowl, shellfish—hard spirits, and desserts, the more refined, seasonal fare of the French eateries was scanted. Yet Gerot's Restaurant on Bank Street between Ninth and Tenth presented the luxurious alternative to hotel carnality: "One need not blush to take a prince there accustomed to Parisian luxuries and cooking, to get a sumptuous dinner or any other meal."

Because the North Carolina French culinary scene was brought into being by the Rutjes family featured in the profile of Charleston pastry chefs that follows, I will pass over the state's history here, turning to Georgia. Of Savannah eateries, midcentury travel guides attested, "The best is the Restaurant Francais, in Whitaker Street, between Bay and Bryan."[13] Up the Savannah River at Augusta, Girardey's Restaurant combined the features of a Philadelphia or Baltimore oyster cellar (New York, Norfolk, and Savannah oysters advertised part of the season; Brunswick oysters, at other months), and a Parisian restaurant with M. Washington, "an excellent and experienced French Cook," presiding.[14] While Girardey's upheld the standard of haute cuisine during the antebellum period, its place in the postwar scene was taken up by Alfred Esmerey's French Restaurant on Ellis Street.[15]

St. Augustine, Florida, though the most ancient city on the eastern seaboard, did not become a sufficiently metropolitan place to support hotels and restaurants until the second quarter of the nineteenth century. Its finest hotel, the Magnolia House, combined standard hotel fish and game with French confections. Even after the Civil War, certain of the city's boardinghouses, those of Mrs. Brava and Mrs. Gardner particularly, had greater reputations for meal service than the city's hotels. Delot's Restaurant was the flagship of French cuisine in Florida. A thoroughly cosmopolitan and contemporary institution, it boasted a back billiard saloon for sporting men.[16]

In the 1800s the Gulf states, Mississippi and Alabama, were culinary outposts of Creole cuisine—or French fare à la New Orleans. The kitchens of the resort hotels and restaurants of Biloxi and Pass Christian were colonized by New Orleans talent during the summer season, and sometimes owned by one of the Louisiana hotel families, such as the Denechauds. Mobile, Alabama, a French colonial city, had its own Gallic tradition. Outside of New Orleans, it boasted the most splendid tables of any southern urban area, with restaurateurs Louis Verneuille, V. L. Lefort, Louis Launoy, and Madame Frozine Madrid all vying for culinary supremacy in the 1850s and '60s.[17] Like the cities of the Gulf Coast, those on the banks of the Mississippi took pains to recognize their French heritage. Natchez's hotels—the Steamboat, whose table "was far better furnished than Richardson's at New Orleans"—the Mansion House, and Parker's Mississippi Hotel intermixed Creole dishes with standard hotel entrées from the 1830s to the outbreak of the Civil War.[18] St. Louis possessed a sequence of excellent French restaurants throughout the nineteenth century, the most splendid of which was Furcy & Thompson's French Restaurant at 48 and 50 Olive Streets, the premier dining place in the city in the 1840s and '50s.[19] While Memphis, Tennessee, had a noteworthy French restaurant run by W. Philibert at 38 Jefferson Street, it differed from nearly every southern city of the century by being a hotbed of Italian culinary activity, with six Italian restaurants active in town during Reconstruction.[20]

Certain dimensions of French culinary aesthetics—dimensions experienced in all parts of the South by urbane diners—were preconditions for southern cooking as it emerged in the second quarter of the century. Foremost of these was a focus on ingredients—particularly vegetables, fruits, and herbs—that made kitchen gardening and orchard-keeping activities upon which home and market depended. What was most distinctive about original southern cooking was its ingredients—not any penchant for frying, hot dishes, or one-pot meals, but rather the natural provision of its waters, forests, and flyways; the plants that grew in its semi-tropic climate; and its various soils.

THE TREASURY OF GARDEN VEGETABLES

Two quests have heretofore shaped historical understanding of nineteenth-century southern kitchen gardens: the search for the secrets of the slave garden and the attempt to understand the vision of horticultural possibility brought to life in Thomas Jefferson's plantings at Monticello. The desire to know the contents of the Huck patch has been fueled by the hope that there might be found cultivars traceable to Africa—okra, benne, guinea squash, and peanuts—suggesting that gardens might be a means of materializing the ways of life before captivity. Peter Hatch's thorough explorations of Jefferson's garden books and planting beds have revealed how an Enlightenment agriculturalist with a global imagination and an experimental inclination evolved several adaptations of the West's botanical legacy to the local conditions of Piedmont, Virginia.

For all the interest of these inquiries, neither informs us greatly about the normal practice of kitchen gardening in the South, particularly in its nineteenth-century heyday. How then to get at an understanding of what was grown, when, and where? While archaeology (used with particular nuance at Monticello) can give us the particulars of what was grown in specific sites, it is a costly knowledge with so narrow a set of findings that one hesitates to impute larger regional patterns to them. There is, however, one body of evidence that can supply a general picture: the stocks of southern seed brokers purveying garden seed to local purchasers. A print record of their offerings exists from the founding of the Republic to the present day in the form of advertising handbills, newspaper advertisements, and seed catalogs.

Located in cities and towns, the brokers engaged in one of four sorts of activities. They might be (1) market gardeners/seedsmen, (2) grocers, (3) druggists, or (4) commercial agents of one of the major seed-producing and seed-selling enterprises located in the North or in Europe. Every farmer or gardener of any size had to journey to a market center at several junctures during the year. In South Carolina, from the Revolution to the

Civil War, upstate farmers went to Augusta, Georgia; midland farmers to Columbia or Camden; and Lowcountry planters to Charleston. Grocers in smaller towns sold seed for the commonest plants—the sugarloaf, drumhead, and early York cabbages, the Windsor, long pod, and kidney beans, the silver skin onion, the Irish potato, the large orange carrot, the salmon radish, the Norfolk and short top turnips. These grocers depended upon the state's major seed brokers for supply; the brokers, in return, existed in partnership relations with suppliers beyond the bounds of the state.

South Carolina did not differ materially from Virginia, Maryland, Georgia, or Louisiana in its relation to the market for garden vegetable seed during the first quarter of the nineteenth century. It mutated into something distinctive in the second quarter. In every state there existed a succession of key seed brokers, usually settled in the state's metropolis. In South Carolina, the first were based in Charleston: gardener Robert Squibb, who farmed lots on the inland end of Tradd Street in the 1780s until securing a prime piece of land when allowed to farm the Orphan House tract in the 1790s, and John D. Vale, gardener and proprietor of the Cash Store at 111 Broad Street.[21] In 1796 the enterprising spirits merchant and grocer Henry Ellison expanded into the seed trade at his stores on Coates Row and East Bay. After the turn of the nineteenth century, George Revell, a grocer at 142 Broad Street, and gardener James Nesbet of Funchal farm out on King Street past the race grounds took up the vocation. Revell's seed importation business was quickly outstripped by the partnership of Tait & Wilson, who showcased the inclusion of new varieties into their shipments after 1803. Any new broccoli that emerged in Europe came to Carolina through Tait & Wilson. Their success prompted merchant-grocers McKenzie & McNeill to enter the business. They imported in 1805 culinary sorrel into the Carolinas, permitting the enjoyment of the wonderfully astringent spring soup and the sharp salad green into the local bowl. They also shipped classic herbs into the Lowcountry.

Because a mystique built around imported seed, numbers of merchants besides grocers tried to develop the business, perhaps the oddest being bookseller W. P. Young, who offered London seed at his store at 41 Broad Street for several years beginning in 1804. A salad lover, Young introduced new lettuce varieties into the Lowcountry. In 1807 grocer G. F. Gennerick entered into competition but only supplied the commonest items. In 1808 a Seed Store appeared at 220 King Street. In that same year, Wilson & Tait transmuted into the partnership of Wilson & Paul. Thomas Cochran, another grocer, began to import seed in 1809, as did Samuel Nobbe, whose store was on the corner of St. Philip and Radcliffe. Patrick McClure joined the fraternity in 1810. Thus by the 1810s, a nationalist anxiety about the production of seed used in America by Britons and Europeans had spurred a North American seed-production agriculture in the Middle Atlantic states and in New England.

Pennsylvania, New York, and Massachusetts were the centers of American seed production early in the century. The first broker in the Carolinas to tout American product over English was George Shievely, whose Philadelphia Seed Store was located at 137 Meeting Street in Charleston. In 1815 Joseph Simmons, located conspicuously at the corner of Broad Street and East Bay, entered into competition with Shievely. Simmons would become in time the chief contact with the French plant-breeding community. During the same year, Mrs. Piere also entered into the business out on King Street.

In 1816 the hegemony of Charleston as seed capital of the state was challenged by Phineas Thornton of Camden. From a modest beginning, he steadily built a market gardening empire that would eclipse any seedsman in Charleston, excepting Robert Landreth in the 1820s. Encouraged by Thornton's example, druggist George Fitch established in 1819 a seed depot in the South Carolina state capital, Columbia, near the post office. He favored beans. The Robb family also entered into business at this time, with James Robb vending turnip seed and garden vegetables in Charleston, and with his two older brothers establishing a seed store in Columbia.

In 1818 an importer of iron garden tools in Charleston, A. Smylie, expanded his business to seeds. The multiplication of sellers and evidence of a willingness of farmers to buy American seed caught the attention of the Landreth brothers, who presided over the oldest seed company in the United States. Organized in 1784, headquartered outside of Philadelphia, and still in operation in 2012, David Landreth & Company Seeds thrived by attending to the demands of persons throughout the United States. Realizing that Charleston was the key to the southern market, the family dispatched Robert Landreth to set up a seed brokerage in 1819 at 228 King Street. Supplying berry and fruit tree cuttings, Landreth's operation expanded well beyond the usual constraints of garden seeds-manship. George Cox—a seed broker for field crops, particularly cotton and grains—expanded his business into garden seeds in 1820. An adept businessman, he took care not to duplicate Landreth's offerings.

In the 1820s James Wilson expanded his seed business from garden seed importation from Philadelphia and London into barley, wheat, and rye seed. He dominated the local trade in onion sets and celebrated the seedsmanship of the Philadelphia horticulturists, his suppliers. In the mid-1820s, druggist J. Rickard on East Bay entered into the seed import trade. In the 1830s, John Gidiere, a merchant with strong ties to Parisian merchants, entered the business, bringing in Parisian seed. The persons who entered the business in the 1830s and '40s tended to be merchants, whether transatlantic hardware traders such as William Dewar at 34 East Bay, or merchant grocers such as G. E. Ring at 202 King Street, his neigh-bors John Thomson at 254 King and F. Whittpen at 335 King, and Dawson & Blacksmith at 17 Broad Street.

From 1780 to 1820, premium garden seed came primarily from En-gland; indeed, a provenance from Battersea or Norfolk, or an important London or Liverpool supplier, proved a selling point. Plants propagated by sets and slips—onions and sweet potatoes—had local producers. But to speak of the garden as being somehow expressive of a region was non-sense when one looks at the origins of the seed. How the seed suited the soil and climate—that was local. Also local was a handful of cultivars that operated submarket in their seed production and distributions (okra until 1821, tomatoes until 1821, collards [colewort] until 1822, and eggplant until 1827). Elite planters, particularly those with the most experimental tendencies, operated at times independently of the seed market, securing roots, corms, nuts, and seeds from a transatlantic fraternity of agricultural experimentalists. Some vegetables—rhubarb, for instance—were exten-sively grown by elite gardeners before its roots were imported for general sale by James Wilson in 1834. Indeed, the Charleston Horticultural So-ciety offered prizes for the best rhubarb in 1831. In the 1830s, after the so-ciety instituted regular exhibitions and prizes for the best fruits and vege-tables, the winners' seed would be exchanged among society members.

In table 1, I indicate the variety name, the year in which the variety is first advertised for sale within South Carolina, the seller, and the origin of the seed. One notes immediately the plant categories that magnetized gardeners: beans, cabbages, lettuce, peas, and turnips. Certain items do not appear here: field cultivars such as sweet potatoes, potatoes, benne, sugarcane, field peas, and the various grains.

Let us restate the obvious immediately. When it came to seed, for the vast majority of garden vegetables it was nonsense to speak of a local origin. The seed market was transatlantic until the 1830s. After the 1830s, American companies from Philadelphia northward became active in the commercial supply of seed. In Charleston in the 1830s, the Charleston Horticultural Society's vegetable and fruit exhibitions made breeding and growing a matter of local competition (see the chapter on markets below), and the decade marks the popularization of local strains of flowers, vegetables, and fruits. During this decade, South Carolina growers supplied New York horticulturist William Prince with okra seed for development and sale to northern growers.

I have obtruded this lengthy list of vegetable varieties in the body of this book both to demonstrate how richly elaborated the world of the Lowcountry kitchen garden could be early in the nineteenth century, and to question more insistently that kind of food history derived from cookbooks. Each of these varieties had different growing habits, tastes, and culinary applications. Look into America's nineteenth-century cookbooks, one finds recipes that call for "a turnip," "a cabbage," "a cauliflower." While we can celebrate the fact that Mary Randolph, Sarah Rutledge, and Lettice Bryan offer recipes for okra, tomatoes, cymlings, field peas, and sweet potatoes, the disparity between the extensive list just presented and the laconic designations found in the three founding texts of southern cookery is stark.

Consider a case—a significant sample recipe: an early elaboration of the recipe using field peas for the southern New Year's Day standard hoppin' John. In her cookbook Mrs. A. P. Hill offered the following instruction:

> Pick out all defective ones from a quart of dried peas; soak them several hours in tepid water; boil them with a chicken or piece of pickled pork until the peas are thoroughly done. In a separate stew-pan boil half as much rice dry; take the peas from the meat, mix them with the rice, fry a few minutes until dry. Season with pepper and salt. This may be made of green English peas.[22]

TABLE 1. South Carolina Garden Seed Sources

Vegetable	Year	Broker	Origin
ARTICHOKE			
Globe	1808	Wilson	London
Green	1799	Ellison	London
ASPARAGUS			
Battersea	1799	Ellison	London
Dutch	1831	Smith	London
Giant	1820	Thornton	NY-NE
Gravesend	1799	Ellison	London
BEANS			
Bush	1820	Thornton	NY-NE
Canterbury	1809	Cochran	London
Chocolate Coloured Cranberry	1819	Fitch	NY
Dutch Runners	1820	Thornton	NY-NE
Dwarf	1800	Vale	SC
Dwarf White Kidney	1806	Wilson	London
Early Dun	1807	Cochran	London
Early Kidney or Liver	1820	Thornton	NY-NE
Early Mazagin	1820	Thornton	NY-NE
Early Mohawk	1853	Dawson	
Early Six Weeks Comfort	1820	Thornton	NY-NE
Early Speckled	1820	Thornton	NY-NE
Early Yellow Bush	1820	Thornton	NY-NE
Green Nonpareil	1809	Cochran	London
Hallum Bush	1819	Fitch	?
Helegoland	1820	Thornton	NY-NE
Kidney or Snap	1803	Ellison	London
Lima	1820	Thornton	NY-NE
Long Pod	1803	Moser	London
Negro	1807	Cochran	London
Pale Cranberry	1820	Thornton	NY-NE
Red Eye Chinese Bush	1819	Fitch	?
Refugee Bush	1819	Fitch	?
Rob Roy	1827	Robson	SC
Scarlet Runner	1803	Moser	London
Speckled Kidney	1803	Moser	London
Speckled Dwarf	1806	Wilson	London
Valentine Bush	1847	Ring	PA
White Albany Bush	1820	Thornton	NY-NE
White Battersea	1803	Moser	London
Windsor	1803	Moser	London

TABLE 1. Continued

Vegetable	Year	Broker	Origin
BEET			
Blood	1820	Thornton	NY-NE
Blood Turnip	1822	Thornton	NY-NE
Early Blood	1822	Thornton	NY-NE
Early Scarcity	1820	Thornton	NY-NE
French Sugar	1831	Gidiere	?
Long Blood	1850	Dawson	?
Red	1804	Revell	London
Yellow	1820	Thornton	NY-NE
BROCCOLI			
Early Purple	1803	Wilson	London
Early White	1803	Wilson	London
Fine New Cape	1816	Wilson	London
Green	1804	Young	London
Large Portsmouth	1809	Cochran	London
Late Purple	1804	Wilson	London
New Belvidere White	1816	Wilson	London
Purple	1797	Vale	London
Siberian	1803	Wilson	London
White	1797	Vale	London
BRUSSELS SPROUTS			
Common	1820	Thornton	NY-NE
CABBAGE			
Amsterdam	1821	Thornton	NY-NE
Battersea	1799	Ellison	London
Bergen	1822	Thornton	NY-NE
Bonneuil	1831	Smith	London
Choux de Milan	1804	Wilson	London
Coleworts [Collards]	1822	Thornton	NY-NE
Cornish York	1803	Wilson	London
Curled Green Savoy	1831	Smith	London
Drumhead	1786	Squibb	London
Early York	1820	Thornton	NY-NE
Early Sugar Loaf	1820	Thornton	NY-NE
Early Dwarf York	1804	Wilson	London
Early Dutch	1820	Thornton	NY-NE
Early Battersea	1808	Wilson	London
Early Penton	1808	Wilson	London

TABLE 1. Continued

Vegetable	Year	Broker	Origin
CABBAGE (CONTINUED)			
Early York	1786	Squibb	London
French	1804	Wilson	London
George	1830	Wilson	Liverpool
Green Curled Borecole	1820	Thornton	NY-NE
Green Glazed	1820	Thornton	NY-NE
Green Savoy	1797	Vale	London
Ice Glazed	1799	Ellison	London
Imperial York	1804	Wilson	London
Large Bergen	1808	New Seed	NY
Large Cow	1831	Wilson	English
Large English Savoy	1820	Thornton	NY-NE
Large Ox	1797	Vale	London
Large Scotch	1808	Wilson	London
Late Dutch	1820	Thornton	NY-NE
Red Dutch	1820	Thornton	NY-NE
Red Pickling	1797	Vale	London
Salisbury Fine Dwarf	1822	Thornton	NY-NE
Sugar Loaf	1786	Squibb	London
Tree (or 1,000 headed)	1822	Thornton	NY-NE
Turnip Rooted [Kohl Rabbi]	1820	Thornton	NY-NE
Turnip Rooted Below Ground	1820	Thornton	NY-NE
Wellington	1830	Wilson	Liverpool
Yellow Savoy	1804	Revell	London
CARROT			
Altringham	1831	Gidiere	?
Blood Red	1822	Thornton	NY-NE
Early Horn	1820	Thornton	NY-NE
Large Orange	1797	Vale	London
Long Lemon	1807	New Seed	NY
Long Red	1831	Smith	London
Orange	1803	Moser	London
Purple	1820	Thornton	NY-NE
Yellow	1831	Smith	London
CAULIFLOWER			
Asiatic	1848	Thomson	Paris
Early	1803	Moser	London
Early London	1820	Thornton	NY-NE
Early Paris	1831	Wilson	France
English Dwarf	1831	Wilson	London
Late London	1820	Thornton	NY-NE

TABLE I. Continued

Vegetable	Year	Broker	Origin
CAULIFLOWER (CONTINUED)			
London	1799	Ellison	London
North German	1831	Wilson	London
Walchrinae	1847	Thomson	Germany
White Cape	1831	Wilson	London
CELERY			
Rose Coloured	1822	Thornton	NY-NE
Salad	1797	Ellison	London
Solid	1803	Moser	London
CORN			
Early Tuscarora	1853	Dawson	NY
CUCUMBER			
Cluster	1807	New Seed	NY
Early	1820	Thornton	NY-NE
Green Turkey	1808	Wilson	London
Long Green	1820	Thornton	NY-NE
Long Prickly	1803	Moser	London
Prickly Gherkins (for Pickles)	1820	Thornton	NY-NE
Sub Cluster	1803	Moser	London
West Indian	1831	Gidiere	?
White Dutch	1831	Smith	London
White Turkey	1807	New Seed	NY
EGGPLANT			
Guinea, or Purple	1827	Robson	SC
GOURD			
Mammoth	1820	Thornton	NY-NE
GREENS			
American Cress	1808	Wilson	London
Batavian Endive	1804	Young	London
Black Mustard	1799	Ellison	London
Brown Mustard	1820	Thornton	NY-NE

TABLE I. Continued

Vegetable	Year	Broker	Origin
GREENS (CONTINUED)			
Corn Salad	1813	Shievley	PA
Curled Endive	1803	Ellison	London
Garden Cress	1797	Vale	London
Green Endive	1799	Ellison	London
Fennel	1809	Nobbe	?
Nasturtium	1809	Cochran	London
Sorrel	1805	McKenzie	London
Summer Savory	1820	Thornton	NY-NE
Water Cress	1797	Ellison	London
White Endive	1807	New Seed	NY
White Mustard	1797	Ellison	London
HERBS			
Balm	1809	Cochran	London
Basil	1805	McKenzie	London
Chervil	1797	Ellison	London
Curled Parsley	1803	Moser	London
Hambro Parsley	1809	Cochran	London
Hysop	1805	McKenzie	London
Peppergrass	1820	Thornton	NY-NE
Plain Parsley	1797	Vale	London
Pot Marjoram	1805	McKenzie	London
Saffron	1820	Thornton	NY-NE
Sage	1805	McKenzie	London
Sweet Marjoram	1805	McKenzie	London
Summer Savory	1805	McKenzie	London
Tarragon Roots	1820	Cox	New York
Thyme	1805	McKenzie	London
Winter Savory	1805	McKenzie	London
KALE			
German	1849	Landreth	PA
Scotch	1820	Thornton	NY-NE
Sea	1807	New Seed	NY
LETTUCE			
Brown Dutch	1799	Ellison	London
Cabbage	1803	Moser	London
Coss	1803	Moser	London
Dutch	1803	Moser	London
Early	1820	Thornton	NY-NE

TABLE I. Continued

Vegetable	Year	Broker	Origin
LETTUCE (CONTINUED)			
Grand Admiral	1808	Wilson	London
Hardy Green	1820	Thornton	NY-NE
Head	1820	Thornton	NY-NE
Ice	1820	Thornton	NY-NE
India Cabbage	1827	Robson	?
Imperial	1820	Thornton	NY-NE
Madeira	1831	Gidiere	?
New Large Florence	1816	Wilson	London
Passion	1822	Thornton	NY-NE
Royal Cabbage	1809	Nobbe	?
Roman Cabbage	1804	Young	London
Silesia	1804	Young	London
Tennis Ball	1808	Wilson	London
White Coss	1804	Revell	London
MELONS			
Cantaloupe	1811	Nesbet	London
Musk	1820	Thornton	NY-NE
Nutmeg	1820	Thornton	NY-NE
Paradise	1822	Thornton	NY-NE
Large Water Melons	1820	Thornton	NY-NE
OKRA			
Ochre	1821	Thornton	SC
ONIONS			
Deptford	1804	Young	London
Large Flag Leek	1827	Robson	SC
Large Scotch Leeks	1820	Thornton	NY-NE
London Leek	1797	Vale	London
Red	1820	Thornton	NY-NE
Red Portugal	1822	Robson	London
Shallots	1831	Wilson	PA
Silver Skin	1797	Vale	London
Strasburgh	1809	Cochran	London
Welsh	1809	Cochran	London
White	1820	Thornton	NY-NE
White Portugal	1797	Ellison	London
White Spanish	1807	New Seed	NY
Yellow New Danvers	1853	Dawson	NY
Yellow Silver Skin	1853	Dawson	NY

TABLE 1. Continued

Vegetable	Year	Broker	Origin
PARSNIP			
Large	1797	Vale	London
Swelling	1820	Thornton	NY-NE
PEAS			
Black Eye Marrowfat	1853	Dawson	?
Blue Imperial	1853	Dawson	?
Branching	1810	McClure	London
Chene	1852	Williams	?
Double Blossomed Frame	1816	Wilson	London
Dwarf	1820	Thornton	NY-NE
Dwarf Cluster	1820	Thornton	NY-NE
Dwarf Marrow	1799	Ellison	London
Dwarf Spanish	1807	Cochran	London
Dwarf Sugar	1811	Nesbet	London
Early Charlton	1799	Ellison	London
Early Dwarf	1803	Moser	London
Early Egg	1809	Nobbe	?
Early Frame	1799	Ellison	London
Early Petersburg	1817	Thornton	NY
Early Warwick	1853	Dawson	?
Green Prussian	1809	Nobbe	?
Golden Hotspur	1804	Wilson	London
Imperial Green	1804	Wilson	London
Knight's New Marrow	1816	Wilson	London
Leadsman Dwarf	1811	Nesbet	London
Lord Anson's Vine	1822	Thornton	NY-NE
Marrowfat	1803	Moser	London
Prince Albert	1848	Thorburn	London
Prolific	1809	Nobbe	?
Prussian Blue	1803	Moser	London
Spanish Dwarf	1807	New Seed	NY
Spanish Marrowfat	1809	Nobbe	?
Spanish Moratta	1807	New Seed	NY
Tall Marrowfat	1820	Thornton	NY-NE
Tall Sugar	1804	Wilson	London
Tall Transparent	1804	Wilson	London
True Prolific	1803	Moser	London
White Prussian	1816	Wilson	London
White Rouncivel	1811	Nesbet	London
Wilson's Six Weeks	1820	Thornton	NY-NE
Wilson's Superfine	1820	Thornton	NY-NE

TABLE 1. Continued

Vegetable	Year	Broker	Origin
PEPPERS			
Cayenne	1820	Thornton	NY-NE
Rabbet Nose	1820	Thornton	NY-NE
Squash	1820	Thornton	NY-NE
POTATOES			
Irish	1820	Thornton	NY-NE
PUMPKIN			
Mammoth	1820	Thornton	NY-NE
RADISH			
Black	1803	Moser	London
Black Spanish	1804	Young	London
Early Frame	1820	Thornton	NY-NE
Early Long Rose Coloured	1831	Smith	London
Early Rose Coloured Turnip	1831	Smith	London
Long Black Winter	1820	Thornton	NY-NE
Purple	1820	Thornton	NY-NE
Naples	1803	Wilson	London
Red Round	1808	Wilson	London
Salmon	1797	Thornton	London
Scarlet	1820	Thornton	NY-NE
Short top	1797	Vale	London
Turnip	1797	Vale	London
White Turnip	1808	Wilson	London
RHUBARB			
Large Roots	1834	Wilson	London
RUTABAGA			
Ruta Baga (Yellow Russian Turnip)	1819	Thornton	NY
Skirving's Improved	1849	Dawson	Liverpool
SALSIFY			
Vegetable Oyster	1813	Shievley	PA

TABLE 1. Continued

Vegetable	Year	Broker	Origin
SPINACH			
Prickley	1799	Ellison	London
Round	1799	Ellison	London
SQUASH			
Early Bush	1827	Robson	?
Com. Porters	1820	Thornton	NY-NE
Serpent	1820	Thornton	NY-NE
Summer Bush	1820	Thornton	NY-NE
Winter Crook Neck	1820	Thornton	NY-NE
TOMATOES			
Tomato	1821	Thornton	SC
TURNIP			
Early Flat Dutch	1830	Wilson	Phil
Early Spring	1820	Thornton	NY-NE
Fine Early Stone	1830	Wilson	Phil
Green Round	1811	Nesbet	London
Green Top	1820	Thornton	NY-NE
Large Bullochs Aberdeen (Yellow Scotch)	1820	Thornton	NY-NE
Large Norfolk	1808	Wilson	London
Large Silver	1800	Vale	SC
Large White Flat	1819	Thornton	NY
London White	1804	Wilson	London
New Long White Transparent	1816	Wilson	London
Norfolk	1800	Vale	London
Red Top	1820	Thornton	NY-NE
Red Top Tankard	1825	Wilson	Liverpool
French, or Hanover	1820	Thornton	NY-NE
Short Top	1808	Wilson	London
Snowball	1848	Landreth	PA
Strap Leaf	1849	Dawson	Liverpool
Swan's Egg	1837	Wilson	NY
White Scotch Globe	1823	Robb	?
White Top Tankard	1825	Wilson	Liverpool
Yellow	1808	Wilson	London
Yellow Stone	1811	Nesbet	London

The substitutability of English peas for field peas, the disinclination to specify a type of dried pea, the generic designation of "rice" as an ingredient typify the homemaker pragmatism that characterized the listing of ingredients in nineteenth-century cookbooks generally. Always aware that a reader might not have a particular ingredient available, the author used the most categorical designation possible for vegetables, grains, and meats.

Cookbook authors avoided particularizing varieties of fruits or vegetables. Even fewer (three, maybe four) said *anything* about the production, the growing of the vegetables or fruits indicated for use. Consider briefly the role of famous authors silent about the subject. None of the great matrons of the cooking schools spoke of it. Not Lydia Marie Child, Mrs. Ellis, Mrs. E. A. Howland, Miss Leslie, Sarah Josepha Hale, Elizabeth Ellet, Mrs. S. T. Rorer, S. Annie Frost, Jennie June, Catharine Beecher, Juliet Corson, Maria Parloa, or Fannie Farmer. Nor did the master hotel chefs of the century—William Volmer, Pierre Blot, Felix Deliée, Charles Ranhofer, and Alexander Filippini. None of these figures noted the stupendous increase in the variety of types of vegetables available.

I do not impugn the abilities or knowledge of these influential authors. The creativity registered in their works lay elsewhere than the meats and vegetables sections; it appeared in the sections on baked goods, puddings, and confections, wherein the cooks and chefs reported the results of energetic experimentation analogous to their contemporaries, the experimental horticulturists. The extraordinary achievements in baking and confectionery deserve a separate historical study and appreciation.

American cookbooks (and I include the canon of southern classics by Mary Randolph, Sarah Rutledge, Mrs. A. P. Hill, Mrs. Lettice Bryan, Mrs. Maria Barringer, Mrs. Sarah A. Elliott, Miss Tyson, Marion Cabell Tyree, Mrs. B. C. Howard, Lafcadio Hearn, the Christian Woman's Exchange of New Orleans, A. G. Wilcox, Mary Stuart Smith, and Mrs. Washington)[23] of the nineteenth century did not register the single most distinctive development of the national cuisine—the enormous proliferation of fruit, grain, and vegetable varieties during the 1800s. All of the genius at plant breeding visible in any seed catalog, horticultural journal, or agricultural magazine vanished in the recipes. Authors of gardening compendia attempted to compensate for the shortfall of information. The landmark books all specify the most popular varieties of garden cultivars:

Thomas Fessenden's *New American Gardener* (1835), Thomas Bridgeman's *Young Gardener's Assistant* (1837), Francis Holmes's *Southern Farmer and Market Gardener* (1842), L. D. Chapin's *Vegetable Kingdom* (1843), Robert Buist's *Family Kitchen Gardener* (1850), William N. White's *Gardening for the South* (1857), Alexander Watson's *American Home Garden* (1859), Fearing Burr Jr.'s *Garden Vegetables* (1866), and Burr's *Field and Garden Vegetables of America* (1865). From the 1850s onward, horticultural authors made an effort to designate the suitability of certain varieties for culinary uses (e.g., red Dutch was a favorite "pickling cabbage," or long green turkey was a salad rather than a pickling cucumber). When authors commented on typical modes of preparing a vegetable, the explanations tended toward the rudimentary. William N. White's remarks upon frying eggplants, for example, were representative of a multitude of cooking observations in contemporary gardening manuals:

> Cut the egg-plant in slices a quarter of an inch thick. To remove the acrid taste, pile the slices on a plate with alternate layers of salt; raise one side of the plate, that the juice may run off. In half an hour wash them well in fresh water, and fry them quite brown in batter.[24]

No mention of the frying medium, the constituents of the batter, the time of cooking, or the required degree of heat grace this minimal instruction.

For the past twenty years, Wendell Berry has been excoriating the state of affairs that has led to a disconnect between the production and preparation/consumption of food. His demand that we conceive of eating as "an agricultural act" sounded the tocsin against food ignorance. The "farm to table" aesthetics of many current chefs responded to the call to bridge the gap. Yet when we look to the canon of American national and regional cookbooks before the rise of industrial agriculture and commercial food processing and marketing, witness that the disconnect between production and cooking and eating has existed since the nation's founding. It has been a fixture of American print culture since the early nineteenth century. Inscribed in two mutually exclusive bodies of print (garden books and cookbooks), we witness a cultural fissure firmly in place in the mid-nineteenth century.

Surely the more capable chefs and cooks of that time possessed the knowledge that bridged the gap. François Lagroue, the chef of the Maryland Club who concocted the Maryland Feast, and Eliza Seymour Lee, preparer of the Jockey Club banquet in Charleston, encountered the plenitude of southern vegetable culture every time they visited their cities' produce markets. They selected items calling upon a fund of experience about which varieties suited which dishes best. This ingredient wisdom gave the best cooks distinct advantages over rivals, and thus became part of the withheld knowledge of culinary practice. It is precisely this profound practical knowledge of ingredients that regionalist chefs most wish to recover in the present day.

Is there any book in the vast archive of nineteenth-century American cookbooks that reveals the kitchen wisdom about produce? Did any cookbook bridge the divide between the market, garden, and stove? Of the multitude of cookery manuals that sprang from the press during the heyday of agrarian America—from 1820 to 1920—few connected the kitchen to the garden, the table to the farm field: Mary L. Edgeworth's *Southern Gardener and Receipt-Book*, published in Philadelphia on the eve of the Civil War, and its model, Phineas Thornton's *Southern Gardener and Receipt Book* (1839, 1845), remain of interest for their elaborations of the use of sugar to preserve fruit. Yet their recipe sections were cursory. Fortunately, one work, composed by one of the greatest cooks in North America, reveals the mind of the chef—Jules A. Harder's *Physiology of Taste; or, Harder's Book of Practical American Cookery*—published by the author in San Francisco in 1885. Harder alone exposed the whole knowledge of the master chef, after decades of securing ingredients and tending the stoves at Delmonico's in New York and at the Palace Hotel in San Francisco. He supplied what others kept as privy intelligence: the deep farm-to-table knowledge of the ingredients.

Artfulness in vegetable cookery lay in conceiving of preparation in terms more nuanced than the simple application of cooking methods to an item: boil it, bake it, roast it, pickle it, fry it, dry it. At minimum, the capable cook knew the most suitable method of bringing the peculiar qualities of a product to the fore, whether dressed as a side dish or as a component of a composite dish. The compatibility of a dish to the other preparations on the menu for a meal comprised another level of artistry. Mastery in vegetable cookery lay in a systematic knowledge of all the possible modes of preparation of any ingredient available in the cycle of seasons. Harder was concerned with this last.

Harder commended his *Physiology of Taste* to readers as "the result of a lifetime of study, constant observation, and practical experience in the best culinary establishments of both Continents. He, therefore, brings to his task a thorough knowledge of the subject, and asserts, fearless of successful contradiction, that the result of his labors will be the only competent treatise—applying culinary science especially to the material conditions of this country—ever written. He intends it for a trustworthy guide to all what to eat and drink, and what to avoid." His treatise discussed "vegetables and all alimentary plants, roots, and seeds grown on the American continent," presenting "the best varieties, their mode of cultivation, cooking, and other matters of interest connected with this branch of the culinary art—one, by the way, of no small importance, but to which generally scant attention is paid by the household, and even by the club and hotel, cook."[25]

The *Physiology of Taste* was the first of six projected volumes, covering all aspects of food. The five remaining volumes never saw publication; they would have explored "soups, fish, flesh, fowl, farinace, sauces, conserves, liqueurs." The encyclopedic design derived from Marie Antonin Carême's survey of French cuisine, *L'Art de la cuisine française au dix-neuvième siècle: Traité élémentaire et pratique* (1833–47, 5 vols.). Yet Harder's title also nodded to the other great theoretician of European gastronomy, Jean Anthelme Brillat-Savarin, whose *Physiologie du goût* proposed a "transcendental gastronomy"—that is, a system in which taste and a philosophy of consumption combine to make the experience of eating the highest sort of human activity.

Harder, however, abandoned Brillat-Savarin's intuitive order of matters and his pre-scientific speculations on the mechanism of the tongue, to explore the range of things grown and tasted. What Harder shared with Brillat-Savarin was the ambitious scope of inquiry. Just as Brillat-Savarin thought the Parisian restaurant table the nexus of a global system bringing by boat and oxcart an array of comestibles from every corner of the planet to the plate of the gastronomic citizen of the world, Harder conceived of the metropolitan food market and urban luxury hotel kitchen as the twin foci of America's national food production system. Only someone who

had cooked at the greatest restaurant (Delmonico's) in the most gastro-
nomically obsessed city (New York) in the country in the period after a
national rail transportation system had been built could have spoken from
experience of so vast an array of products as is contained in this volume.

How comprehensive was his scope? Thomas F. De Voe's 1867 *The Market
Assistant*—which described every article of food sold in the Philadelphia,
New York, Brooklyn, and Boston markets—treated 224 vegetables, herbs,
fruits, and nuts with no specification of the chief varieties of these cultivars and no indication of their agriculture. Harder treats 240 vegetables
and herbs (no fruits and berries, except the tomato), and details all of the
significant varieties, their cultivation, and preservation. Separate tables of
contents using French and German plant names appear after the English
contents. Organized alphabetically like the post-Enlightenment guides to
plants, it begins with a general discussion of a category of cultivar—its cultivation, care, harvesting, processing—followed by a listing of the favorite
varieties available in the United States, then recipes.

Harder's employment of the vegetables available to him in the New
York and San Francisco markets was hedged with rigorous judgment. In
the early nineteenth century, the great American metropolises were ringed
by huge glasshouse gardens growing produce suited to forced and controlled planting regimens. With the improvements in canning over the
century, an increasing percentage of the vegetable component of the city
diet was so preserved. Harder, in the name of taste and hygiene, spoke the
ban on both for the realm of gastronomy. "Preserved vegetables should not
be used for the table, if they can be possibly declined." "Vegetables forced
in hot-houses are not as good as those grown in the open air, and subjected
to ordinary natural conditions" (Harder, vi). This latter dictum gave the
seal of approval for the extraordinary market farming system that developed in the United States after the Civil War.

Jules Harder knew the South generally and the Lowcountry particularly through the superlative vegetables he encountered in New York from
1865 to 1874 that were shipped from Charleston, Savannah, and Jacksonville. (See the truck-farming chapter below.) In 1872–73 he cooked a season in Savannah, Georgia, but the death from disease of his three-year-old
son, Theodore, drove him north again in May 1873 to head the kitchen of
the Long Branch Hotel in New Jersey. Having every comestible item in

the country available for his inspection, he judged the virtues of produce with a circumspection and depth of knowledge unequaled by anyone of his era. He knew of Lowcountry preferences for sea kale, the southern cultivation of goosefoot (white quinoa), the inclusion of cuckoo-flower cress in Georgia salads, the use of strawberry tomatoes (*Physalis alkekengi*) in preserves, the African American benne puddings of Carolina. He knew that seven top turnips were cultivated for their greens, while the early white flat Dutch strap-leaved turnip grew in kitchen gardens for the table. Only in Harder's compendium do we learn of the affinity of the South for the drumhead short stem cabbage (62), or its fascination with the heat tolerance of the late-season green glazed cabbage (63). No other print source records the taste that southerners had for Burlington early Adams corn as a white table corn. Harder also notes the southern avoidance of sugar and cream in salad dressings (187), and he revels in the varieties of southern sweet potatoes. Trained in classic French technique, but kitchen-taught in American vernacular cookery to suit the taste of hotel patrons in Saratoga, New York, he approached each ingredient with a sense of possibility, hoping to discover what might bring its distinctive features to the fore.

That is how to approach the newly restored ingredients of classic Lowcountry cuisine. To the twenty-first-century tongue, these ingredients' tastes contain all the novelty and possibility that a Lowcountry guinea squash (long purple eggplant) did when Harder first encountered it as chef at Delmonico's. Harder fulfilled in the kitchen the accomplishments that the age of experiment had managed in the fields, orchards, and gardens. By returning to use the range of grains, roots, berries, and greens created during that time when taste mattered so greatly in plant breeding is to restore an aesthetic promise to cooking in this region. A living tradition does not foreclose creativity by ritually repeating a repertoire of dishes.

When Harder moved westward in 1876, he knew the finest fruits and vegetables grown in the country from his deep engagement with the New York produce market, their sources, and exactly how the regional truck-farming systems worked.[26] Upon arriving in San Francisco in 1875, he encouraged the construction on the West Coast of what existed in the East. His kitchen in the Palace Hotel in San Francisco became the *locus primus* of demand for fine produce. His encouragement to California farmers and his promotion of their finest creations contributed to the elevation of the

Golden State to the first rank among vegetable-growing regions. His fame in California was such that when Los Angeles vied to become the cultural capital of the Southland, it built a hotel to rival the Palace, the Nadeau House, and lured "the best cook of modern times" from San Francisco to head its kitchen.[27]

Adherents of the locavore movement will find Harder a redoubtable opponent. He understood that cities can never be sourced by the immediate locale. He believed that the finest dining depended upon the finest ingredients procured from wherever they may come without too great expense and peril to the quality of the product. Indeed, it was to serve this sort of vision of possibility that the country's infrastructure of transportation was elaborated so intensely from 1860 to 1960.

This is what can be ascertained of his career: Jules Arthur Harder was born in Alsace in 1830. His initial training occurred in Paris under Jean-Louis-François Collinet, the brilliant chef who created sauce Béarnaise and les pommes soufflés. He underwent seven years of training in the various branches of cuisines. He came to the United States in 1852, hired by Lorenzo Delmonico, and worked at his restaurant for ten years until hired by its chief rival, the Maison Dorée, in 1862 to replace its chef Charles Ranhofer. Some during the 1860s thought that "it was the best restaurant in the city." He then cooked at the Union Club in New York City. From there he was hired to be the French chef at the Union Hall hotel in Saratoga and was still there in 1869 when the hotel was rebuilt as the Grand Union, the largest resort in the United States. Because of the expansion of Delmonico's in New York into three premises, chef Charles Ranhofer hired him to be chef de cuisine at the Fifth Avenue branch, circa 1871. In 1875 when Warren Leland went west to establish a world-class hotel in San Francisco, Jules Harder accompanied them. He was the inaugural chef of the Palace Hotel, the landmark of California cuisine A decade later, in December 1886, he was hired to be the chef de cuisine at the first great luxury hotel in Los Angeles: Nadeau House. The death of Remy Nadeau and an inheritance struggle prompted him to move to the Hotel Delmonte in Monterey in 1888. After a decade in the kitchen at the Delmonte, the Macfarlane family lured him to Honolulu to become head chef at the Royal Hawaiian Hotel in November 1898.[28]

When he moved to the West Coast in 1875, the Hispanic dimension of his cooking took on additional prominence. In *Physiology of Taste*, Harder's recipes reflect an acute attention to the proper ingredient, the best kitchen technique, and knowledge of the strongest dishes making up the eclectic mélange of traditions that comprise American cooking. He has had to wait over a century to be recognized as the prophet of American regional cookery.

When regional cooking revived in the last decades of the twentieth century, a generation of chefs spearheaded the rehabilitation of dishes and cooking methods. Their cookbooks, their appearances on ETV, their writings in *Gourmet*, and the burgeoning lists of culinary magazines ignited a curiosity about the food identities of places. Chef Donald Barickman of Magnolias in Charleston made shrimp and grits a national icon of the Lowcountry. Elizabeth Terry of the splendid Elizabeth's on Thirty-Seventh in Savannah restored the fried grits cake to its honored place in Lowcountry cuisine. Yet it was the West Coast chef Alice Waters whose fetishistic concern with well-grown vegetables most raised consciousness about ingredients among culinary professionals. I do not doubt that the heady combination of regional revival, ingredient mystique, and the historical explorations of figures such as Karen Hess and John Martin Taylor contributed to the transformation of Glenn Roberts from a restaurateur to a grower and miller of landrace grains in the 1990s. Roberts's advent on the culinary exchange marked the conjunction of the world of the seed savers such as David Bradshaw and John Coykendall with the world of the chefs. What was needed was a guide—a key to the flavors and how they operated in cooking. It was among this circle that Harder's book became the grimoire wherein the properties of the storied ingredients could be divined. It should therefore come as no surprise that Sean Brock, the most celebrated chef among the "lardcore" revivalists of southern food, declares that his "favorite cookbook of all time" is Harder's *Physiology of Taste*[29] for its encyclopedic coverage of produce varieties—cultivation and cookery—and its challenging recipes. It is the greatest American cookbook because it is the one that most permits us to find a way to celebrate a world of traditional ingredients.

When Harder moved to Los Angeles, a reporter noted that the *Physiology of Taste* "comprises six large volumes of four hundred pages each. Dissertations on and instructions how to cook every known article of food are given, and the work is an undoubted authority."[30] Apparently, Harder had finished two volumes of his magnum opus. The unpublished volumes constitute the great lost treasure of American gastronomic literature. Yet the one volume that *did* get published would exert its influence—in the South as well as on the West Coast. Jane Eddington, the New Orleans cooking writer for the 1920s *Times-Picayune*, in the midst of a reflection on the proper employment of "sweet herbs," invoked the chef's expertise. "Anyone who can get hold of that rather rare book 'Harder's Practical American Cookery,' will find described in it an astonishingly long list of herbs with recipes sometimes for their use, and always a paragraph how to grow them. . . . His influence has gone on to this day."[31]

Now that Google Books has made a PDF copy of Harder's magnum opus available to the public for free, there is no reason why anyone should *not* take Eddington's advice. Its pages make visible the nineteenth-century convergence of horticulture, agriculture, gastronomy, and culinary art. Only in its comprehensive view of the continent's cookery does the distinct pattern of cultivars, aesthetic preferences, and dishes that signify southern cooking stand revealed against a background of general national practice. It came into being between 1830 and 1885, just as the South became a communal identity, post-1828. Farmers and cooks in the region organized a material expression of place and taste that served as a register of that identity.

THE INSTITUTIONS

Jules Arthur Harder's career makes visible the institutions that established social standards of practice and taste in cuisine in the United States. His European training inflected by ingredients in the New York and San Francisco markets resulted in fine food served in restaurants, hotels, and gentlemen's clubs. An active participant in professional associations and an instructor of a succession of American cooks, he conceived of his work as an art that answered to a tradition of culinary excellence, while giving pleasure to the public. In California, he engaged with a community of growers and meat packers to articulate a standard of quality in taste, configuration, and freshness for produce and meat. He codified his knowledge from the field, butcher shop, market, and kitchen in print for the benefit of culinary professionals and talented home cooks. His engagement with the existing postcolonial Spanish ingredients and Hispanic American preferences within the public caused him to explore and incorporate these features into his cosmopolitan repertoire. Around these institutions and practices, the food world of California was constituted in its enduring form. Only the later incorporation of Asian culinary dimensions altered in any fundamental way this constitution. He only encountered these toward the end of his career when he moved to Hawaii.

My order of business now is to document how these same institutions (European professional training, the hotel, the club, the restaurant, the market, and the book) shaped aspects of regional food identity in the South. We will see how European professional training, hotels, and restaurants shaped the formation of the world-famous professional culinary scene of antebellum New Orleans. In the Chesapeake, a French-trained chef created a menu that elevated local products to the level of artistry in the Maryland Club—and the world of gentlemen's clubs spreads its fame throughout the North and across the Atlantic. In Charleston, three dynasties of caterers spanning the nineteenth century—one French and two African American—trained in continental pastry cooking and elaborated the cuisine of the Lowcountry in civic banquets and society dinners. The apotheosis of this professional development of Lowcountry cooking was a banquet for the South Carolina Jockey Club in 1860.

These opening studies supply what has been missing from a history that has long been fixed upon domestic cookery and vernacular foodways. After suggesting how the institutions of professional cookery became differentiated in different parts of the South, I will examine the function of Lowcountry food markets to show their role in inspiring local vegetable and fruit breeding, calling into being market gardening and truck farming. I also will show how the market connects the towns of the South to a national system of provision and exchange while simultaneously focusing local production. Finally, I will explore several of the most critical ingredients of Lowcountry cuisine, showing how they developed and were taken up by cooks.

THREE *Madame Eugène and Nineteenth-Century Restaurant Cuisine in New Orleans*

No place in the United States obsesses about food heritage more than New Orleans. Yet the history of the city's cuisine remains oddly incomplete. What is missing, strangely enough, is the cookery that won the city its international reputation as the premier center of gastronomy in the United States: the restaurant fare of the nineteenth century. Instead, the domestic cookery of the city matrons and their *Creoles du colour* servants have been preserved and canonized as traditional Creole cuisine.

Two cookbooks stand as founding scriptures for the Creole tradition: the New Orleans Christian Woman's Exchange's *Creole Cookery Book* and Lafcadio Hearn's *La Cuisine Creole*—both issued from the press in 1885 in response to the World Industrial and Cotton Centennial Exposition held in New Orleans (1884–85). The Christian Woman's Exchange, a benevolent association of genteel women who collected funds to assist the female poor of the city and maintained a lunchroom, compiled their collection as a money-raising project, deriving material from "housekeepers experienced in the science of cookery as practiced throughout the South, and more particularly as it is understood and applied by the Creoles of Louisiana."[1] Hearn's famous collection also depended upon the manuscript recipes of city housewives, particularly Adrienne Goslé Matas and Lylie O. Harris.[2]

Historian Rien Fertel has recently determined that the third classic recipe collection of the New Orleans tradition, *The Picayune Creole Cook Book* (1901), was composed by Marie Louise Points. Its first five editions made explicit the purpose of the collection: to arm white housekeepers with kitchen skills at a time when the number of African American cooks was declining.[3] It, too, was domestic in focus. Fertel writes that the sixth edition attempted to obscure the collection's domestic *raison d'être*, insisting that its contents derived from the famous nineteenth-century chefs conveyed father to son in restaurant families. This is precisely what the cookbook was *not*. The domesticity of the contents remained evident despite the representations of the editor, and in the seventh and subsequent editions, the fiction of masculine transmission disappeared. Nevertheless, the sixth edition's invocation of the resonant names was telling. It revealed that the publishers wished the collection to have been a treasury of recipes from New Orleans' culinary heroes. It was not. Yet it makes one wonder, where *were* the records of the creations of the masters?

Chefs?

Perhaps there are still living many of the older generation who haunted the old French restaurants, they of the sanded floor and the incomparable cuisine. The names of the great chefs which became identified with New Orleans in those long-gone years may be still unforgotten. What of the delight "Mme. Eugène," who presided at Moreau's, when it was near the French Market? All of the gourmets of that time used to eat there, and many a visit was paid to New Orleans simply that one might sit at the table where Mme. Eugène's famous dishes could be set before them.[4]

The preface from the sixth edition continued by speaking the resonant names: Moreau, Victor, Miguel, Boudro, Leon, Antoine. Perhaps the editor was not old enough to have accurate memories. During Madame Eugène's reign at Moreau's from 1880 to 1887, the restaurant was located at 127 Canal Street on the boundary between the French and American sections of the city, not near the market. Moreau's had moved from Chartres Street near the market in 1850, three years before Madame Eugène arrived in America. While her cuisine at Moreau's inspired great celebration, her fame arose during the twenty years from 1860 to 1880 when she presided over Le Pellerin at 15 Madison Street. The only accurate expressions in the editor's rhapsody were that an extraordinary cook named Madame Eugène operated in New Orleans, and that her unnamed creations enjoyed the favor of gourmets.

Let me here give this artist a name and vocation. She was Sophie Dorn Flêche, Mrs. Eugène Flêche; after her marriage to Jean Baptiste Laporte in 1887, she was Mrs. Sophie Laporte.[5] She lived from 1836 to 1906. She characterized herself as a cateress. She viewed her *métier* as French cookery, not Creole. Nevertheless, she was the only of the city's restaurateurs to have recipes included in *any* of the founding trilogy of Creole cookbooks—a bisque and a crème in *The Creole Cookery Book*.

To understand Madame Eugène's art and career, we must first jettison the category of *chef* when regarding her vocation. In the twenty-first century, *chef* has become an honorific title bestowed upon anyone who demonstrates mastery running a commercial kitchen. In the early nineteenth century, *chef* had a more precise usage: it denominated an office in a household or institution. Chefs were superintendents of hierarchies (aristocratic households, hospitals, officers' billets, clubs) charged with processing food from purchase or selection to disposal and cleanup. A chef commanded staff. He (or she) rarely interacted personally with the consumers. In New Orleans, only the great hotels after 1837—the St. Charles, the St. Louis, and the Veranda—could be said to possess the scale that necessitated a crew overseen by a chef.

While the creation of the St. Charles Hotel (1835–37), the finest American hostelry of its day, brought national notice to the city's gentility and served as a catalyst to the city's emergence as a center of haute cuisine, the hotels almost never promoted the reputations of their chefs and confectioners by name.[6] While the management would advertise that "the Cuisine is supplied with the best French talent,"[7] the identities of the chefs creating food for the saloon, the gentlemen's dining room, and the women's ordinary of the St. Charles never appeared in print during the antebellum period so as not to distract from the repute of the hotel managers—the hosts.[8] Baptiste Moreau and Walter Van Rensselaer were chefs at the St. Charles during the era when it won its fame.[9] John Galpin was chef at the Veranda Hotel during its antebellum heyday, before opening a restaurant bearing his name.[10] Census records suggest that in 1850 the Hotel St. Louis had four resident kitchen staff: chef Prosper Bounecage, cook Michel Tromale, and two confectioners, Auguste Petremant and L. Testoratzi.[11]

The public representative of the kitchen in New Orleans restaurants used *caterer* to refer to himself or *cateress* to herself during the 1800s. English nouns derived from *acatour*, a French verb meaning to secure by purchase; they came to mean a *provisioner*, and it implied one who directly engaged with the public for which he or she provided. If "chef" spoke of a culinary master's relation with his staff, "caterer" spoke of the master's relation with the consumer. When a restaurant launched—or announced—a new kitchen virtuoso, or publicized a reopening, or trumpeted its seasonal offerings, a paragraph would appear in the *Daily Picayune*: "New Restaurant—The Cadeau Bleu, 49 Chartres Street, kept by A. Bruant, a caterer long and favorably known, is now said to rank among the very best restaurants in the city" (January 25, 1841); "John Galpin's New Restaurant—Who in New Orleans does not know the well earned and well deserved reputation of John Galpin, as a caterer of the creature comforts of life?" (December 2, 1860); "Pino's Reopening—The patrons of the well-known restaurant and oyster saloon, No. 23 St. Charles Street, known as Pino's, which is presided over by the famous host and caterer, Mr. A. Camors, will be delighted to know that, after a thorough overhauling and refurnishing, it has once again thrown opens its doors to the public" (September 4, 1869); "Bidwell's Phoenix House, 96 St. Charles Street, re-opens to-day in a state of entire rehabilitation with the renowned caterer Charley Yeager in charge" (September 25, 1881); "ACME OYSTER BAR—This favorite saloon is open to-day under [Gerome M.] Borges, the great caterer, who has laid in for this occasion the most liberal supply of good things" (August 12, 1876); and so on. While a caterer's responsibilities at times encompassed being host, primary emphasis remained on preparing fine things to eat. When the *Times-Picayune* commenced publishing recipes with "The Art of Soup Making" in November 1884, these instructions were signed "The Caterer."[12]

"Madame Eugène, who keeps the restaurant on Madison Street, is certainly one of the most successful and popular caterers in this city. She is the worthy successor of Victor, and the bon vivants of the city are accustomed to wend their way down to Madison Street to get a good meal, composed of the best material and always prepared in the most artistic and appetizing style."[13] This appreciative blurb presents in epitome some of the peculiar features of the world of the caterers. The most famous (like twenty-first-century pop stars) were known by single names. Grace King, author and preservationist, noted the bon ton's favorites in *New Orleans: The Place and the People* (1917), recalling evenings of racing and opera, "and the dinners afterwards, at Moreau's, Victor's, Miguel's, and the famous lake restaurants, with their rival chefs and rival cellars! And after that again the grand salons of the old St. Louis and St. Charles, filled with everybody; and all enjoying themselves."[14] The famous lake restaurants at Milneburg were likewise known by the single names of the caterers in charge: Boudro's, Miguel's, and, later in the century, Astredo's.[15] One of the challenges of sketching a history of this professional culinary world is getting behind the names to lives and kitchen practices. Grace King gives us only a sense of a kind of gastronomic achieved civility, a firmament of fixed stars.

Before we can appreciate Madame Eugène, we must understand how the scene she entered in 1853 came to be and came to recognize her talents.

THE SHAPING OF NEW ORLEANS' GASTRONOMIC FIRMAMENT

Before the restaurant were the tavern and the café. An eighteenth-century traveler to New Orleans might find accommodation and refreshment at several inns[16] if he or she did not seek the hospitality of one of the religious orders. Everyone in the common rooms of these public houses dined from a set bill of fare. One could choose beverages, not meat. In contrast, the restaurant distinguished itself by the range of dishes available to a diner. The customer could order à la carte. As an institution, the restaurant mushroomed overnight in Paris in the wake of the French Revolution's destruction of the aristocracy.[17] An army of unemployed household chefs sought their fortune in the metropolis, tempting the public with their creations. The Haitian Revolution similarly loosed a number of household chefs onto the North American continent, giving rise to the first American restaurants in Boston and the eastern coastal cities. New Orleans, the most French of the continental cities, would prove most congenial to the novel institution.

The restaurant became an adjunct to another novel institution: the hotel. Purpose-built public accommodations—with assembly areas, ballrooms, dining rooms, as well as sitting salons and sleeping rooms—first appeared in North America in the last decade of the eighteenth century. The first building so designed was the Union Public Hotel in the District of Columbia (begun 1793). The first successful functioning hotel was Manhattan's City Hotel (1794). The Boston Exchange Coffee House (1809) was the most impressive of the early erections. Size, stylishness, splendor, and service were hallmarks of these palaces of hospitality, marking them from the inns and taverns of the eighteenth century.[18] In New Orleans, several buildings bore the designation "hotel" from 1799 to 1832, none of which quite attained the dignity—the Hotel d'Orleans (1799–1907), the Hotel des Etrangers (1812), and the Hotel de la Marine ("the Navy Hotel"). The latter became significant in the development of the city's food culture, for its patrons dined at a fully fledged restaurant, R. Ravel's Le Veau-que-tete (the Sucking Calf), immediately contiguous. Le Veau-que-tete, according to the early commentators on the Crescent's City's civil culture, was the first to offer entrées à la carte as well as on the table d'hôte. The Hotel de la Marine, in its appointments and spaces, more approximated an inn than a hotel. Proprietor Bernard Tremoulet opened a second hostelry that aspired to the evolving international standard, the Hotel Tremoulet at St. Peter and the Rue de Levee, which had meeting rooms and a dining area.

John Davis nearly single-handedly wrote the next chapter of New Orleans' world of entertainment and hospitality. This moneyed refugee from Saint-Domingue wished his adopted home to have the cultural amenities of a European metropolis. He purchased the Hotel Tremoulet and dressed it in empire fittings. He opened a ballroom/banquet hall, the Salle d'Orléans. He founded a café, the Orleans, whose selection of liquors famously eclipsed the varieties of coffee served.[19] And he oversaw the completion of the Théâtre d'Orléans, "French Theater," near the junction of Bourbon Street and Orleans in 1819. Securing operatic talent from Europe and traveling dramatic troupes, he elevated the theater to the most consistently artistic and advanced in North America.

The glamour of the theater caused places of sociability to gravitate around it. If the first decades of the nineteenth century saw the culinary world of the city concentrated near the riverfront on Levee and Chartres, the third decade saw a restaurant world bloom around the intersection of Bourbon and Orleans in the vicinity of the theater and Davis's Orleans Coffeehouse. Other restaurants included the following:

Restaurant Guillaume was opened by the proprietor of the Hotel de la Marine on Rue d'Orleans, at the corner of Bourbon across the street from the Orleans Coffeehouse. It thrived in the late 1820s. For a period of time in 1830, it operated under the proprietorship of Cheri & Lafaye as the Paris Restaurant. They failed, then sold it back to Guillaume, who reopened the restaurant under his name in December 1830.[20]

The Paris Coffee House was located beneath the Restaurant Guillaume at Orleans St. and Bourbon under the direction of M. S. Chapus & Andre. This partnership dissolved in April 1831, leaving Chapus as sole proprietor. It rivaled the establishment upstairs in terms of its offerings: "Breakfast, Dinner & Supper, and the best dainties will be found there. Also Oyster soup and Gumbo, and oysters cooked in every style."[21] Because the audience of the theater included women as well as men, caterers made an effort to address their tastes particularly. Confectioners belonged to the staff of these establishments, and ice cream became chief among the "dainties" offered.

Café Louisianais opened on the corner of Orleans and Bourbon Streets in 1828 with L. D'Letra as proprietor. It gained a reputation for its confectionery department, advertising "Ice Creams and Sherberts of every variety and of the finest qualities being made by expert ice-men."[22]

Café Tricolore on the opposite corner of Bourbon and Orleans was opened by Plumard and Cheri in 1831. It sought a clientele that favored refinement in its dining experience: "Le service de la table ne saissere rien a desirer pour la proprete et la delicatesse des mets." [The table service leaves nothing to be desired in terms of cleanliness and delicacy of dishes.][23]

In February 1830, the number, profitability, and power of the café and restaurant owners had grown to such an extent that they organized a society of coffeehouse keepers to resist what they perceived as exorbitant taxation of their business by the municipal authorities.[24] Another mark of the public importance of these establishments was their use as places of public vendue. Goods and slaves were regularly auctioned at the Exchange Coffeehouse or Hewlitt's Coffeehouse on the corner of Chartres and St. Louis.

Flush times came to New Orleans in the late 1820s and with it a regular tide of merchants and traders from the Mississippi Valley. These seasonal occupants of hotels and lodging houses began to contract out regular boarding arrangements with restaurants, providing a steady source of income from October through April. Cooks, such as Jean Toy, who had worked at the hotels went on to found restaurants under their own names. Toy premiered his establishment in October 1831 at the corner of St. Pierre and Dauphine. The Cotton Boom culminated in the construction of the three great hotels during the 1830s—the St. Louis, the St. Charles, and the Verandah—announcing to the world that New Orleans offered accommodation and pleasurable entertainment on a scale competitive with any city in the Western Hemisphere.

The challenge posed by the great hotels to local eating house operators can be judged by the response of coffeehouse keeper John Hewlitt. The English-born Hewlitt, after the opening of the St. Charles in 1835, switched his base of operation to Banks' Arcade on Magazine Street. He jettisoned the name "coffee house" and styled his house a restaurant and imported the best cooking talent. His cuisine became decidedly French and stylishly refined.[25] By 1844 Hewlitt had developed a sufficient following to take over Bishop's Hotel. Rebranding the hostelry "Hewlitt's Hotel," he invited the city's bon vivants to an opening banquet at his Exchange restaurant. "From his turtle soup to his dessert, everything was surpassingly excellent. Those broiled pompanos were superlative, while the boiled capons, with oyster sauce, were what boiled capons should be. But the beef, the roast beef—we plant ourselves upon that—*was* roast beef."[26] His cook was a young Frenchman, John Marie.[27]

The period 1840–55 saw the maturation of restaurant culture in the city. During this period, Victor Martin (born in France in 1812) and Jules Martin (France, 1818), Baptiste Moreau (France, 1815), Madame Eugène (Sophie Dorn Flêche; France, 1812), Antoine Alciatore (Italy, 1822), John Strenna (Corsica, 1820), and Fritz Huppenbauer (Germany, 1825) emigrated from Europe and commenced their storied culinary careers in the city. These became the single names that designated the star restaurants— Victor's, Moreau's, Madame Eugène's, Antoine's, John's, and Fritz's.

Each of the great name restaurants possessed complex lineages. Unlike domestic Creole cookery that emphasized a maternal heritage of recipes and foodways, the legacies of the name restaurants did not have a Louisiana nativity (the caterers were literally not Creoles, having been born and trained in Europe). Furthermore, they transmitted their culinary art to protégés or collateral family members, rather than descendants. (The direct descent of Antoine's from Antoine to son Jules Alciatore is exceptional among the early name restaurants. The Deneschauds were the only other restaurant-hotel family that managed succession by lineal descent from the nineteenth century to the twentieth.) Take the case of Madame Eugène's being "the worthy successor of Victor." Madame Eugène was literally not the inheritor of the culinary legacy of Victor Martin. Her restaurant Le Pellerin did occupy a locale on 15 Madison that once housed Victor's. She could be said in a general sense to have taken on the mantle of champion of French cuisine. But the actual culinary inheritors of Victor's were his brother Jules (France, 1818), and nephew George Martin, and finally, and somewhat accidentally, Victor Bero.[28] When Victor's Restaurant burned on January 10, 1874, a newspaper reporter mused on its history.

> For forty years Victor's was the restaurant of the city, and until its removal to Canal Street [in 1865] and for some years thereafter, but not of late, was regarded as the best French restaurant in the United States. . . . Victor, the original first established himself on Madison street. . . . We believe that Madame Eugenie, that genial and stout hostess from Strasbourg, now keeps a most excellent restaurant in the building where Victor

began his career. . . . Victor . . . next opened on the old Place d'Armes, now Jackson Square, in one of those mouldy, old Spanish buildings, which were supplanted by the fine brick rows erected by Madame Pontalba in 1850. Here Victor's became a famous resort of the bon vivants of our city. In fact, its reputation extended throughout the valley of the Mississippi. Strangers of luxurious tastes and cultivated appetites, on visiting our city, regarded breakfast or dinner at Victor's as one of the chief enjoyments of our city, ranking it with a seat at the Orleans Opera or at the then magnificent old St. Charles. Victor's next move was to Toulouse Street, between Chartres and the Levee. Here the restaurant was greatly enlarged—in capacity, as well as in its business and popularity. Though several rivals had, in the growth of our city, sprung up—among which Moreau's pressed closely on the heels of Victor's—the latter continued to maintain its superiority. The elder of the brothers . . . about this time was tempted to go to Mexico and engage in some speculation, which deprived the restaurant of his valuable services, skill and supervision. He died in Mexico. His brother, Jules Martin, proved a worthy successor, and with the aid of his nephew, who afterward became so familiar with our people as the genial George Martin, maintained the reputation of Victor's as long as it remained on Toulouse Street. A model French dinner, equal to the best served in Paris, could always be obtained at Victor's. . . . The superiority of French cooking, supplemented by many Creole improvements, was thus demonstrated to even appreciative American stomachs, so that a taste for the gastronomic art became largely developed among our people. . . . After the death of George Martin [in 1873], Victor's declined greatly in the popularity, and Moreau's under the admirable management of Charley Rhodes, passed it in the race for public favor.[29]

This brief memoir revealed that both rival claimants to the title of best restaurant during the first age of New Orleans cuisine were institutions passed from a founder to a successor.

Charles Morton Rhodes Jr. (1822–1893), the caterer who piloted Moreau's Restaurant to supremacy in the 1870s, had been trained personally by Baptiste Moreau in the 1830s and by Moreau's appointed successor, Chef Moulin.[30] Moreau, a restless genius, had founded his restaurant on Custom House Street in 1837, the year of the St. Charles Hotel's completion. He hired Rhodes as a waiter and cook F. Moulin as his assistant. The instant success of the establishment did not satisfy Moreau, who moved the restaurant to Chartres Street. Then in 1839 he sold the restaurant to Moulin, who ran the restaurant with Rhodes as his assistant and maître d'.[31] Moreau was hired to take over the kitchens of the St. Charles Hotel and worked there for a decade, establishing its reputation as an international culinary destination. The strain of directing a corps of a dozen cooks and pastry chefs took its toll, and in the early 1850s, he turned the kitchen over to Fritz Huppenbauer. Moreau left the city to the Spanish Fort to found one of the great resort seafood houses. In 1849 Moulin and Rhodes moved Moreau's to Canal Street. Rhodes departed during the Civil War to serve in the Louisiana Defense Forces. In 1866 Moulin, by this juncture a wealthy man, decided to return to France. He contacted Rhodes, then presiding over a resort at Pass Christian, who returned to New Orleans and took over the kitchen at 127 Canal Street.[32] In 1880 Rhodes, fatigued at running Moreau's for twelve years, turned the restaurant over to Madame Eugène, who presided over the period of its greatest fame in the 1880s until marrying the wealthy merchant Jean Baptiste Laporte in 1887 and retiring herself.[33] Rhodes returned to the proprietorship and kept the restaurant running smoothly until his death in 1893. From 1893 to 1899, the cuisine declined at the hands of his son W. J. Rhodes, who saw the great merit of the establishment to be its location. Moreau's closed in 1899 when the younger Rhodes sold the premises to developers Macon & Kernaghan.

One encounters similar succession patterns and concerns with continuity in the famous Lake Pontchartrain and Bayou St. John resorts: Miguel's Phoenix House and Boudro's. During the 1840s, the lake resorts—Milneburg, the West End, and Spanish Fort—became famous for their seafood cookery. Railroad service between New Orleans and Milneburg by steam car began in 1832. During the same year, the New Orleans Navigation Canal from the city to the West End commenced construction. In 1838 a shell road was completed next to the canal for draft animals to haul barges and made carriage travel to Lake Pontchartrain easy. The Old Spanish Fort, a fortification erected at the mouth of Bayou St. John, was decommissioned in 1823. The Pontchartrain Hotel was erected there during the second decade of the nineteenth century.

During the 1840s, all three resorts became from May through September favorite day trips for citizens. Some of the hotels remained open until winter. There Boudro, Miguel, Moreau, and Bell transformed game and seafood into Lucullan feasts.

Miguel Brisolara (sometimes spelled Brisolari) was born in Genoa, Italy, the son of a pasta maker. When a child, his family moved to Barcelona, where Miguel underwent his culinary education. In his early twenties, he emigrated to Louisiana, secured a boat, and set up as a fisherman.[34] Yet his skills cooking the fish he caught secured him a position as cook at the Arcade, a porticoed wooden summerhouse on Lake Pontchartrain. He married a cook and the industrious couple—backed by Daniels and Bidwell, owners of Phoenix House, a picture gallery/bowling alley/oyster saloon in the French Quarter[35]—built their own unpretentious wooden dining facility in Milneburg, also called Phoenix House. Here, novelist William Makepeace Thackeray dined in 1853: "At that comfortable tavern on Lake Pontchartrain we had a bouillabaisse that which a better was never eaten in Marseilles."[36] Though Louisianans took pride in the novelist's compliment, they preferred others of Miguel's offerings: "Fresh fish and turtle soup and soft shell crabs, and game of all kinds, with the earliest vegetables, berries, and fruits, can always be had at Miguel's; and then one can sit down to a meal out upon his verandahs, with the cool breeze coming in from the waters of the Lake, with a feeling of satisfaction and enjoyment which can be sought for in vain in the city."[37] Fish were prepared variously, "from the plain fry to the most delicious of court-bouillons."[38]

Miguel insured that his legacy would survive when his powers began to decline in the 1870s by training "Leon" (Leon Dubuc Sr.?) to take over his kitchen and married his daughter Sarah to John Tresconi (1837–1902), an ambitious partner in a New Orleans oyster saloon. Tresconi, a native of the Italian Piedmont, had emigrated while a boy. Eighteen when he arrived in New Orleans, Tresconi's industry, instinct for business, and attraction to the role of public provisioner made him an ideal heir. In 1874 he assumed control of the Phoenix House, keeping his father-in-law involved as superintendent of cuisine.[39] He expanded his hospitality empire by becoming the proprietor of the Washington Hotel in Milneburg in 1886. His fortune was made when he rented the French Market from the city and collected vendors' fees.[40]

Miguel's friend and rival Lucien Budro (1810–1867) was born and trained in France, coming to America as a young man. He made his name presiding over the kitchen at Davis's Hotel in Mandeville. In 1843 he opened his resort, the Shell Road Hotel, at the West End.[41] When the Pontchartrain Railroad was built, its terminus ran proximate to his restaurant. Beginning the last week in April, citizens might take the half-hour ride from the city, take a table on the broad piazzas or in the airy apartments, and enjoy the glory of the restaurant pompano. "Sprung, like Aphrodite, from the foam, and his silvery sides sparkled in the sunlight with prismatic hues," this fish, grilled over charcoal and seasoned by Boudro, stood as the head of Louisiana's seafood cuisine.[42] Upon his death in 1867, a literary gastronome asserted "that no other man has ever arrived at such perfection in the art of cooking fish. Pompano was not pompano without Boudro cooking them. Court-bouillons were tasteless unless seasoned by Boudro."[43] Boudro trained two collaborators, Henry Borno and Philip Billman. The latter would become his successor. "The mantle of Boudro, the famous Lake End restaurateur, whose memory is so inseparably associated with pompano, court-bouillons, and all that is delicate and savory in pescatory cuisine[,] has fallen upon worthy shoulders. Philip, a long time attaché, has succeeded the great master, under whose skillful tuition he became second only to him whose fame was not limited by geographical lines."[44] Two years after Boudro's death, the anxious were reassured that "seasons come and go, and men with them; but Boudro's knows no change."[45]

One of the great resort caterers, Charles L. Bell, proprietor of the Washington Hotel and Restaurant during the mid-1840s, failed to secure a succession, so memory of his greatness evaporated in the latter decades of the nineteenth century. Yet he also managed sublimity in creating seasonal seafood feasts. On a weekly basis from, April through November, Bell would alert the newspaper readership about what was available at his restaurant: "Eels, Flounders, Soft Crabs, Croakers . . . [and] those delicious birds known as Caille de Laurier."[46] One of the most elaborate representations of a seasonal meal surviving from nineteenth-century Louisiana is Bell's autumnal feast reported in the November 2, 1843, issue of the *Daily Picayune*:

> Whetting the appetite to the finest edge by two or three oysters, whereon lemon juice had been sprinkled, we entered at once upon a potage d la tortue.—Bell's turtle soup is indeed what a turtle soup should be . . . all the delicacy of flavor which you demand in it is preserved, while that extreme richness . . . is avoided. To the soup succeeded a Sheepshead [the fish], baked aux huitres, and slightly flavored with tomatoes. . . . The beefsteak aux truffes, the "blue winged teal," broiled, the delicious green peas, the potatoes—the true mealy murphy, not waxy, sodden ground nuts—of these deserves a separate mention, but we have not room. Of an *omelette soufflé*, we will only say that is was the best we ever ate in New Orleans. But how to do just to the salad! . . . how crisp and tender were its leaves, rejoicing the sweet emollient admixture. . . . We come now to exotics; cheese of highest flavor, which had traversed the broad Atlantic, fruits, golden fruits, which had ripened in foreign climes, and wines of generous quality.

If Bell was regarded as the least of the Lake caterers, then the creations of Miguel and Boudro were sublime, indeed.

Boudro's had such high repute that in the year after the end of the Civil War, he opened "Boudro's Confectionary and Lunch Saloon," manned by Henry Borno. For a great name to open a satellite restaurant to spread fame and collect a franchise percentage became a matter of course in the 1850s. Baptiste Moreau had opened a resort out on Bayou St. John on the eve of the Civil War. Victor's opened branches in Carrollton and in Baton Rouge. The latter, launched in October 1860, was "on Boulevard Street, in the house lately kept by Mad. Eugène."[47] In an odd irony, Victor Martin was having his forces occupy a place previously held by a woman who had departed for New Orleans to take up residence in 15 Madison, a place previously occupied by Victor's. Eugène went to New Orleans to become the successor to a master French caterer, Jean Baptiste Auguste Broue, who founded a restaurant whose name spoke to the condition of so many of his sort, Le Pellerin—the Pilgrim.

All of the great caterers—all of eminences who went by a single name—

had a non-Louisianan nativity, crossed the Atlantic or the continent, were pilgrims in search of their culinary destinies, and when they aged, sought to preserve their legacies. Most chose artistic heirs who either had a similar European background and training, or persons whose tutelage they personally conducted. Creoles—persons born in Louisiana—had relatively little to do with the commercial world of the caterers until late in the nineteenth century. An analysis of census records confirms this point. Consider the listing in 1850 of culinary professionals in the ward (3-1) in which Victor Martin resided and worked in 1850. Nine residents were listed as cooks: six Frenchmen, two Germans, and one Creole. Six residents were listed as restaurant keepers: three Frenchman, two Italians, and a Spaniard. There were but two confectioners—a Frenchman and an Italian. Restaurant cooking in antebellum New Orleans was Eurocentric and would remain so until the 1880s.[48]

Madame Eugène—a native of Reichshoffen, Alsace, and trained as a cook in France—came with her husband to New Orleans in 1853.[49] She worked anonymously in New Orleans restaurants until 1858, when she moved to Baton Rouge to take over the restaurant over the Gem Saloon, creating a restaurant under her own name that was regarded as the best in Louisiana outside New Orleans.[50] In 1860 she answered the appeal of her aging countryman Auguste Broue (1803-1870) to return to New Orleans and preserve his legacy and restaurant. She was twenty-four years old.

Auguste Broue never won the fame of his compeers among the city's caterers; indeed what we know of him derives from an epicurean newspaper reporter who thought him an unappreciated genius laboring in obscurity. Broue had risen from scullion to chef in France, serving as staff cook for an admiral. The officer's death prompted Broue's removal to New Orleans, where he opened Le Pellerin in 1841. "His cooking was superb, and . . . his prices were little over half those of other establishments." His admirers likened him as a culinary artist to his contemporary, the famous Alexis Benoist Soyer, but lamented a modesty that threatened to see him "unwept, unhonored, and unsung."[51] He turned Le Pellerin and his recipes over to Madame Eugène in 1860, returning to his native country, where he found loneliness and boredom rather than retired serenity. In 1865, hearing news of the Confederacy's defeat and the return of peace to Louisiana, he returned to New Orleans and, despite his advanced years, collaborated with Madame Eugène at 15 Madison Street before opening a place, the Encampment, that served more as a home to conversation than ingestion. His enduring contribution to New Orleans cuisine was popularizing curries.[52]

Madame Eugène undertook the management of Le Pellerin with more resolve than Broue. In 1867 Giulio Adamoli during his tour of New Orleans listed Le Pellerin with the St. Charles, Moreau's, and the Cosmopolitan as sharing "the reputation of being the best dining place in town."[53] From 1860 to 1880, Madame Eugène made Le Pellerin "the rendezvous of the people prominent in the theatrical history of the town—the Jeffersons, the Davenports, Augustin Daly, Davidge, Barton Hill, George Clarke, Marie Wainwright, and Georgie Drew."[54] The theater and the opera constituted the two chief amusements of the New Orleans haute monde. Madame Eugène's cultivation of this traveling clientele insured the good word would be spread along the stock company touring circuits while enlisting a following among the most mobile members of America's artist class (a clientele markedly contrasting with the commercial class pursued by the Canal Street restaurants).

Women were prominent, indeed dominant, in the touring theatrical and operatic companies. Madame Eugène knew how to capture the gustatory favor of women—something that many of the restaurateurs fixated on cultivating the business lunch trade did not do. She had come to New Orleans at the moment—1853-58—that several confectioners of genius had perfected the women's luncheon venue.

The introduction of the purple-ribbon cane from Georgia amplified sugar production in Louisiana in the 1830s. Things made with sugar became cheap and popular. *Confiseur* Gabriel Julien, whose sweet shop occupied No. 30 Rue de Conde, was the first sugar artist to make a name in the city. It was a wonderland of bonbons, sugared fruits, pastilles, jujubes, candied flowers, chocolates, brandied fruits, and flavored syrups.[55] These syrups were poured over shaved ice for a chilly confection. Even before the sugar boom, consuming ice cream and sorbet had become a local craze in the 1820s because of the artistry of M. Serreau at the corner of Chartres and St. Louis Streets. The next generation of cold confectioners, such as Lazzaro Dancevich and James Mathes, made the ice cream saloon a fixture in the cityscape. The pinnacle of antebellum confectionery service was Vincent's at the corner of Canal and Carondelet. The quality of his goods—"from a sherbert to champagne, and from a paté de perdreaux aux truffs to a bonbon"—brought in an ample walk-in trade from women promenading Canal Street.[56] As much a store as a saloon, the luncheon offerings ballooned when Vincent's disciple F. Lefevre took over the master's shop and opened a second store at the corner of St. Peter and Royal Streets. Lefevre made the lady's lunch the focus of his establishments. The refinement of these meals is suggested by a carte published in 1856:

A Splendid Lunch Every Day

Composed of very choice dishes; such as

Galatine Truffée,　Mayonaise de Volaille,

Turkey, truffée,　Westphalian Ham,

Beef filet,　Stuffed Tongue,

Vol au vents, with Mushrooms.

Suprême de Volaille,　Salmon filet à la Tartare,

Cuisse-de-poulard, à la maréchale,

Charlotte Russe,　Rum Jelly,　Maraschino,

Rice and Milk,　Café au lait,　Black Mocha, &c.

Beaujolais Wine,　Bordeaux Wine,

Grave sec,　Chablis,

Lunel Muscat,　Froutignan,

Tokay,　Dressed Marseilles,　Champagne.[57]

The excellence of this luncheon is best understood when it is contrasted to the lunches offered by the businessmen's restaurants in the city that I treat below.

I have chosen Lefevre's Confectionary Saloon as a final demonstration of the maturation of New Orleans culinary institutions in the antebellum period for a particular reason. It is with François Lefevre that Charles Ranhofer, the greatest Franco-American chef of the nineteenth century and chef du cuisine of Delmonico's in New York from the 1860s through the 1890s, trained during his four years (1856–60) as a resident of New Orleans. It was in preparing these dishes, and serving the women of this city, that Ranhofer learned how to adapt American ingredients to the recipes and cooking techniques of classic European gastronomy. What he learned with Lefevre would become the professional standard for excellence and creativity against which all American cuisine in the final decades of the century would be measured. Lefevre's, Ranhofer's, and Madame Eugène's cuisines all imagined dining as a heterosocial occasion, requiring the satisfaction of tastes inflected by culturally induced gender preferences.

Creole ladies welcomed Madame Eugène into their imagined sorority because she had invited them into a space where their tastes would be served. No mistake that besides Eugène's signature dish, crawfish bisque, the Christian Woman's Exchange included a confection, Crème Eugène, in their handbook of Creole cookery.[58] Confectionery was the culinary art in which Creole women most looked to culinary professionals for guidance. Whatever the particulars of the case, in the 1880s, while she led Moreau's kitchen, Madame Eugène consolidated support among the residents of the French Quarter by appearing as a French friend of Creole culture at a time when national interest seized upon the Francophone natives of Louisiana.

THE CREOLE BOOM

Creole cookery became a fashionable brand suddenly in the national world of print in 1885. The World Industrial and Cotton Centennial Exposition and the appearance of the two local cookbooks stimulated a national interest in Creole cookery. National magazines beginning in 1884 welcomed sketches delineating the characteristic dishes of New Orleans. Cookbook authors—cognizant that "America's French City" somehow melded the gastronomic excellencies of the Gallic kitchen with the distinctive vegetables, game, fruit, nuts, and seafood of the American South—took notice of Creole dishes. In 1884 celebrity chef Felix Deliée of New York had excited the culinary public with the prospect of a synthesis of French and American approaches to food in his *Franco-American Cookery Book* (1885), which revealed that such a synthesis had already taken place organically in the Creole cookery of Louisiana. Professional cookbook writers of the 1880s and 1890s immediately took up the signal accomplishments of Creole cookery, accenting their collections with preparations *à la Créole*.

Historians of American culture understand the Creole emergence into national conspicuousness as a literary phenomenon, its landmarks being the 1879 publication of George Washington Cable's *Old Creole Days*, Lafcadio Hearn's "invention" of New Orleans as the American city of mystery in his periodical sketches of the 1880s,[59] and the local color news reportage surrounding the 1884 World Industrial and Cotton Centennial Exposition. The literary Creole was intended for a national audience, as the most exotic species of local color types being promoted by the editors of national magazines published in New York, Boston, and Philadelphia.[60] Their editorial project—reknitting a sense of national comity by promoting a touristic desire to view the characteristic traits of varieties of regional communities and landscapes—resulted in issues filled with tour reports, sketches, and literary portraits of local characters and descriptions if not recipes of local dishes. The problem of defusing animosity against the recent enemy—particularly when news reports of lynchings filtered northward regularly (fifty-three in 1883, fifty-one in 1884, seventy-four in 1885)—led to several representational strategies. Southern places were written into the past. White southerners were rendered anachronistic, their manners quaint, their ambitions immaterial to the commercial industrial world of the post–Civil War United States. So Virginia became Thomas Nelson Page's Ol' Virginia; Charleston and Savannah became the charming spinster sister cities; and, by a curious literary transmutation, the French and Spanish families who had been dispossessed from political power by the Anglo-American takeover of Louisiana came to stand for New Orleans. Quaint and alien, mysterious and interesting, yet nonetheless American, New Orleans was served up for national consumption *à la Créole*. The Cotton Exposition's publicity exposed the uses and contradictions of New Orleans: the world would be enticed to the city by its quaint charm . . . in order to discover the modernity of its industrial cultivation and processing of cotton.

The Creoles who seized the national imagination in the 1880s were Franglish creatures, presented by Anglo-American literary ethnographers. They were not the same Creoles who peopled the Francophone literature of Louisiana published in the wake of the war. Black and white Creoles published poetry, prose, and journalism in volume, ranging from the liberationist and socialist *La Tribune de la Nouvelle-Orléans* to the naturalist fiction of Alfred Mercier and the race and class explorations of novelist Sidonie de la Houssaye (Louise Raymond). Because English-speaking readers had little cognizance of this Francophone outpouring, their sense of what French-speaking citizens of Louisiana thought or felt derived from a few bilingual Creoles, Charles Gayarré and T. C. De Leon particularly. Both were fixated on revising the image of Franco-Americans being promulgated by Cable and Hearn, particularly their concern with the African American contributions to Louisiana culture and the issue of miscegenation. Gayarré's recourse to jeremiads about the dilution of a pure Gallic/Creole culture in the mid-nineteenth century barely concealed its racism. Yet his claims that Creole food had suffered dilution and decline mapped onto a conviction held by numbers of black and white Creoles in the city who thought that the explosion of oyster saloons and cosmopolitan restaurants threatened the city's distinctive style of cookery. The fear of an inundation of American taste could make the Creole matrons form common cause with the largely male non-Creole European culinary professionals.

Deviation into American cosmopolitan cookery first took place in the grand hotel barrooms when the free businessman's lunch became standard. William Head Coleman's 1885 *Historical Sketch Book and Guide to New Orleans and Environs* recounted this development:

These free lunches were instituted by Alvarez, who ran the bar-room in the old St. Louis Hotel in 1837. Gentlemen doing business in New Orleans, which was mainly conducted in what is now the French portion of the city, complained that, as many of them resided as far down as the lower cotton press, and some as high up as Julia Street, they could not find time during the middle of the day to go home and get a bite and they did not want to pay restaurant prices for a mere plate of soup and a sandwich. To gratify this large class and secure their custom, the then only first-class bar-rooms in the city—St. Louis Hotel, Hewlitt's (afterward City Hotel), Arcade, Veranda, St. Charles Hotel inaugurated free lunches.[61]

In 1846 an ex-chef of the St. Charles Hotel, Walter Van Rensselaer, triggered a boom in oyster saloons, adaptations of the oyster and porter cellars of Philadelphia and Baltimore, that featured businessmen's luncheons. A culinary fashion not particularly French in inspiration or execution seized the city and did not let go. Coleman's guide listed the typical daily offerings of five such establishments at the time of the Cotton Exposition. The listing reveals how commonplace the offerings of the new style of commercial eateries were. One could get similar fare in any port town south of Philadelphia. Here is the bill of fare for the Acme Saloon in 1885:

ACME SALOON, ROYAL STREET

Monday—Vegetable soup, roast beef, beef stewed with potatoes, stewed kidney, baked macaroni, corn, tomatoes, lettuce, green onions, potato salad, beets, cold slaw.

Tuesday—Gumbo, roast beef, dry hash, stewed liver, boiled Irish potatoes, baked beans, boiled rice, lettuce, green onions, potato salad, beets and cold slaw.

Wednesday—Pea soup, roast beef, beef stewed with tomatoes, sauerkraut and boiled pork, stewed carrots, green peas, baked sweet potatoes, lettuce, green onions, potato salad, beets and cold slaw.

Thursday—Bean soup, roast beef, beef stewed with potatoes, boiled onions, fried tripe, baked macaroni, stewed tomatoes, boiled turnips, lettuce, green onions, potato salad, beets and cold slaw.

Friday—Oyster soup, baked red snapper, roast beef, boiled ham, mashed Irish potatoes, stewed corn, rice jambalaya, lettuce, green onions, potato salad, beets and cold slaw.

Saturday—Gumbo, roast beef, beef stewed with green peas, corned beef and cabbage, baked beans, baked sweet potatoes, boiled Irish potatoes with jackets on, lettuce, green onions, potato salad, beets and cold slaw.[62]

Two signature local dishes—gumbo and jambalaya—nod to Creole style, but the bulk of the menu reflected the Anglo-American businessman's norms of taste. (If the city's name restaurants operated on the model of "French cuisine with Creole improvements," these restaurants operated on the model of "American cuisine with token Creole add-ons.") In the wake of the Civil War, the following New Orleans restaurateurs operated on this model:

M. Andrews, Restaurant, 67 North Market

Thomas Appoloni, Restaurant, Orleans corner of Dauphine

Hugh Cassidy, Cassidy's Oyster Saloon and Restaurant, 174 Gravier

Tobias Christianson, Restaurant, Patterson, Algiers

A. T. Curry, Restaurant, Dryades near Perdido

Jacob Frederick, Coffeehouse and Restaurant, 13 Old Levee

Jonathan Gunnine, Coffeehouse and Restaurant, St. Charles, 474
    Felicity

John Hosch, Coliseum Beer Saloon and Restaurant, 51 Bienville

John Justin, Restaurant, 199 Poydras

Peter Labatt, Bar and Restaurant, 252 Common

John Leary, Restaurant, 211 Tchoupitoulas

Laurence Mas, Coffeehouse and Restaurant, 231 Customhouse

J. E. McClure, Sam's Oyster Saloon and Restaurant, 101 St. Charles

A. B. Mitchel, Restaurant, 20 Baronne

George Morris, Coffeehouse and Restaurant, Customhouse corner of
    Franklin

B. Mumford, Restaurant, 205 Baronne

Richard Murphy, Hotel and Restaurant, 98 and 100 St. Charles

Mark Nicholas, Oyster Saloon and Restaurant, 72 St. Charles

Simon Seiglan, Restaurant, 11 Madison

H. Stouber, Restaurant and Beer Saloon, 49 Customhouse

Evariste Sugasti, Restaurant, 17 St. Philip

G. W. Watkins, Restaurant, 116 Carondelet

L. Winson, Restaurant and Oyster Saloon, 19 Royal

Those who operated French cafés and French restaurants (no one labeled such venues Creole until after the Cotton Exposition)[63] did so conscious that they defended a tradition and conducted a culinary resistance.[64]

Madame Eugène was pivotal in the coalescence of the Creole and French culinary interests. She, E. Deneschaud, and Miguel Brisolara were three of the names who had established themselves before the Civil War and were still active in New Orleans in 1885. Only Leon Lamothe, the French-born heir of the Camors restaurant tradition of the younger generation, approached their repute.[65] Among members of the Woman's Exchange, the institution that most actively promoted the domestic tradition of Creole cookery, a pride in female mastery attained by Madame Eugène's prevailed. She made manifest a fantasy figure who haunted the Creole imagination: the kitchen savant. The Jewish Creole novelist T. C. De Leon[66] best captured the fantasy of the French Quarter eatery presided over by a female genius. In a chapter of his novel *Creole and Puritan* entitled "Déjeuner à la Fourchette" ("Brunch"), De Leon tells the tale of the 1866 visit of Union General Dale Everett to the Catfish Café. Passing into a building so modest as to dispense entirely with signage, he encountered the "unsurpassed cuisine" of "Madame Pietro Bartol," French Creole wife of a Spanish innkeeper. Her court bouillon was the "veritable essence of the red snapper of the Gulf, boiled into an almost jellied form and flavored with a dozen individual condiments that tempered, without disguising, the inevitable chile pepper." This commenced a feast of rare excellence.

Next . . . came the triumph of the Maison Bartol,—its name-specialty,— the rare green perch, flopping ten minutes before in the osier basket that brought them that dawn from the high waters at Metairie Ridge; royal perch, with broad backs and clear fins, and with firm flaked meat of such bouquet as held its own, with the knowing ones, even against that of the far-praised pompano. Then were served cutlets of startling thickness, brown in coat, but weeping blood like martyrs at the least cruelty of the knife; and with them real French peas, small, plump, and with flavor.[67]

Certain features of De Leon's representation of Madame Pietro were standard features of the mystique of name caterers: the cultivation of a signature dish for which she was generally acknowledged the supreme practitioner, mastery of all areas of kitchen craft, an exquisitely refined taste, conviction of the rightness of her culinary art, and great force of character. She was treasured by an ardent and select circle of gastronomic devotees. While the annals of New Orleans gastronomy spoke of several such savants—Madame Bégué, Madame Venn,[68] and Mrs. Coutoulas— and Mobile boasted the talents of that "delightful housekeeper and cater-ess" Madame Frozine Madrid,[69] it particularly conformed to the reputa-tion of Madame Eugène.[70]

M.A.B.'s sketch of Creole cooking in an 1887 issue of *Good Housekeep-ing* included the following accolade: "To the Creole is due the honor of having invented a most goodly conceit—crawfish *bisque*. The crawfish, here, is not regarded as unclean, as in other parts of the country, but is estimated at its true value. The recipe given for it is from Madame E, of New Orleans, a cook who is simply inspired, and whose famous hostelrie is enshrined in the stomachic affections of every *gourmet* in the state."[71] Madame Eugène's recipe for crawfish bisque was so famous that it appeared in print four times from 1885 to 1890. It was a central creation in the canon of New Orleans cuisine:

> Take fifty crawfish, wash them in several waters, and put them in a saucepan over a brisk fire. Add to them salt, whole black pepper, and butter the size of an egg, with a little grated nutmeg. Stir with a spoon for one-half hour, when cooked drain the crawfish, free them from the shells, and mash the meat in a mortar. Boil one cup of rice in the crawfish *bouillon* for a quarter of an hour, drain it and put it in the mortar with the crawfish, pounding it well. Put all back into the saucepan, thin it with the *bouillon* and pass it through a sieve. Mash the crawfish shells, add *bouillon* in which they were cooked, and strain it through a sieve into the crawfish and rice puree. It should then be of a reddish color. Put this into a saucepan over a moderate fire, not letting it boil, but it must be very hot. Put some toasted bread in the tureen, add to the broth one wineglassful of Madeira wine, and pour over toast. Serve immediately.[72]

Is this Creole? Or is this essentially a French receipt rebranded as Creole? While the recipe owes a debt to French renditions of *potage à la bisque d'écrevisse* such as that found in Antoine B. Beauvilliers's *L'Art du Cuisinier* (1814), one notes the refinement of the soup's texture by the incorporation of a *crème de riz* made of pureed boiled rice, and the enrichment of the taste by the dollop of Madeira before plating.[73] In short, a French dish with Creole improvements, making use of the Carolina Gold rice grown in south Louisiana.

The other presentations of her signature dish all differ. Consider the version contained in *The Creole Cookery Book*:

BISQUE POTAGE—MADAME EUGÈNE

Take 50 or more shrimp; wash them in 5 or 6 waters; put them in a saucepan, adding salt and big black pepper, a little nutmeg (grated) and a bit of butter, on a brisk fire; stir with a spoon for ½ hour; when cooked let the shrimp drain; remove the meats and mash in mortar; boil rice in bouillon ¼ hour; strain, and put it in mortar with the shrimp; when well pounded, put in saucepan, and thin with bouillon, and pass through a sieve; thin this puree (Cream) so that it be neither too thick nor too thin; then mash the shrimp shells, and juice or butter in which the shrimps have been cooked, and strain the puree in a cullender; it should then be of reddish color; put this in a saucepan on a moderate fire; do not let come to a boil, but should be quite hot; put crust of bread in soup dish and pour on a little broth, hot, and when ready to serve add a little Madeira. (210)

One notices immediately the substitution of shrimp for crawfish. Since *The Creole Cookery Book* avoided any culinary treatment of crawfish, one might attribute the alterations of this recipe to an editorial calculation, based on some perception of the squeamishness that Anglo-American tourists might have about eating mudbugs. The basic order of action and times and measures are roughly commensurate, though details diverge (the suggestion that the shrimp might be cooked in butter as well as bouillon), and the timing of the Madeira splash upon plating differs. Was there no written template upon which these recipes were based? Was Madame Eugène responding to requested information off the top of her head? When we confront a third version, published in Mrs. Washington's *Unrivaled Cookbook* in 1885, suspicion grows to certainty. Madame Eugène, like most master cooks of longer professional experience, kept no recipe book per se; when asked for recipes by the curious, she responded impromptu from memory. In version number three, from the *Unrivaled Cookbook*, we have a supplemental feature of the dish, crawfish forcemeats:

[CRAWFISH] BISQUE À LA CRÉOLE (MADAME EUGÈNE)

Take a peck of fat crawfish, wash them through several waters to clean them, and boil them in salt and water which you use later for your bouillon; take off the heads; peel your crawfish; reserve twenty-four heads to stuff for your bisque; take all the rest of the heads and all the peeling, carefully removing the sand-bug, and pound them in a mortar; pour them in the bouillon, in which they were boiled, with a soup-bunch, a head of celery, salt, and pepper; let it simmer slowly two hours; in the meantime pound the tails of the crawfish you have peeled in a mortar, mix them with butter, chopped onions, chopped ham, salt, and pepper; bind it with the beaten yolk of an egg and fry it; stuff the heads with this; strain the bouillon, make a soup, in which you fry a chopped onion, till it colors; strain this in your bouillon, and pour it boiling hot into your tureen over the stuffed heads and fried croutons of bread; a moment before serving stir in a tablespoonful of sweet red-pepper powder that is used for coloring. (23)

This version of bisque reads more like a transcript of an oral instruction than that in *The Creole Cookery Book*, which employs grammatical elisions like the elimination of articles—"put crust of bread in soup dish"— characteristic of written epitomes.

Why has culinary history failed to capture the glories of restaurant cookery in the era when the great names gave New Orleans its gastronomic glory? Because the kitchen culture of the caterers depends much more on apprenticeships of practical instruction and constant re-creation of dishes than writing. Bakers and pastry chefs may have required receipt books for reference, particularly given the changing chemistry and need for exact measurement of ingredients; experienced caterers did not.[74] Then, too, there are proprietary issues at work. Restaurant cooking is a ferociously competitive business. Your dishes were and are your stock in trade. A caterer thinks carefully about giving out instruction or putting onto paper one's fund of knowledge, so the sum of one's work can be copied or pilfered. So we are faced with a situation where we know what the signature dishes of the great chefs were. Boudro-Pompano & Courtbuillion, Miguel Bouillabaisse and Soft Shell Crabs à la Creole, John Galpin's Creole beefsteak, Victor Martin-Red Snapper à la Chambourg, Auguste Broue's curried fish, and Baptiste Moreau's Gelatine Truffée à la Gelée. But the only recipe that survives by any of the named chefs was taken from the legendary Moreau,[75] taken down from the cook's lips by a midwestern businessman touring New Orleans midcentury:

MOREAU'S OKRA GUMBO SOUP

Put a spoonful of lard in the soup pot on the fire. Cut up a chicken, a few onions, and a little ham. Brown, add sliced okra, mix, add a few tomatoes, cut up, and a small quantity of flour. Put all over a quick fire for a minute or two. Add water or beef broth, according to number of persons to be served. Season with salt, pepper, thyme, and bay leaf. Veal will do instead of chicken. Serve with boiled rice.[76]

One notes that the roux has not yet become the base of the soup.

So when we turn to Madame Eugène, we face a relative wealth of information. The *Unrivaled Cookbook* includes four additional recipes, and *The Creole Cookery Book*, one. Why was she more forthcoming with her treasures? Perhaps because the devotees of her cooking were Creole housekeepers who would never be professional rivals.

"Mrs. Washington's" *Unrivaled Cookbook* is one of the more interesting collections of recipes to be published in the last quarter of the nineteenth century. Mrs. Washington (a pseudonym) styles herself as editor,[77] contributing a single recipe to her collection, but compiling a wonderful grab bag of recipes from Europe and America, with clusters of Russian, German, English country, French, Italian monastic, Virginian, Wisconsin, and New England recipes. The heart of the assembly—two hundred Creole recipes from "Madame" (whose name was not given)—was itself a collection of favorite recipes from a Creole madame's friends. Besides the selections from Madame Eugène, there are several recipes each by "Dina," "Desiree," "Daddy Jim," and "Old Humphrey." A dedication identifies these as honest cooks who "have as good a right to be 'among the stars' as more illustrious worthies." A thorough examination of Soard's *New Orleans Directory for 1880* finds no one identified as cook or confectioner who fit these names. So in all likelihood these cooks fall under the category of housekeeper, like the informants who supplied the content of the two founding Creole cookbooks of 1885.

The *Unrivaled Cookbook* was an immediate indication of a public for Creole cuisine in the national print market.[78] Other cookbooks by authors from other parts added recipes *à la Créole* forwarded by authentic informants. From 1885 to the publication of the first edition of *The Picayune Creole Cook Book* in 1901, between 270 and 280 "Creole" recipes came into print differing from those found in Hearn's and the Christian Woman's Exchange's collections. Some were supplied by housekeepers of the Creole diaspora, such as Olympe Boudinot, who supplied the Creole contents in Chicago's *Daily News Cook Book*. Others were collected by enthusiasts for the cuisine, such as Sara Van Buren Brugière, whose 1890 book *Good-Living* has several splendid Creole vegetable recipes. More recipes found their way into large circulation magazines. The hallmark of the bulk of these offerings was the tag *à la Créole*.

Two of Madame Eugène's recipes collected in the *Unrivaled Cookbook* bear this designation. Interestingly, both exemplify restaurant fare rather than home cookery. Snipe was the butt of decades of newspaper witticisms about restaurateurs charging 50 cents or more for a bird so minuscule. Sweetbreads were a favorite luncheon offering at French bistros. From the *Unrivaled Cookbook*:

PUREE OF SNIPE À LA CRÉOLE (MADAME EUGÈNE)

Snipe should always be kept *four days* at least, before cooking. Never pluck them until you are ready to cook them. Hang them in a cool, dry place. Take a dozen snipe, pluck them and draw them; cut off all the meat, and put it aside, with the entrails, in a mortar; put the remains of the birds in a saucepan with bouillon, parsley, laurel leaf, a clove, and two glassfuls of white wine; boil this till it is reduced to half, and strain it; pound your birds and entrails in a mortar with three ounces of fat pork, moisten with the above sauce, and pass this puree through a colander; put it in a saucepan, let it heat through without boiling, and serve on a dish surrounded by fried croutons. (169)

SWEETBREAD CROQUETTES À LA CRÉOLE (MADAME EUGÈNE)

Soak the sweetbreads an hour in warm water, and blanch them in boiling water until the larding needle can pass through them without tearing them; cut them in dice; cut the same quantity of mushrooms, also, in dice; stew them together in a little white sauce; make them into shapes like a pear, sticking a clove in the end; powder them with bread crumbs and fry; serve with a tomato sauce. (104–5)

SHRIMP OR CRAB MAYONNAISE (MADAME EUGÈNE)

Boil and peel your shrimps or crabs; make a rich mayonnaise dressing, and serve over them; garnish your dish with tender lettuce leaves. (68)

SALPICON (MADAME EUGÈNE'S ENTRÉE)

Make a white roux; moisten it with bouillon and a glassful of white wine; add a soup bunch, salt, and pepper; let it boil and thicken; take for your ragout equal portions of whatever cold meats, fowl, game, livers, ham and tongue, mushrooms, bottoms of artichokes, you may have, and cut them in little dice; let them simmer and color; take out the soup bunch; thicken the sauce with a little flour if necessary; fill little pâtés and vol au vents, and serve. (541)

A half-dozen recipes may seem small a corpus upon which to determine the extent of a talent's greatness. But other evidences survive of Madame Eugène's versatility. In Christmas season 1877, she prepared a feast for Sheriff T. H. Handy and twenty-five guests that saw her reproduce the most famous feast of another American region:

> The dinner was a *chef d'oeuvre* in its way. Its most prominent features were the introduction of those vaunted delicacies of the Maryland market and menu, terrapin stew and canvas back duck. . . . They fully justified in the appreciation of the gourmets present, the fame, which has become worldwide, of their richness and excellence. These, with entrees prepared in M'me Eugenie's best style, and accompanied by the choicest vintages, including Santime, Burgundy, sherry, old Madeira and champagne au naturel and frappeed, and concluding with fruit, omelette, soufflé, cheese, coffee and punch, made up one of the most complete and artistic dinners ever given in this city.[79]

Her menu—first formulated by the French chef of the Maryland Club in Baltimore on the eve of the Civil War, and explored in detail in chapter 4 below—had become in the eyes of world the exemplary adaptation of local American ingredients in the service of haute cuisine. It was the Chesapeake equivalent of French cuisine with Creole improvements. Madame Eugène grasped the principle and could perform the Maryland version of the culinary adaptation she performed every day. Snipe may not trump canvasback duck in the mouths of culinary aesthetes, but the little bird was tasty and local.

Perhaps we should not wonder at the small number of her surviving recipes, but her unprecedented generosity in distributing transcripts of her creations. Why didn't Madame Eugène suffer the same wariness that kept the other star caterers' wisdom locked in the kitchen and in the skull? Perhaps she had attained everything one could desire in the world in which she worked, having taken one of the two renowned restaurants of that time and place to its greatest culinary eminence. Then, too, there was the question of succession. She had no heir in waiting. Whether because of the dicey gender politics of men learning from a cateress, or because her own disinclination to train a successor, she did not have an acolyte to be the vessel and beneficiary of her secrets. So perhaps the Creole house-keepers and their cooks could be her successors. Those who asked received. This is supposition, of course. What we *do* know for a fact was that upon her marriage to retired merchant Jean B. Laporte in 1887, Eugène turned Moreau's back over to Charles Rhodes and enjoyed for a brief spell domes-tic pleasures. But in 1890 her daughter Sophie Flêche Ecuyer died, leaving four young children; then in 1892 her husband died. She moved into the Ecuyer household at 1244 Esplanade to supply a maternal presence for her grandchildren. So deeply had she retired from the culinary world into the domestic sphere that when Walter Hale published his elegy on the passing of Old New Orleans in the *Uncle Remus Magazine* in 1908, he believed that she had returned to France to live out her life in Provence.

One wonders what Sophie Laporte thought when Madame Bégué in 1901 published her brief collection of recipes used at her breakfast house. This would be the sole glimpse of the professional world of the New Orleans caterers published during Madame Eugène's lifetime. Bégué's during its heyday was considered humble, quaint, and somewhat Bohe-mian. Moreau's had been the finest eatery in the city.

I've used Madame Eugène's career to provide a preliminary sketch of the world of the caterers in nineteenth-century New Orleans. I suspect certain of the multitude of New Orleans recipes that found their way into print during the Creole boom may derive from restaurant practices. The Sheepshead à la Créole published by Delmonico's chef A. Filippini in *100 Ways of Cooking Fish* (1891) and the Shad à la Créole found in Charles Ranhofer's magnum opus *The Epicurean* (1893) both have the fragrance of restaurant fare. Numbers of the items included in the *Unrivaled Cookbook* aspire to more than household cookery, even for an aristocratic ménage. But the critical analysis of recipes has only recently begun with Susan Tucker's *New Orleans Cuisine: Fourteen Signature Dishes and Their Histo-ries* (2009). The tools of digital humanities should allow us to undertake genealogical studies of every recipe in *The Creole Cookery Book*, *La Cuisine Creole*, the Creole portion of the *Unrivaled Cookbook*, and the first edition of *The Picayune Creole Cook Book*.

An expansion beyond New Orleans to explore the French and Creole fare in the French-speaking enclaves of nineteenth-century Mobile, St. Louis, Galveston, and Baton Rouge would give a more general cooking vernacular. A starting point in this investigation would be Jessup Whitehead's account of the Creole cooking he witnessed while working as an ice cream maker for a Creole caterer that was added to the fourth edition of *Hotel Meat Cooking* (Chicago, 1886). His collection of Creole recipes in this book is the second largest, after the *Unrivaled Cookbook*, published between *La Cuisine Creole* and *The Picayune Creole Cook Book*.

I've suggested here the ways that antebellum hotels and restaurants produced a repertoire of dishes and inculcated a standard of taste; I've explored the problem of the lack of a southern literature of cooking instruction from professional caterers; I've particularized some dimensions of the exchange of information between home cooks and professional cooks; and I've documented how persons trained in French culinary technique took up local ingredients (*crème de riz* in the crawfish bisque) in the service of making the local edible in a way that stimulated a cosmopolitan public. We'll now turn to the single most famous southern menu that illustrated the artistry possible when regional ingredients were taken up by classically trained cook—the Maryland Feast designed by François Lagroue for the Maryland Club.

FOUR   *The Maryland Club Feast*

Maryland's government has recognized the importance of the state's traditional foodways in its online *Maryland Manual*.[1] There we learn that in 2011 the "Maryland-most" foods in order of listing are (1) Beaten Biscuits ("Dinner biscuit made from dough beaten with a wooden mallet or dowel for twenty to thirty minutes"); (2) Chicken, Maryland ("Pan-fried, then steamed, breaded chicken, served with a white cream gravy"); and (3) Crab Cakes. Mention is made of ham, oyster fritters, and Lady Baltimore cake. If one surfs into the seafood section, one discovers that rockfish and soft-shell clams rank as favorite local commodities. In the eyes of twenty-first-century conservators of culinary traditions, this list includes the most resonant and traditional of Maryland dishes.

Yet 150 years ago, when Maryland epicures envisioned a banquet of characteristic Chesapeake dishes, none of the above listed items appeared. The Maryland Feast—a menu of the most splendid gastronomic treasures of the "land of pleasant living"—was formulated by François Lagroue on the eve of the Civil War at the early autumn dinners of the Maryland Club in Baltimore (founded 1857).[2] After the war, it spread to the great restaurants of the East Coast, became a fixture of dining in the private dinners of the bon ton from Newport to Virginia Springs, and appeared in the menus printed in many cookery guides to haute cuisine. The following is the least elaborate form of the feast:

> *Four small Lynnhaven Bay oysters.*
> *Terrapin, à la Maryland.*
> *Canvas-back Duck.*
> *Salad of Crab and Lettuce.*
> *Baked Irish Potatoes. Fried Hominy Cakes. Plain Celery.*[3]

So famous was this meal as an exemplification of American gastronomic ability that in 1863, during the height of the Civil War, Mr. H. L. Batemen used it as a template for an American feast in London, to which he invited England's gastronomes. He shipped the ingredients from New York. Chef William Blanchard prepared the meal at his restaurant on Beak Street. More elaborate than the Maryland Club menu, Bateman's feast featured turbot instead of crab. The event was written up in the first volume of *The Epicure's Year Book and Table Companion* and the menu reproduced:

> *Saddle Rock oysters.*
> *Oyster soup à l'Americaine.*
> *Turbot, lobster sauce.*
> *Canvass-back ducks; celery.*
> *Saddle of mutton.*
> *Diamond-back terrapin à la Maryland.*
> *Dessert*
> *Wines*
> *Sauterne, amontillado, claret, champagne.*[4]

Since Bateman shipped his ingredients from the New York market, the Saddle Rock oysters from Little Neck Bay (Long Island) substituted for the Lynnhaven oysters from the mouth of the Chesapeake.

Because the Maryland menu became so celebrated, it deserves particular study. The circumstances of its formation, the creation of its constitu-

ent dishes, the history of its ingredients, the circumstances of its consumption, and, finally, the eclipse of the menu as the quintessence of both
American and Maryland cuisine all require understanding.

First, we must understand that the menu was created as a standard
bill of fare in a social club. While clubs have been fixtures of American
sociability since the second quarter of the eighteenth century, Baltimore's
Maryland Club was decidedly a new phenomenon, a gentlemen's club on
European models. Like a London club, it was open daily from morning
to evening every day of the year. Like a Parisian club, it possessed its own
dining facility and posted a daily *table d'hôte*, requiring that members reserve tables. The Union Club of the City of New York pioneered the renovated form of clubbing in America, opening its doors on Broadway near
Fourth Avenue in 1836 and erecting a purpose-built clubhouse on the
corner of Twenty-First Street and Fifth Avenue in 1855. The dining room
occupied the third floor, the kitchen, the fourth and topmost floor, so that
odors would dissipate and not invade the meeting and eating areas.[5] A
trained chef de cuisine serviced the one thousand members. In the 1860s,
the Union Club's chef was Jules Arthur Harder. Club dining by the Civil
War rivaled the best hotel dining in Boston, New York, Philadelphia,
Baltimore, and Cincinnati.

The Maryland Club occupied a colonial mansion on Franklin Street
in Baltimore. Like the Union Club, its initial membership drew from the
region's old established families.[6] As with all such organizations, it es-
poused a desire to be a haven from commerce and politics. It existed to
keep "alive a civilization in some respects peculiar, and which was endangered by the rude but vigorous strides of Young America. It at present
numbers among its members gentlemen from all portions of Maryland,
and the close communion thus established has resulted in the perpetuation
of that traditional hospitality of which every true Marylander is proud."
It differed from many gentlemen's clubs by naming women to honorary
membership, "and a number of the most gifted in Baltimore have availed
themselves of this privilege."[7] During a crisis in identity at the end of the
nineteenth century, when it moved to a new clubhouse and Europeanized
its fare, member Stephen Bonsal sought to capture in words the endangered culinary tradition of the Maryland Club.

The following will give the reader who has never enjoyed the actual experience an idea of what the Maryland Club dinner, as eaten and digested by the members of the older and original stock, really is. We will begin our Maryland dinner with oysters from Lynnhaven, Virginia—a step which will surprise those who do not know that six generations of surveyors have been unable to indicate the frontier lines between the two States, most probably because (alack! that this should have been said before, and in Congress) there are none. A consommé is then to be recommended, whereupon the terrapin in real Maryland style is ushered in with an air of becoming solemnity. Upon this mystery follows a saddle of mutton from the mountains, which will have "hung" for two weeks; and then appears the second mystery of the repast—a wild duck with celery, and hominy, which has first been boiled and then fried—the hominy, and not the duck. Now do not be obstinate and insist upon the wild-duck being a canvas-back, if Tom whispers in your ear that the "hunter" of the club writes to say that this peerless bird is flying high and doing "poorly." A good red-head or a baldpate, or even a mallard in good condition, is much better eating than a canvas-back which has been doing poorly. As a matter of fact, the baldpate—better known to ornithologists as the sheldrake—is the best eating·duck. He does not seem to have the nice nervous organization which worries the canvas-back thin, and you will understand his succulent plumpness, his easy-going eatable nature, when from your blind or sink-box you have watched the rogue steal the crisp wild-celery which the diving canvas-back has spent an afternoon in uprooting. Your feast should conclude with an Eastern Shore ham, two years old, and baked a rich claret-color, and then coffee, cigars, and liqueurs, according to your fancy. The wines with which you may decide to discuss your dinner will be very good, wherever your choice may fall, but the Maryland Club whiskey and Madeiras cannot be found elsewhere.[8]

Several points: Maryland pride gave way to a more expansive sense of gustatory region when Virginia's Lynnhaven oysters were granted a place at the table. The Maryland portions of the Chesapeake Bay did and do not possess sufficient salinity to supply the savor of a first-rate oyster. In true epicurean fashion, taste trumped locality.

The club retained its own hunter to supply wild fare. Indeed, part of the masculine ethos of the gentlemen's club, its identification as a community at odds with the business of contemporary commercial production, was its preference for game. Game, of course, was available in the Baltimore market. But the club retained its own huntsman to insure that the larder was directly provisioned from the wild. One indication of the primacy of wild food in the Maryland Feast was the exclusion of the two proteins that depended upon livestock agriculture—mutton and ham—on the simplest version of the Maryland menu that began this meditation. H. L. Bateman in London knew that mutton was served as part of the standard carte in the Maryland Club so felt no compunction about including it in his menu.

In the 1880s, the scarcity of the canvasback duck caused club members to excuse the substitution of other wildfowl for the canvasback. Bonsal's literary finessing of the matter cannot distract a reader from the truth of the matter: what was once insisted upon in the 1860s was no longer available. A consequence of the club's amplifying the mystique of the canvasback in the world of haute cuisine has been intensive market gunning that has stressed the wild population. (For more on this, see chapter 10 below.)

When *Scribner's Monthly* in November 1877 mused why Baltimore had become the "gastronomic capital" of the country, it did not ponder long for reasons. "Baltimore rests not its reputation upon the precarious tenure of a single dish; it sits in complacent contemplation of the unrivaled variety of its local market and calmly forbids comparison. While the Chesapeake continues to give it its terrapins, its canvas-backs, its oysters and its fish, this may be done with safety."[9] The conditional nature of the final statement deserves notice. What begins as a paean to Maryland gastronomy shifted quickly to a meditation on the nature of hunting—the "wholesale murdering" of market gunning, drifting up on sleeping shoals of ducks in a sink boat with a "night reflector" on the bow to blind the birds for easy shooting. "From twenty to thirty ducks to each shot fired is a common experience" (3). Opposed to this indiscriminate slaughter was sport hunting in blinds over decoys deployed on the waters skirting the vast private estates around the Chesapeake. Sport was shooting in the semi-dark with skilled retrievers on icy mornings. The two breeds that fed upon water celery—the canvasback and the redhead—stood highest in hunters' estimations.

The great Baltimore sportsman and editor of the *American Farmer*, John

Stuart Skinner, gave instructions on how to cook the canvasback in an 1845 book, *The Dog and the Sportsman*; it became culinary holy writ in Maryland:

> Take it, as soon after the *leaden messenger* brings it down, as possible, even while it is yet warm, if it can be so, and cook it in a "tin kitchen," turning and basting it frequently with a gravy, composed in the bottom of the oven, with a little water and a grain of salt, and its own drippings. The fire should be a brisk one (hickory the best), so that it may be done "to a turn" in twenty-five, or at most thirty minutes. Serve it up immediately, in its own gravy, with a dish of nice, well-boiled (and then fried) milk-white *hominy*.[10]

If one had a proper cookstove at one's disposal, the time of cooking could be reduced. Alexander Filippini, chef at Delmonico's, considered eighteen minutes the optimum. The Maryland Club and Filippini belonged to the sect believing that "the canvas-back cannot be too little cooked, and that to carry it three times round a hot kitchen is quite sufficient." Only when rare does the celeriac tang make the flesh sing. "An over-cooked canvasback is no better than any barnyard duck."[11]

In the Maryland tradition of cooking duck, the kitchen should maintain the simplicity of a campfire. The duck was picked, drawn, and wiped dry, no water ever touching it. The head was left on. A light strew of salt seasoned the fowl sufficiently. Its own juice formed the gravy. On the plate it only appeared with three complements: fried hominy cut in geometrical shapes, a spoonful of currant jelly, or celery.

A note about fried hominy: people around the Chesapeake, like the inhabitants of the Carolina Lowcountry, preferred that their hominy be prepared from white flint or white gourdseed corn. By lye curing or other processing, the outer shell of bran was removed from the white kernel. The large kernels, boiled and fried, became a staple at southern and western breakfasts. Kernels that had been milled coarsely became hominy grits and, ground finely, samp. The fried hominy that appeared with canvasback employed either grits or samp, depending on the degree of toothsomeness desired. Jules Arthur Harder, who presided over the kitchens of both the

Union Club and Delmonico's, supplied directions for preparing the golden fried corn shapes:

> Soak two pounds of Hominy over night, and when it is ready to cook, have in a saucepan six quarts of boiling water, lightly salted, into which put the Hominy slowly, while stirring it with a wooden spoon. Let it boil slowly, occasionally stirring it from the bottom, until it is well cooked, and when cooked it should be similar to mush. . . . When it is well cooked put it into square, buttered pans, about two inches thick, and set it aside to get cold. When cold, cut the Hominy in slices and dip them into beaten eggs, diluted with a little milk. Then flour them and fry them in clarified butter. It is occasionally served with roast wild ducks.[12]

Other chefs fried the slices in duck fat or lard.

As the mystique of the canvasback became ever more entrenched in the clubroom and restaurant and ever more celebrated in the burgeoning world of epicurean letters, market gunners strove to meet the swelling demand. As the ducks became rarer, the price became dearer, fueling gunners' desire to get more of the highest-paying item in the market. The vicious cycle would have continued to the duck's extinction if the sportsmen's backlash against commercial killing hadn't led to the outlawing of many market-gunning practices and the imposition of bag limits. Conservation was a rich man's movement directed against the ambitions of laissez-faire profiteers from the wild.

Canvasbacks survived into the twentieth century to endure a second peril, the destruction of the habitat of wild celery (*Vallisneria americana*). Wild celery occurs naturally in the tidal freshwater shallows of the upper Chesapeake Bay, particularly the Susquehanna Flats and certain tributary rivers, such as the Potomac. Throughout the autumn months, the ducks feed on the plant, building fat stores during the stopovers on their migratory flights southward. Pollution of the watershed and the disruption of bottom sediments from heavy private boat traffic in the last half of the twentieth century led to the destruction of the celery beds. In the 1990s, botanists observed that wild celery in the Chesapeake had been nearly eliminated, and biologists argued that it could be directly correlated with the decline of the canvasback population.[13] In the twenty-first century, several restoration initiatives have been attempted under the direction of R. L. Orth and Kenneth Moore. Every method—the hand planting of seedlings, the dispersion of intact seedpods, the planting of seeds within netted zones—entails costs and requires wetland zones free of pollution and water traffic, stiff requirements in the twenty-first-century Chesapeake.[14] Yet the conviction that the health of the waterway will only be restored with the regeneration of aquatic vegetation has set several bodies in action replanting the wild celery. If the wild celery burgeons, so too will the canvasback ducks, and they will no longer taste of the clams they consume when no celery exists upon which to graze.

LYNNHAVEN OYSTERS

Two miles east of the southern terminus of the Chesapeake Bay Bridge Tunnel, Lynnhaven Bay empties into the most oceanic section of the bay. Now the shores of Lynnhaven River and Bay bristle with single-family dwellings and suburban streets. Here, English colonists found oysters as large as shoes. One of the oldest surviving dwellings in the Old Dominion, the Adam Thoroughgood House, overlooks its waters. For much of the last half of the twentieth century, the chemical runoff from lawn fertilizers and weed and bug killers has rendered the waters of the river and bay unfit for mariculture.

One might think that the Lynnhaven oysters suffered a parallel history to that of the canvasback ducks, but that is hardly the case. Never did the indiscriminate harvesting of Lynnhaven oysters take place. By the mid-nineteenth century, a regimen of cultivation was established among the community of oysterman who tonged the Lynnhaven River and the various coves of the bay. Colonel M. McDonald devised a system of oyster planting, dredging seed oysters from Lynnhaven Bay and planting them in the Lynnhaven River, thus inspiring the private gardening of the population on staked beds.[15] What caused the extraordinary plumpness and flavor of the Lynnhaven oysters was a matter of speculation. The ebb and flow of salt water and freshwater seemed to nineteenth-century observers the reason for their extraordinary quality.

Lynnhaven River is simply a branching arm of Chesapeake Bay, and has been made by the tidal ebb and flow. It is fed by very little surface-drainage, the rain waters of the back country gliding their way into it by percolation through the porous subsoils that form the banks. When the tide is out the fresh water flows out on all sides by infiltration, and dilutes the salt water in the coves and all along the shores. When the tide is at the flood the saltiness is in a measure restored. It is to these incursions of fresh water twice in 24 hours, that the extreme fatness and flavor of these oysters are probably to be attributed.[16]

Despite the intense demand for Lynnhaven oysters, a communal discipline maintained among the Virginia oystermen kept the brand lustrous and the harvest restricted. Shortly after the turn of the twentieth century, the US Bureau of Fisheries reported that the "demand for Lynnhaven Bay oysters is greater than the supply, and the prices paid are higher than for any other shell stock in the state. The output from the beds in 1904–5 was estimated at 8,000 barrels, or 18,000 bushels, valued at $40,000. The superiority of Lynnhaven oysters is due to the fact that more care is taken in their cultivation and fewer oysters are laid down in a given area."[17] Barrels of Lynnhavens in the shell were shipped out of Norfolk. Because of the premium upon freshly shucked top-quality oysters, Lynnhavens were never canned. Nor were Horn Harbor, York River, or Sleepy Hole oysters, the Chesapeake bivalves next in the estimation of connoisseurs. Packers in Norfolk shucked and canned oysters from the Elizabeth, York, Nansemond, Pocosin, Chuckatuck, Weir, East, Piankatank, and Rappahannock Rivers, and Mason's, Tanner's and Back Creeks, shipping tins north to New York, Baltimore, Philadelphia, and Washington for the tides of oyster stew served in hotel restaurants.[18]

In 1915 the oysters in the Lynnhaven River developed green gills, inspiring buyer suspicion and the beginning of market resistance to the brand. Marine biologists immediately began studying the phenomenon, speculating whether ingestion of the diatom *Navicula ostrearia* was responsible.[19] While the phenomenon had been noted previously in parts of the Lynnhaven marine complex for isolated seasons—in 1888–89, for instance—after 1915 the greening of the oysters became regular, and the esteem that they enjoyed declined. Certain families—the Croonenbergs foremost among them—attempted heroically to maintain the quality of the population, but by 1935 they surrendered; the unbridled development around the bay and river and the degradation of water quality had taken its toll on the Lynnhaven oyster.[20] From the Depression to the end of the century, the Lynnhaven was a memory, a regret, a proof that the quality of life in the Old Dominion was declining with every passing decade.

Legends are surprisingly resilient. When scientists began discovering multitudes of native oysters growing in the Lynnhaven River in 2002 and 2003, despite the degraded water conditions, the idea of restoring the waterway as an exploitable habitat took hold among the Virginia marine science community.[21] A contiguous body of water to the east, Broad Bay, because it was bounded by First Landing State Park, remained relatively free of the bacteria and chemical runoff that afflicted the Lynnhaven basin. There, in 2004, a group of local entrepreneurs began seeding oysters and incorporated the Lynnhaven Oyster Company.[22] Determined efforts to clean Lynnhaven Bay, and particularly Lynnhaven River, have resulted in the upgrading of the river's water quality to B status. Beds have been seeded and in March 2011, 40 percent of the river was opened to unrestricted oyster and clam harvesting.[23] The environmental issues remain daunting. Dermo and other oyster diseases remain active in Chesapeake waters. Getting water quality to the level that the estuary enjoyed in the nineteenth century will take years of work and public money. In 2013 the oysters that most closely approximate the classic Lynnhavens come from the relatively pristine waters of the eastern shore, grown by Shooting Point Oyster Company and H. M. Terry Company's Sewansecott Clams & Oysters. But the hope that the Lynnhaven Oyster Company might fully renovate that salty, fat, and deep-shelled oyster of yore is much closer to reality than it has been at any time since 1915.

SALAD OF CRAB AND LETTUCE

In her chronicle of family cooking published in 1874, Miss M. L. Tyson, Maryland's "Queen of the Kitchen," supplied a recipe for this classic cold collation, stunning for its lack of detail. Presumably the dish was so well known to her readership that it required no elaboration: "Crabs for Salad. After boiling the crabs, pick them carefully, and serve the crabs cold with salad dressing, and lettuce."[24] No one would have mistaken which crabs were being referenced: the Chesapeake blue crab (*Callinectes sapidus*, "the tasty beautiful swimmer"). The most resilient of the wild foods included in the Maryland Feast, the crabs have been plentiful from colonial times to the present day. Despite a population decline early in the twenty-first century from overfishing, careful management by the states of Maryland and Virginia have seen a rebound in numbers in 2010 that bodes well for its future.[25]

Picked crabmeat for salad was cooked in water with no seasoning. "Mrs. Washington" supplied all that one needs to know about the art in the *Unrivaled Cookbook*. First, one filled a pot with water and set it boiling. Bring the crabs to the kitchen and "plunge them alive in boiling water; if they show signs of weakness, throw them away—they are not good; let the crabs boil until they are bright red, then pour off the water, and break open the shells; remove the fingers (which lie between the outer and inner shell), and remove also the sand-bags; all the of rest of the crab is good, especially the fat, which is usually of a reddish yellow, and found in the cavity of the shell; break the crab in half, and you will find the meat re-vealed like the kernel of a well-cracked shell-bark."[26] Picked meat would be stored in a bowl set on ice immediately.

Both lettuce and celery were cultivated widely in Maryland and deemed of superior quality.[27] The favorite lettuce varieties of the 1870s around Baltimore were the loose-headed Hanson lettuce, butter lettuce, the early curled Simpson, and the curled Silesia. The cos lettuces were deemed too bitter to be paired with crabmeat.

What dressing went on the classic crab salad? In *Fifty Years in a Mary-land Kitchen* (1880), Mrs. B. C. Howard provided what Miss Tyson pre-sumed the reader already knew. Not salt and mayonnaise. Not vinaigrette and red pepper. Rather, "a large table-spoonful of butter creamed, with mustard, salt, pepper, vinegar, and the yolks of two raw eggs. After mixing well together, put it on the fire and stir until it becomes the consistency of mustard."[28] This dressing had more than a little piquancy, playing off the chill of the crabmeat and ripped lettuce leaves. The Maryland conviction that crabmeat tasted sufficiently sweet to require no enhancement caused Baltimorean cooks to eschew the tablespoon of sugar that northern cooks employed in this dressing.[29]

TERRAPIN À LA MARYLAND

Dr Cheever: "Isn't Baltimore the home of the diamond back terrapin? I have always wanted to taste some terrapin cooked in Baltimore."

I assured him that he was in the proper place, at the Maryland Club, where they pride themselves on cooking terrapin à la Maryland. By the time the terrapin arrived it was after ten o'clock. To my surprise Dr. Cheever ate with evident relish a generous portion of terrapin and fixings such as would have done credit to anyone, a pretty good contract for that time of night. When he had finished, he expressed great satisfaction and said that the merits of terrapin had not been in the least exaggerated. I felt some trepidation about leaving him at his hotel after this late feast, for "terrapin à la Maryland' is a rich dish, and with my impression as to the good doctor's faulty digest, I wondered how the terrapin would sit. However, next morning when I called for him, he appeared to be in excellent shape, and said that he had had a splendid night and continued to enjoy greatly in retrospect the terrapin of the night before. I never had seen him in better form.

The Autobiography of J. M. T. Finney: A Surgeon's Life

The terrapin lives in the coastal waters of the south from the Georgia Sea Islands to the Patapsco River in Maryland. In the post–Civil War era, most of the diamondbacks consumed in Baltimore came from the James River in Virginia, where freedmen would poke the bottom mud with slender sticks to find dormant turtles.[30] After mid-September, a captured terrapin would survive until spring without food or water, and eating establishments often maintained a barrel of live terrapins in the coolest, darkest corner of the cellar. The female "cow" (not the male "bull") was Maryland cooks' decided preference when preparing stews and soups. Turtle eggs were greatly desired as well and were conventionally incorporated into the Philadelphia version of terrapin stew.

The cachet of Terrapin à la Maryland after it became part of the Maryland Feast resulted in a demand that, over the thirty years following the founding of the Maryland Club, led to the diminution of the breed in the

Chesapeake. In 1877 a commentator wrote, "Thirty years ago the largest dealer in Baltimore had hard work to dispose of the terrapin he received at $6 a dozen. . . . That day, however, is of the past, and it is doubtful if this valuable article of food is not gradually becoming extinct. The negroes who make a business of sending them to market complain of their increasing rarity, and nothing but the high price has stimulated them to keep up the supply."[31] The demand for terrapin in the clubs and restaurants of the Northeast, particularly Philadelphia and New York, gave rise to specialist brokers who collected terrapin and canvasback for shipment there: Mr. A. T. LaValetta of Crisfield, Maryland, controlled the flow of terrapin northward.[32] S. R. Scoggins of Scoggins Game and Terrapin Depot in Baltimore provided canvasback and some terrapin sourced from Virginia's rivers.

What exactly was the dish that imperiled the terrapin? Turtles require substantial initial preparation before incorporation into a dish. Some had the terrapin swim in several changes of water to clear out their system before cooking. Once cleansed, "plunge the terrapins alive into boiling water, and let them remain until the sides and lower shell begin to crack—this will take less than an hour; then remove them and let them get cold; take off the shell and outer skin, being careful to save all the blood possible in opening them. If there are eggs in them put them aside in a dish; take all the insides out, and be very careful not to break the gall, which must be immediately removed, or it will make the rest bitter. It lies within the liver."[33] The meat was chopped into small pieces and put into a saucepan. Marylanders invariably added the blood and juice exuding from the terrapin when being cut up. Chef Alexander Filippini describes the process from this point: "Carefully cut up two terrapins . . . place them in a saucepan with half a wine-glass of good Madeira wine, half a pinch of salt, and a very little cayenne pepper, also an ounce of good butter. Mix well a cupful of good, sweet cream with the yolks of three boiled eggs, and add it to the terrapin, briskly shuffling constantly, while thoroughly heating, but without letting it come to a boil. Pour into a hot tureen, and serve very hot."[34]

To insure that Terrapin à la Maryland came to the table piping hot, the Maryland Club erected a battery of chafing dishes along one wall of the dining room. Two African American cooks assembled the dish and dispensed it to patrons throughout every evening in terrapin season. The invariability of the dish's place on the menu—indeed the fixity of every dish of the Maryland Feast on the club's menu—prompted an English visitor in the early 1880s to remark that the club was "pitilessly monotonous in its *carte*."[35]

Filippini insisted that good Madeira be used in preparing the dish. The Maryland Club's cellar of sherries and Madeiras was legendary; it had, upon its founding in 1857, inherited the stock of two previous Baltimore clubs, one of which dated back to the eighteenth century. It owned Sercial dating from the 1770s. And the cellars housed "wines of fabulous age, including the famous Glenn, Hoffman, and Noble Madeira bottled in 1810, 1819, and 1826."[36] While Madeira remained the preferred accompaniment to the Maryland Feast into the 1890s, burgundy began to supplant it in the tastes of the younger generation in the 1880s.

Ironically, the necessity for Madeira in Terrapin à la Maryland saved the turtles from extinction in the early twentieth century. Prohibition in 1919 put an end to the public consumption of dishes employing fortified wines. The decade of non-consumption caused terrapin populations to rebound. When Prohibition was repealed, the taste for the old Chesapeake classic had declined to an extent that few temples of haute cuisine restored it to the menu. Even in Baltimore and Washington, DC, it gave way to oyster stew and clam chowder in popularity. Terrapin populations climbed into the 1960s, when degradation of habitat caused by coastal development and wetlands population reversed the trend. Since the 1970s, the status of the terrapin verged on being "threatened," and localities have prohibited or scaled back harvesting of the special breed. In South Carolina, where the population is most robust, state law permits the harvesting and sale of terrapin, but the Department of Natural Resources as an administrative policy has issued no permits since 2000.[37] The primary risk to populations in the Chesapeake, North Carolina, and South Carolina, besides the degradation of nesting habitat, has been the capture of adults in the multitudes of crab pots deployed in coastal waters.

In sum, if you know someone in the Carolina Lowcountry with wetlands, and if they harvest the creatures on their own property and give them to you, you can make one of the essential components of the Maryland Feast. If you secure canvasback ducks from one of the Midwest flyways, where wild celery restoration has gone on for some time, you can roast them as the Maryland Club did. If you secure hominy grits from one of the suppliers that employ historic strains of white flint or white gourd-seed corn (such as Anson Mills), you can make the fried hominy diamonds that accompany the duck. If you contact Shooting Point Oyster Company, or Sewansecott Clams & Oysters, you can approximate the taste of the classic large Lynnhavens on the half shell. We hope that we will be able to hail the restoration of the Lynnhaven population in the coming five years. The dish most easily reproduced from the Maryland Feast remains Crab and Lettuce Salad. Butter lettuce remains a favorite green, and lump back-fin crab from the East Coast is widely available.

In 1908, when Escoffier, the "king" of Parisian chefs, came to New York to organize the kitchen of the second Ritz-Carlton Hotel, he sampled the best American food that the city offered. The dishes that most entranced him all came from Maryland—soft clams, Chicken à la Maryland at Martin's Restaurant, and the two linchpin dishes of the Maryland Feast, canvasback duck and terrapin.[38] One can perhaps see this as the pivotal moment, that juncture when the old splendor began being supplanted by the new—when fried chicken insinuated its way into the feast. It wouldn't be too long before the Alston Club's fried soft-shell crabs, crab patties (croquettes that began to appear in cookbooks around 1870), and beaten biscuits (which, in the mid-nineteenth century, was identified as a Virginia preparation) elbowed the Lynnhaven oyster, the canvasback duck, and the terrapin to the sidelines of favor.

In Baltimore, New York, Newport, London, and Paris, the Maryland Feast stood as the pinnacle of American cuisine until the First World War. After the war, a new culinary world emerged, and the feast receded into legend.

Wisdom consists in understanding the accomplishments of past ages and the costs and benefits of achieving great things. Aesthetics teaches us that old pleasures can be revived and delight us anew.

FIVE   *Charleston's Caterers,*
1795 to 1883

In nineteenth-century New Orleans, culinary fame came only to those who could make a restaurant meal memorable. The finest French wine, the freshest seasonal ingredients, and the most delicate French kitchen technique earned a handful of caterers glory. In nineteenth-century Charleston, culinary fame came to those who triumphed in preparing banquets for the multitude of societies and associations in the city. While providing an attractive bill of fare at a restaurant assisted in making one noteworthy, fame came only to those who fashioned the splendid food expected at anniversary occasions and fêtes. Because so many of these events took place in meeting halls or public spaces, a mastery of logistics—carting, constructing trestle tables, preparing food on site, and laying out the spread—mattered as much as quality ingredients and kitchen craft in success. There were a very few names that echoed through the gazettes over the century as masters of the mobile culinary art. John and Eliza Lee, the proprietors of the Jones Hotel; Nat Fuller, proprietor of the Bachelor's Retreat restaurant on the corner of Church Street and St. Michael's Alley; Thomas R. Tully, whose eating house was located at 124 King Street; and

A. J. Rutjes and Madam T. M. Rutjes, proprietors of the Mount Vernon Restaurant. The first four were free black caterers born in South Carolina; the latter two, Euro-American pastry cooks. Their styles of cooking, while inflected by French practices, were recognizably southern and American. The conspicuousness of African American talent in the shaping of the city's haute cuisine paralleled the catering tradition of Baltimore and Richmond[1] rather than the Eurocentric New Orleans's restaurant world.

The world of Charleston's restaurateurs during the age when Lowcountry cuisine came into being has never been explored. A history of the great cooks, their venues, and their menus will enrich our understanding of how this distinct tradition came to be.

Paralleling developments in other southern cities, Charleston's restaurants emerged out of the welter of taverns and barrooms when hotels projected a standard of fine dining. This happened in March 1838 when the newly opened Charleston Hotel alerted the public to the splendor of haute cuisine with its superb saloon and à la carte menu.[2] Rival establishments—the Planter's Hotel (elevated from inn status in 1809 by proprietor Alexander Calder) and the Victoria Hotel (erected from 1838 to 1839 on King Street)—strove to upgrade and equal the Charleston Hotel in appointments and cuisine. The Planter's Hotel took the challenge seriously, renovating its kitchen by installing Dr. Nott's Patent Portable Baker and Boiler when intimations of the Charleston Hotel's intended erection surfaced in late 1834.[3] In 1847, in the face of declining family custom, proprietor Charles H. Miot refurbished the building, creating a "Ladies' Ordinary" on the model of New Orleans's St. Charles Hotel, to ensure that women did not feel discommoded at meals.[4] The Victoria countered not with equipment, but with personnel, securing the talented Charles Frazier as caterer.

As in New Orleans, the ratcheting up of the culinary quality of the hotel dining rooms in Charleston challenged coffeehouse keepers to upgrade their facilities to the status of restaurants. From the 1820s to the '50s, at least two such freestanding establishments operated in the city at any given time. In the 1850s, there was an efflorescence of eateries. The important eating houses in Charleston from the 1820s through 1840s were as follows:

1820s: The Carolina Coffee House, Tradd Street, Angus Stewart, prop.

1820s: Charier's, 59 Queen Street

1830s: French Coffee House, 125 East Bay, R. Mignot, prop.

1842: Joseph Coche's (pastry and charcuterie), 5 North Market Street

1845: The Exchange Café, Meeting and Market Sts., Thomas Baker, prop.

In the heyday of restaurants from 1850 to 1865, the following freestanding eating houses operated in the city:

Bachelor's Retreat: 77 Church Street, Nat Fuller, prop.

Chupien's Restaurant: 105 East Bay (after 1861, Litschge's Restaurant)

First Class Restaurant: 61 Hasel Street, George E. Johnston, prop.

French Coffee House: Church Street, Thomas Baker, prop. (after 1858, Henry Mertens)

Greer's: 535 King Street, Louis Kenacks, prop.

Ladies' Fashionable Restaurant: 170 King Street, A. J. Rutjes, prop. (early 1850s)

Madame Favier's: State Street (after 1863, 39 Broad Street), Madame A. Favier, prop.

Maison Dorée: (restaurant and billiard saloon), 119 Meeting Street

Mott's Restaurant: 3 and 5 Princess Street, William Mott, prop.

Mount Vernon Restaurant: 174 King Street, A. J. Rutjes, prop. to 1858 (W. Hammond to 1860)

National Exchange Restaurant: 125 Meeting Street, Jonathan J. Jowitt, prop.

New Restaurant: 6 Broad Street, J. Silva, prop. (later W. J. Riding; closes 1858)

Palmetto Shade Restaurant: 115 East Bay, R. Daly, prop.

Phoenix Restaurant: 39 Queen Street, "Dr." William B. Thompson, prop.

Sideboard Restaurant: 6 Broad Street, Mrs. Watson, prop. after 1858

Vanderhorst and Tully's: 124 King Street, Thomas R. Tully, prop.

PASTRY COOKS

Of all the kitchen offices, that of pastry chef in the late eighteenth and early nineteenth century was regarded as most skilled and valuable. While the mastery of dough—particularly puff pastry—constituted a requisite of pastry cookery, the skilled practitioner had to be equally adept at handling savory dishes, such as meat pies. The first professional cook to become a public figure in Charleston, Charles Moore, was a pastry chef who provisioned gentlemen at a private mess held in his home at 20 Meeting Street in the 1780s. The scope of his talent is suggested by his promise to serve "Portugal, Plumb, and seed cakes . . . turtle dressed . . . soups from 11 to 2 o'clock, tea and coffee every day."[5] Within a year, a rival Londoner Adam Prior set up at 40 Elliot Street, advertising "Rich Cakes, French Pies, Patties, Trifles, every kind of Cut-Pastry, Jellies, and all sorts of Confectionary. Note. Hot meat pies of all kinds."[6] He would train Sally Seymour.

Of slaves, among the most valuable, rating next to skilled carpenters, were pastry cooks. Always distinguished from mere "cooks," pastry cooks often occasioned encomiums in the calls for sale, even when the name of the woman was not supplied: "A Pastry Cook, very perfect in her business."[7] The usual descriptor for a kitchen artist of the highest accomplishment was a "complete pastry cook."

The history of one such cook has garnered the attention of historians of free black women: After her manumission in 1795, Sally Seymour, the mistress of planter Thomas Martin and mother of his children, opened a pastry shop on Tradd Street in Charleston. As Larry Koger has documented, she bought and trained a slave workforce to bolster her production.[8] Sally trained her daughter Eliza and son William alongside her slave staff. After Sally Seymour's death in 1824, Eliza assumed control of the shop and married John Lee, a free mulatto tailor whose shop was located close to the Seymour's kitchen. Lee, a member of the Brown Fellowship Society, the association of the free mixed-race elite, possessed substantial business acumen and the credit of the network of African American artisans and professionals. Eliza Lee, meanwhile, won a formidable reputation for cooking among the white citizenry. The Society of the Cincinnati met regularly at her establishment on Tradd into the mid-1830s.[9] During the 1830s, John secured the contract with the Charleston City Council to provision the assemblies of the Citizen Guard.[10] Given his wife's talent as a caterer and his own administrative ability, John determined to change vocations, becoming both a public caterer and boardinghouse proprietor. From 1840 through 1851, they collaborated on running four establishments: the Mansion House on Broad Street (1840–45), the Lee House (1845–48), the Jones Hotel (1848–50), and the Moultrie House on Sullivan's Island (1850–51).[11] The death of John in 1851 forced Eliza on an independent course. Opening a famous restaurant on 18 Beaufain Street, she reigned as the matriarch of Lowcountry cooking until she retired in 1861. An 1856 advertisement (fig. 1) indicates both the range of her culinary prowess and the specialties upon which her fame rested.

Eliza's sense of vocation conformed exactly with that of most pastry cooks. Cakes, pies, and jellies stood foremost among the creations at her command. Hosting society dinners was her primary evening business, not boarding diners. Drop-in customers would be served at all hours, but lunch was commended particularly to the public. Of savory dishes, oysters—the signature dish of coastal eating houses from Portland, Maine, to Galveston, Texas—was the only savory item receiving particular mention. If turtle had been in season, it too would have been mentioned.

Pastry cookery was a cosmopolitan art, its tenets codified in majestic tomes, such as M. A. Carême's *Royal Parisian Pastrycook and Confectioner*, whose English edition was advertised in the *Charleston Courier* through spring of 1837. There is no suggestion in any of the surviving records of the Seymour-Lee family of any West African ethnic dimension to their production. Admittedly, the record is scant. Yet baking was not a regular mode of food preparation among most of the West African nations, so one does not expect it.

The premium placed on complete pastry cooks in slave sales strongly suggests that persons apprenticed and trained by literate cooks, such as Sally Seymour and Eliza Lee, made up the majority of the skilled listings during the final decades of slave culture in South Carolina. One reason that the Seymour-Lee family inspired great regard in Charleston was the quality of the servants they trained. Whenever one of the numbers of slaves that Sally Seymour or Eliza Lee instructed came upon the market, an advertisement appeared in the city gazettes and a private sale, rather than a public auction, would settle the person with a master. On a unique

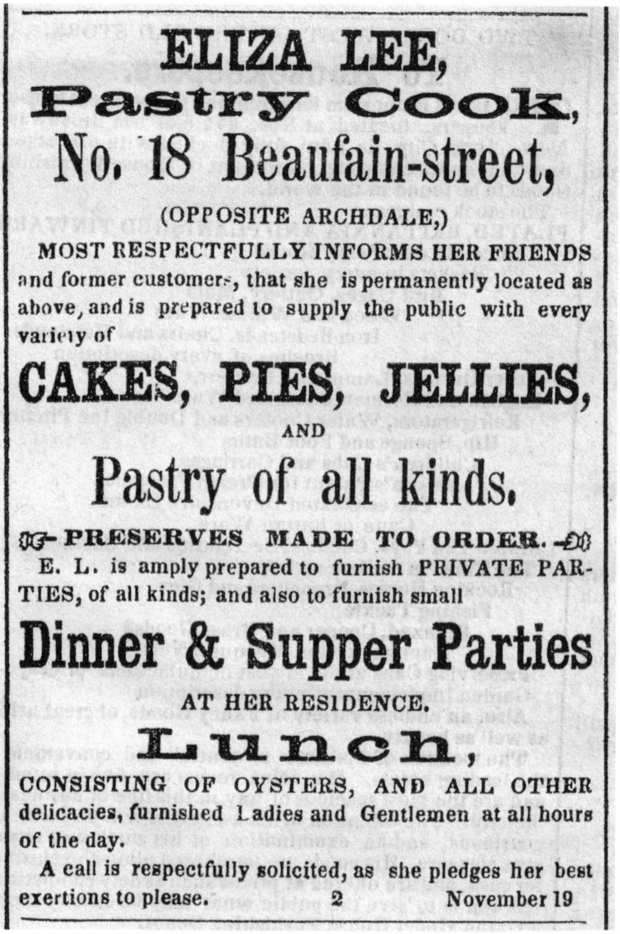

ELIZA LEE,
Pastry Cook,
No. 18 Beaufain-street,

(OPPOSITE ARCHDALE,)

MOST RESPECTFULLY INFORMS HER FRIENDS and former customers, that she is permanently located as above, and is prepared to supply the public with every variety of

CAKES, PIES, JELLIES,

AND

Pastry of all kinds,

☞ PRESERVES MADE TO ORDER. ☜

E. L. is amply prepared to furnish PRIVATE PARTIES, of all kinds; and also to furnish small

Dinner & Supper Parties

AT HER RESIDENCE.

Lunch,

CONSISTING OF OYSTERS, AND ALL OTHER delicacies, furnished Ladies and Gentlemen at all hours of the day.

A call is respectfully solicited, as she pledges her best exertions to please.   2   November 19

FIGURE I. Ad for Eliza Lee, pastry cook.
Courtesy Lowcountry Heritage Education.

occasion on February 20, 1844, the *Charleston Courier*, in separate ads, announced the private sale of a "very superior" male cook "brought up" by Eliza Lee; and "a very like Mulatto woman, 35 years old, a complete pastry Cook, in all of its branches, served her time with Sally Seymour." During Lee's years at Tradd Street, white Charlestonians apprenticed out black boys and girls to learn the art. It could be argued that the Seymour-Lee family did more than any other persons in the antebellum era to improve the quality of cooking available in Charleston, influencing elite domestic consumption through the pastry cooks they trained to expertise, as well as the public fare available in city. The other free black pastry cooks who owned slaves—Camilla Johnson, Eliza Dwight, Martha Gilchrist, Hannah Hetty, Elizabeth Holton, Mary Holton, and Cato McCloud—performed similarly.[12]

Charleston differed markedly from New Orleans in the relation between its restaurant and upper-class home food cultures. In New Orleans, the restaurateurs were invariably Europeans who cultivated French cuisine and did not train household cooks, either in slave times or during Reconstruction. In Charleston, the great city household cooks were regularly trained by free black pastry cooks during the antebellum period. The household cooks were nearly invariably African American and trained in an urbane cosmopolitan style. One must look to plantation "meat cooks" operating in the country, and the few black city cook shops, for the formulation of the African American dishes that come into the domestic repertoire codified in *The Carolina Housewife* and other southern post-Civil War cookbooks. Professional cookery in Charleston—like Baltimore, Richmond, Washington, DC, and Savannah—employed local fish, game, fowl, produce, and regional fruit in preparations that called for French cooking technique, supplemented by a body of fried dishes inflected by West African practices.

If Eliza Lee established a kind of norm for good cuisine in Charleston, the fashionable horizon was expanded most by confectioners Théonie and Adolphus John Rutjes.

THE FRENCH CONNECTION

Rémy Mignot, coffeehouse keeper, first set up in Charleston in 1823 at 193 East Bay Street. Coffeehouses in that masculine and mercantile sector of the city dispensed as much alcohol as caffeine. So there is little surprise in the fact that Mignot's first appearance in the public prints announced his application for a liquor license in October 1823.[13] Careful management of his revenues enabled in a short while the purchase of a more favorable space at 170 King Street, which by the 1820s had become the fashionable promenade in the city. In partnership with Charles Rame, Mignot opened the Cheap Confectionary Store purveying ice cream and pastries.

The house dispensed food and drink at a refreshment bar, and tea and tea cakes "baked daily, and a constant supply" sated the morning or mid-day pedestrian.[14] On October 1, 1831, the terms of partnership expired, and Mignot took over sole proprietorship of the confectionery business on King Street.[15] Rame would eventually open an ice cream shop at 165 Meeting Street. Mignot, like Rame, touted ice cream for the warm season, yet one-upped his old partner by offering Roman punch and cakes fresh baked each day.[16] He also became adept in the manufacture of fruit syrups, obtaining sugar from New Orleans and lemons from Florida, selling his concoctions at 37½ cents per bottle.

The cause of French cuisine in Charleston advanced immeasurably in January 1837 when Mignot partnered with cook Louis Lefeve and coffeehouse keeper Alexis Galliot to remake the United States Coffee House at 129 East Bay Street into the premier eatery in the city. The triumvirate promised the public that it would stock the Coffee House's larder "with all that is rare and delicious, in Fish, Flesh and Fowl." It announced that in "addition to the customary lunch and refreshment, an Ordinary or Table d'Hote, will be prepared and ready every day, at half past 2 o'clock, got up under the management of Mr. Lefeve, in the style of the Parisian and New York Restorat."[17] As an added incentive to sporting gentlemen, the Coffee House secured one of the city's three permits to maintain a billiard table.

Mignot had a genius for business, and when specie dried up in the region during the summer of 1837, hindering the ability to tender coins as change, the United States Coffee House issued scrip, a private paper currency analogous to that issued by private banks at the time.[18] The experiment in entertainment lasted a year before Louis Lefeve decided to let the partnership expire, hoping to wrest the property from Alex Galliot. Mignot would have none of it, brought suit, and forced Lefeve to sell the building and kitchen stock in a sheriff's sale in February 1838.[19] Two months later, using the proceeds from the sale, Mignot purchased Eude's Café at 125 East Bay, rebranded it as the French Coffee House, reanimating his idea of a cosmopolitan Gallic eatery.[20] Widow Eude, having witnessed the expansion of business accomplished by Mignot, yearned to have the property back under her control. She married P. Ligniez, a man of means, and convinced him to buy back the house at a price Mignot could not refuse. And in April 1840, Mignot did not refuse.

Mignot, flush with cash, contented himself with being a subsidiary interest in a number of partnerships, including a saloon at 2 Market Street, and a grocery and dry goods business run by J. P. Legrix in Aiken. But his active engagement in catering only resumed in 1842 when he reactivated his confectionery at 160 King Street (a renumbering of 170). To mark his reopening, Mignot set the price of ice cream at 6½ cents a plate, a price that would stand for nearly two decades. The confectionery in the 1840s became more Parisian in its offerings because of the influence of his wife, Théonie Rivière Mignot.

Théonie was the daughter of Baron Jean-Pierre Rivière, a refugee of both the French and Haitian Revolutions who finally found security in Charleston as a grocer specializing in luxury goods. Born in Philadelphia and educated in Paris, Théonie had learned the luxury goods trade in the French capital before returning to Charleston at age twenty-two. In 1834 she married the newly widowed Rémy Mignot, then eighteen years her senior. Child rearing occupied the early years of the marriage, but by 1842 her imagination required vent in other than domestic affairs. She began ordering materials from Paris for the King Street store. Her tastes are reflected in the billet of sweets published during Christmas season of 1843: "Mint Candy, Rock Candy, Horehound Candy, Flaxseed Candy; Sugar Plums: Almond & Coriander, Marble Sugar Plums, Cinnamon & Citron, Burnt Almond, Vanilla Almonds, Lemon Almonds, Preteen Rose, Chocolate Drops, Cherries Crystallized, Raisins Crystallized, Coriander Drops, Cordial Beans, Citronel, Apenvinette, Raspberry Sugar Plums."[21] She had an enduring fascination with toys that found expression in extravagant Christmas selections from France and Germany. She exercised an increasing influence on the stock of the confectionery through the 1840s. In 1847 Rémy contracted cancer, and as he declined he turned management of affairs entirely into the hands of his wife. Rémy expired in 1848. For two years, Théonie performed the responsibilities of motherhood (including raising the future luminist painter Louis Rémy Mignot) while serving as proprietor of the store and restaurant on King Street.

The revolutionary ferment that disturbed Europe in 1848 set many fleeing the capitals in search of safety and support. In January of that troubled year, Paris became profoundly unstable; in February the monarchy collapsed. Those whose livelihoods depended on entertaining or serving the tastes of the privileged orders found themselves set loose. The most enterprising of these sought their fortunes in America. In February 1848, the pianist T. A. Rutjes relocated to Charleston.[22] Shortly thereafter, he sent for his brother, Adolphus John Rutjes, a confectioner. Both had been born in Zevenaar, Netherlands, and had removed to Paris to try their fortune. However, fortune in the year of revolution turned against them.

Adolphus John was already a close friend of the Mignot household. Rémy's eldest son, Adolphus John, was named after him. Worldly, bold, talented, and congenial, he appeared in Charleston precisely at a moment when Madame Mignot felt a need for a partner and confidant. She was an energetic and unabashed spirit, with a genius for event catering and party planning; he was an inventive pastry chef and sugar baker. On January 2, 1850, they formed a matrimonial alliance and business partnership.[23] Madame Rutjes announced the rebranding of her store in the public papers:

ICE CREAM ICE CREAM ICE CREAM

AT THE CHEAP CONFECTIONERY

174 KING STREET

Mrs. T. Rutjes, formerly Madame Mignot, would respectfully inform her friends and the public, that she will be prepared this day, to serve them with the best ICE CREAMS and SHERBETS, together with a large assortment of Confectionaries of all kinds and the best quality. Mrs. T. Rutjes has fitted up a Saloon for the accommodation of ladies, in the most modern style.[24]

What Adolphus John brought to the partnership received public airing in advertisements later that year. He declared that "he has commenced making a very great variety of substantial and FANCY CAKES; many of them of his own, or the latest inventions of Paris; which may be had every day, Fresh. OYSTER, and every description of Pattys, of the most original style and savoury taste, made on the shortest notice. PYRAMIDS of every kind, of great splendour, from two to fifty dollars each; FANCY PIECES, for ornamental tables; and every article which can tempt the most refined taste."[25] Like a classic pastry chef, Rutjes had mastered the savory pies and patties as well as the sweet cakes. Pyramidal arrangements of fruits and cream puffs had become a Parisian fashion as part of the post-Napoleonic Egyptomania that had seized the metropolis. Fancy cakes required extraordinary temperature control. No doubt Madame Rutjes owned a new-style bake oven at the confectionery.

These two ambitious spirits kindled commercial creativity among them. Adolphus John converted a portion of the ground-floor space into a store and display hall for "Bonbons, French Toys, Parisian Preserves and Candies," and seasonal fireworks. In May 1851, they hired the German Brass Band to serenade diners during the evening hours.[26] In August he purchased the adjoining property at 170 King. The combined establishment was called "The Ladies' Saloon"[27] or "Ladies' Fashionable Restaurant." Its rules of admittance appeared in October. The space was "expressly for the Ladies of Charleston. Gentlemen visiting the Saloon in the company of Ladies will be admitted."[28] Hours were from 7:00 a.m. until 10:00 p.m. Adolphus John indicated as well that a French cook had been hired to prepare delicacies and game. Early in the social season, he refitted one of his rooms, knocking out an interior wall so that it accommodated fifty persons, in order to entice clubs and associations to meet. This did not result in a surge in business, and the responsibility of superintending two properties troubled Rutjes, so that shortly after the New Year he put 170 King Street up for sale. To supply additional space at 174 King, Adolphus John landscaped an exterior yard (172 King) and opened in the spring of 1852 the Mount Vernon Ice Cream Garden.[29] By November 1852, Rutjes's taste for business had palled, and he offered his entire establishment, 174 and 172 (an open lot that served as the garden), for sale. The price Rutjes desired was never met, so he continued to occupy his restaurant and garden, refreshing his love of catering by undertaking an increasing volume of association dinners through 1853.

In June 1854, when cholera coursed through the city, and because miasmic theory made people chary of eating outside, the business at the Mount Vernon Ice Cream Garden appeared fated to fail. Rutjes became proprietor of the up-country Aiken Hotel for the summer season, touting it as the seat of health.[30] In August he withdrew. In autumn he was back on King Street, hiring confectioners and expanding his service. For the next years, the cycle of activity proved stable. During the warm-weather months, the Mount Vernon Ice Cream Garden would operate late into the night, illuminated by gas fixtures. In October, at the arrival of cool weather, it would close entirely, and the restaurant would ramp up to full service. Madame Rutjes's fancy goods shop would open at that time as well. In January 1856 Adolphus John, noting the rising prosperity of game provisioner and cook Nat Fuller, contracted with New York shippers to supply him game for resale in Charleston. Rutjes began selling "Turkey, Grouse, Pheasant, Capons, Geese, and Pigeons" out of his restaurant.[31]

One of Adolphus John's weaknesses was a penchant for real estate speculation. He purchased on credit a number of properties in Charleston and Mount Pleasant. In 1856 these investments went sour, and the first of several equity proceedings began against Rutjes. An equity suit engaged by his wife's oldest son, Adolphus, seeking to gain control of property in Adolphus John's name since his marriage, prompted the sale of the Mount Vernon Ice Cream Garden and Ladies' Fashionable Restaurant to a third party.[32] In September 1856, Adolphus John sold 172 and 174 King Street, the restaurant's equipment, and the store's contents to William Hammond. Hammond, having won awards for confectionery at the Franklin Institute Exhibition in Philadelphia, kept Rutjes on staff for six months. After a period working solely as an event caterer, Adolphus John opened a cigar stand and sweet shop at 6 State Street, another of his properties, and bided his time. Hammond's business, lacking the vivacious force of Madame Rutjes in the front of the house, tailed off. In autumn 1858, Adolphus John regained control of the King Street property, and on November 11 began advertising for apprentices.[33] On December 6—just in time for the Christmas trade—he reopened the Mount Vernon Restaurant and Store. To impress the public with the range of his culinary skills, he hosted a banquet on December 13, to which most of the bon ton was invited.

The second incarnation of the Mount Vernon restaurant differed from the first in two respects: women were no longer the target customers, rather "Societies and Clubs" were; and alcoholic beverages and cigars found their way onto the carte of offerings.[34] Adolphus John began producing candy on a commercial scale early in 1859. Madame Rutjes reconstituted the store and enhanced its offerings, including Parisian-made china and stemware. She also operated as event planner for catered occasions off premises. The restaurant remained the city's standard-bearer for

French cuisine, offering on its menus "Pates fois gras, Olive Farcer, Truffels, Champignons, Petet pois au Beurre, Petit Pois Naturelle."[35] When Rutjes reopened the Mount Vernon Ice Cream Garden in late March, the rise in commodity prices prompted him to raise prices of a plate of ice cream from 6½ to 10 cents, a hike steep enough to require public explanation in the city papers.[36] In May 1860, Adolphus John's health began to decline, and on June 9 he announced the appointment of his wife as his attorney, for his condition forced him to leave Carolina.[37]

On June 11, the property at 172 and 174 King Street was sold to F. Chapeau, who permitted Madame Rutjes to remain as a lessee. Théonie Rutjes took over the complete management of the restaurants and store. Addresses to the public appeared under the heading "Madame T. M. Rutjes" thereafter. She followed the long-established pattern of shuttering the restaurant and store in late March to run an ice cream saloon during the hot months. In mid-October, the saloon would be shut down and the restaurant service reinstituted. Aided by "the best French Cooks" and "her own personal knowledge and experience," she offered Parisian fare suited to Carolina tastes: "Mock Turtle Soup, Oysters—Fried or Stewed, Meat and Oyster Patties, Beef Steak, Mutton and Veal Chops, Sardines, Ham and Eggs, Omelette, French Styles Beef Alamode, with Jelly, Cakes, Ice Cream, Coffee, Chocolate. &c., &c."[38] The reign of T. M. Rutjes over the kitchen of the Mount Vernon would be short, for on December 15, 1861, the Great Fire destroyed all of that section of King Street and Madame Rutjes's home on Horlbeck Alley.

The economic and civic distress wrought by the fire precluded Théonie from attempting a rebuild in the city. She removed to the state capital in Columbia and in May 1862 opened Central House, a "First-Class Boarding House."[39] After the war, she returned to Charleston to open the Mansion House hotel and restaurant on Broad Street. Adolphus John returned, declared bankruptcy in the Charleston courts, and convinced Théonie to move to Raleigh, North Carolina, where they opened an array of boardinghouses and eateries. So ended, in 1868, the efforts of the two greatest champions of French confectionery and restaurant cuisine in the Lowcountry during the antebellum era. For thirty-five years, from 1823 to 1867, the Miguot-Rutjes combination had made French confection the standard for delicious sweetness and had strove to acquaint the public with other features of French cuisine. They recognized women as a clientele, creating the first women-focused eating space in the city, and the most elegant one at that.

The two cooking dynasties we've examined thus far expired during or shortly after the Civil War. Only one professional succession took the antebellum cuisine deep into the Reconstruction and made use of the explosion of seafood and vegetables occasioned by the bounty of the Reconstruction era: Nat Fuller and his pupil, Thomas R. Tully. These free black caterers were reckoned the greatest culinary artists of the city and the definers of the festive board in the Lowcountry.

THE ARTISTS

In certain respects, the emergence of Nat Fuller (1812–1866) as a major force in Charleston's culinary firmament mirrors that of butcher John Galpin in New Orleans. Galpin brought in the best beef, mutton, and pork to his city; learned from his hotel purchasers how to cook and dress them; opened his own restaurant; and eventually took over the kitchen of the hotelier who first instructed him. Fuller became a major purveyor at the Charleston Game Market at 68 King Street in the 1840s, developed concurrently a popular mobile catering business, and eventually opened the finest eatery in Charleston. At 68 King Street,[40] he sold grouse, quail, pheasants, capons, bear, geese, turkeys, mutton, geese, venison, and whatever the railroads could bring from the West or steamers from the North.[41] Game was premium offering on hotel menus. Fuller studied his clientele and learned their art. The game market, like the produce and meat markets, opened at dawn and closed at noon. In actuality, business in meat was usually finished by ten in the morning. This enabled Galpin in New Orleans and Fuller in Charleston to switch vocations from market vendor to caterer during the course of a single day. While Fuller may have changed hats, he did not change premises. Working out of 68 King, he marshaled the materials needed to create banquets and party collations.

He has imported from Europe a supply of china-ware (sufficient for the use of the largest balls) and table ornaments, such as candelabras (plated and gilded), fancy skewers, punch bowls . . . which can be taken to any part of the country. His supply for forks and spoons do away, in small families, of borrowing from one's neighbors and friends on occasions of entertainments, and any one who had the pleasure of assisting at the St. Cecilia and Jockey Balls of last year, not to mention many private parties, can testify to the talent which our own people can display with encouragement.[42]

The emphasis upon china and flatware reminds us that the business of a banquet cook included supplying the table finery as well as the comestibles.

When the Elmore Insurance Company erected an office building on Broad Street, it hosted a banquet on the new premises. "In the upper hall a handsome collation had been spread, and all present sat down, without ceremony, to discuss the choice liquors and tempting viands. . . . [T]o the thoughtful attention of Nat Fuller, the caterer of the occasion, the guests are much indebted for much of their comfort and enjoyment."[43] Fuller's supply of alcohol drew particular praise and reminds us that the masculine world of associational dining fueled sociability with spirits. No doubt Fuller had commercial arrangements with the grocers who controlled the trade in alcohol in the city. Fuller was the most popular banquet provisioner in the 1850s, overseeing meetings and meals by the Phoenix Fire Company, the Charleston Light Dragoons, the St. Andrew's Society, and the Chamber of Commerce. He also mastered the trickier art of supplying refreshments for balls—heterosocial occasions requiring wine (champagne) as well as liquor, confections as well as viands, and a combination of hot and cold dishes. He catered the two major occasions on the city's social calendar, the St. Cecilia Ball and the Carolina Jockey Club Ball.

By autumn of 1860, Fuller had accomplished everything a banquet chef could hope to achieve in Charleston. He was the "renowned" "prince of caterers." He determined to follow the model of A. J. Rutjes and Eliza Lee, in opening a restaurant. On October 10 he announced the opening of his establishment at 77 Church Street, on the northwest corner of its intersection with St. Michael's Alley. "He has prepared neat and comfortable Chambers, Parlors, and Sitting Rooms, Dinner and Supper Halls, capable of accommodating Parties from Twenty-five to One Hundred persons."[44] He called his restaurant the Bachelor's Retreat, offering "Breakfast, Dinner, Supper, Lunch and Oysters, served up at any hour and in every style."[45] Though Fuller continued to cater weddings, balls, and events in city town houses, he wished, like Rutjes, to draw the club meeting trade into his restaurant. To this end, he announced that the use of rooms in the Bachelor's Retreat would be "tendered to Military Companies, Committees or Clubs without charge."[46] He would make his profit supplying refreshments.

As a dining and food retail structure, the Bachelor's Retreat eclipsed every other venue in town, except perhaps the Charleston Hotel. Backed by a two-story brick kitchen, the brick restaurant stood three stories tall. A huge cistern dominated the yard: "The main building contains, on the first floor, a very large store and a small Store. On the second and third floors three large rooms, and two finished attics on the fourth floor; under the first floor there is a deep paved cellar, and gas throughout the house."[47] As the description suggests, Fuller transferred his game business into the ground-floor store. The dining areas were all on the second and third floors. The fitting of the household with gas suggests that Fuller employed a gas stove and oven, the cutting edge in 1860 in temperature control, essential for fine sauce work and baking.

Fuller's specialty was meat cooking, and his mastery of his métier showed in his menu for the Tuesday evening dinners in autumn. The bill of fare included "Lamb Mutton of rare quality, with Green Peas, Duffield Hams, Oysters in Soup, Pies and Patties, Calf Head Soup, À la Mode Beef, Chicken Pies, Ducks, Boned Turkey . . . with vegetables and dessert courses."[48] The most remarkable item on the menu was the Duffield ham, a brand popularized by Charles Duffield in Cincinnati, and therefore an item procured from enemy territory.

Running a temple of luxury during wartime can be a dicey business. Fuller's business continued well enough until the fall of 1863, when Fuller fell gravely ill. The house closed for at least two months, and when it reopened for Christmas 1863, Fuller had fallen in arrears on his lease.[49] The war was going badly for the Confederacy, and upon the termination of the contract in March, the building's owner put 77 Church Street up for sale, hoping to cash out and head for the hinterlands. Nat Fuller relocated to 25 Washington Street, a space whose qualities no way approached the grandeur of the Bachelor's Retreat. There he offered tried-and-true recipes: green turtle soup, shrimp pie, and wild turkey.[50] He resumed his mobile catering business, expanding to service waterborne excursions. Indeed, the final public glimpse of him finds him giving pleasure to a boatload of firemen cruising Charleston Harbor: "Nat Fuller, the renowned presiding genius over many a fine dinner and supper, has a cunning way of fixing up water so as to take all the bad taste out of it. We did not get the exact receipt, but believe that ice, brandy, mint and sugar are some of the condiments used. There was an abundant supply of this preparation; and it was in constant quest, as it was recommended as a panacea."[51]

Though he had spent his entire life promoting the pleasure and comity of various associations of white southerners, when the day of liberation came, Nat Fuller rejoiced. Frances Porcher, a Charleston *salonière*, noted in a letter to her friend: "Nat Fuller, a Negro caterer, provided munificently for a miscegenated dinner, at which blacks and whites sat on an equality and gave toasts and sang songs for Lincoln and freedom. Miss Middlein and Miss Alston, young ladies of color, presented a colored regiment with a flag on the Citadel green, and nicely dressed black sentinels turned back white citizens, reprimanding them for the passes not being correct."[52] The one immediate benefit Fuller accrued from the new political order was permission to reoccupy the building at 77 Church Street. His place of business restored and his world expanded by new rights, Fuller enjoyed liberty for a little over a year. Taking sick again in autumn 1866, he died on December 16 and was interred in the Heriot Street Cemetery. He left a culinary heir, Thomas R. Tully, who became during the later 1860s the premier caterer in the city.

Tully (1828–1883) had the good fortune to be born into a free black family who had settled on Edisto Island, South Carolina. This enabled him to leave the countryside for Charleston, seeking training as a baker while a teenager. In the city, he attached himself to Nat Fuller, sixteen years his senior, at 68 King Street. In Fuller's employ, Tully specialized in aspects of cooking complementary to Fuller—that is, baking and confection, rather than Fuller's métier, meat cooking and pastry chef work. Sometime in 1849, Tully brought his seven-year-old sister to live with him in the city.[53] The need to support a household in the 1850s compelled him to leave the employ of Fuller and establish a partnership with the

mulatto pastry cook Martha Vanderhorst (1812–1902) in a catering business headquartered at a luncheon room at 117 King Street. In 1859 business had proved sufficiently profitable to enable a move across the street
to 122 King Street, a building that contained rooms large enough to ac-
commodate club meetings. Vanderhorst and Tully announced that they
could serve "gentlemen's Suppers, Dinners, Meetings." Tully's signature
dishes—"Black Cakes, Fruit Cakes, and Cakes of Every Kind"—received
conspicuous mention in the notice.[54] The partnership thrived for four
years, but as the economic situation unraveled in the city during 1864, the
business failed and the partnership dissolved. After the armistice, Tully
alone reactivated the restaurant in April 1866.[55]

A decade's collaboration with Vanderhorst and substantial training
with Fuller had thoroughly schooled Tully in every aspect of cookery. His
culinary range may be seen in the menu for a dinner catered for the St.
Andrew's Society in December 1866:

BILL OF FARE

Fish: Rock Fish, lemon sauce; Fried Whiting,
Scalloped Oysters, Fried Oysters.
Roast: Turkeys, gravy sauce; Geese, apple sauce;
A la mode Beef, Mutton, mint sauce.
Salt: Ham, Tongue, Round of Beef.
Side Dishes: Fricasseed Chickens, with mushrooms, Pigs' Feet,
tomato sauce, Stuffed Peppers, Haggis.
Game: Wild Turkey, Venison, currant jelly; Ducks, Grouse,
Pheasants, Partridges, Chicken Salad, Lobster Salad.
Vegetables: Rice, Potatoes, Green Peas, Asparagus.
Dessert: Fruit Cakes, Jelly Cakes, Apple Pies, Cranberry Pies,
Peach Pies, Prune Pies, Small Tarts, Calves' Feet Jelly,
Ice Cream, Charlotte Russe.
Fruit—Coffee.[56]

Wine was served during the period of toasts after the banquet.

Several things may be observed about this menu: that Tully had access
to glasshouse gardens to provide asparagus in December; that French-

style sauces had been supplanted by fruit sauces and gravies; that dimensions of Lowcountry vernacular cooking (pigs' feet with tomato sauce) combined with classic Franco-American items, such as fricasseed chicken and beef à la mode; that game remained the climax of the meal (Fuller's legacy); and that pies were assuming an equal status with cakes on the dessert table. The carte makes plain Tully's ambition, and the appearance of rare entrées indicates his avidity to secure the rarest and finest ingredients for a repast. This feature of Tully's practice would eventually bring him difficulties, as the association world of Charleston inclined more to economy than gustatory splendor in the 1870s.

Tully's professional plight becomes a theme in the cogent biography of the caterer published in the *Charleston News and Courier* shortly after his death. This obituary appreciation is the longest discussion of any Lowcountry chef published in the nineteenth century. It deserves extended quotation for the view it gives of the rewards and liabilities attending the profession of cooking, especially for African Americans:

DEATH OF A CULINARY ARTIST

Thomas R. Tully, the well-known coloured caterer, died at his residence in King street yesterday morning. Tully was essentially and peculiarly one of the landmarks of Charleston. He was born on Edisto Island in November, 1828, and he came to the city while a boy. Here he picked up such an education as could be obtained by free persons of color, and at an early age developed the instincts and genius of a culinary artist. His early education was acquired under the tuition of Nat Fuller, who will be remembered by old Charlestonians as the leading caterer of Charleston. Tully, however, soon outstripped his teacher, and went to the front of the profession in a city where the work of gastronomic artists was always properly appreciated and handsomely rewarded. For nearly half a century the name of "Tully" has been associated in this city with everything worth remembering in the way of good living. For nearly half a century Tully had served he suppers of the Hibernian and Fellowship Societies, of "The Cincinnati," the German Friendly Society and all other associations that delighted to meet around the festive board and discuss the good things of life. Tully had no peer in the preparation of oysters and shell fish. His "stews" were unapproachable, no one could touch him in "fries," no one to this day has ever attained the art of frying an oyster like Tully and his deviled crabs and deviled terrapin were unequalled. In the matter of preparing "daubes" Tully had no peer. After the war he had a large business, but he seemed unable to realize the results of the war and his prices were found to be too high. He had besides turned out several apprentices, and the bulk of the catering business was transferred to other caterers. Still it was acknowledged that no one could equal Tully in preparing a feast, and those who desired epicurean repasts, independent of expense, always went to Tully. His latest and brightest achievement was a dinner given here in compliment to Gen. Fitz Lee last year—a repast which it is said has never been equaled anywhere in the South. The gourmands who had transferred the preparation of their monthly dinners elsewhere were seriously discussing the propriety of resuming their relations with Tully when his death was announced. Tully had always lived in King street. He was a staunch Democrat in politics, but always conservative in views. His wife died last year, and his only son about five years ago.[57]

Who were the culinary progeny who supplanted him? Henry Carroll, Jeremiah Seabrook, and Walter Dennison (cooks at the Charleston Hotel), Porter Brown (cook of the Waverly House), and Thomas McNeill (cook at the Pavilion Hotel). All of these African American chefs conveyed aspects of the Fuller-Tully tradition of Lowcountry cuisine into the twentieth century. They brought the splendor of antebellum society banqueting to the hotel table to the verge of the Charleston Revival in the 1920s.

SIX   *The Jockey Club Banquet of February 1, 1860*

On the first Wednesday of February, promptly at 6:00 p.m., the culinary apex of the social year occurred in Charleston. Two hundred members and invited guests of the South Carolina Jockey Club assembled in the banquet room. The club president stood, and with his rising the club stewards removed a cloth covering the dishes on a huge sideboard. "Every body, however vociferous a few moments before, is hushed into a profound silence." The president then broke into song, leading the guests in a turf anthem, "The High-Mettled Racer." As the last note died away, the diners began hammering the table and rattling the glass, the loudness of the din expressing their enthusiasm for the first day's racing and the feast ready to be consumed.[1]

In 1860, with rumors of war rife in Carolina, a correspondent from New York's sporting periodical, the *Spirit of the Times*, traveled to Charleston for race week and secured an invitation to the club banquet. Upon viewing the sideboard, he opined, "It would seem that the entire animal and vegetable kingdoms had been placed at the command of the Club's caterer, that Heaven itself had furnished the cooks." The witness did not know that club regulations stipulated that the expense of the dinner could not exceed $1,000. The unnamed caterer was Eliza Seymour Lee.[2] Lee's cooking was famous among American epicures. Actor-gourmand George Vandenhoff attested to the affection the country's gastronomes held for her work as a hotel caterer, particularly at the Jones Hotel, that "little snuggery in Charleston, where the finest gentlemen of the day were wont to meet at dinner. . . . The bill of fare . . . was always *tout ce qu'il y avait de plus excellent*; not so *recherché* on paper, not so high-sounding, nor so remarkable for a long list of ill-spelt *entrées* of impossible French dishes, — but liberal, ample, substantial, appetizing, well-cooked dinners, to which you sat down with full intent to do justice, and from which you arose content, as from the performance of a good action."[3] When we look upon the banquet bill of fare,[4] we find precisely those qualities commended by Vandenhoff: avoidance of pretentious menu French, liberality of offering, promise of excellence. It is the most ample menu from the nineteenth-century Lowcountry:

BILL OF FARE

Turtle Soup.   Fins and Steaks.

FISH.
Rock Fish, melted butter.   Black Drum, Worcestershire sauce.
Fresh Salmon.   Broiled Shad.

BROILED.
Mutton, caper sauce.   Capons, mushroom sauce.
Turkey, oyster sauce.   Vol au vent Oysters.
Westphalia Ham.   Round of Beef.   Smoked Tongue.
Pig's Feet, with tomatoes.   Fricasseed Terrapin.

ROAST.
Turkeys, brown gravy.   Beef, Radish.
Geese, Cranberry sauce.   Saddle of Lamb, mint sauce.
Capons, gravy.   Saddle of Mutton, gravy.
Maccaroon Pies.   Pigeon Pies.
Boned Turkey, in Truffles.   Vol au vent of Sweet Bread.

GAME.

Venison, Currant Jelly.   Canvas Back Ducks.
Wild Turkeys.   Black Head Ducks.
Grouse.   Teal Ducks.
Pheasants.   Snipe.
Quails.   Partridges.
Pate de foi Gras.   Pate de foi Doie.
Chicken Salad.   Lobster Salad.

VEGETABLES.

Green Peas.   Asparagus.   Parsnips.   Carrots.   Spinach.
Rice.   Bread.   Potatoes.

DESSERT.

Plum Puddings.   Charlotte Russe.   Apple Tarts.
Lemon Puddings.   Blancmange.   Cranberry Tarts.
Orange Puddings.   Jellies.   Almond Cakes.

ORNAMENT.

Candied Fruits.   Vanilla Ice Cream.   Pine Apple Ice Cream.
Fruits, Nuts, Etc.

COFFEE.

In 1863 the celebrity chef Pierre Blot explained how a bill of fare should be formed and offered instructions to diners about parsing one. His explanation took the form of a series of maxims, whose cogency aided memorization.

Bills of fare vary according to the season of the year, and therefore to the produce in the market.

A dinner, no matter how grand, is composed of three courses, and seven kinds of dishes. The first course comprises dishes of four kinds, viz.: soups, releves, hors-d'oeuvre, and entrees. The second course comprises dishes of two kinds, viz.: rots and entremets. The third course comprises dishes of one kind, the dessert.

The number of dishes of each kind is generally according to the number of guests. It may also be according to the importance of the occasion for which the dinner is given; to the honor the giver or givers wish to show the personage or personages invited; to the amount of money they are willing to spend.[5]

The Jockey Club bill of fare revealed the club's cosmopolitan eating habits by conforming strictly to an international ideal of the banquet, despite its restraint in employing French terminology. It was entirely seasonal—the fish, fowl, and vegetables being those available in the Low-country in midwinter. (The first shad appear in the Cooper River in mid-January.) The feast had three courses, despite its multiple headings; all the soups, fish, and broiled meats fell within Blot's rubrics—"soups, releves, hors-d'oeuvre, and entrees"—comprising the first service. The roasts and game dishes were Blot's "rots," and the vegetables, his "entremets," made up the second serving. The third-course desserts and ornaments (confections adorning the dining tables) were not as numerous as would appear on a Parisian or New York bill of fare, where thirty dessert dishes might grace the menu; yet the decision not to include cakes at the end of so substantial a repast reveals gustatory intelligence.

The Jockey Club's bill deviated most markedly from Blot's norm by including the hors d'oeuvres ("Lobster Salad, Chicken Salad, Pate de foie Gras, Pate de fois Doie"—although in some quarters the salads might be viewed as entrées) in the second course. The number of soups, entrées, and *relevés* served in the first course, fifteen, approached the eighteen that Blot presented as the maximum provision. Blot had indicated that the number of dishes depended upon the importance of the occasion, and the Jockey Club's dinner was the supreme social expression of Lowcountry gentility. In this rite, the plantocracy projected its most cherished public image. "You can form no adequate idea of its magnificence without being present to see the vast number of the elite of South Carolina, every countenance beaming with intelligence and good humor; to hear the flow of eloquence, wit, and repartee; to partake of the good things which are spread before you."[6] The races, the dinner, and the Friday evening ball were highlights of the national sporting calendar, and turfmen, society matrons, military officers, flash bachelors, and southern debutantes converged on Charleston and the Grand Saloon of Washington Racetrack for the diversion, conviviality, and balmy Lowcountry climate. Club stewards reserved a substantial number of the seats at dinner for members' guests, and months of negotiating kinship obligations, school friendships, commercial connections, military ranks, and public reputations ensured that the manners and pleasures of the Carolina elite showed to best advantage to the attending men and women of the regional and national elites.

For the plantocracy to appear in a northern periodical as a class of humane, intelligent, and companionable human beings in 1860 was something of a minor miracle. The abolitionist press in the North had invested years of energy to envisioning the great planters as violent, grasping creatures of passion, sadistically obsessed with oppressing slaves. The *Spirit of the Times* supplied a rare discursive space in which the southern elite shared values of civility, good taste, sociability, and a love of sport with likeminded persons in other sections of the country. In the periodical's pages, Saratoga Springs was in the same cultural vicinity as Washington Park.

Cultural and social equivalency becomes apparent only when a high degree of commensurability appears between the manners, fashions, values, and diversions of geographically disparate people. We must keep this in mind when examining the club's bill of fare. It had to be recognizable as the haute cuisine enjoyed by genteel people in the great cities of the Western world. Only the wild harvest of a region received universal approbation as the appropriate culinary expression of the genius loci: hence the emphasis on fish and fowl. Distinctively local vegetables or preparations from grain, however, risked appearing peculiar or parochial. Winter banquets everywhere featured root vegetables, and three appear on the Jockey Club's menu—parsnips, carrots, and potatoes—yet the two favorite roots in the Lowcountry, the sweet potato and the tanya, did not grace the dining tables. While Carolina rice, because of its global fame, appeared, the other staple grain of the region, corn, did not. No corn on the cob or hominy, no grits or corn bread. Other hallmarks of southern cooking, particularly the products of West Africa—the guinea squash, benne, okra, sorghum, watermelon—are nowhere to be seen.

Comparing the contents of the Jockey Club's first course with the list of dishes Blot supplied as representative entrées and *relevés*, one sees that every dish, except one, "Steaks and Fins," appeared in some form in the chef's listing of appropriate fare. "Steaks and Fins," however, is the Low-country version of Terrapin à la Maryland, a staple of the Maryland Feast.[7] If this were not enough, a fricasseed terrapin gave diners a second stewed turtle option. We should not be surprised to find other components of the Chesapeake dinner—canvasback and black ducks, as well as oysters (though here prepared vol-au-vents, napped with béchamel sauce and nestled in pastry shells, a Seymour-Lee family specialty).

The stewards of the Jockey Club were not simply content to acknowl-edge the creations of their neighbors immediately south of the Mason-Dixon Line; they included half a dozen dishes that advertised adherence to a "southern" taste. The inclusion of Westphalia ham and pigs' feet with tomatoes nods first to traditionalism, then to innovation with pig meat. Westphalia designated any ham that was dry-smoked at low heat with aromatic wood; it is the "country ham" cured in southern smokehouses since early in the colonial era. Pigs' feet with tomatoes, in contrast, was new to the Lowcountry table, emerging after the spread of tomato culture in the American 1840s. The idea may have come from Florida or South America, where the Spanish Creole dish, *manitas de cerdo en salsa*, enjoyed some popularity. A peppery stew, the dish enjoyed broad popularity when prepared thusly:

> Eight pigs' feet, 1 pint tomatoes, 1 teaspoonful chopped onion, 1 cupful boiling water, 1 bay leaf, 1 tablespoonful of butter, tablespoonful flour. Boil pigs' feet with bay leaf and salt until tender; take out bones and cut meat in small pieces; heat butter and flour, onions, tomatoes and water, cook about 15 minutes, then add pigs' feet, season with chili powder and cook ½ hour longer.[8]

Versions of this recipe have become fixtures in African American cook-books, appearing in Edna Lewis's *Gift of Southern Cooking* (2003) and Carolyn Quick Tillery's *African-American Heritage Cookbook* (2000).

Southern taste in the twenty-first century does not map well upon the preferences of the mid-nineteenth century when it comes to proteins. In 2015 a banquet table in the Carolinas would feature the meat of pigs, cows, and chickens. The Jockey Club featured the flesh of sheep, ducks, and turkeys. The prevalence of mutton and lamb over beef will come as a surprise to persons who believe that the Lowcountry's climate was and is too tropical for sheep. Yet sheep herding began in earnest in the 1840s when the success of Colonel Wade Hampton and B. F. Taylor's flocks in the midlands sparked a fashion for grazing merino and African broad-tailed sheep (the Tunis sheep) in areas not suited to cotton culture.[9] Both breeds proved hale and hearty in the heat, supplying wool and fat mutton. The dishes featured on the Jockey Club bill of fare were transatlantic classics that enjoyed favor for several generations. Mutton—the meat of sheep killed and dressed at three years of age, then hung for two weeks to ripen—required a longer cooking time than lamb and was reckoned more nutritious. Mutton with caper sauce, a cooking-school staple, called for a leg to be stripped of its caul fat, boiled until tender, then browned in an oven. The caper sauce was a white sauce, charged with three tablespoons of butter and a cupful of capers.[10] In the American imagination, roasted saddle of mutton with mint sauce vied with rare roast beef as the quintessential English main dish. The saddle is the whole loin of a sheep removed before splitting the carcass. Traditionally, some of the contiguous bones were removed with the cut and the flank ends rolled and fastened with wooden skewers. "It is always roasted. The fat on its surface is scored in squares; the skin previously separated from the fat by the butcher, is generally skewered on by the cook as a preservative of the fat, but which is removed in time to froth and brown the surface."[11] The melted fat served as the base for mutton gravy; a favorite version called for flour, ketchup, seasonings, and white vinegar. The saddle of lamb, being more tender and delicate, paired more readily with mint jelly, which in the antebellum era could be quite sharp in taste, combining a cup each of vinegar, sugar, and mint, a teaspoon of gelatin, and a dash of pepper, paprika, and salt.

Ducks were the most conspicuous in an array of seasonal game birds offered at the table. Grouse, pheasant, quail, partridge, and snipe competed for attention. The ruffed grouse (*Bonasa umbellus*), native to the Carolina hill country, sported a genus name, *Bonasa*, that translates as "good when roasted." "The meat of the grouse is all dark, the breast very full and large, and the legs (unlike the pheasant), very tender. . . . The flavor of the grouse, when cooked as a canvass back, is not unlike it, and meat is just as tender. When over-done the grouse is unfit to eat."[12] Pheasant varied greatly in taste and texture depending on age. Young birds were roasted on an open fire and seasoned; old birds, braised. More than any other game bird, the pheasant required ripening. So it was plucked and hung to encourage flavor; again, the older the bird, the longer the hang— up to two weeks.[13] Quail, a favorite sport bird in the Lowcountry because of their small size, ran the risk of overcooking. After plucking, they were split and grilled. "Wash in salt water, split down the back, wipe dry, rub with butter, pepper, and salt. Put on the grid-iron over clear coals. Cook principally from the underside. Take up, rub with butter, sift over browned powdered crackers. Serve with currant jelly."[14] Partridge (or dove, as it is now called in the Lowcountry) was prepared in an identical fashion. Wilson's snipe, a member of the woodcock family, is most plentiful in South Carolina from mid-November until early March. These birds were plucked and pan-fried with their heads on. In a hot skillet larded with bacon fat, the snipe were laid out and covered with bacon strips. After a quick browning, a cup of stock or wine was added to the skillet. After the birds were cooked tender, the eyes and skin about the head were removed and a nut or mushroom put in the bird's bill before serving.[15] Pan-fried snipe, split doves and quail, broiled pheasant, and roasted grouse can all be had at autumn and winter hunt club feasts throughout the Carolinas and Georgia in 2015. Only the population of ruffed grouse has declined to a point provoking concern.

While we have explored the classic techniques for dressing duck in the Maryland Feast, we must recall a point that cannot be emphasized too often: wild ducks like the teal, the black duck, and the canvasback have less fat than their domestic cousins. For this reason, the meat dries out upon protracted roasting or baking. Duck is better served rare than well done.

The crowning glory of the Jockey Club Banquet was turkey. Both domestic and wild birds appeared in the first two courses—boiled with oyster sauce, roasted with brown gravy, plain roasted in the case of the wild bird, and boned with a truffle-based forcemeat as a cold galantine. In February, turkey hunting season was entering in the phase when mating calls lured male toms to their doom. Hunters in blinds near the birds' favorite haunts enticed solitary birds roaming the brush. Earlier in the season, turkey hunting had a different cast. Gangs of turkeys roamed the woods. A trained dog ran in and dispersed the gang, scattering them far and wide. By calling to one another, the turkeys attempted to reconsolidate their flock. Hunters used social calls attracting scattered individuals thinking they were rejoining their company.[16] Being an intelligent, difficult bird to hunt successfully, "they are generally hunted more for their meat than the sport they afford."[17] Wild turkey was invariably roasted in a tin oven.

"Turkey, Oyster Sauce" might be had any place along the Atlantic and Gulf Coasts with an abundant supply of bivalves: "Fill the body with oysters, and let it boil by steam, without any water. When sufficiently done, take it up; strain the gravy that will be found in the pan; thicken it with a little flour and butter, add the liquor of the oysters intended for sauce, also stewed, and warm the oysters up in it; whiten it with a little boiled cream, and pour it over the turkey."[18] Cooked in a pan suspended in a covered vat of boiling water, the turkey took several hours to cook. In some recipes, the skin is removed before the flesh is drenched in sauce. Breast-side up, it is a resplendently white dish with a lusciously unctuous taste. In the South, it appeared in Christmas and New Year's dinners at refined households.

More splendid than the oyster-bedizened steamed turkey was the boned galantine of turkey filled with truffle forcemeat. On the banquet table, it vied with the round of roast beef as the ceremonial center of the feast. Of French origin, it became a fixture of ceremonial occasions throughout the Western world in the nineteenth century. Early in the twentieth century, the editors of *The Picayune Creole Cook Book* declared, "The boned turkey is the triumph of the New Orleans cuisine when serving cold turkey. No great reception or buffet luncheon is complete without it. It is the standing dish on New Year's day, when the Creole ladies receive their gentlemen friends, and, on occasions of marriages in the family, every father will insist that there shall be a boned turkey for the wedding feast."[19] A recipe appeared two decades after the Civil War in *The Unrivaled Cookbook*. The recipe suggests the general level of culinary accomplishment achieved by the strata of southern caterers to which caterer Eliza Seymour Lee belonged:

BONED TURKEY

Cut off the neck and claws, remove the drumsticks, and leave the wings, which must be carefully boned; then put the turkey on a clean cloth, cut open the back, and very carefully remove all the bones, taking care also not to spoil or gash the skin; then, with a larding needle, carefully lard the breast of the turkey and whatever other part admits of larding; make a stuffing of veal, fillet of beef, fat pork chopped into small dice, bread crumbs rolled fine and mixed with savory herbs, salt and pepper to taste, small triangular bits of cold tongue, a few truffles sliced fine, and yolks of two or three hard-boiled eggs cut into thick slices; fill the interior of the turkey with alternate layers of this stuffing and the thinnest possible slices of cold veal and lean ham; when stuffed sew up the aperture carefully, and rub the turkey over with lemon juice; do this thoroughly, and then envelop the turkey in thin slices of ham; sew it up afterwards in a clean muslin cloth, which should previously have been dipped in sherry wine; cook it for three hours, proceeding as for turkey alia Triestina; when quite cold remove the cloth, and serve the turkey in the jelly in which it was cooked. This jelly should be clarified.[20]

For all the interest that the Jockey Club Banquet has as a register of the use of game birds in ceremonial cooking, the unexpected revelation in the menu lies in what it shows about Lowcountry preferences in domestic poultry: the capon trumped the chicken. Capons, the double-size birds created by castrating immature roosters, have been a minor fixture in the poultry yard since Roman antiquity. Because the flesh of the bird does not become saturated with sex hormones as it grows, its meat is less gamey and more tender than that of unaltered hens and roosters. Yet only experimental farmers caponized fowl in Georgia and Carolina. In the years before the war, the Dorking fowl, a breed native to Scotland, enjoyed particular favor for caponizing in the Lowcountry, promoted energetically by Thomas Spalding of Georgia.[21] By the end of the century, the Brahma, Cochin, and Langshan breeds had demoted the Dorking into the second rank of preference.[22] A capon was ideal for cooking when it had "a fat vein under the wing; thick belly and rump; comb short and pale; spurs short and blunt and legs smooth."[23] Capon with mushroom sauce was a favorite English dish, with the capon boiled and napped with a gravy made of veal stock, mushrooms, flour, butter, and seasoning. For a more pronounced flavor, cooks employed beef stock and mushroom ketchup. Roasted capon and gravy used the rendered fat of the bird, flour, chicken stock, salt and pepper, and sometimes the yolks of hard-boiled eggs for the sauce.

No fried chicken appeared on the menu—it was regarded more a Virginia than a Lowcountry dish. But chicken salad (using mayonnaise) has endured as a constant year-round party dish from the antebellum period to the present day.

Given the plethora of roasts, boiled fowls, hot soup, and broiled meat, the third-course desserts provided relief by being cold, from the frigid pineapple ice cream to the room-temperature tarts and puddings. The spectacle dish in the assortment was the charlotte russe, the invention of French baking for the haute monde in the eighteenth century. Coffee was the accompaniment. But many attendees maintained a plate of almond cake or a slice of apple tart for the post-banquet round of toasts. Then the legendary stock of Jockey Club Madeira was dispensed among the assembly, loosening tongues and firing bonhomie. The sale of the Madeira collection (714 bottles buried during the Civil War) in 1877 enabled a brief revival of racing in Charleston before the final meet in 1880.[24] It is rumored that individual bottles have survived into the twenty-first century in private collections in Savannah and Connecticut.

For lavishness and scale, the South Carolina Jockey Club's midwinter banquet has no recorded equal in the antebellum Lowcountry. While cosmopolitan, it projected local bounty in its game and fish offerings. While nodding to French gastronomic finesse, it in no way showed the Francophilic excesses of banquet menus elsewhere, and offered traditional British favorites and local items, such as pigs' feet and tomatoes. It was seasonal, yet managed to include occasional out-of-season rarities, such as February lamb and midwinter sweetbreads. The number of man-hours involved in preparing charlotte russe, boned turkey with truffles—not to mention dressing deer, a multitude of game birds ranging in size from wild turkeys to snipe, and turtles—required a kitchen regiment. Eliza Seymour Lee must have possessed the logistical genius of an adjutant general, particularly if her staff prepared the cold collation at the end of the feast as well as the first two courses. The magnitude of the accomplishment can be grasped instantly by glancing at another bill of fare describing a banquet three months later in Richmond, Virginia, honoring writer John R. Thompson. A spring feast, it served a company a quarter of the size of the Jockey Club Banquet:

COMPLIMENTARY DINNER

TO

JOHN R. THOMPSON, ESQ.

Tuesday, May 15th, 1869.

BILL OF FARE

SOUP.
Green Turtle.

FISH.
Boiled Salmon. Anchovy source.
Turtle Steaks Sautes, Port Wine sauce.

ENTREES.
Tenderloin Beef, larded aux Truffles.
Sweet Bread, glazed with Tomato sauce.
Vol au Vent with Chicken Liver a la Financière.
Timballes de Maccaroni, a l'Editeur.
Lamb's Fries, fried with Herbs.
Cotelettes d'Agneau Sautes, with Green Peas.

VEGETABLES.
Green Peas,   Asparagus,
Spinach,   Mashed Potatoes,
Stewed Tomatoes,   Raw Tomatoes,
Lettuce,   Radishes,
Beets,   Boiled New Potatoes.

ROAST.
Roast Capon, stuffed Truffles and larded, with Lobster Salad.

DESSERT.

Bavaroise with Strawberries.

FRUITS.

Pine Apples,   Oranges,

Strawberries,   Almonds,

Raisins,   Figs,

English Walnuts,   Prunes.

Cheese and Crackers, French, Coffee, Chartreuse, Cigars.[25]

While the Richmond literary feast follows the same order of march (soup, fish, entrées as course one; roasts and vegetables as course two; and desserts and fruits as course three), and while the turtle soup, turtle steaks, and salmon map closely upon the inaugural tastes of the Jockey Club feast, the heart of the Thompson dinner deviated greatly from the Charleston dinner. Here, beef and spring lamb featured as the proteins. No game—no samples of the Old Dominion's wild harvest—appeared on the menu. The decidedly French bias of the bill of fare extended to the coffee and after-dinner aperitif. Where were the hallmarks of local Virginia cuisine: The bay oysters? The fried chicken? The Smithfield hams? The Virginian peanuts? Instead we have English walnuts and strawberries prepared Bavarian style. In short, the cuisine evidenced here was French cosmopolitan, not Virginia or southern.

The cuisine served at the Jockey Club feast was cosmopolitan, but it was also southern, and more particularly Lowcountry. Authentic cuisines express the distinctive occasions of their originating regions and communicate the festivity of the day in a manner intelligible to guest and local celebrant alike. Race week was the great social occasion on the Charleston calendar, and it elicited a feast whose splendor proved newsworthy to visitors from the most cosmopolitan city in the country, New York. A century and a half later, it still inspires awe for its richness and variety.

SEVEN   *Possum in Wetumpka*

I've recovered the professional world of early southern cooking in some detail because the received picture is so decidedly skewed to pictures of the extremes: plantation feasts and poor eats in the cabin. A professionally elaborated standard of taste and a creative experimentation with regional ingredients existed from the 1820s in all parts of the South. This was not to say that the funky vernacular cooking of common people—the greasy greens, gravy sumps, and fried things—was a myth. Rather, it was a set of foodways always subjected to alteration, critique, and refinement. Certain of the institutions—hotel, restaurant, market, print culture—that made cooking in New Orleans, the Tidewater, and the Lowcountry develop into cuisines worked to ameliorate the unsavory dimensions of vernacular cooking. Indeed, they could make a silk purse out of a sow's ear. Consider the evening's repast at a hotel in Wetumpka, Alabama.

In a comic character sketch of an antebellum bon vivant, "The Colonel," humorist Johnson Jones Hooper tells of his hero's trek in 1845 through the counties of Alabama in search of the ideal town in which to settle the state capital. Much of the rumination came down to the sorts of meals that prospective delegates to the Alabama Assembly would experience in the local hotels. The Colonel, an epicure, favored the fare at the hotel in

Montgomery, the menu of which featured oysters, boiled turkey, roast pig, pies, and champagne. The Wetumpka Hotel, in contrast, offered decidedly more plebian dishes. Humorist Hooper banked on his readers recognizing the menu as containing resonantly common cooking, the stuff served at a plain eatery in any second-rank town in the Deep South.[1]

Soup—Cowpea.
Boiled—Bacon and Greens.
Roast—'Possum.
Entrees—Tripe and Cow-Heel.
Dessert—Fritters and Molasses.
Fruit—Persimmons, Chestnuts, Goobers.
Wines—Black Malaga.

If we wish to understand what got the middling sort salivating, this menu offers a good place to start. First, we must realize that this bill of fare is public food, not home cooking. It has the ceremonial organization of those meals that feature a different style of cooking for each course. It abides by the general expectation that game appears as one of the meat courses at a hotel repast—in this case, possum. And wine—not whiskey, not beer, not cider—appears as the favored beverage. No doubt there is a satire of dissonance at work in the menu—in the Wetumpka Hotel's abiding by the form, but not the content, of a proper hotel table d'hôte. Yet the satire only works to the extent that someone recognizes that these are indeed the dishes one is likely to encounter at a provincial hostelry.

One thing that may not be apparent on first reading of this menu is that the Wetumpka dinner is not seasonal. Cowpeas might be had dried at any time of year. Some type of green could be put into the pot any month of the year from midsummer mustard to winter collards. Possums do not hibernate and they forage year-round. Tripe and cow-heel were available anywhere that butchering occurred. While freshly butchered beef was sometimes rare in the summer because of spoilage issues, it did come to market even in smaller towns. Persimmons, while ripening in fall, were often dried in the South for consumption at other times. Nuts and even goober peas had long shelf lives in the shell. In short, this was a durable menu.

We have already encountered the cowpea or field pea. But the plant deserves more extensive appreciation. Conveyed from Africa on the slave ships, patch grown in private plots through the colonial era, it came into its own in the wake of the soil exhaustion crisis of the first decades of the century. Farmers realized it possessed powers to replenish soils taxed by "hungry" cash crops, such as tobacco, corn, and cotton. Plowed under as green manure, it provided a double measure of good to fields. The dried stalks — pea hay — found great favor as a food for livestock.[2] Deer preferred it to corn. For this, and the mutual benefit in terms of weed suppression and nutrition, both would be intercropped in fields.[3] Certain varieties proved so viable that a farmer could cast them on unplowed acres and have them germinate. Hence, it saved labor. The most popular varieties were drought tolerant. And certain of the varieties — the white lady pea, the black-eyed pea, the Sea Island red pea, the iron pea, the clay pea, the Tory pea — tasted good, if cooked long in liquid with bacon or a pig knuckle. Of all of the remedies for declining soil floated in the agricultural press of the 1820s, the growing of field peas would be the one that enjoyed the broadest embrace. While it first found favor in the coastal plains planted with staples — such as tobacco, cotton, rice, and wheat — the spread of pea culture into the hog and corn hill country saw it established through much of the southern interior by 1830.

Southern cooking's founding books — Mary Randolph's *Virginia House-wife* (1824), Lettice Bryan's *Kentucky Housewife* (1838), and Sarah Rutledge's *Carolina Housewife* (1847) — contained recipes treating field peas. The range of preparations attracts notice — Randolph's is the most African in its cooking technique, with plain fried field peas, pea fritters, and plain boiled peas. Both Bryan and Rutledge offer pea soup recipes for which an ancestry to European dried pease porridge shines forth. Rutledge's "Red Pea Soup" is the simpler of the two dishes, unprepossessing common food:

One quart of peas, one pound of bacon (or a hambone), two quarts of water, and some celery, chopped; boil the peas, and, when half done, put in the bacon; when the peas are thoroughly boiled, take them out and rub them through a cullender or coarse sieve; then put the pulp back into the pot with the bacon, and season with a little pepper and salt, if necessary.

If the soup should not be thick enough, a little wheat flour may be stirred in. Green peas may be used instead of the red pea.[4]

Rutledge specifies the particular sort of pea preferred for the preparation, the Sea Island red pea. This very tasty pea enjoyed a singular reputation in the Lowcountry, being the basis for classic dishes such as red pea gravy and reezy peezy. With less chalkiness and more nuttiness than the majority of field peas, it remained in private cultivation until the twenty-first century. It returned to commercial cultivation in the past six years, planted and sold by Glenn Roberts.

Lettice Bryan, the "Kentucky Housewife," observed, "There are several kinds of field peas, some of which are unfit for soup, being very dark; there are two kinds that are white, and very nice for the purpose; the one is large, and the other quite small, being far the most delicate of this species. They should be full grown, but not the least hard or yellow."[5] Bryan adhered to a decidedly Anglo aesthetic when it came to soups, favoring cream colors, forcemeat balls, and butter to give it lustrous finish. Of the multitudes of cowpeas grown in the South, the two with the highest culinary reputation were the lady pea (the large white mentioned above) and the rice pea (the small white). Planter James V. Jones, the premier cowpea breeder in the antebellum South, described the former as "a delicious table pea" and said of the latter, the "most valuable table variety known, and should be grown universally."[6] The rice pea's qualities were celebrated by cooking magazines until the eve of the First World War, when a Bostonian testified that the all-white pea

> is even more delicate of flavor than black-eyed peas; these are as delicate as early June peas, and they retain their natural color when cooked, and do not change the color of meat cooked with them. Perhaps the reason rice peas are not grown more generally is that they are not as hardy as black-eyed peas and other field peas. These delicately flavored rice peas, cooked with tender young pork, are far and away more appetizing than pork and beans, and almost or quite as nutritious. They are good, either cooked after they have become dry in the autumn and winter, or when young and tender in the late spring and early summer. Southern ladies often cook the tender young peas, pods and all, as snap beans are cooked.[7]

The rice pea became featured in an ultra-refined Charleston all-white variation on hoppin' John with the peas hardly distinguishable from the grains of Carolina Gold rice.

It is difficult to imagine the cowpea soup at Wetumpka being made of pureed rice peas. They were and are difficult to grow, too vulnerable to rough handling on the stove, and less productive than virtually any other variety to grow. Indeed, there is little to suggest that the patrons at Wetumpka shared Lettice Bryan's genteel preference for white peas and soups. The Alabama traditions of cooking cowpeas did not get comprehensively recorded until the final decade of the nineteenth century. But when George Washington Carver did transcribe the best kitchen practices for handling them in *The Tuskegee Agricultural Experiment Station Bulletin* no. 5 (1903), he did so with unrivaled thoroughness. The first differs very little from the Rutledge red pea soup recipe, the simple difference being the freshness of the peas.

GREEN PEA SOUP

Put two quarts of green peas with four quarts of water, boil two hours, renewing waste by adding boiling water when needed; strain from liquor, return that to pot. Rub the peas through sieve, chop an onion fine and small sprig of mint and parsley, let boil ten or fifteen minutes, stir a teaspoonful of flour into two of butter, add a pinch of pepper and two teaspoonfuls of salt, stir carefully into the boiling soup. Serve with well buttered sippets of toasted bread.

PLAIN PEA SOUP

Take one quart of hulled peas, boil until perfectly soft, allowing four quarts of water to one of peas, mash peas, add flour and butter rubbed together, also salt and pepper to taste; cut cold bread into small pieces, toast and drop into soup, with a bit of minced parsley.

PEA SOUP NO. 2

Put in a sauce-pan two ounces of bacon chopped fine, six onions, peeled and chopped, salt and pepper to taste add four quarts of hot water; boil twenty minutes; meantime rub through sieve a quart of peas that have been previously boiled, add them to the first ingredients, boil one hour longer and serve hot.[8]

Carver combined a scientific grasp of system with the sense of social engagement and mission that Booker T. Washington had vested in the Tuskegee Institute. Hence, his bulletin surveys the nineteenth-century print record with the thoroughness conventional to a scientific report supplying a multitude of recipes employing cowpeas; yet it also records matters not found in the print record, collected by his assistants from the best local practices. Indeed, Carver's various agronomic investigations into cultivars, because of their employment of oral as well as written data, reveal the vernacular cookery of the Deep South, and particularly its African American traditions, with unequaled thoroughness. Upon these grounds, Carver erects his own experiments and creations, particularly in terms of non-culinary employments. The Carver portraits of peanuts, cowpeas, sweet potatoes, tomatoes, and plums suggest, among other things, that African American cookery was not a make-do tradition using leftovers; rather, like West African cookery, there was a ramified employment of several key ingredients, employing frying, roasting, boiling, and baking of each item.

Which pea soup was served in Wetumpka? On a good night, Pea Soup No. 2.

BACON AND GREENS

No common dish inspired more poetic feelings among American enthusiasts of the table than bacon and greens. The pairing of cured pork and seasonal greens (turnip, mustard, kale, colewort, or cabbage) had ancient European antecedents. In England, Sarah Harrison commended the pairing in her *House-Keeper's Pocket-Book, and Compleat Family Cook* (1739). William Kitchener, the oracle of the kitchen, believed it to be the ideal accompaniment of veal dishes. It became standard sea-voyaging fare on the transatlantic routes and quickly established itself in the southern colonies as proper food for persons of every class. When George Bagby, the humorist, pondered "How to Make a True Virginian" (ca. 1870s), he opened his meditation with an observation worthy of Brillat-Savarin: "There is a connection between diet and the ethnological characteristics of the human race, and I take it for granted, first, that a Virginian could not be a Virginian without bacon and greens." If you are what you eat, then a Virginian comes to be because of the following diet:

> He must, of course, begin on pot-liquor, and keep it up until he sheds his milk-teeth. He must have fried chicken, stewed chicken, broiled chicken, and chicken-pie; old hare, butter-beans, new potatoes, squirrels, cymblins, snaps, barbecued shoat, roas'n ears, buttermilk, hoe-cake, ash-cake, pancake, fritters, pot-pie, tomatoes, sweet potatoes, June apples, waffles, sweet milk, parsnips, artichokes, carrots, cracklin-bread, hominy, bonny-clabber, scrambled eggs, gooba-peas, fried apples, pop-corn, persimmon beer, apple-bread, milk and peaches, mutton-stew, dewberries, batter-cakes, mus'melons, hickory nuts, partridges, honey in the honey-comb, snappin'-turtle eggs, damsom-tarts, cat-fish, cider, hot light-bread, and cornfield peas all the time. But he must not intermit bacon and greens.[9]

But Virginia maintained no monopoly on the sapid dish, and every state in the region laid claim to its formative powers. Alabama, in particular, enjoyed a particular connection with it because the Tuscaloosa lawyer Bakus T. Huntington penned the best-loved ode attesting to its glories, a hymn set to music and performed in parlors, minstrel shows, and tavern rooms from 1850 to the end of the century:

BACON AND GREENS

I have lived long enough to be rarely mistaken,
And borne my full share of life's changeable scenes,
But my woes have been solaced by good greens and bacon,
And my joys have been doubled by bacon and greens.

What a thrill of remembrance e'en now they awaken,
Of childhood's gay morning and youth's merry scenes,
When, one day, we had greens and a plate full of bacon,
And, the next, we had bacon and a plate full of greens.

Ah! well I remember when sad and forsaken,
Heart-wrung by the scorn of a miss in her teens,

How I rushed from her sight to my loved greens and bacon,
And forgot my despair over bacon and greens.

When the banks refused specie and credit was shaken,
I shared in the wreck and was ruined in means;
My friends all declared I had not saved my bacon,
But they lied—for I still had my bacon and greens.

Oh! there is a charm in this dish, rightly taken,
That, from custards and jellies, an epicure weans:
Stick your fork in the fat—wrap your greens round the bacon,
And you will vow there is nothing like bacon and greens.

If some fairy a grant of three wishes would make one
So worthless as I, and so laden with sins,
I'd wish all the greens in the world—then the bacon—
And then wish a little more bacon and greens.

POSTSCRIPT.

I return to confess that for once I'm mistaken,
As much as I've known of this world and its scenes,
There's one thing that's equal to both greens and bacon,
And that is a dish of—good bacon and greens.[10]

Given the poetic expansiveness of these effusions, one wonders what exactly was meant by bacon . . . and also by greens.

Mrs. P. W., one of the experienced Tidewater matrons whom Marion Cabell Tyree enlisted to help document *Housekeeping in Old Virginia* (1879), submitted a recipe that has an aura of age to it:

BACON AND GREENS

The middling is generally used for this purpose: cut a piece about a foot square, boil three hours. Take a good head of cabbage, cut, quarter, and wash clean; press the water out as dry as you can. Boil them one or two hours with half a pod of red pepper; put them on a dish and the middling on top. You can fry the cabbage next day, and make a savory dish, but it does not suit dyspeptics. The thin part of the middling is used for frying, and is called "breakfast bacon."[11]

Middlings, that fatty layer of pork extending from the ham to the shoulder, was also designated salt pork after its curing. Early recipes call for a rather large expanse of middlings boiled in the pot. It would be sliced into strips once cooked at the table. One did not boil strip bacon in traditional recipes.

In Virginia, cabbage was frequently designated as the green of choice. Cabbage, however, collected a multitude of meanings. P. W. clearly indicated a headed form of the *Brassica* genus, a cabbage such as the large York or the flat Dutch, both popular in the coastal South. Yet other Virginians leaned toward other brassicas. Reporting on Virginia preferences in an issue of *Table Talk* at the end of the century, Mrs. Grayson noted, "The greens were kale, a species of cabbage which does not form heads, but has leaves somewhat resembling spinach, only very much more curled. It is generally boiled with a piece of smoked bacon or flitch."[12] Kale, because of its ability to draw up salt from fields, became popular in crop rotations in seaside counties where salinization of the soil posed a problem. Colewort, a non-heading variety of cabbage, or a cabbage harvested before the head was formed, also found its way into the pot—but by midcentury most southerners had substituted "collard" for colewort as a name. In the 1870s in Georgia, a blue variety of non-heading brassica gained enough popularity to be picked up by northern seed brokers as the Georgia collard or the blue collard. Writer Bret Harte observed of the collard that it "is the kind of Cabbage found everywhere in the south, whose leaves, not heads, furnish the greens for the inevitable dish of bacon and greens."[13]

While Euro-Americans may have decidedly favored some version of a brassica as their greens, African Americans, who often worked in the kitchens of the nineteenth-century South, welcomed a broader latitude of greens into the pot. Besides the expected turnip and beet greens, recipes indicate that the following found their way into the bacon boil:

Poke (*Domestic Cookery*, 1859)
Dandelion (*Appledore Cookbook*, 1872)
White Mustard (*Gardening for the South*, 1868)

Nettle (*Harder's Book of Practical American Cookery*, 1885)

Purslain (*New York Gardener*, 1824)

Rape (*Field and Garden Vegetables of America*, 1874)

Swiss Chard (*Unrivaled Cookbook*, 1881)

Sea Kale (*Family Kitchen Gardener*, 1850)

Shepherd's Purse (*Harder's Book of Practical American Cookery*, 1885)

Having determined a rough range of probability for the contents of the pot, we turn to the most contentious point: the length of time the bacon and greens must be cooked together. Mrs. P.W.'s very approximate one to two hours supplies sufficient latitude for taste. One hour was enough for the meat and the vegetables to "swap" flavors. In 1881 a clerk for the South Carolina Board of Health explained the salubrious ideal: "For pickled or smoked meats, boiling is the best process of preparation. The old fashioned bacon and greens offers an admirable instance of the latter. The juices of the meat are intermingled with the tender leaves of the collard, and this commingling tends to soften the meat, which is permeated by the vegetable juices." [14] The dish must be cooked sufficiently long so that the major components no longer projected their flavors separately and distinctly. But there was a school of cooks and eaters who thought this threshold insufficient. They opted for the second hour, and for "slippery" greens, a consistency in which the cell integrity of stalks and leaves has begun to break down, and the green need not be masticated for it to slide down the throat. The US Department of Agriculture launched a publicity campaign against overcooked greens in 1894, yet both approaches survived into our century in home cooking and southern diner cuisine. Among devotees of southern cuisine, however, the second approach has gone decidedly out of favor and the cooking time for collards, the most robust of greens, reduced to half an hour.

POSSUM

De books cyarnt spell what cooks in de pot,
Nor 'scribe de tas'e of de roas' dat's hot

—"Carve that Possum"

Possum's reputation as a comestible has never entirely shaken its insistent nineteenth-century literary associations with the caricature of the African American life of Blackville. In the minstrel show Dixie of yore, enthusiastic "darkies" saluted "dat hebenly food" in song and story. The possum "is preserved in the negro songs which the negroes never sing; he has been the theme of lofty gastronomic eloquence and the 'negro humorists' have found him more useful than the mother-in-law, and excelled only by the razor and the hen-roost."[15] To the extent that the caricature has seemed freakish, so has the celebration of roasted possum. African Americans, of course, had no monopoly on its preparation or consumption in the 1800s. During the Civil War, Napier Bartlett consumed it cooked on campfires of Tennessee: "No more delicious morsel was ever placed on a table than the fine roasted opossum of Tennessee; it has somewhat the quality of the erstwhile popular roast pig of New England, with an added richness and the piquancy of a certain gamey flavor."[16] Jessup Whitehead of Chicago and Georgia, author of *The Steward's Handbook*, characterized the dish as an "American Country Luxury."[17] Southern boardinghouse keeper Sarah Elliott attested that possum and sweet potatoes was "the favorite dish with Chapel Hill students in Olden Times."[18] No African Americans attended the University of North Carolina in the antebellum era.

That African Americans in the South savored roasted possum is well attested. Solomon Northup, who escaped bondage on a Louisiana plantation, wrote in 1853, "verily there is nothing in all butcherdom so delicious as a roasted 'possum."

They are a round, rather long-bodied, little animal, of a whitish color, with a nose like a pig, and caudal extremity like a rat. They burrow among the roots and in the hollows of the gum tree, and are clumsy and slow of motion. They are deceitful and cunning creatures. On receiving the slightest tap of a stick, they will roll over on the ground and feign death. If the hunter leaves him, in pursuit of another, without first taking particular pains to break his neck, the chances are, on his return, he is not to be found. The little animal has out witted the enemy—has "played 'possum"—and is off.[19]

Northup's introduction to the marsupial introduces a second ground of resistance to the possum: its rodent-like appearance. Even epicurean Virginians questioned the culinary aesthetics of placing in the center of a banquet table a creature "reminding one of a roasted rat sodden in castor-oil."[20] For some, this resemblance could not be put out of mind. But if prepared discreetly, with enough sweet potatoes strewn about, the analogy did not occur to diners.

Two methods of roasting possum prevailed throughout the South. The classic preparation paired the possum with sweet potatoes. A boarding-house alternative employed a Dutch oven, stuffing the possum with bread crumbs and onions. In 1898 the *Atlanta Medical and Surgical Journal* printed a transcript of an old man's oral account of how to roast possum with potatoes:

> You cleans him fust. Den you puts him into de pot with cold water, and put de pot over a hot fire an' den you parbiles him—not too much—fur you don't want to lose any of his nice sweet fat. Den you takes him out of de pot an' you dries him in a clean towel. Den you puts him in a big frying-pan; den you scrapes de skin off you sweet potatoes an' you puts dem into de same pan wid de 'possum. Den you has you stove red, and den you puts de pan an' 'possum an' potatoes into de oven and den go away for a little while, but not too long. Den when you come back you puts in a little hot water, an' den you begins and bastes de 'possum an' de sweet potatoes an' you keeps on a-basting and a-basting till de 'possum is a good brown . . . an' de sweet potatoes is soft and juicy an' de gravy is almost black, and plenty of it. Den you takes it out ob de oven an' den you sots de table, and den—well den, you bars de doors, fo' the smell of cooked 'possum goes a long ways, an when you have only one 'possum you doesn't want much company besides yourself.[21]

The boardinghouse method of roasting possum appeared in Frances Emogene Owen's *New Cook Book* of 1899:

> Clean like a pig—scrape, not skin it. Chop the liver fine, mix with bread crumbs, chopped onion, and parsley, with pepper and salt; bind with a

beaten egg, and stuff the body with it. Sew up, roast, baste with salt and water. In order to make it crisp, rub with a rag dipped in its own grease. Serve with gravy thickened with browned flour. Serve whole on a platter, with a baked apple in its mouth. Opossum. It is very nice stuffed with apples peeled and sliced.[22]

The fact that boardinghouses and hotels featured possum—a wild creature much more difficult to secure than pork, mutton, or beef—attests to the intensity of the regard it inspired among persons. Hunted by dogs at night, the possum was taken live from a tree and kept alive in a dark barrel for days. Hotels in provincial towns and cities that served game made it known to the local hunting community that it would purchase wildfowl, venison, turtle, and possum. Turtle and possum only sold if live. They would be kept in barrels in a storeroom until needed. Two days before serving, the cook killed the creature and hung it in a cool place.[23] A vat of boiling water would be prepared and the carcass dipped repeatedly. The cook then scraped the fur to the skin—a process similar to that of scalding and scraping the bristles off a hog. It was then parboiled but never left in the water long enough to rend fat. Then the possum was ready for roasting.

Wetumpka, located on the highest navigable point on the Coosa River in Alabama, afforded the usual sorts of freshwater fish—bass, bream, crappie, and cat. None appeared on the Wetumpka Hotel bill of fare. Preserving caught fish from spoilage in the nineteenth century presented a vastly more difficult problem than storing game. Venison benefited from hanging, as did hare, and even possum. Besides its traditional association with hotel and inn dining, game was a far easier product to store than fresh fish. Only oysters in the shell in barrels had a shelf life that warranted shipping and holding in a hostelry's cold cellar.

> Jes' roasted right to a turnin' o' brown,
> Wid taters piled in a row all aroun',
> De gravy dreenin' an' greasin' um down;
> Don't you lose no lean nor fat,
> For possum ain't lak hyar.[24]

TRIPE AND COW HEEL

Ox hooves and cattle guts, scalded and rinsed, were signatures of British town cookery from the 1600s through the 1800s. These humble remnants of the butchering of livestock were sold in offal shops ready boiled or cooked and carted about the streets of the big cities.[25] "Tripe requires endless cleaning, and is best managed at a river side in the first instance. Afterwards, to assist in the cleaning and blanching, a piece of quick-lime may be dissolved in the water in which it is scalded and scraped. The scalding must be frequently repeated. When bought in the shops, choose it thick, fat, and white; and see that it be fresh."[26] Because of the hours of labor needed to clean tripe and cook cow heel (from six to nine hours, depending on the degree of gelatinization one desired), it proved economical for town specialists to undertake the task, cleaning and cooking on a large scale. Cooking often took place overnight on banked fires.

Sarah Josepha Hale, the New England–born editor of *Godey's Lady's Book* and scrupulous theorizer of American household management, observed of tripe and cow heel, "Ox-feet, or Cow-heels, are rarely eaten by Americans, but in Europe, and particularly in Great Britain, they are always cooked. They contain much nutriment, and may be dressed in the various ways already stated for tripe, with which they are commonly boiled. They are frequently eaten cold, with mustard and vinegar."[27] Daughter of a New Hampshire tavern-keeper, Hale undoubtedly knew the foodways of her region. Yet Wetumpka was in another region, one that in the 1840s had already distinguished itself for its distinctive tastes, including a savor for chitterlings, the cooked intestinal tract of pigs. Another hallmark was the retention of British practices of tavern cooking and entertainment. In London, Glasgow, Edinburgh, Bristol, Liverpool, and Dublin, a steaming bowl was expected during the cold season. "The public diners-out of Dublin are, in winter months, partial to partaking of the dish denominated tripe and cow-heel, which, at moderate prices, well dressed, is supplied to them in various taverns of Dublin, on exclusive days in each week of the tripe and cow-heel season."[28]

The method for cooking tripe and cow heel differed little in America and Great Britain. The first imperative was to clean the product. Mrs. Annabella P. Hill, one of the authoritative southern cooks of the Reconstruction period, has a particularly clear exposition of the modes of preparing both.

TO BOIL TRIPE

As soon as possible after the animal is killed, have the stomach emptied and well washed in cold water; sprinkle lime or ashes over the inside, fold it carefully and lay it in a jar or small tub; cover it with tepid water for six hours; scrape off all the dark part. When all this is removed, wash in several waters and again lay the tripe away for a day and a night in weak salt water (use another jar than the one first used, or scald that well and sun it). Boil the tripe (putting to it cold water) until a straw can be easily run through it and the edges look transparent; skim closely, and when the tripe is tender, take it up and cut it in uniform slices of convenient size for serving; pour over milk, or milk and water, to cover it, and keep it closely covered; should the milk turn a little sour it will not injure the tripe, as it is usual to add vinegar in cooking it. It should not be kept long; either fry, stew, or make into a pillau or hash.[29]

TO BOIL COW HEEL

After being well cleaned boil them until the bones can be removed easily; skin them and serve with parsley and onion sauce. Clean the feet by immersing them in boiling water; let them remain long enough to loosen the horny part; run a knife around and under the horn; fork it off, scrape and wash well. This is an economical dish, nutritive and agreeable, when well prepared it is good fried, after being boiled, or stewed and dressed with cream and butter; cut it in pieces of convenient size for serving.

In the winter tavern version of tripe and cow heel, they were boiled together for a substantial length of time until becoming quite unctuous. This hearty bowl was invariably accompanied by the following sauce:

SAUCE FOR TRIPE, COW-HEEL

Stir into half a pint of oiled butter, (that is, butter melted and strained,) a table-spoonful of garlic-vinegar, and a tea-spoonful each of made mustard, ground black pepper, and brown sugar.[30]

Robust and glossy, the dish enjoyed a reputation for healthfulness. If one imbibed too freely the black Malaga wine, it mitigated the discomforts of the belly and the head. Since the eighteenth century, it had become part of the standard diet prescribed for consumption (tuberculosis) and respiratory disorders. So, for a dining room full of travelers and locals suffering colds, no dish enjoyed more wholehearted a welcome.

FRITTERS AND MOLASSES

From the 1830s through the 1880s, the fritter enjoyed a heyday in American kitchens. Traditional to the cookery of southern Europe and West Africa, the fritter incorporated fruits, vegetables, or meats into a batter of wheat, corn, buckwheat, or rice flour, and fried it in rendered lard or a vegetable oil. A fritter could be savory or sweet, it could eschew ingredients other than the batter, and it could be consumed hot or cold, though most preferred hot. In Louisiana, they were called beignets; in the Midwest, dodgers; in the South, fritters. They might be dusted with sugar, drenched in syrup or molasses, dipped in gravy, wine, melted butter, or honey. Sometimes they were salted.

Since the menu did not specify that the fritters in question featured any fruit, vegetable, or meat, we should presume that this was a basic cornmeal fritter of the sort repeatedly discussed in American cookbooks of the nineteenth century. In the early decades of that century, the dish might be called an "Indian Meal Fritter." Since 1937 in the southern United States, the fritter has been called a "Hush Puppy." Christian Isobel Johnstone includes it in *The Cook and Housewife's Manual* (1847):

INDIAN MEAL FRITTERS AND PANCAKES

Beat four eggs very well, and mix with a pint of milk, into which stir gradually ten spoonfuls of Indian meal. Work the mixture well till it is a smooth batter, when drop a ladleful at a time into half a pound of boiling lard in a deep frying-pan. Lift out the fritters, when done, one by one with a perforated skimmer, and drain and serve hot and hot. More lard may be required, and the fritters must be carefully kept separate in the frying fat. The above batter will make pancakes of Indian meal, in the usual way.[31]

Like all fritters, these would be served either with butter and salt, molasses, or with nutmeg, wine, and sugar. There is a decided proclivity for sugaring Indian fritters in northern cookbooks. The famous Eliza Leslie recommends that treatment for her Indian fritters in *New Receipt Book* (1850), a version noteworthy for the lightness of its batter (eight eggs, one quart of milk, and twelve tablespoons of meal).[32] Southern cooks sweetened with molasses and appreciated salt and butter as accompaniments if they served it as savory snacks. If molasses was intended, a tablespoon of sugar might be added to the batter. When sauced with butter, it would be left out. While milk was the standard liquid in the batter, buttermilk is called for in Quaker Baltimorean Elizabeth E. Lea's recipe for "Indian Meal Fritters" in *Domestic Cookery* (1859).

Fritter batters could be made of wheat flour, and in the case of beignets de riz, rice flour. Yet the rhetorical point of the menu is the commonness of the public fare. A cornmeal fritter was more homely than a wheat flour fritter, just as molasses was more homely than refined loaf sugar.

How, exactly, did a hotel patron consume a fritter dripping with molasses? Fortunately, southern literature provides a portrait in one of the sketches contained in Joseph G. Baldwin's *Flush Times of Alabama and Mississippi* (1854). The hotel gourmand was Squire A.

> He had a way of eating them with molasses, which gave them a rare and delectable relish. Accordingly seating himself the first at the table, and taking position next to the door nearest the kitchen, he prepared himself for the onslaught. He ordered a soup-plate and filled it half-full of molasses—tucked up his sleeves—brought the public towel from the roller in the porch, and fixed it before him at the neck, so as to protect his whole bust—and stood as ready as the jolly Abbott over the haunch of venison, at the widow Glendinning's, to do full justice to the provant, when announced.[33]

When the plate piled with fritters emerged from the kitchen, three other fritter-lovers conspired to hijack it, so when the platter came to Squire A, it was bare.

PERSIMMONS, CHESTNUTS, AND GOOBERS

The American persimmon (*Diospyros virginiana*) grows wild across much of the American South. Prior to the twentieth century, its cultivation was haphazard. While farmers might plant trees from seed or sprouts around the perimeter of cornfields to distract deer and raccoons, few amateur pomologists saw the merit in improving the native stock by breeding. The astringency of the green fruit, the length of time the tree had to grow before bearing, and the tendency for transplanted trees to fail or bear fruit poorly inhibited growers from experimenting with it when apples, peaches, pears, plums, and quinces were so much more forgiving. The roundish fruit can range from one to two inches in diameter. Wild varieties tend to contain large seeds. When systematic cultivation began in the last quarter of the nineteenth century, the number of seeds reduced to two or three per fruit. The taste, according to reports, differed greatly from stand to stand of trees: some were sugary as dates; others never lost their astringency, even after frost. Like apples grown from seed, each persimmon tree possesses distinctive characteristics. The introduction of the Japanese persimmon varieties into California and Florida in the early 1880s stimulated efforts in America to consolidate varieties of native fruit. In the 1890s, the US experimental stations tested these varieties—Shoto, early bearing, gold gem, Daniel Boone, Hicks, Kansas, early golden—propagated by grafting and layering.

Since the Wetumpka Hotel operated at a time before the development of distinct varieties, the fruit it served must have been harvested from the wild. Harvesters carried long poles and jostled fruit from the twenty- to thirty-feet trees freestanding in fields. Old forest persimmon trees might grow over sixty feet high; but their fruit fall did not tend to be collected for market or sale to hotels.

Once picked, the persimmon tended not to rot. If kept it a cool place with air circulation, it would dry. If humidity posed problems in one's neighborhood, the fruit would be packed in sugar or placed uncooked in a glass jar and covered in simple syrup.[34] Dried persimmons were a favorite holiday fruit in the South, but a hotel might have served sugar-cured persimmons at the end of the meal. The one classic southern dish made with the fruit was persimmon pudding, for which a multitude of early recipes exist. But this appeared at breakfast rather than dinner or supper. It did not appear on the bill of fare.

Before the outbreak of blight in 1904, the American chestnut grew from Maine to the Gulf Coast on any soil drier than marsh, thriving in hilly terrain particularly. The degradation of the chestnut in the South from another scourge, *Phytophthora*, began sometime after the Civil War, commencing in lowland areas of the Deep South, working its way gradually into the mountains of North Carolina and Virginia by the 1890s.[35] Arkansas of the 1840s was blissfully ignorant of the plague that would come in the lifetime of many of the Wetumpka Hotel's patrons.

The kernels of the American chestnut were sweeter and smaller than those of its European and Chinese cousins. Eaten raw, boiled, steamed, or roasted, they first appeared in the market after the first frost in a region. In winter, the roasted chestnut enjoyed wide favor, parboiled, nicked on the shells, then parched in a Dutch oven on an open fireplace in a tavern common room or a hotel bar. Coastal newspapers throughout the South would regularly print the notice "Many Chestnuts in the Mountains" until the 1890s.

The most refined dishes made with the nut required that the steamed nut meats be pulped, married with cream, sugar, and rosewater, to be baked as a chestnut pudding.[36] Perhaps the most interesting southern employments of chestnut used the ground flour of cured and dried nuts. The flour substituted for cornmeal in making the Indian meal fritters/hush puppies noted above, or chestnut skillet bread, or using meal as a coating when frying fish. Occasional visitors to the Piedmont regions of the South also reported encountering homesteads preparing chestnut grits using coarse groundnut meat. At the Wetumpka Hotel, the chestnuts were probably roasted.

Goobers in all likelihood referred to roasted peanuts. In actuality, the goober pea was the African *Amphicarpaea monoica*, a subterranean legume that produced one kernel per pod and required boiling for consumption. It became confused with the pindar or peanut, of South American origin, although introduced to the West Indies and North America via West Africa when transported to America on slave ships as food. The peanut could be eaten raw and boiled, but by the first quarter of the nineteenth century had become popular roasted and served in public places—city streets from carts, hotels, theater foyers, and newsstands. In 1845 the variety would have been the North Carolina, or African, peanut. The large Virginia roasting peanut had only just been introduced into cultivation from Bolivia (see chapter 16 below).

Black Malaga wine accompanied the plain fare available at this provincial southern hotel. Having suffered the general devaluation of sweet fortified wines that took place in Europe and America during the twentieth century, Malaga has become unfamiliar; few now have tasted this once-popular dessert wine made of the Pedro Ximénez grape in the south of Spain. Deep ruby in color, regular Malaga was and is laced with brandy for a higher alcohol content. A super-sweet version of the wine was made by allowing the grapes to dry and concentrate their sugars. Unscrupulous vintners in North America sometimes concocted wine from red grape raisins, laced it with apple or peach brandy, and called the final product "black Malaga," because of its dark brownish-black hue.[37] It was, perhaps, this high-octane substance that accompanied the meal in Arkansas.

As the patron pushed away from the table at evening's end, he could be content in the roundedness of his intake—cowpeas and peanuts supplied his legumes, collards his green vegetables, fritters his grains, molasses his sugars, persimmons his fruit, chestnuts his nuts, and three different proteins, none of which were "red meat" per se. Tripe and cow heel were offal. The bacon was cured fat. Possum was the "other" other white meat. If one did not indulge too freely in the black Malaga, the night's digestion would not have proved too troublesome. True, if Justus von Leibig, the pioneer nutritionist and plant chemist, had been in attendance, he would have wondered at the absence of root vegetables. And if one of New England's sumptuary philosophers of the Alcott ilk had sampled the dinner, the preponderance of meats and absence of bread would have probably induced a crisis about the carnage involved in eating. But the usual patrons— the men such as Squire A and his rivals—would have entertained few qualms at the offerings. Indeed, they would have seated themselves near the kitchen door.

PART TWO
Selling

EIGHT *Touring the*
City Markets, 1810 to 1860

In June 2011, the City Market Preservation Trust, LLC, completed a $5.5 million renovation of the four historic Charleston open-air market buildings. For over two hundred years, the roofed open-air complex has extended from Meeting Street—built on the spine of the Charleston peninsula—to East Bay, the major street paralleling the Cooper River waterfront. Decades of exposure to the elements had damaged roofs, dissolved mortar, and degraded wood. The signature market hall, built in 1841, underwent extensive renovation in recent decades, but its shops required extensive refurbishment. The trust built a broad pedestrian aisle to the three open sheds, relieving the pedestrian crush during the tourist season.

I toured the Charleston City Market within two weeks of the opening. Like other well-wishers of Charleston's public spaces, I felt gratified that the structural stabilization would ensure another century of use. When I passed under the shady eves of the shed closest to East Bay, I couldn't help thinking how greatly the scene before my eyes differed from what a consumer would have seen from 1807 to the First World War. Then, the stalls featured vegetables, fruits, meat, and fish; now, souvenirs, clothing, craftwork, and collectibles. After World War II, produce was restricted to the shed closest to East Bay Street, but by the mid-1960s the produce vendors had ceased to be a significant presence. During the market's first century and a half, the great majority of vendors were African American; now they are mostly Caucasian. Then, the streets adjacent to the market would have been filled with turkey vultures jostling over scraps; now they are filled with automobiles, descendants of the machines that frightened the "Charleston Eagles" away from the market in 1920 and 1921.

Certain things have not changed. Now, as then, the market bustles with commerce. The loudness—the oral din and street cacophony— endures from the earlier era. But in 2011, the market was primarily a picturesque alternative in Charleston's rich array of shopping choices. Then, as the central fresh food market of the city, it was a place of necessity. Until the city's grocers took over the produce trade in the third decade of the twentieth century, a family could not avoid going to the market regularly.

Its importance was attested by the multiple lines of transport focused upon it: up-country cattle and fruit crowded the King's Highway (King Street) to its intersection with Market Street; the railroad (recall Charleston's "The Best Friend" was the first railroad engine in operation) hauled corn and flour from Augusta, Georgia, and parts inland to a terminus at North Market; canoes and barges floated down the Cooper River to the market wharves; the oceanic smack fleets hauled fish to those same wharves; coastal steam packets carried fruit from Cuba, candy from Philadelphia, butter and cheese from New York, and salt cod from Boston. A small fleet tied Charleston to the Lowcountry port towns, each market a focus of subsidiary networks of trade and transport: Wilmington, Georgetown, Beaufort–Port Royal, Savannah, Darien, Brunswick, Jacksonville, and St. Augustine.[1]

THE EARLY MARKET

In 1807 the city council of Charleston consolidated the various markets arrayed across the city into the "Centre Market" extending from the Cooper River wharves along North and South Market Streets to Meeting Street. The Queen Street Market was stripped of its right to sell meat and vegetables, as was the ancient market on South Bay Street. The council directed a panel of commissioners to erect a fish market on Market Street east of Governor's Bridge and temporary stalls to permit the selling of vegetables from Maiden Lane to Church Street on Market. The council directed that any free person caught selling meat or vegetables outside the Centre Market had to pay a fine of $20; any slave caught doing so would be confined to the stocks erected at the Centre Market for an hour and receive ten to twenty lashes administered by the Clerk of the Market, or secure payment of $20 from his or her master.[2]

Because meat had the most value of any commodity at the market, the council's directions to butchers were particularly thorough. Butchers did not possess the right to transfer their stall to another's administration; they could not slaughter neat cattle within the city, nor could they cart it uncovered within the city. They could not keep goats, shoats, lambs, or other small livestock penned except in designated locations. The weights and measures maintained by the Clerk of the Market had final authority in any controversy about the weighing of meat, fish, or produce. In 1814 the city council legislated a dress code for butchers: they had to be neatly clad and wear a white cotton apron.

Sales commenced at daybreak every day of the week except Sunday. The tolling of the market bell indicated the start of business. Meat and vegetables vendors plied their wares until 11:00 a.m. on weekdays from June through September, and until noon from October through May. On Saturdays, the market remained open until sunset. Fishmongers and fruit sellers operated by a different clock. They could sell during daylight hours every day except Sunday. Fishmongers could sell their stock on Sundays from daybreak to 8:00 a.m. and from 4:00 p.m. to sunset.

By 1820 citizens ceased using the name "Centre Market" and called it simply the "Charleston Market." In the area between the parallel North and South Market Streets stood the roofed open-sided wooden buildings wherein butchers and vegetable sellers maintained their stalls. After the erection of permanent structures, the Charleston Market became one of the more picturesque, exotic, and varied open-air emporia in the United States. Edward Brickell White's Hall, erected in 1841,[3] was the chief work in a renovation of the complex, which also saw a shortening of the market's length by the destruction of the shed on the Cooper River side of East Bay Street.

The Duke of Saxe-Weimar-Eisenach visited in 1825 and thought the five structures then making up the market resembled those in Philadelphia. He noted, as every tourist did, the throng of turkey buzzards roosting on the brick market house and adjoining buildings and marveled how they kept the streets and floors spotless. He found the contents of the stalls worth extended description: "The quantity of the most beautiful tropical fruit therein arranged, oranges from Florida, pistachios, and large excellent pineapples from Cuba, interested me much. These large and delicious fruit cost only twelve and a half cents each, of course a dollar for eight. There were nuts of various descriptions; many sorts of potatoes, cabbages, and white and red radishes."[4]

By 1830 no market in New Orleans could match the variety and quality of fruits and vegetables found in the Charleston Market.[5] In 1831 a New Englander observed, "There are oranges, the growth of Carolina, and the earth produces few larger or better; there are clusters of bananas, weighing twenty pounds; there are cocoa-nuts, figs, peaches, melons of vast dimensions, cones of lemons, and pyramids of yams."[6] Anne Royall, who also visited the market in 1831, found the fruit stalls a pomological wonderland.

> Besides every species of orange is to be seen, in astonishing quantities, even to the wild orange, which grows in the neighborhood; this is about the size of an egg, supposing it to be round, they are of a deep yellow, and sour as a lemon. Lemons in cart loads, and the banana; this is in taste, substance and color, like our pawpaws, but not, in shape: it is long, perhaps four inches, and crooked like a longnecked squash; it has a sweetish, insipid taste, and grows in clusters upon a small twig, to the amount of a peck, and are brought into market hanging upon the stalk. Besides these, there were a great variety of fruits, and all the nuts of the globe, the names of which I could not learn.

Mrs. Royall in early March "saw all kinds of vegetables, excepting green beans; peas, cabbages, onions, turnips, and every other species of garden vegetable, were in great profusion."[7]

Certain vegetables appeared regularly in the market stalls in Charleston and few places else on the mainland. Wild-picked chainey briar (a smilax prepared like wild asparagus) appeared for two weeks every spring. The chayote—a member of the squash family—was long a local favorite, and only grew in Louisiana (as the mirliton) and east Florida. James Stuart, a British gentleman, encountered another local specialty in 1832: "The Tanya, a very pleasant root, somewhat resembling the Jerusalem artichoke, I have seen, within the last day or two, for the first time."[8] The city adopted the tanya (a cousin of the taro) as a local emblem. Mrs. D. M. W. recalled in the 1880s the vogue for this root vegetable: "On my arrival in Charleston, S.C., more than forty years ago, Tanyas, 'Caladium esculentum,' were commonly sold in the Charleston market as a vegetable; and among other things sent by a friend as gifts to us as strangers, on our first going to housekeeping, was a bag of tanyas."[9] As for the standard vegetables, their availability in winter amazed northerners.

While some of the exotica—particularly in the fruit stalls—can be ascribed to the extensive trade that occurred between the port and the West Indies, much of the citrus fruit came from the Lowcountry (see chapter 17 below). Much fruit and the very great majority of vegetables came from orchards, fields, and gardens within eighty miles of the city. An ambitious community of horticulturists and kitchen gardeners improved the quality of local supply. When it organized into the Horticultural Society of Charleston in 1830, it instituted a bylaw concerning the award of premiums for superlative vegetables at the annual exhibition: "The whole market is considered as in competition: that is, if any vegetable has appeared in market any time during the season, finer than that exhibited, no premium is awarded, although it may surpass all those exhibited, this prevents any premium being bestowed unworthily."[10] The city's great kitchen gardens supplied the market vegetable stalls, and growers haunted the market to view the best productions of rivals. Certain growers gained reputations for particular fruits and vegetables. E. W. Bounetheau had the best onion beds on Charleston Neck, producing both Madeira and silver varieties. He grew fine leeks and salsify as well. Dr. H. R. Frost loved working with brassicas and grew colewort, cabbage, and award-winning kohlrabi. Joseph O'Hear, secretary of the Horticultural Society, was unrivaled as a grower of Irish potatoes. James Legare experimented with rhubarb (a tough grow in a warm humid climate), but had enduring success with parsnips. Dr. B. B. Strobel created a sensation in the mid-1830s by successfully cultivating the garbanzo bean for the first time in the United States. Professional gardener J. Tobin, who tended three major city gardens, grew the best broccoli and battled with Mrs. F. Rutledge's gardener in growing the largest and whitest cauliflowers. Joseph A. Winthrop worked with squashes, growing them in separate fields on James Island to prevented crossings. He introduced both the California and coconut squashes to the region.[11] He also grew the first patch of sugar beets in South Carolina.

While praise in the marketplace and silver medals at the Horticultural Society exhibitions rewarded Charleston's talented kitchen gardeners, local growers bestowed a more profound respect for those who mastered the cultivation of fruits and berries. Henry Horbleck excelled at growing nectarines. Henry Stifley gained a local reputation as master of the apricot. T. F. Purse had learned from a friend in Savannah the best way to grow mulberry. Charles Bassacker grew splendid peaches. William McKown grew apples, though the market tended to be supplied by Woodstock Farm in Goose Creek. Edward De Cottes specialized in figs. Simon Magwood in nearby St. Andrews famously grew seckel and brown beurre pears.[12] No group of growers was more adventurous than the arborists and pomologists. Periodically John Legare, editor of the *Southern Agriculturist*, published wish lists of fruit and nut trees gleaned from conversations among the local tree lovers. One such list, published in November 1834, envisioned the extraordinary benefits that would follow upon acculturating the following trees to the Lowcountry: Chinese mulberry, green tea camellia, sweet-scented olive, jujube, English walnut, pistachio, stone pine, Ogeechee lime, *Salisburia*, teak tree, camphor tree, hazelnut, cork oak, paper mulberry, soapberry tree, cherimoya, pawpaw, and buffalo berry tree.[13] All would be attempted before the outbreak of the Civil War, and many were grown in the experimental orchards of a single adventurous grower. John Michel was acknowledged to be the most curious and capable botanist of the region, a man who rivaled Philippe Noisette as a floriculturist and William Summers of Pomaria as a pomologist. After Noisette's death in 1835, Charlestonians desiring to know the mysteries of grafting, pruning, fumigating, and healing plants turned invariably to Michel.

A VISIT TO MICHEL'S GARDEN

If one walked to the Meeting Street end of the Charleston Market, crossed Meeting, and continued straight ahead for two blocks, turned right on Archdale, striding the few paces to that street's terminus in Beaufain, one could see the south end of St. Philip Street. Crossing over, one might head north on St. Philip, entering into the neighborhood of the College of Charleston. In the block beyond the old College Hall, where Maybank Hall now stands, stood the original home of John Michel. Appointed Justice of the Quorum in 1824, Michel owned nos. 59, 61, and 63 (where he resided with his wife, Ann). Behind the buildings, a garden and orchard extended through the block's interior. Michel walled the plantings to protect them from rapacious college students. Arrayed along the Calhoun Street west wall were the plants that most needed sun, his tropical trees. In the spring, the interior beds were filled with strawberry plants. Numbers of persons who visited the garden in the antebellum era felt moved to comment:

> We have been highly gratified with a visit to the Flower, Fruit, and Vegetable Garden of our enterprizing and tasteful fellow townsman, J. Michel, Esq., attached to his residence in St. Philip's street. Notwithstanding the extreme and desolating severity of the past winter, and the lateness and coolness of the spring, his garden exhibits a most luxuriant and enchanting appearance, teeming with a prolusion of rich, rare and useful products, abounding in the choicest gifts of Flora, Pomona and Ceres, and forming, with its varied and lovely hues, an optical feast, and with its delightful odors, an olfactory concert. The floral wealth of his enclosure is immense; about 400 Rose trees, embracing 250 varieties, unfold their banners of beauty, and open their fragrant censers—and of these no less than 250 are Moss Rose Trees—the white, red, dark red and royal Moss—in full bloom. The Plumeria (B.) or Franchipane (F.), the Microphylla Rose, the stately Lady Tankerville, and the Root and *Tree* Peony, (the bloom of the latter of these being a novel triumph of horticultural skill in this State) contribute their respective charms to the attraction of the scene. In the fruit department, we perceive the Strawberry—including the Bishop Superb and the Wilmot Superb—as inviting to the eye as it is luscious to the taste—four varieties of the Cherry, already of brilliant red, and nearly ripe—with twenty varieties of the Pear and French Prune, covered with the richest profusion of young fruit; and among the hothouse exotics, are the Lime Tree, and three varieties of the Banana, from

which fruit is expected next year, and would probably have been realized this season, but for the Siberian aspect of the past winter in our Southern clime. The Kitchen-Garden, too, is vigorous *and forward* in its growth — manifesting either favoring influences or unwonted skill.[14]

The aesthetics of this account are floricultural, with sight and smell given priority over taste. But Michel's aesthetics were whole-bodied, with taste and touch mattering as greatly as sight and scent. He collected fruits and vegetables for the rarity of their tastes and textures. In 1840 he managed to secure a *Solanum crispum*, a Chilean climbing potato, that he called a "yam massicot."[15] Though he believed that the plant had an African origin and an American acculturation in Santo Domingo, this South American plant bears more resemblance to the Peruvian potato than the sweet potato. Michel observed that it is "superior in flavor to the Irish potato. It is not sweet. It is cooked in the same way with all other potatoes — may be boiled, baked or roasted, and when cooked is said to be of a bright gamboge color."[16]

Though Michel collected to challenge his tongue as well as his eyes and nose, his understanding of the world of plants, and particularly the world of fruits, was informed by the most cosmopolitan sort of reading. No form of cultivation was more bookish than pomology, fruit culture. The quest for the best fruits from around the world became passionate for a network of orchardists in Britain, America, France, Germany, Spain, Italy, and Portugal. Michel read the books, the nursery catalogs, and the correspondence of a network of growers of exotica. While his reading informed him what to collect, his success in the orchard derived from extensive practical experience. "It is in the processes of grafting, and budding or inoculating, that he has achieved some of his greatest triumphs — the former being done with so much nicety, as almost to hide from detection the point of union between the parent stem and the inserted shoot; and the latter shewing, in one instance, no less than nine varieties of the rose on a single bush."[17] His preeminence as a nursery man was such that he became the region's principal supplier of garden plants and fruit trees after the death of Noisette in 1835.[18] From a host of reports, we can fill in more details of his orchard. We know, because of a Horticultural Society award in 1835, that one of the three banana varieties was the rare "purple banana." He exhibited a "sweet guava" in that year's exhibition as well. He had a fruiting coffee tree that survived the freeze of 1835.[19] A trellis supported the vines of the Chasselas de Fontainebleau grape. At the second annual Charleston Horticultural Society exhibition at Seyle's Long Room, Michel displayed pears and plums, the reporter noting that he had "taken great pains to introduce the finest fruits of France."[20] Elsewhere, we learn that he grew Perrigaud plums and Portugal quinces.[21] These quinces won a silver medal in the 1834 Horticultural Society exhibition, as well as his display of apples and strawberries. In the published commendation, we read that "the cherries produced by this gentleman, merit particular notice, as they show that this delicious fruit may be successfully cultivated here."[22] Little wonder that tourists marveled at the fruit available at the Charleston Market, when Michel's surplus supplied the stalls from 1830 to 1855.

Michel's contributions as an experimental kitchen gardener have not produced so ample a record. Besides strawberries, his one vegetable fascination appears to have been the globe artichoke. With James Bancroft and John Van Rhyn, he vied for the annual medal for artichokes. It was the only vegetable he sent to market. Throughout the 1830s, a core of Horticultural Society growers kept the market stalls filled with "very fine" vegetables: "Messrs. Edward Barnwell, J. Hartman, Wm. McLean, E. Witty, A. G. Rose, Lapenne, James Fraser, R. K. Payne, J. S. Payne, P. Javain and J. F. O'Hear."[23] Lapenne grew guinea squash (eggplant) on a tract on upper King Street. Edward Barnwell's cabbages and celeries became draws at Baker's Grocery Store in the city. Hartman grew potatoes and regularly introduced new varieties to market, such as the Napoleon in 1838.

The market provided a focus for the efforts of the Charleston horticulturists. Their association and exhibition alerted the growing community who had grown the best produce during the season. Winners enjoyed a demand for seed, so their improved strains might be interbred with the best versions of a cultivar maintained by the buyers. In this way, a local seed exchange developed producing regional variations of the standard varieties available in the transatlantic seed market. Only in the 1830s does the organized improvement of fruits and vegetables give rise to what might be called regional creations—a body of variants whose seed circulated among a gardening and orchard tending community.

If the 1830s saw the dominion of the experimental kitchen gardener in the Charleston Market, with a grower specializing in a few sorts of vegetables, the 1840s saw the rise of a new creature, the market gardener, who, like Michel with fruits, attempted to grow the entire panoply of grains, legumes, greens, and roots consumed in a region. We know from Francis S. Holmes's 1842 book, *The Southern Farmer and Market Gardener,* exactly what the new breed of commercial grower raised for the Charleston Market.[24] The grains (in order of appearance in Holmes's book): barley, rye, oats, millet. The roots (beginning with those used in livestock feeding, suggesting where value lay in the market): rutabaga, mangelwurzel, Dale's yellow hybrid turnip, carrots, parsnips, Jerusalem artichoke, sweet potatoes, potatoes, Indian corn, cowpeas, fodder corn, guinea corn, broom corn, and sunflowers were next in importance among commodities. Then mustard, benne (sesame), rhubarb, arrowroot, melons, watermelons, cucumbers, running beans, mushrooms, groundnuts (peanuts), cabbages. Holmes devotes a separate section to herbs: balm, fennel, lavender, marjoram, mint, pennyroyal, sage, sorrel, tansy, thyme, and wormwood.

Holmes's guide presented several mysteries: the absence of variety listings for tomatoes, sweet potatoes, rhubarb, and onions chief among them. (Did other regional growers specialize in these?) The elaboration of varieties of beets and turnips reminds us of the absolutely centrality of root vegetables for farm systems, where they operated as winter livestock feed as well as table vegetables. The gusto for turnips in particular has been lost to twenty-first-century southern taste. Holmes instructed readers that certain vegetables had to been grown from seed from specified sources. Carrots and certain of the cabbages he believed still had to come from European seedsmen. Onion slips had to be secured from growers in Charleston.

The profusion of nuts (a multitude of unknown varieties in the eyes of some) was a distinctive feature of the market in the eyes of visitors. Pistachios and coconuts were named specifically. Holmes commented on the market demand for groundnuts (peanuts/pindars/goober peas) and treated the black walnut and hickory nut in his volume as well. Pecans grew in profusion in the neighborhood. Joel Roberts Poinsett grew hazelnuts on his farm near Charleston. Chestnuts from the western part of the state no doubt stocked the market in season. An article in an 1834 issue of the *Southern Agriculturist* noted the presence of pine nuts in the market, though *Pinus pinea* did not grow locally.[25] It was obviously imported. What else came in from parts beyond is now difficult to determine.

With the rise of market farming, more vegetables grew outside the city limits. Material was either carted into the city along King Street Road from the interior or rowed down the Cooper River by slaves in canoes. The transport took place in the dark, and in the hour before dawn, carts and canoes disburdened their contents at the stalls. African American market women arranged vegetables in wooden stalls under the market roof. Each stall featured a wooden table/platform with a railing that contained the vegetables. On the street end was a hinged wooden gate to permit easy loading from dispatch carts. Market women earned a reputation for flamboyance of dress and manner. They characteristically wore "gay turbans of Madras, and whose manner of sitting beside their merchandize, has a very Turkish appearance."[26]

Black butcher/purveyors presided over another section of stalls facing onto North and South Market Streets. Because the sight and odor of slaughter offended people, the abattoir stood at some remove from the market, located on a low piece of land abutting a creek in the city's Eighth Ward. There the scalding, flaying, gutting, and rending of flesh took place amid a cloud of buzzards. Lidded carts conveyed sides and cuts of meat to market. In market, butchers portioned and trimmed beef, pork, mutton, lamb, venison, rabbit, and other game to salable size. One practice of the Charleston meat stalls was distinctive—the heaping of the varieties of flesh contiguous to one another. "The beef is not kept apart from the mutton, nor the pork from both." The mutton derived from Merino sheep grown in Colleton County or Tunis sheep (fat-tailed) in the midlands. Cattle and pigs came from throughout the region. Venison was seasonally present in fall and winter. William Bingley, on an 1821 tour, grumbled about the quality: "The beef, mutton, veal, and pork, of South Carolina, are seldom in perfection; and the hot weather renders it impossible to keep meat many hours after it is killed."[27] During the summer months, this section of the market wrought great anxiety in the eyes of tourists scared of spoilage. The butchers assuaged this anxiety by making liberal use of ice, shipped in bulk to the Charleston Market (and the Savannah Market as well) by Frederick Tudor of Massachusetts, the most energetic ice purveyor in the United States from 1817 through the 1830s.[28] While the meat

in the market never fully lost its aura of trepidation for northern visitors—
except for hams and bacon—fowls, which were kept live in parts of the
market, were shackled in pairs and were always fresh.

The story of fish in the Charleston Market requires rather elaborate
telling, so has been reserved for chapter 9. Game came to market, supplied
by African American hunters in seasonal waves. Venison appeared less frequently than one might suspect, since the Lowcountry deer population
was nowhere near as great as it is today. Wildfowl, on the other hand, appeared in great abundance. With the rise of the railroads in the 1840s and
'50s, game from the American interior supplanted local supply.

A market's greatness may best be measured by the meals it enables—
both the home-cooking and hotel-dining varieties. If we are to judge by
the wealth of surviving descriptions of feasts, the Charleston Market was
among the greatest in America. John Lambert in 1817 observed of the
city's hosts: "Every article that the market can supply is found at their
festive board. The wine flows in abundance, and nothing affords them
greater satisfaction than to see their guests drop gradually under the table
after dinner."[29] James Stuart attended a private dinner party in March
1830 and wrote:

> I dined with a large party this day in a very handsome house of some an-
> tiquity, the rooms fitted up with figured wainscot in the old English style.
> Twenty persons sat down to dinner at about half past four o'clock. We
> had a most abundant feast, of which I mention the particulars merely to
> show the style of such a dinner here. It was attended by an upper servant
> and three servants in livery, all of course slaves. The table was covered
> with turtle soup, fish, venison, boiled mutton, roast turkey, boiled turkey,
> a ham, two boiled salted tongues, two tame ducks, two wild ducks, some
> dressed dishes, boiled rice, hominie, potatoes, cauliflower, salad, &c. The
> whole dinner was at once placed on the table before we sat down. When
> it was removed, a complete course of pastry and puddings succeeded,
> and then a most excellent dessert of oranges, shaddocks, bananas, and
> a variety of West India fruits, with iced cream in profusion. The liquids
> consisted of champagne, Madeira, sherry, port, claret, porter, lemonade,
> &c.[30]

An English traveler remarked on the fare available at Charleston's Planter's Hotel in 1832: "The table at these hotels is generally spread with great abundance. Turtle and terrapin soup, fish, venison, wild turkeys, and meat of all kinds, are the common dishes. Very little wine is drank, and rather too much brandy. The wine is almost always Madeira, to the perfection of which the climate is very favourable."[31]

Profusion of meat was the hallmark of the city market and the hotel kitchen. The abundance of fruits and vegetables in market found its greatest expression in town-house cookery. So the ample testimonies of visitors and city residents make clear. Yet a question remains: Why does no one mention grain in his or her tour of the stalls? Rice and corn were the two edible staples produced in the region. And what of wheat, rye, barley, and oats?

With the exception of the firm of Campsen & Ellerhorst, grain was not sold in the Charleston Market. Dealers in grain tended to be located on the Cooper River waterfront, with offices on East Bay and South Bay Streets: E. M. Beach, Otis Phillips, D. S. Stocking, R. C. Browne, George Kinloch, Otis Mills, and J. C. Miller. Here wholesale grain might be purchased and distribution made to the network of grocers in the South. (Charleston's grocery world is described in chapter 13 on sugar below.) The bake house had a different supply system than the kitchen.

Provided a cook had the wherewithal to pay, the Charleston Market could supply kitchens with fruits and vegetables as splendid as available anyplace in the United States. Social competition among a community of growers fueled improvement in market staples, and the development in the 1840s of a professional aesthetics among market gardeners ensured that the common supply in the Charleston Market was wholesome and tasty. Only Savannah of the other Lowcountry markets enjoyed Charleston's level of supply for meats, fruits, and vegetables.

THE SAVANNAH MARKET

When the colonial capital of Georgia was laid out in its distinctive grid of squares, Percival Square served as site of the city market. Several acts of the colonial legislature in the 1750s established and regulated its operation, specifying its daily opening except for the Sabbath, the tolling of a bell at sunrise to herald the start of business, and appointing a clerk to maintain a set of public scales and to collect rents and fees. In 1763 the market relocated to Ellis Square, where it would remain thereafter, except for 1820 to 1821, when the ravages of the Great Fire caused its short-term transfer to South Broad Street. Five commissioners policed the Savannah Market, empowered to seize meat and produce that had spoiled or had been adulterated. The city owned the stalls and rented them to purveyors on a yearly basis, the contract beginning on the first Wednesday in December. The city also owned the scale, until the volume of the meat trade in the 1830s grew to the extent where the city required each butcher to provide his own scale and submit it to regular inspection by the Clerk of the Market.

Despite efforts at regulation, untoward things happened periodically. A fire in a market bake house in 1797 destroyed 229 houses in the city. Sellers began operating on the morning of the Sabbath. A visitor in 1831 observed, "The greatest market is on Sunday morning. The godly ought to petition Congress to stop the market."[32] A continuing source of aggravation to the Georgia plantocracy was the number of African American slaves who sold produce (sometimes off plantations without permission) and amassed money. Enough cash and a slave could buy his or her freedom. Since many of the regular market sales force consisted of free black butchers, stall women, and bakers, determining whether an African American was free or bound took effort. Since some planters granted slaves written permission to sell in the market, the issue was further complicated.

The market, located on the elevated plateau upon which Savannah's principal buildings stood, depended upon supplies carted up the steep paths traversing the forty-foot bluff that rose from the waterfront. "Oyster-boats and fishing craft with torn, discolored sails, truck-boats filled with all manner of green things, coasters from the sea-islands, dash past to land at the market-warf,—the one dock where all supplies for the city market are received."[33]

Like the Charleston Market, the Savannah Market prided itself on its selection of local fruit. The old German settlement of Ebenezer, twenty-five miles from Savannah, carted in "peaches, apples, pears, quinces, grapes,

&c. Melons of delicious flavour are produced."[34] Of the over 150 varieties of apples grown in Georgia, the favorite southern market varieties were the berry, wonder, buff, and English crab. They grew several popular northern varieties as well—the Esopus Spitzenberg, Newton, and northern spy.[35] While civic boosters branded Georgia the "Peach State," it could just as well have been designated the "Melon State," so great was the national reputation of its cantaloupes and watermelons. Notoriously prone to mutation and cross breeding, melons conformed to recognizable varieties only by scrupulous superintendence by communities of gardeners and farmers. The nineteenth-century shopper recognized two categories of melons—the rough textured muskmelons and the smooth, thick-skinned watermelons. The Savannah Market featured several varieties of each. Of the muskmelons, the citron inspired admiration for its sweetness, richness, and pronounced flavor,[36] the ribbed nutmeg for forward musky flavor and large size. Until the 1850s and the introduction of the Summers Brothers' varieties, Savannah's favorite watermelons were the round, dark green-skinned Spanish black, the mountain sweet, the small round orange watermelon, the early ripening Carolina, the Japanese apple-pie, and the pickling citron. After 1860, the rattlesnake and Bradford watermelons ruled. Ogeechee limes—the scarlet fruit of the *Nyssa candicans*, or tupelo tree—enjoyed great local favor, being pickled or preserved in sugar.[37]

Of vegetables proper, visitors were stupefied by the splendor of the cabbages appearing in the market stalls. Again, the Germans took the lead in creating these "perfect" vegetables. In the 1830s, they undertook a concerted effort to grow cabbages and employed trucks for shipment to Savannah and parts north.[38] In the eyes of northern visitors, the meat in Savannah appeared "indifferent," but "fruit and vegetables were fine, peas were plentiful and had been for ten days; radishes, turnips, and lettuce, grow here all winter."[39] Okra, sweet potatoes, potatoes, and field peas abounded in season. Lettuce, white mustard, cress, collards, and spinach made their appearance around the calendar.

Of grains, locally grown gold seed rice flowed through the market in abundance. Wheat refined at the Etowah Mills made Savannah a major bourse for flour. Because its lands were not suited to cotton culture, Effingham County, home of the Salzburgers, grew sugarcane, rice, corn, rye, peas, potatoes, and wheat—with the latter two commodities becoming significant crops. Their home-manufactured cane syrup enjoyed greatly popularity at the market.[40] Rye and oats were always available.

The city code offered a legal snapshot of the usual offerings of the market in its table of fees. Each purveyor had to pay a stipulated amount of money for each item sold. The Clerk of the Market oversaw the collection and checked butchers' records of the markings of slaughtered livestock to insure rustled cattle, hogs, sheep, and goats were not being fenced. While antebellum fee schedules have not survived, one from 1888 contains nothing that was not encountered in the 1850s:

For every beef, twenty-five cents; for every calf, sheep, lamb, hog, deer or goat, fifteen cents; for each piggin, pail or firkin of butter or lard, ten cents; for each drum fish, bass, snapper, grouper, or other large scale fish not sold on string, five cents; for each turtle, five cents; for each pair of terrapins, five cents; for each shad, three cents; for each string of fish not less than one cent nor more than two cents; for each basket of shrimps or prawn, twenty cents; for each pail of open oysters, twenty cents; oysters and clams per bushel, five cents; for weighing on the public scales, each draft over thirty pounds, ten cents; and under thirty pounds, five cents; for every lot of vegetables sold from a stall or bench, ten cents; for every pair of wild English, black or canvas-back ducks, five cents; for every other kind of wild ducks, per pair, three cents; poultry sold from country carts, not taxable; fowls per pair, five cents; turkeys, five cents each; geese, five cents each; from vendors of sausages, twenty-five cents for each day's marketing, and the same for the Saturday afternoon's market; for every coffee stand, twenty-five cents per day, and the same for Saturday afternoon's market; for each saddle of venison sold from a stall or bench, ten cents; for each lot of vegetables, fruit or other produce sold from a two horse wagon or cart at the market during market hours, fifty cents; for each lot of vegetables, fruit or other produce sold from a one horse wagon or cart at the market during market hours, twenty-five cents; for every basket of vegetables, fruit or other produce sold at the market, five cents; for every lot of jerked or dried beef sold at the market, twenty-five cents; for every basket of rice, ten cents; for every lot of watermelons or cantaloupes sold at the market, one cent for each melon or cantaloupe sold; for every sturgeon sold at the market, twenty cents.[41]

The code recognized any cart dispatched by a purveyor during the hours that the market operated as an extension of the market. Carts operating after closing time had a different scheme of taxation and regulation.

Of all the products sold at the Savannah Market, meat underwent the most scrutiny. The cuts offered, the penning of animals, the freshness, and the source were all regulated. No pens were allowed within a mile of the market, no dogs within thirty feet of the stalls. Early in the century, the Savannah Market suffered from scarcity. In 1817, "the market is tolerably well supplied with fish and poultry, but not with butcher's meat."[42] Supply improved in the 1820s. Late in the antebellum era (the precise date cannot be now determined), the bonding of butchers began. Butchers maintained dispatch carts to transport sides and cuts to steady customers. As an ancillary business, large butchers set up sausage vendors in the market as a conduit for unsold cuts. Politically active, social, and dollar savvy, the butchers thrived to the extent that they could cultivate networks of husbandmen to supply stock and regular customers. Invariably, the most successful cultivated connections with the ship captains, supplying barrels of pickled meat and boxes of jerked beef and venison for sailors' rations. These were processed from subprime flesh that came to market.

Georgia's finest pork came from two breeds of hog: the Woburn and grazier. The grazier was sometimes bred with the Chinese guinea if a smaller pig was preferred. Pumpkins and sweet potatoes cycled with barley and the gleanings of wheat fields as feed. The beef that came to market derived from indeterminate local breeds of cattle. In 1851, when a quarter century of breeding had convinced much of the country that pure breeds were the best sorts of neat cattle, a Clarksville husbandman reported to the US Patent Office, "We have neither the pure blood nor crosses of the Devon or Hereford cattle; but our native breeds are as thrifty, and take on fat as readily as the Durhams."[43]

While shrimp, oysters, and clams received notice in the city code, crabs did not. Nevertheless, they were a seasonal item of sale. In her *Reminiscences of Georgia* (1850), Emily Burke observed that "shell fish, such as crabs, shrimps, and prawns, were more saleable than those with fins."[44] Oysters reigned in terms of taste. A traveler on the eve of the Civil War observed, "The inhabitants of Savannah, rich or poor, free or slave, consume immense quantities of oysters. For breakfast, for dinner, and for supper, oysters, in one form or another, are sure to be supplied to all above the poorest classes of the population; and here there are few who can be called as absolutely poor as their compeers in Europe. The result is, according to the calculation of a notable inhabitant, that Savannah consumes in a year a sufficient quantity of oysters to leave shells enough for the construction of one mile of road."[45] In 1840 Andrew Nelson began laying shells on Georgia bottoms to build oyster beds. During the subsequent forty years, beds in the Burnside and Thunderbolt Rivers spread south of the city. The idea of transporting seed oysters from Wassaw Sound and Tybee Island to waters more convenient to Savannah took hold, and numbers of developers nourished beds repeatedly refreshed with castings of year-old seed.[46]

Shrimp also enjoyed great favor. Caught by net, they were sold head on by the pail, peeled, steamed, and sauced in shrimp pie, the favorite local preparation. Shrimp also played an important role as bait in catching market fish. Undersize shrimp were not thrown back but used for fertilizer in coastal fields.

This bustle of commerce continued into the twentieth century when, like Charleston, well-capitalized grocers and wholesale food merchants in Savannah, such as W. T. Belford, absorbed the sale of produce into their operations. Public vendue of fruits and vegetables declined with each decade of the twentieth century until, in the late 1950s, the city's Market Hall in Ellis Square was razed to build a parking garage. In 2011, when tour guides directed one to the Savannah Market, they proudly told how Ellis Square was reclaimed by putting the parking garage underground and erecting a children's playground on a greensward laid above the garage. The market now is a district of souvenir shops, eateries, craft stores, and galleries. If you want fresh local vegetables, you can get them one day a week, Saturday, in the morning from April to mid-December in Forsyth Park. Charleston, too, since 1989, has had an April to December Saturday local farmers' market at Marion Square, where one can have access to the bounty of the Lowcountry's fields and gardens. Presumably, enough fresh produce is available in the local groceries—including the organic groceries—to satisfy demand during the winter months and the other six days of the week.

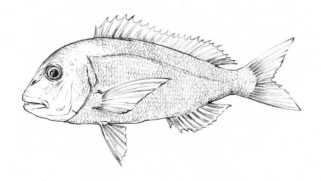

NINE *Fish Master:*
C. C. Leslie and the Reconstruction
of Charleston Cuisine

The Charleston, Savannah, Wilmington, and Jacksonville markets during Reconstruction saw their abundance of exotic fruits and quality garden vegetables supplemented by a range of inexpensive asparagus, radishes, potatoes, strawberries, lettuce, tomatoes, and cabbages. Charleston's market improved in one other area as well—fish supply. While the antebellum city has come down in memory as a place where the privileged orders enjoyed extraordinary luxury of table and cellar, it actually suffered an undersupply of seafood before the war, an odd state of affairs given its status as an Atlantic port city with immense resources swimming the coastal waters. The slave system did not allow the efficient harvest of the oceanic bounty nor the timely transport of freshwater seafood to market. Only with emancipation did the market abound in fish, shellfish, and turtles, when a largely African American workforce plied the waters under the direction of an African American market savant, Charles C. Leslie.

One axiom of capitalism from the time of Adam Smith's *Wealth of Nations* (1776) was that slavery hinders the efficient operation of an economy because it restricts the free exchange of goods and services. Work under slavery is driven by negative incentive (you will be punished if you don't work) rather than positive reward, so a worker's ambitions are never enlisted in an undertaking.[1] The idea that the freedom of persons to act in their own self-interest contributed to the expansion and enrichment of markets seemed a resonant truth to some antebellum writers. Thomas F. De Voe's history of the rise of the New York food supply system, *The Market Book* (1862), envisioned an increasingly expansive and enterprising network of growers, livestock raisers, hunters, butchers, and fishermen coalescing to service the demand of America's hungriest city. De Voe's story recounts the power of the invisible hand arising from the Dutch colonial Burgher Right and the competitive energies of a multitude of private enterprisers in fashioning a succession of commercial organisms of unprecedented scope and efficiency.[2] The preconditions for the existence of something as potent as the Washington Market in New York were the liberty of sovereign citizens to act on their own initiative to grow, process, and sell; a government that supplied a stable currency and a domestic transportation system; and the power of the law.

The Charleston Market emerged in a political system with restricted liberty, in a state with an underdeveloped skein of roads, and a code of laws that dispensed justice inequitably among portions of the population. From De Voe's perspective, the Charleston Market must have suffered inadequacies of supply, processing, and demand. It did—not so much in the availability of vegetables, fruits, and meat, but rather in the supply of fish and, to a lesser extent, game. This inefficiency becomes obtrusively apparent when we contrast reports about the state of the fish market from the 1870s and '80s with those of the 1840s and '50s.

Given the fulsome descriptions of the abundance of meat and produce in the Charleston Market by visitors from 1810 to the Civil War, reports that the port city suffered a regular dearth of fish and seafood in the market stalls comes as something of a shock. Yet we can infer nothing less than an endemic paucity of fish at market during the period when we read in "The Prospects and Policy of the South" (1854) a widely published critique of southern political economy:

Our rivers abound in fish, some of which are unrivalled in flavor by that of any fresh-water in America, but they never find their way to Charleston, while the cod from Boston may be obtained fresh in its season; and if our market abounds in shad in their season, we are indebted for it to Northern enterprise. The lovers of this fish in Charleston may congratulate themselves that every Northern river abounds in shad, otherwise we should have the mortification of seeing the produce of our rivers pass by our wharves on their way to a New York or Boston market.[3]

Little freshwater fish came to market? Yankees controlled the market supply of saltwater fish and were shipping shad from northern rivers? However counterintuitive these claims may seem, they had a basis in fact. The anecdotal reports of a multitude of antebellum tourists support the general characterization that Charleston's seafood market suffered undersupply and limited choice. During his tour of the southern states in 1826, the Duke of Saxe-Weimar-Eisenach visited the Charleston Market and reported: "Fish were not presented in so great a variety as I expected. Of shell fish, I saw oysters only, which are roasted in the shell at market, and consumed by the negroes with great avidity."[4] No clams, no shrimp, no scallops, no crabs—just oysters. The availability of fish proved variable. It was not at all unusual to encounter reports, such as that of Daniel Blowe in 1820, that "fish were very scarce and dear."[5] When fish were in market, their variety was invariably limited. Mrs. Ann Royall observed in 1831 that the fish were "bass mostly, they were fresh and neat."[6] Of the hundred-plus fish caught in a day's sail of Charleston Harbor, the market featured only six saltwater varieties—those named in Sarah Rutledge's *Carolina Housewife*: bass, sheepshead, drum, shad, mackerel, and blackfish.[7] Only bass and drum had more than episodic presence at the market.

The restriction of saltwater supplies of fish arose from two circumstances: (1) the commercial smack fleet being controlled by northern fisherman who reserved a substantial portion of the catch for northern ports; and (2) a black and Cuban mosquito fleet that either (a) supplied plantations directly with food, or (b) preferred landing fish out of market for distribution on wharves on the various Lowcountry sounds. George Brown Goode, the nineteenth century's greatest historian of American fisheries, observed of the antebellum Charleston Market:

For many years prior to the rebellion the fisheries were controlled largely by Northern fishermen, together with Spaniards [from Cuba], free negroes, and a few others who bought their time from their masters. At that time the vessel fisheries were very extensive, and a greater part of the supply was landed by the smacks. In 1860, according to Mr. J. S. Terry, the oldest fish dealer in the city, there were about fifteen New England smacks engaged in fishing for the Charleston market during the winter months. These came South in the early fall and remained till the middle or last of May. They engaged chiefly in the capture of blackfish (Serranus atrarius).[8]

Goode explained two features of the antebellum anecdotal descriptions: the lack of fish in certain seasons and the restriction of catch to a certain few marketable varieties—primarily blackfish (sea bass). All of the larger vessels—the ten- to thirty-ton smacks that fished with hand lines the coral banks ten to twenty miles offshore from Bulls Bay in the north to Santa Helena Island in the south—were northern owned and manned. The mosquito fleet—the small boat fleet locally manned by free blacks, Cubans, and some slaves working at task fishing—did not venture to the oceanic fishing grounds. Their primary access to the market took place in summer when the northern vessels decamped. Their catch consisted of coastal fish, of which only the sheepshead paid a premium at the market, crabs, shad in winter, and bait shrimp.[9]

If we are to credit the representations of the author of "The Prospects and Policy of the South," the paucity of fresh fish and game at the Charleston Market could be directly attributed to the disinclination of the great planters who controlled the commercial system to support enterprises that might develop trade in items other than the staples—cotton, rice, corn, tobacco, sugarcane—that concerned them. Because labor was not free to develop niche markets, slaves could not respond to market demand in any concerted or consistent way. When northern market gunners began making annual forays into the Pee Dee River basin in the 1850s, after being driven out by legislation from Delaware, Virginia, and the Outer Banks of North Carolina, the local grandees tolerated their industry briefly, permitting them to supply the Charleston Market for a percentage of the proceeds. The plantocracy's willingness to tolerate white outlanders to perform the fish and game harvest rather than allocate their own slaves to the task had unforeseen consequences. The northerners performed as market gunners typically did: "A large body of aliens who frequent that neighborhood during the whole winter, destroy all the game, and as soon as the spring is opened, destroy all the fish that frequent these waters."[10] The decimation deprived locals of sport and sustenance, so the planters stopped the gunning and fishing by legislation. The dearth of freshwater fish and game was restored to the market in 1856.

On the eve of the Civil War, the country tables of the Lowcountry enjoyed a plentitude of fish and game that the residents of Charleston did not. In New York and Paris, in Baltimore and London, the markets drew in the broadest spectrum of meat and fish, domestic and wild. Charleston and Savannah did not. While Lowcountry cities consumed the abundance of domestic pork, beef, and mutton that came to the butcher stalls, it suffered a curious undersupply of wildfowl, game, and fish, even the tastiest creatures of the forest, field, air, and water. "It is well known that in Autumn the rice birds frequently darken the air on Cooper River and are killed in great abundance. Who ever sees a rice bird for sale in the Charleston market?"[11] The paradox: the country table was more richly laden than the city because hunting and fishing by black and white inhabitants supplied it. Only with the emancipation of the labor force and the collapse of restrictions on the mobility of black workers did the Charleston Market enjoy a rich supply of game and fish. Because questions of access to wild creatures were much less fraught on the waters than on land, the fish market would undergo the greater transformation as a mass of freedmen took to the coastal waters. Their efforts would be organized, often without their initial acquiescence, by Charles C. Leslie. Furthermore, his curiosity about and broad firsthand knowledge of fish drew him to ichthyology. In the 1880s, he became the primary supplier to the scientific community of fish specimens from Atlantic waters. His involvement with the scientific community led to concrete benefits: the creation of the first soft-shell crab nursery in the United States, the rationalization of shrimp harvesting in the coastal waters, and the protection of stressed fish populations. The efflorescence of Charleston seafood cookery took place during the four decades after the Civil War because Charles Leslie enabled it to occur.

THE EMERGENCE AND ENTERPRISE
OF CHARLES C. LESLIE

Born into freedom at Chandler, South Carolina, a plantation cross-roads settlement in Mount Pleasant, South Carolina, on April 12, 1841, Charles C. Leslie was home-schooled in mathematics and writing, skills that would eventually elevate him above most of the African Americans who gravitated toward the relative liberty of the coastal fishing trade. His parents belonged to the region's "brown elite," mulatto, literate, and Episcopalian. Leslie's story does not conform in key particulars to the picture of the politically active, abolitionist watermen described by David S. Cecelski in his classic study of North Carolina's black maritime laborers, *The Waterman's Song*.[12] Around Charleston, the free black butchers in the market, not the watermen, spearheaded resistance to the excesses of the slave regime. Rivalry with the Yankee captains, who supplied the bulk of offerings at the city seafood market, forced members of the mosquito fleet into partnership arrangements, since solitary actors could not get much traction in the market; most tried setting up private supply arrangements with wharves outside of the city, or with the quasi-illegal street vendors who cried wares in Charleston's streets. Leslie, while a teenager, realized his greatest advantage in the coastal fishing world lay in acquiring as much knowledge as possible of the complicated pattern of bars and shoals in the harbor and coastal waters. Because the smack fleet worked miles offshore, it didn't cruise the coastal waters and occasionally suffered mishaps in the shifting channels of the harbor. On the eve of the Civil War, Leslie became one of the supreme pilot-navigators of the coast. His skills were such that his services were sought by Charleston merchants and the Cuban ship captain and fisherman A. Francis Lopez. In April 1861, when Carolina's artillery opened fire on Fort Sumter, Leslie was twenty years old. He spent the war running guns for the Confederacy.[13]

Details of Leslie's service to the Confederacy are difficult to ascertain. His diary—the primary source for information about his early life—was misplaced forty years ago by his sole surviving daughter, Julie Leslie. Its contents were conveyed only in the most general terms to one of Charleston's black heritage keepers, Feldreth Hutchinson, and recorded by historian Lee Drago of the College of Charleston in the 1980s. So, Leslie's reason for taking so active a part in the defense of his native state can only be speculated. Perhaps he thought on the stories about the fate of Thomas Jeremiah that circulated in the African American community. During the American Revolution, Jeremiah, a free black Charleston pilot with skill rivaling Leslie's, chose not to side with local revolutionaries and fell victim to the gallows for his loyalty to Britain.[14] One had a choice: turn against the local power and leave, or support the power and stay. If one resisted and stayed, one faced the fate of Thomas Jeremiah. Many other persons black and white could handle boats and use navigational instruments. Leslie's trump card was his exquisite knowledge of the local waters. Leaving Charleston would forfeit his greatest advantage over other waterman. Whatever his reasoning for aiding to the Confederacy, its defeat did not prove ruinous to him. By the surrender, he and A. Francis Lopez had collected a small fleet of vessels. Leslie had sufficient assets to take advantage of the commercial and administrative disorder after the cessation of hostilities.

It is instructive to contrast Leslie's course of action with that of another black pilot, Robert Smalls. Smalls used his knowledge of coastal waters to steer the Confederate transport ship, *The Planter*, to Union naval forces outside of Charleston Harbor in May 1862. After the war, Smalls realized that if he settled in Charleston, his activities would be hindered by the city's resentful white population. So he returned to his native city, Beaufort, and became a Republican politician and US representative renowned for his energy in defending full citizenry and the franchise for African American men. Paradoxically, the ex-Confederate gun-runner Charles C. Leslie, during Reconstruction, accomplished as much for Carolina's African Americans in the commercial sphere as Smalls did in the political one. Service to the Confederacy did not preclude service to the African American community.

In late 1865, the commercial world of Charleston was in a chaotic state. The destruction and disenfranchisement of the old propertied order and the emancipation of the slave populace led to a laissez-faire dystopia. As George Brown Goode recalled in 1888:

> The emancipation proclamation threw a large class of people upon their
> own resources, and the first impulse of freedom led many to forsake their

old masters and plantation life, and to seek employment in the city. With their natural love of boating and fishing many of them drifted into the fishers as a desirable way of obtaining a livelihood. Finding their earnings equal to those of any other class, and the work usually light, the number of fishermen has gradually increased until in 1880 there were nearly 600 people either catching or handling fish during some portion of the year, with about 1,700 people depending upon them for support. Of this entire number, 94 per cent are negroes, about 4 per cent are Spaniards, and only 2 per cent are [white] Americans.[15]

One prewar fish seller remained in the city with sufficient resources to restart business, J. S. Terry, whose connections with the Chesapeake oystermen enabled him to reboot the shellfish market in Charleston. His Norfolk connection proved invaluable because the Civil War had wrought a complete transformation in the Charleston labor market.[16] Terry was white. The fishing freedmen didn't want a white boss or broker superintending the sale of their catch; indeed, most sold to black women street vendors, who saturated the city with so much product that a free fall in prices would take place with each visitation of fish to the coastal waters.

A second consequence of the increase in fishermen was the decimation of fish populations. If antebellum shad was imported by northern vessels hauling the catch from northern rivers, the postwar period saw shad come to Charleston from the Edisto, caught by stringing nets across the entire river, intercepting the season's breeding run. By 1869 the depopulation had grown so critical that the South Carolina legislature passed "An Act for the better protection of Migratory Fish," outlawing the entire blockage of rivers and streams with nets and an imposing moratorium days on fishing every week.[17] The number of moratorium days were increased in two successive emendations of the bill in 1871 and 1872.

Furthermore, a condition of outlawry prevailed on the waters among the boatmen, each fisherman striving to advance his chances, violating traditional grounds and beds, and engaging in piracy and theft. In January 1868, Lopez and Leslie fell victim to a theft sufficiently large to make the columns of the *Charleston Daily News*. The news story's tone was jocular, but the contents singularly informative:

Piscatorial: There are some disciples of the gentle Isaac who like to lure the finny tribe from their native element, but others more impetuous, continue to catch them when at school and induce them to enter a net which at once encloses them. Those hauls are frequently quite large, and in order to secure the fish they are put in a floating trap and brought from the fishing banks to the city. One of these traps, belonging to Lopes & Leslie, well-known fishmongers, containing nearly twelve-hundred fine blackfish, was stolen from the head of union Warf on Thursday night. The Thief endeavored to secure another trap which was fastened near by, but was frustrated. The loss was almost irreparable, for though as good fish were in the sea as ever came out of it, yet they were like Mrs. Glasee's hare, they had to be caught before they were cooked, and many of the customers of Lopes & Leslie were constrained to do without their fish dinners.[18]

Much can be adduced from this report: Lopez and Leslie concentrated their retail business in the market, rather than on the streets as the newly free black fishermen did, and they had done so sufficiently long before 1868 to become "well-known" in town. They had the vessels and skills to harvest vast quantities of oceanic fish and transport them over ten miles of sea to Charleston Harbor. Their competitors who attempted to steal the fish lacked the competence to manage the nets and traps, losing the catch. Further things can be inferred: the quantities alluded to were sufficiently large to determine the town price of fish. Besides controlling quantity of supply, they had the advantage of superior quality, keeping their fish alive in the Cooper River until the stalls needed supply; the independent fishermen transported dead fish caught on hand lines the ten miles to Charleston and had them carted about the city streets until being sold. Under the circumstances, it is easy to infer how Leslie asserted his dominance over the community of fishermen. He apparently offered an either/or to his freedman competitors—either ally with him by giving him first offering of a catch, or be undersold by him and left with unsold perishing product. Allying would bring immediate benefits. He paid suppliers immediately in cash and kept his word on every contract made. This policy became codified in an advertising slogan addressed to customers and suppliers: "All orders promptly attended to. Terms cash or city acceptance."

Cash, credibility, and market muscle did much to impose a growing order of the freedman's fleet around the Lopez and Leslie partnership. But a further dimension of this rationalization may be discerned in Leslie's reference for horizontal rather than hierarchical relationships in business and society. Leslie was not the self-interested individualist adventurer beloved by the celebrators of free-market capitalism. Instead, he believed the betterment of groups of persons formed into institutions and bound by charters, creeds, and contracts should be his directive.

Leslie particularly sought to concretize the social and political gains that had emerged for African Americans with Reconstruction in institutions, and he participated directly in the formation of several of them. When the Grand Lodge of South Carolina of the Prince Hall Masons organized in Charleston in 1867, Leslie was the prime local mover and undertook the post of grand secretary.[19] He would be instrumental in the lodge's support for past National Grand Master Richard H. Gleaves in his successful bid to be elected lieutenant governor of South Carolina over lapsed Prince Hall Mason and black nationalist Martin Delany. In 1869 Leslie was the moving force in securing the charter for the Unity and Friendship Society, a benevolent association that insured the welfare and burial of members.[20] He formed a partnership group with several black merchants and artisans to petition the South Carolina legislature for the right to mine phosphate on the Coosaw River.[21] He combined with the group of black Episcopalians who formed St. Mark's Church and would be elected a vestryman.[22] In the world of business, Leslie thrived by contracting partnership. By 1870 the vessels that plied the waters off Carolina had one of four relationships with Leslie: they were part-owned by Leslie through partnership arrangements; they maintained informal but routine contractual relations with Leslie; they were operated by Leslie's rival, J. S. Terry, or by white entrepreneurs in the sport fishing-for-hire business; or they were remnant independent freedman operators who attempted to sell directly to the public through street vendors.

Central to the Lopez and Leslie business was the reconstituted smack fleet, a Charleston-based flotilla replacing the Yankee fishing vessels that dominated the antebellum harvest. "Charleston is no longer dependent upon the northern fishermen, but is supplied chiefly by her own citizens; and instead of the fifteen northern smacks of 1860, there is now but one, with ten addition owned in Charleston, seven of which fish during the entire year."[23] Lopez and Leslie both owned vessels (Leslie's smack was the *Thomas R. Crocker*) and existed in partnership arrangements with others, such as with Captain Samuel M. Corker in his failed effort to create a Menhaden fishery in Carolina waters.[24] Certain of these were used in the shipping trade off-loading product at coastal towns in North Carolina, South Carolina, and Georgia for railroad shipment to the interior. Leslie also put product onto the steamers transporting market vegetables to Philadelphia, New York, and Boston.

Besides refracting influence through partnerships and institutions, Leslie accrued power and wealth by happenstance and by one act of direct initiative. In 1870 his partner Lopez died, so the whole business devolved to his hands. When the market commissioners in 1869 determined to relocate the fish market as part of a major rearrangement of the market, converting the old fish market to the market scale house,[25] they built a new covered area for seafood across East Bay from the bulk of the city market. Editorialists dubbed the project a boondoggle and noted the reluctance of vendors to move into the new premises. It stood vacant some months, being used to store petroleum and other dangerous fluids coming into the market. In 1870, after securing a very favorable rent rate, Leslie moved his sellers in, leasing stalls one and two, the most conspicuous in the market. He maintained his office on 24 Market Street.

Ensconced in a building more convenient to water, Leslie determined to renovate the fish business by greatly expanding the category of marketable product. In the era before the war, the mosquito fleet had caught and sold porgy, scup, and adult drum to poor whites and blacks on the wharves around coastal Carolina. These "trash" fish had not come to market. Leslie wished to bring everyone, poor or rich, to the market, so he devoted stall space to less desirable fish sold by the string at low prices. To attract high-end trade, he expanded the offering beyond the standard six varieties offered before the war. Blackfish remained the best seller, but Leslie promoted the taste for pompano, jacks, red snappers, bastard snappers, grunts, bream, squirrelfish, and hake. Variety when added to low price proved magnetic to a broad public. Because of this expansion, Leslie found himself increasingly involved in the shellfish trade.

Because many of these fish preferred shrimp to every other bait, Leslie and rival Terry were greatly interested in the shrimp fishery that operated from April until mid-November. As fishing became a local industry, shrimping expanded until two hundred persons were involved in it. Those shrimp not used as bait were carried into the Charleston streets, distributed to vendors, who cried out for custom on the city streets.[26] (Because shrimp did not fall under market regulation in the city ordinances, it could be sold anywhere.) It became ubiquitous in season, and its availability stimulated the culinary exploitation of the crustacean in the city and particularly in hotel restaurants.

By 1880 the expansion of supply, labor, and demand attracted commercial rivals. Terry remained a constant—and the Terry family would remain in the fish market until evicted by the city government in the 1920s. But new players entered the scene—M. Alsina, J. DeAntonio, T. L. Marshal, and S. Shivers. Leslie's advantage over these new brokers was his curiosity. The rewards of expanding variety set Leslie questing for more product. He informed boatmen and smack crews to show him anything unusual caught during the fishing trips. Sometimes they produced creatures no one had ever seen or heard tell of. He would disgorge the fish's stomach to see what it ate. He inquired as to the whereabouts of its capture and recorded the information on a maritime chart kept in his office.[27]

To supplement his practical knowledge, Leslie began reading scientific literature during the 1870s, studying particularly John Edwards Holbrook's *Ichthyology of South Carolina* (1855). One of Leslie's regular customers was Dr. G. E. Manigault of the College of Charleston, a marine scientist who gathered specimens at Leslie's stalls. Perhaps he suggested that Leslie reach out to members of the ichthyological community about fish in Carolina waters. When George Brown Goode, curator of the US National Museum, visited Charleston in 1878, he used Leslie as his guide, sailing from Charleston Harbor to collect the Charleston bream, the bastard snapper, and the black grunt.[28] Later in the year, Leslie corresponded with Goode about menhaden.[29] At Goode's request, Leslie shipped a specimen of the pinfish to Dr. T. H. Bean of the Smithsonian.[30] He assisted the National Museum's collector R. E. Earil in hunting for hake and kingfish in 1880. Sometime before 1880, Leslie communicated with Professor David Jordan and his protégé Charles H. Gilbert[31] at the University of Indiana just as they were undertaking their landmark survey of the fishes of the Pacific coast. In 1880, when Jordan returned to consolidate their collections and data at Indiana, Gilbert headed south, continuing to collect along the Pacific coast of Central America. He crossed the isthmus and continued collecting through the Gulf of Mexico. In the summer of 1882, he arrived at Charleston, intent on making it his headquarters for a protracted stay. He immediately contacted Dr. Manigault of the College of Charleston and Charles C. Leslie.

Leslie arranged for Gilbert to travel in the fishing smacks. But the scientist found the market as rich a place for specimen collecting. Leslie's expansion of the fish offerings available in the stalls made Charleston the richest locally sourced bourse for seafood in the United States.[32] We can reconstruct what appeared in the market from Gilbert's report in the *Proceedings of the U.S. National Museum*. In the prefatory remarks, Gilbert testified that "especial acknowledgments are due to Mr. Charles C. Leslie for aid of various kinds rendered Mr. Gilbert while in Charleston. It was only through his co-operation that the present collection was made possible."[33]

Publication of Gilbert's report made Leslie a known resource among the scientific community. Requests for specimens came from Harvard University, the Smithsonian, the University of Cincinnati, the Academy of Natural Sciences at Philadelphia, and the University of Indiana. Dr. David Jordan, while president of the University of Indiana and shortly before accepting the call to become the first president of Stanford University, published a set of "Notes on a Collection of Fishes Sent by Mr. Charles C. Leslie from Charleston, SC" (1887), clarifying the categorization of flounders and other flat fishes.[34] Leslie's peculiar merit in the eyes of professional ichthyologists lay in an acquaintance with Atlantic fishes so comprehensive that he alone of laymen knew whether a rare fish was new to knowledge or not.

Leslie's correspondence about issues concerning the American fishery appeared in national publications throughout the 1880s. Most often, he conveyed information, such as the depletion of blackfish populations off Cape Hatteras in June 1882.

We have noticed for the past four or five years the scarcity of blackfish in the summer, and especially this summer. The smacks here have not made their expenses for the past two months. I have just seen Capt. S. M.

Corker, one of our most expert blackfish fishermen, who has been in the business for thirty years. He states that he has never seen them so scarce as they are, and that in former years they could catch enough to pay expenses during the summer. Captain Corker told me also, about the first of June, a vessel came into this port; her captain reported that he sailed through acres of codfishes floating belly up between Hatteras and Cape Henry. The fishes were not dead, but very weak.[35]

Leslie realized that the society of maritime scientists operated by an economy, predicated on the exchange of information, rather than cash. He never demanded payment for specimens shipped to universities and museums and personally covered shipping costs. But after he had put numbers of persons in his debt, he asked for information that would benefit his business in Charleston. In 1884 he dispatched a letter to the United States Fish Commission, which it circulated through the scientific community.

"ON THE CULTIVATION OF SOFT SHELL CRABS" BY CHARLES C. LESLIE

In our harbor and along our coast are found millions of the common blue sea-crab, and I have for the past two years been considering why it is that, with the number that are to be found here, we cannot get a supply of soft-shell crabs. The same crabs are found along the coast of Maryland and other States adjacent, and yet I have hunted and failed to find many. At one time I found three and at another time four. But in no instance have I found a half dozen, even after hunting a whole day.

I would be greatly obliged to you if you would kindly tell me if there is any artificial way by which I could secure a supply.

Charleston, S.C., April 24, 1884.

REPLY BY PROFESSOR BAIRD

If you have the same blue crab (which I presume to be the case) as the one furnishing the "soft-shells" of the Chesapeake Bay, there is no reason why you should not find them in this condition, which is merely their state after the old shell has been thrown off and the new one is being formed.

You might try the experiment of penning up the crabs in a shoal pond, fed by the tide, into which small fish and other marine refuse can be brought by the tide through a grating.

By taking flat stones, bundles of brush, or other substances of a similar character, and laying them over the bottom, you furnish a refuge under which the crabs can crawl. By lifting up these branches from time to time you can find the crabs under them.

This process has, I believe, been actually made the subject of a patent, but the inventor is dead, and the patent, probably, has long since run out.

Of course the defenseless crabs are readily devoured by their stronger relations, and it is therefore advisable to keep them where they can be properly protected from such destruction.

Washington, D.C., April 26, 1884.[36]

In 1885 Leslie organized the soft-shell crab nursery on the Cooper River in Mount Pleasant. Leslie's expansion and regularization of supply of this shellfish took business away from his chief rival, J. S. Terry.

During the last twenty years of his business, from 1885 to 1906, Leslie flourished. He expanded service into South Carolina's inland towns and cities—Sumter, Georgetown, Edgefield, Columbia, Greenville—providing wholesale and retail "Fish, Game, Oysters, Turtles, Terrapins, Poultry, Eggs, &c."[37] The game, poultry, and eggs came from inland suppliers. His coastal boatmen gathered the turtles, shellfish, and fish. One can understand the market logic of bringing the harvest of the ocean to the interior, and the harvest of the forest to the city; the 1880s expansion into the poultry and egg business is more difficult to fathom, except that Charleston's demand for chicken seemed inexhaustible. Wealth accrued and Leslie made use of it. He used a portion of his profits to underwrite a savings and loan for African American workingmen. He also contributed funds to the Avery Normal Institute, Charleston's academy for the sons and daughters of the African American elite.

Nothing symbolized his eminence more than his purchase in 1904 of the Kohne Mansion at 72 Anson Street, a three-and-a-half-story brick side-hall pile with vast piazzas across the front. This was a big house and was meant to serve as big houses do, as both monument and homestead for his family. Shortly after the purchase, sometime in 1906, Leslie sold his business to Englishman Thomas W. Carroll and retired. He enjoyed entertaining in his mansion and whiling away his time reading and doing church work. He died two days after turning seventy in April 1911. His daughter Julia Brennan Leslie would preside over the homestead until the 1950s, becoming an elder and storyteller in Charleston's African American community and continuing the family's strong support of St. Mark's Episcopal Church. By any register—social eminence, public beneficence, personal wealth, expertise, repute in the world of marine biology— Charles C. Leslie mattered. He was an exemplary African American entrepreneur, a lay scholar of marine life, and a champion of an institutionalized black presence in civic life in the South during a period of racial animosity.

Leslie's life transit—his nearly uninterrupted ascendancy to wealth, social influence, and professional reputation—lacks the sorts of conspicuous confrontations with racial prejudice that we see in the careers of other major African American figures in the South. There is no attempt to diminish his potency by a white propertied class attempting to reassert political authority, such as the engineered bribery trial directed at US Representative Robert Smalls in 1877. Leslie grounded his place in Charleston on multiple foundations: his knowledge of fish and fish selling, his money, his strict adherence to market ethics in terms of contracts, judgment of catch, and employment of approved public scales and measures. He had schooled himself in law, particularly regarding property, partnerships, and the chartering of corporations. Certain venues in the public world of Charleston may have been closed to him, but he had taken pains to bring into existence a penumbra of associations that could serve the African American world as a public sphere. His recognition by the national community of marine scientists and his regular appearance in print made his voice something not contained by the parochial conversations of the city. Did his service as a Confederate gun-runner earn Leslie the benign patronage of Charleston's old white families? It certainly didn't hurt, yet it was probably less consequential than the fact that he consistently provided more types of fresh fish than any seller. Until the 1880s, most of the butchers and vegetable sellers in the market were black; so patronizing a black seller was the usual course of business for everyone in the city. No other African American in the region enjoyed the sort of success that

Leslie did; so one might be tempted to attribute the sort of exceptional enterprising spirit and capitalist genius to him that a De Voe would. Yet I've tried to suggest that Leslie was hardly the auto-dynamic enterpriser of capitalist mythology. The association, network, corporation, partnership always framed his actions, diffusing risk, insulating him from public animosity, sharing rewards, and enjoying cooperative betterment.

What Leslie accomplished with the fish market was unparalleled. It depended entirely on his ability to enter into contractual and partnership relationships with the freedman's mosquito fleet and the smack fleet of fishermen. This could have happened only on a limited scale during the antebellum period, given the northern ownership of the smack fleet and the bound status of numbers of African American fishermen. Leslie's ability to offer the city so extensive a choice of fish depended upon his own willingness to test the breadth of the market, the natural bounty of the coastal waters, and the trusting cooperation of a community of watermen willing to indulge Leslie's curiosity. The liberty of that community to do so gave rise to plentitude.

In terms of culinary history what does this story suggest? Just this: that the Reconstruction, not the antebellum period, was the era in which the fullness of Charleston cuisine came into being. While a wealth of meat, vegetables, and fruits existed in the market prior to the Civil War, the bounty of the waters and game were known primarily to country plantation cooking. After the Civil War, Leslie's fish market, Campsen's mills, and the rise of truck farming on the Charleston Neck concatenated to supply the ingredients that we now recognize as the signatures of Charleston cuisine—the marriage of seafood, grains, and vegetables found in dishes such as shrimp and grits, crab pilau, and limping Susan.

TEN   *The New York Market: National Supply and Demand*

Two years after Appomattox, the butcher-antiquarian Thomas F. De Voe noted a revolution in the operation of the New York market. At the beginning of the nineteenth century, the producer and consumer often met face-to-face in the marketplace. In 1867, he noted, the "producer is often hundreds of miles in one direction, while the consumer may be as many hundred in another, from the mart at which the productions were sold and purchased. Through the course of the year, the products of the North, South, East, and West, are to be found in our large public market-places; from which great quantities are disposed of, to be consumed in other cities, towns, or villages, or on the many ocean or rivers steamers or other vessels, as well as in foreign countries."[1]

Cities have never been self-provisioning enclaves. While one can speak of a locavore countryside of farmsteads and towns, when a populous urban center requires provisioning, the multitude of people needing food demands sourcing from beyond. At the beginning of the nineteenth century, when New York, Boston, Philadelphia, Providence, and Charleston were not greatly populous, demand could be served by a constellation of glasshouse gardeners and suburban farmers. Indeed, the earliest American horticultural guides—Bernard McMahon's *American Garden Calendar* (1806) and William Cobbett's *American Gardener* (1823)—envisioned greenhouse provisioners as their prime readership. De Voe chronicled the moment just before the Civil War when the great cities of the Northeast commanded the service of a nation to feed them.

A supply system that brought distant and sometimes unfamiliar things to the stalls made caveat emptor the rule of purchase. A customer did not see or know the producer to trust him or her. Adulteration of prepared foods, misrepresentation of meats, water injection of melons to balloon weight, and other shady practices required vigilance and knowledge. No governmental agency policed the food system, no professional association set standards of behavior for producers or sellers, and the various municipal governments tended to minimize regulation to questions of weights, hours, rentals, and fees. Into the laissez-faire hubbub of the city markets, De Voe sought to inject reason by supplying each seller and shopper with an aid, *The Market Assistant, containing a brief description of every article of human food sold in the public markets of New York, Boston, Philadelphia, and Brooklyn, including the various domestic and wild animals, poultry, game, fish, vegetable, fruits, etc.*

Some idea of the purposes and quality of information that De Voe supplies can be had from his treatment of melons.

MELONS

It is said that there are but two species of this fruit—at least, that we cultivate successfully: the rough or embroidered coated is called the *musk-melon*, and those with a smooth thick skin are called *water-melons*. These are divided into many varieties. From the *musk-melon* are the *nutmegs, citron, cantaloup, pineapple,* etc. Of these, the citron is most valued for its sweetness, richness, and high flavor. They appear from the South—usually from Charleston and Savannah—about the 1st of August. The nutmeg is preferred by most people for its high musky flavor and large size, and the skin appears as if covered with a net, ribbed or crossed like the nutmeg spice. They are in season a short time previous to the former, and are found more numerous. The cantaloup is the first ripe *musk-melon,* but it is not so much cultivated as the two former. It, however, enjoys a sweet and pleasant flavor. The *musk-melon* appears not to have been generally cultivated around New York, prior to 1818. . . . Among the best varieties of the *water-melon* are the Spanish, mountain sweet, orange, Carolina, apple-pie, citron water-melon, etc. The Spanish variety is certainly one of the best, being very sweet, rich, and excellent. The skin is of a dark green, and slightly marbled rind, moderately thick, with a red, solid flesh. This variety is extensively cultivated on Long Island, New Jersey, etc.

The orange *water-melon* is of a round shape, and of a smaller size, and, when ripe, must be cut through the skin like an orange, and the rind taken off without breaking the pulp, then divided by cutting between the lobes, when it will be found delicious eating. The Carolina *water-melons* are very good here when fresh, and are found here in the latter part of July. The citron *water-melon* ripens late, and is quite small and round, with a very thick skin or rind, and generally used for preserves.

Apple-pie *water-melon.*—This Japan species of melon is but lately introduced here, and appears, with the aid of a little lemon-juice, to make excellent apple-pie, or one that you cannot hardly tell the difference. It will keep quite well all winter.

To judge *water-melons,* when ripe and fit to eat, they should, when pressing them between the hands and knees, make a sort of cracking noise, and, when knocked on by the knuckles, will emit a sort of hollow sound, but never by their great weight. It, however, requires practice to judge them properly. (380–81)

De Voe's treatment of watermelons reveals the market gap, the disconnect between consumers and plant breeders. Buyers in New York, Boston, and Philadelphia in 1867 looked to the old established types of watermelon—the mountain sweet and the Carolina—varieties whose liabilities had southern horticulturists creating better-tasting alternatives in the 1850s. Nathaniel Bradford's Bradford watermelon, Augusta, Georgia's rattlesnake watermelon, and the Summer brothers new introductions—the Ravenscroft, Souter white, and Pomaria watermelons—may have been the gold standard for melons in the antebellum and Reconstruction Charleston and Savannah markets, but northern demand remained fixed on the two names that had in the 1830s and '40s come to define watermelon—hefty, oblong, green skinned, red fleshed. Icon trumped taste for the northern buyer. These newer, tastier melons did not take hold until circa 1868.

New York's preference cannot be ascribed to ignorance. Northern horti-culturists knew and celebrated the superlative sugary Bradford, Ravens-croft, Odell's, Pomaria, and Souter melons. Indeed, Fearing Burr Jr., New England's greatest student of edible plants, featured these varieties in his landmark *The Field and Garden Vegetables of America* (1865).[2] But a law of mass markets was at work in post–Civil War New York: familiar branding trumps all other considerations in the sale of products for which a demand has been established.

It was easier to get someone to purchase a novelty such as an apple-pie watermelon,[3] since it performed an unusual function as pie filling, than to buy a variety that supplanted one of the tried-and-true brands. Indeed, a new breed of watermelon only attracted buyers at the market if it (1) ap-peared some weeks earlier in the season than the standard brand, (2) cost substantially lower than the standard brand, or (3) permitted a new culi-nary treatment of the product.

Where taste and other aesthetic considerations *did* bear was in the seed markets. The foremost devotees of taste were kitchen gardeners growing their own plots of vegetables, tending their own orchards, and maintain-ing their own herb and medicinal plant beds. These gardeners tended to be suburban, townsfolk, or literate agriculturists in the countryside—not city dwellers. These subscribed to the farming journals, belonged to the agricultural societies, participated in the annual regional contests of su-perlative vegetables and fruits, heeded who won, secured a place on the mailing lists of the important seed brokers, and concerned themselves with the processing of the food they grew. America's great seed companies expanded by appealing to the imaginations of these growers/consumers.

A starker contrast between the minds of the city market consumer and the grower/consumer can be had by glancing briefly at De Voe's entry on squash. A rather bald demonstration of the dominion of brand conscious-ness, it lists names, no descriptions. What *did* receive mention was the date of the first appearance at the market. "The varieties of this vegetable are very numerous and most extensively cultivated. Among the most esteemed are the Boston marrow, Valparaiso, summer and winter crook-necked, yel-low butter, acorn, or Turkish cap, apple, custard, early bush, etc. The latter is one of the earliest, or first ready for use, about the middle of June, the yellow butter about the 1st of July, the Boston marrow about the 1st of

August, and some of the varieties continue by proper care to be good until the 1st of January" (352). When we turn to James J. H. Gregory's *Squashes: How to Grow Them*, published in New York the same year as *The Market Assistant*, we encounter the qualities of the various sorts. Each variety is illustrated with an engraving and supplied a history. The first listed of De Voe's squashes, the Boston marrow, appeared as the autumnal marrow squash in Gregory. The horticulturist informed his readers that it "was introduced to the public by Mr. J. M. Ives, in the years 1831–32. When introduced, it was a small sized squash, weighing five or six pounds, fine grained and dry, with an excellent flavor. Marketmen found that by crossing with the African and South American varieties, they could increase the size of the original Marrow; they did this without troubling themselves about any risk of deteriorating the quality, and I doubt not that much of the present inferior quality of the Marrow squash is due to this vicious crossing."[4]

Reading De Voe, one would not know that the first-listed "market favorite" had been undergoing a quality decline. Gregory supplied that verdict and a cause—"vicious crossing" by "Marketmen." By marketmen, Gregory did not refer to city vendors such as De Voe, but market farmers—persons who cultivated exclusively to supply city demand. These constituted a separate contingent of the plant breeding and growing community—a group driven by profit rather than any intuition of what constitutes an ideal plant. The marketmen had opted to increase size, knowing that family economies (we should recall that the 1860 census indicated the average family size in New York to have been 6.2 persons) placed a premium on quantity; quality was sacrificed. Gregory stood as a defender of quality. This is the invariable role of the specialist seedsman during the mid-nineteenth century. The horticultural specialist projected himself or herself as arbiter of vegetable or flower aesthetics—taste, conformation, appearance, size, texture, and robustness. The vendor, the consumer, even the cook might sacrifice taste for something else (size, good looks, price, familiarity, earliness to market, shelf life). But breeders, such as Gregory, Colonel A. G. Summer, Hiram Sibley, B. Riggs, James Fick, D. M. Ferry, W. Atlee Burpee, and Peter Henderson, in their quests for superlative produce, sought the most exquisite tastes, heeding the desires of the amateur community beyond the corps of market gardeners.[5]

Sometimes the kitchen gardener and the specialist breeder created varieties of vegetable so distinctive that the major markets and the seedsmen embraced them. Gregory had turned the Hubbard squash into a New England staple in the antebellum period. The Jackson white potato, developed in Maine in the 1860s, improved the popular Carter potato and became the standard market potato grown in northern states. The Nansemond sweet potato, bred on the eastern shore of Virginia late in the antebellum period, became the favorite gardening and market potato in the North (sometimes renamed as the Jersey), where cooks preferred boiling to baking as a mode of preparation. Dutton eight-row field corn became a milling standard in northern and midwestern states. Many of these varieties achieved their dominion by the assiduous promotion of seed companies, several of which had developed a national clientele by the mid-nineteenth century.

While a metropolitan food market might have a nationwide source of supply, the agricultural and horticultural seed markets, as we have seen, were international. Gardeners and plant breeders regularly looked to the best creations of the best breeders in Europe, Japan, and South America. The group of Prussian breeders (the Schmidt, Benary, and Lorenz families, particularly), concentrated about Erfurt, Thuringia, enjoyed the highest repute in American growing circles—and seed for their finest creations (the early Erfurt red cabbage, Erfurt's early and dwarf mammoth cauliflower, Erfurt's early celeriac, the Erfurt kohlrabi) were eagerly sought by growers. The Parisian Louis de Vilmorin, head of the family seed company Vilmorin-Andrieux, may have been the most influential scientific breeder of vegetables in the world during the antebellum period, offering improved versions of a range of garden cultivars from beets to the cardoon.[6] Russian rhubarb, garlic, cucumbers, and sunflowers were embraced by American growers. Every major seed introduction into British horticulture found an American following. Of these various foreign introductions, few became market stars—the Arguenteuil asparagus from France, the Charleston Wakefield cabbage from Britain, the Erfurt kohlrabi.

In 1867 De Voe described a market somewhat hidebound in its support of familiar vegetables. Yet he also showed big cities avid in their desire for superior meat, game, fowl, and fish. In nineteenth-century markets, butchers were characteristically the most forward public persons, active in civic life, politics, and legal actions. Butcher De Voe had the additional talent of being well-read, an autodidact who fell in love with old books and manuscripts and who before the war wrote the history of New York's markets from Dutch beginnings to the eve of the Civil War.[7] Because he knew the old ways so thoroughly, the distinctive character of innovations struck him with particular force. His introduction to *The Market Assistant* supplies an interesting reassurance to the reader about the guild pride and sense of responsibility among butchers, telling of their initiative in keeping "casualty flesh" (livestock dead by accident or disease) off the market. Yet it warns of the general unreliability of what any vendor says concerning the quality of the produce being displayed.[8] The hungry ears of the buyers have incited the sellers' hyperbole: "To induce them to buy the dealers must bespatter their articles with a dozen falsehoods, and sometimes fifteen or twenty per cent above the market price, before the purchasers are fully satisfied with their bargains."[9]

What strikes a twenty-first-century reader about De Voe's treatment of meat is his inattention to breeds of cattle. According to the butcher, what influences the taste of beef is the cut of meat. Quality also depends upon whether the meat comes from (in order of fineness) a spayed heifer from four to seven years old, a steer of bullock (never worked) from four to six years old, a free martin (barren heifer) eight years old or younger, an ox from five to eight years old, a heifer three to four years old, a cow from three to eight years old, a stag from three to eight years old, or a bull from two to six years old. Finally, quality depends upon whether the livestock was grazed on grass (producing tender but relatively flavorless beef) or stall fed on grain and roots (more nutritious and wholesome to De Voe's mind). Whether a Holstein heifer or a Highlands cow provided the meat does not enter into the butcher's consideration. Given the amount of ink spent on arguing the various advantages of breeds exhibited in the New England cattle fairs of the antebellum period, one might wonder at the inattention, except that the chief points of argumentation dealt with milk production and quality. The husbanding of cattle varieties in the early nineteenth century directly related to the promotion of dairying in the United States.

More surprising is the absence of comment on breeds of hogs in De Voe. Farmers bred pigs exclusively for meat. By the 1830s, several breeds had become established in various regions: the clean white Irish grazier;

the large-bodied, small-hammed Leicestershire; the varicolored Wo-
bourn, favored in Kentucky; the light-skinned Westchester found south
of Philadelphia; the China; the Mackay, an improved China popular
around Boston; the dark-colored Berkshire; the Hospital, a Massachusetts cross between the Mackay and Berkshire; the naked Neapolitan; and
the black Essex and Suffolk pigs that Colonel Adam G. Summer made
popular in South Carolina and Georgia. Breeders such as A. B. Allen of
Buffalo determined to create hogs weighing a half ton, importing champion Berkshires such as "Windsor Castle" from England and breeding
them into behemoths.[10] The Berkshire pig first made a mark on the minds
of American drovers in 1832 when imported animals came into New York,
Kentucky, and Massachusetts. The breed dominated the imaginations of
livestock breeders for the next two decades. (Colonel Summer purchased
New York–bred boars and sows of the Berkshire early in the 1840s.)

What concerned breeders was size, speed to maturity, efficiency in
turning feed to meat, and ease of maintenance. No one cultivated breeds
with the conviction that a variety's flesh tasted superior to the others. Indeed, the prevailing theory concerning swine flesh was that its flavor depended upon what you fed hogs, particularly in the months immediately
before slaughter. Those who wished to earn a flavor premium for their
meat gorged their hogs on apples or parsnips.[11] De Voe, who had a market
butcher's fixation on the reliable uniformity of product, favored the grain
feeding of hogs rather than masting. He wrote in *The Market Assistant*, "If
the animals are allowed to run at large . . . eating whatever they can pick
up—their uncleanly character is too well known, both as to habit and the
filth and animals substances they select for food—there can be no doubt
that pork from such animals offers unfit and unwholesome food" (78). De
Voe's trepidations have grounds, for certain lazy stockmen allowed swine
to feed on the farm dung heaps. It was the market butcher paying a premium on "regular" pork that compelled increasing numbers of farmers to
feed swine on grain and root vegetables in stalls and yards. Only in areas
of the South did a taste for masted hogs remain into the twentieth century, giving rise to the peanut-fed hog in Virginia in the 1910s and '20s.

Customers did not commonly encounter fresh pork during the summer
months, because of fears of spoilage. Indeed, the market for cured pork—
hams and shoulders—or pickled pork in a pork barrel proved greater than

for just butchered pork. Massive shipments of Western beef, too, came to market salted and pickled. Jerking—air drying sheets of salted pickled beef—was common from 1820 to 1840, according to De Voe, because it was the one way to make diseased beef and game vendible. This negative association eventually killed the demand when large quantities of corned and salted beef appeared in New York in the 1840s. Of the preserved cuts of meat, the ham won the highest regard. Only cider rivaled the ham as a product of expert artisanal manufacture in the farmsteads of the United States.[12] Yet the glory of the New York market was not cured domestic flesh, but freshly harvested fish, fowl, and game.

THE WILD SIDE

Wild meat held a peculiar exotic appeal to city buyers, the hotel and club cooks driving the demand for novelties; game immediately distinguished hotel meals from those served by even blue book cooks in New York and Boston town houses. De Voe described the appearance of antelope, badgers, bears, beavers, bighorn sheep, bison, black-tailed deer, caribou, deer, elks, foxes, groundhogs, guinea pigs, hares, lynx, moose, mountain goats, muskrats, opossums, otters, panthers, porcupines, raccoons, skunks, squirrels, and venison, noting frequency or rarity of appearance at the market and palatability. (Lynx did not appear at market, but De Voe wished to report its edibility from trappers' accounts.) Yet the wealth of the metropolitan market was not registered in game so much as in fish and fowl. The fish section, including shellfish, operated as a shopper's field guide, informing the cook on the basis of description about the color, size, and configuration of fish, shellfish, and turtles. Freshwater creatures appeared alongside the denizens of salt water in an abundance that would only be surpassed in the 1870s by Charles C. Leslie's stall at the Charleston Market. The fowl and game birds would be unequaled in their variety and abundance.

City epicureanism, the cult of fine dining nurtured at Delmonico's and the Union Club, placed a premium on certain game birds: the canvasback duck, the woodcock, the ricebird, the ruffed grouse, and the quail (in that order) comprised the chief wildfowl. The demand for these items marshaled steamships and railroads from the South and West to supply the city tables. High prices gave rise to a creature that would become, by the end of the century, the scourge of the waterways: the market gunner. In 1867 De Voe could already read the historical consequences of the culinary mystique surrounding these birds. The canvasback duck, "the finest and choicest wild duck known for the table," owed its distinctive flavor to its diet of water celery, upon which it feeds during the late autumn in the eastern waterways. The flavor depended upon its feeding, so its season was short—late November to the first week in January—heightening its scarcity. Indeed, the rarity and fame were so great, that large numbers were shipped "by our swift steamers to Europe."[13] Prices in 1867 rose to $3 for a pair of canvasbacks, an amount exceeding by 50 percent any other fowl. He asked how the market could be regularly supplied with canvasbacks during season in the 1860s, when, prior to 1820, few came to the New York market. He then reproduced a report from a Norfolk newspaper about Edward Burroughs of Long Island in Princess Anne County, Virginia. Burroughs had

> twenty men employed constantly since the commencement of the season; and up to the 20th of December, 1856, they had consumed in their vocation twenty-three kegs of gunpowder, with shot in proportion. The ducks which they killed were brought to Norfolk once a week, and piled up in the warehouse of Kemp & Buskey, on Roanoke Square, where, on every Wednesday, they were packed in barrels and shipped for New York by the steamship Jamestown. The number of barrels thus sent off weekly have, up to this time, averaged from fifteen to twenty-five barrels, and one week the number reached as high as thirty-one. They consist of all the varieties of the duck species known in our latitude, such as canvasback, red-heads, mallard, black ducks, sprig-tails, bull-necks, bald-faces (or widgeons), shovellers, etc., to which may be added a good proportion of wild geese."[14]

This indiscriminate harvest of game birds in a region was the hallmark of market gunning. It stood in stark contrast to the sportsman's pursuit of a particular prey, hunting.

Laws existed in most states and some territories defining the hunting season and who could hunt where. Game laws did not, as a rule, limit the kill in season. Because markets abided by the season, yet also served a desire for products not restricted to time of year, poachers and off-season gunners often offered illegal product. The ruffed grouse, for instance, had a two-month season (October and November), but hunting underground brought them to New York at other times, selling them "under the name of owls." De Voe heartily defended the propriety of the law of seasons and cited ill effects of consuming winter grouse, harvested dead from cold or starvation off midwestern fields after huge snowstorms. Such birds, having been "deprived of their ordinary food, become thin, poor, and starved, and are forced to feed upon the leaves of the poisonous evergreens" (159). The ruffed grouse's relative, the pinnated grouse or prairie hen, became after 1852 one of the popular market birds. "Within the last fifteen years they have been brought from the West—Illinois, Iowa, Wisconsin, etc.—in large numbers, in fact, so large as to create a glut in the winter and early spring months. They begin to arrive in October, and continue until the month of April; usually brought in barrels and other packages in a frozen state" (161).

In no other section of De Voe's guide do we see the pressure of historical change more starkly apparent. The rising potencies of demand, the expanding range of the city dollar on rural imagination, the growing hunting pressure on wild populations of birds and animals, the expanding networks of transportation, the shifting domains of the legal and the illegal, and the expanding population of consumers all figure in the entries under "Game Birds." Ironically, one bird appeared in the guide free of De Voe's fretting about supply: the passenger pigeon.

> These numerous birds are found in our markets, both alive and dead, very plenty, and generally cheap in the latter part of September and October; they are also found in less numbers through the winter months. Great numbers are taken alive with nets, cooped up for several weeks, and fed with grain until fat, then brought to our markets as the prices advance; while those that are brought dead have been shot from off the "spar," and sent here at the time of their "flying," which takes place generally in the month of March, when they are going north, and then again in the fall,

about the 15th to the 25th September, when they leave for the Southern climate. Large numbers of the old birds and squabs are sent here from the "West," where they are killed or taken alive at their "roosts."[15]

De Voe's picture of inexhaustible plentitude only gestures at decline in the final pages of his book when his antiquarian memory recalls a moment before the American Revolution when 75,000 pigeons were brought to market in a single week, and when the supply in Boston in 1771 was so great that it drove down the price of all provisions in the market. He does not draw inferences about the disparity of the "great flights" of those years and the normal plentitude of his post–Civil War present. His insensitivity may be attributed to a sense that the game portion of the market was simply a niche. In 1870 the population of New York was 942,292, and Brooklyn, 396,099. Even the storied thousands of birds in a week of the 1770s was a pittance in terms of the meat requisite to feed the population for a day. Only domesticated herds could service the demand for meat. To the extent that game attempted to service this demand, did the wild population of a hunted or fished creature decline.

The market butcher did not see the depredations wrought on the wild; sportsmen did. In the decades after the Civil War, the fisherman and the sport hunter witnessed the depleted trout streams and saw market gunners clubbing thousands of passenger pigeons in their nests. They fought the culture war against the indiscriminate killing of birds and bison. By the end of the century, most states (since the Tenth Amendment of the Constitution acknowledged the regulation of hunting a dimension of a state's policing power) had game laws on the books, indicating who may hunt, what they may hunt, and how they may hunt. The conservation campaign barely managed to halt the killing of bison. It failed to prevent the extinction of the passenger pigeon. In 1895 the New York Market sold its last passenger pigeon. In 1906 the St. Louis Market received a single bird, the last to be sold for meat.

This sad and oft-repeated tale should not distract us from the brutal truth behind the history. The market gunners were attempting to apply in the wild what herdsmen and meat packers were accomplishing in the feedlots and slaughterhouses of America: enacting a level of supply scaled to satisfy the swelling urban population and its rapacious appetites. The city demanded to be fed, and persons further removed from the marketplaces and dinner tables were moved over the course of the century to service that hunger. After the Civil War, the Lowcountry returned to economic viability by becoming the supplier of fruits and vegetables to the urban Northeast, and to New York, particularly. The land where cotton had once been king would become a countryside where asparagus, potatoes, tomatoes, strawberries, and cabbage ruled. Conversely, the Lowcountry imported meat and game from New York, and throughout the South restaurants and hotels boasted that the game served had been secured from New York. Indeed, if one were in an inland city such as Macon, advertising one's connection with the country's capital of cosmopolitanism was a mark of aesthetic ambition: "C. A. Ells & Son . . . are now prepared to supply all, and particular our kind friends who have so liberally patronized us with all the luxuries that can now be obtained in the New York or Savannah Market."[16]

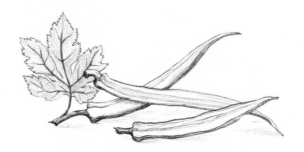

ELEVEN   *Truck Farming*

As Thomas F. De Voe's remarks on antebellum Charleston and Savannah watermelons in the 1850s New York market suggest, the northern city markets began exerting their magnetism upon Lowcountry growers before the Civil War. When peace prevailed after the defeat of the Confederacy in 1865, northern desire for fresh produce revitalized coastal agriculture and injected money into the wrecked southern economy. For the last three decades of the nineteenth century and the first three of the twentieth, the fortunes of the Lowcountry waxed as the urban appetite grew. The Lowcountry became a truck-farming paradise, indeed, *the* truck-farming paradise of America until California supplanted it in the twentieth century.

In 1836 the New York and Charleston Steam Packet Company began shipping mail between Charleston and New York, but the transport of early season vegetables to New York did not occur until the sailing of *The Southerner* (launched 1846) and *The Northerner* (launched 1847). These pioneer coast-wise trading vessels departed every fourteen days from port, making a run in anywhere from fifty-nine to eighty hours, depending upon weather.[1] Because the local market was so robust during the antebellum period, the food trade with New York did not much matter for Charleston producers other than watermelon growers, rice planters, and cotton producers. Carolina's consumers, however, developed a taste for New York butter and cheese. The destruction of the southern economy with the Civil War changed this situation. Necessity made Charleston look northward in 1866, the year when the city's steam packets became the means of servicing the New York market. In that first year after defeat, Charleston shipped 1,800 packages of fruits and vegetables to New York. Every year after in the century, this amount would increase.[2]

Initially, much of the produce shipped northward grew in a 12,000-acre swatch of land on Charleston Neck, between the Ashley and Cooper Rivers, west of the city.[3] Mount Pleasant, too, generated substantial amounts of asparagus and artichokes. In the 1880s, truck farming expanded to James, Johns, and Wadmalaw Islands, south of Charleston. Shipments began in late February, with asparagus, and continued to the fall. The rush, however, began in early April and continued to mid-May, superseded in mid-May when Norfolk's exports flooded the northern markets and undersold Charleston's products. After the steam commerce had established the reputation of Charleston produce in New York, railroads sought the business and by the 1880s had instituted service that could bring items to market in less than forty-eight hours. Produce would be offloaded at Washington, Philadelphia, and New York. Less perishable items went waterborne on the steam packets.

Over the course of the last three decades of the nineteenth century, individual vegetables enjoyed ebbs and flows of demand. The early season tomato, for instance, emerged as a cash crop in the late 1860s, and by 1873 had eclipsed the New Jersey early season produce, driving farmers there to other cultivars.[4] Charleston dominated the mid-1870s early season trade, until canners in the early 1880s perfected cheap preservation of tomatoes and Bermuda shipped its crop three weeks before the Carolina tomatoes ripened.[5] Another victim of the perfection of canning was the trade in early garden peas.

Though William Summer promoted asparagus culture in the Carolina midlands throughout the middle decades of the nineteenth century, it did not become a coastal truck crop until the 1880s, when John Nix and the Jounnet family began growing it. The Jounnets, whose beds were in Mount Pleasant, South Carolina (Christ Church Parish), planted the early giant

Argenteuil, a variety befitting their French background, while their neighbor Nix grew Conover's colossal "until he noticed that his neighbor's Asparagus, under the same conditions, was invariably better than his own."[6] Nix secured roots in 1886 and forwarded some to seedsman Peter Henderson, who branded the variety "Palmetto" and established the important southern cultivar of the late nineteenth century. Nix would make agricultural headlines in the next decade when he first reported the outbreak of asparagus rust in South Carolina. Because of the prestige accorded the vegetables in the great restaurants of the Western world, enormous civic pride attached to asparagus production, and anxiety grew over California's attempt to replicate the truck-farming paradise that the Carolina coast had become. In 1910 a writer for the *Charleston Year Book*, in a rhapsody of boosterism, hymned the vegetable: "Charleston asparagus is the finest grown in the world, and as James Henry Rice, Jr., says, in his story of the truck growing industry to day, 'California can produce nothing comparable to what comes from Christ Church Parish, including men.' Charleston asparagus is served at the principal hotels in New York at 75 cents the helping, and to the Charleston man subsisting on this sort of diet it appeared almost 'a shame to take the money.'"[7] Charleston exported a substantial amount of this vegetable northward. Its quality soon made it the priciest asparagus in the New York markets. Pride precedes a fall. When New Jersey and Delaware decided to make asparagus a cash crop in the 1950s, the low transportation costs to the northeastern city markets undercut that of the Carolina crop. By that time, conventional agriculture and inattention to the quality of the cultivar had lost the Carolina asparagus its cachet. For the last decade, the Fallaw family of Ridge Spring, South Carolina, has been the chief commercial producer in the state.[8] But in 2011, three Lowcountry farmers associated with GrowFood Carolina have planted beds. I have initiated a search for surviving strains of the Palmetto variety and have put GrowFood in contact with suppliers of the classic Argenteuil seed.

Certain steady-seller vegetables brought dependable income from 1866 to the end of the century. New potatoes from Charleston[9] so excited the inexhaustible hunger of New Yorkers that they often commanded $6 per bushel, a stratospheric price after the Civil War.[10] In 1871 one Charleston Neck farmer working a forty-acre plot reported a $15,000 profit in potatoes. This same farmer also produced cucumbers, tomatoes, peas, beans, onions, cabbages, and sweet potatoes from the same land. A reporter for the *Fruit Recorder and Cottage Gardener* magazine calculated the 1871 potato revenue for Charleston at $200,000.[11] While the dollar amount of the crop would be reported intermittently during the heyday of the truck farmer, various state and national governmental bodies regularly published the records of the amount of produce shipped by rail and steam packet. The number of containers was the metric recorded.[12] In 1883, 51,460 barrels of potatoes were shipped; in 1884, 45,349; and by 1885, 60,000.[13]

One reason why the dollar amounts for profit were difficult to calculate and reported only intermittently was the avoidance of record keeping for the payment of laborers working the farms. An 1884 *Charleston and News Courier* report on the "Industrial Life of South Carolina" sheds some light on the labor needed to manage the fields. The report noted that laborers were hired on a job basis at a daily rate of pay. Though rates fluctuated according to the labor supply, with a paucity of workers in spring and fall and a surplus in summer and winter, the average daily pay for a black male laborer was 75 cents, and for a woman, 50 cents.[14] James Island proprietors, because it was a less desirable place to work, offered laborers monthly wages with rations. On Charleston Neck, four-fifths of the labor force was black, one-fifth, white. Of the 157 truck farms on the Neck, 12 used white labor exclusively. No blacks owned property until 1883. Black tenant farmers superintended 19 with all-black workforces under them. One of these tenant farmer families, the Noisettes, excelled at strawberry cultivation, generating the best shipped out of the city, accumulating sufficient capital to buy seventeen acres. As owners, they employed 75 hands, paying experienced men $1 a day, and earned an annual profit of between $20,000 and $30,000 selling berries and vegetables.[15] The women and children who worked on these farms almost exclusively did field labor, picking or weeding strawberries and potatoes.[16]

Of all the crops grown in Charleston's environs, the strawberry pressed most on the imaginations of northern consumers. Henry Laurens had successfully grown the first ever-bearing alpine strawberry in America on his six-acre botanical garden in Charleston in the 1760s. From the 1830s on, agricultural experimentalists in the Carolinas had been advocating large-scale berry culture, but large plantings did not occur until the mid-1850s.

The first cultivars extensively grown were the Hovey strawberry, the 1836 creation of the influential New England horticulturist Charles Mason Hovey,[17] the old pine strawberry, and the Harris seedling. In the 1860s, Charlestonian George Nunan, whose strawberry beds on the west end of Nunan Street were a city landmark, crossed an old pine with a Harris, creating a new, prolific variety. The resulting berry, the Neunan prolific, became immediately popular in the city for its tang and its durability. Seedsman John Thompson on King Street made it a regional hit. He heralded the strawberry's qualities: "The berries are larger, redder, more juicy, ripen earlier, yield more, and stand the climate and change of soil better than other varieties."[18] It prospered in hot growing conditions, making it the regional preference over the Wilson's strawberry that dominated culture in other parts of the United States. Contemporaries described the Neunan thusly: "Medium roundish to round-conic, light crimson; flesh medium red, very firm, acid, fair; runners numerous."[19] It would dominate Lowcountry field culture until the 1880s, when a mutation of the Neunan, discovered in 1877 by H. Hoffman of Charleston, was refined into the Hoffman seedling. Because this offspring had a more regular configuration and a greater resistance to disease, it supplanted the Neunan, becoming the chief market and breeding berry in the South at the end of the nineteenth century. The Hoffman was "large, pointed, a rich, deep color, and are most liked for their keeping qualities."[20] The Neunan and Hoffman berries would be sent north to a ready market until the end of the century. Charleston's strawberries competed with the huge fields ringing Norfolk. It remained a presence in the northern markets primarily because it could place fruit on New York tables three weeks before Norfolk, and because of the quality of the fruit produced. But the success of the Charleston growers inspired farmers elsewhere. By the later 1880s, the four hundred acres of berries under cultivation on the Neck paled behind the thousands planted in eastern Virginia and Thomasville, Georgia. In 1888 a reporter noted ruefully that despite a reduction in acreage and a timely and profitable appearance at market, "an enormous quantity of strawberries was left over, and either sold at home or turned in and used for fertilizing purposes."[21] Because of their delicacy and vulnerability to rough handling during transportation, both the Neunan and the Hoffman seedling varieties, strains that had covered thousands of acres in the

South for years, ceased to be planted by the advent of World War I. In 2011 a canvas of germplasm banks and seed savers' collections failed to turn up a single surviving plant of either the Neunan or Hoffman berries. Yet their legacy remains alive in the Blakemore strawberry, a 1923 cross between a missionary strawberry (a Virginia mutation of the Hoffman) and the disease-resistant Herbert 17. This twentieth-century grandchild of the Neunan-Hoffman lines has been preserved in the National Clonal Germplasm Repository in Corvallis, Oregon.

I am hesitant, however, to have the Clemson Coastal Research and Education Center secure plants for a trial growing, hoping to repopulate the fields of Georgia and the Carolinas with Blakemore clones. If flavor is what we most desire in a strawberry, then growing a market strawberry (heirloom or not) may not be the way to go. The virtues of the Neunan and the Wilson in the nineteenth century lay in their firmness and in their productivity—shipping durability and quantity being market premiums. Charleston contemporaries of George Nunan thought his lady-finger strawberry more flavorsome than the prolific. Epicures of fruit, such as D. H. Jacques, editor of the *Rural Carolinian*, gave an informed and measured judgment of the berry: "In quality, it will compare favorably, when fully ripe, with Wilson's Albany, but cannot claim the high, rich flavors of Triomphe de Grand, Seth Boyden, Lennig's White, President Wilder and others."[22] These garden (no field) varieties of strawberry grew in pomologist P. J. Berckmans's Fruitlands Nursery near Augusta, Georgia. None, alas, were suited to hot weather culture. None were particularly prolific. Yet one of these garden alternatives was a peculiarly interesting strawberry. The Triomphe de Grand strawberry appeared to nineteenth-century botanists to be a rather pure descendant of the original Chilean wild strawberries taken to Europe in the colonial era and interbred with the Virginia strain to form the modern alpine strawberries.[23] Less acid, more aromatic than the majority of cultivars, the old Triomphe de Grand may have indeed offered a different, richer path of strawberry taste.

Genetic science has reached a level of sophistication that it might consider an experimental revisitation of the breeding program that gave rise to the modern cultivars, again taking up the wild Chilean and North American strains and marrying them anew, this time with the greatest premiums placed upon fragrance and flavor rather than size and texture. The

Neunan and the Hoffman no longer exist. But the wild berries do. Why back-breed a good, historically significant strawberry when one can create from the primordial plants something tastier and more fragrant than anything bred thus far?

While strawberries may have been the crop that galvanized the imaginings of winter-weary northerners, the vegetable that captivated the fancy of Charleston growers was the cabbage. In 1908 C. F. Myers reflected upon the period in the 1890s, when planters became "Cabbage Crazy":

> Every available piece of land was planted in Cabbage. Hundreds of acres, which had formerly been devoted to the growing of Cotton, became vast Cabbage fields. No one, not acquainted with the situation, can imagine the amount of Cabbage shipped from this vicinity during one day. As many as 225 solid carloads were shipped in one day. I am satisfied that there is enough Cabbage grown around Charleston annually to supply every man, woman, and child in the United States with a head.[24]

Money was made in great amounts because no northerner grower could compete with Charleston's early date to market . . . until savvy farmers in California and other warm-weather locales saw the money being made, and cabbage culture exploded during the first decade of the twentieth century. The Charlestonians' own success—the sheer amount of product they shipped north—drove prices down. In 1907 Walter Hines Page, a cultural commentator, observed that the city's annual take on truck was somewhere between $7 and $9 million, with the chief crops being, in order of importance, "cabbage, potatoes, asparagus, lettuce, snap-beans, strawberries." Carrots, radishes, cauliflower, onions, tomatoes, eggplants, and peas were also significant crops. (One wonders whether the absence of cucumbers from this list is an oversight on Page's part.) Page noted, "For thirteen miles, in one place, nothing is visible from the seat of a buggy but cabbages."[25] Cabbage farming abounded with rags-to-riches stories. Page told of an illiterate farm laborer from Georgia who began working the fields on the Charleston Neck for $10 a month. His wife taught him to read. He gradually built his holdings until he controlled a thousand acres of cabbages and had seven miles of railroad beds servicing his dispatch depot in Meggett. This was Norman Blitch, "the Cabbage King."[26]

William C. Geraty of Yonge's Island rivaled Blitch as a shipper, moving 40 million heads.

Nearly all of the cabbage grown in the Carolinas for shipment were the Jersey Wakefield and Charleston Wakefield cabbages. Though the latter plant took its name from the town of Charleston near Wakefield in England, the popular linkage of Charleston with cabbages at the end of the nineteenth century naturally caused them to believe that the variety originated in South Carolina. The cabbage plants were put in the ground in November and December, and they began to mature in the middle of March. "From that time until the end of May experienced cutters armed with machetes go through the fields between the rows striking right and left close to the ground and amputating a Cabbage at every stroke. Their experienced eyes are able to select mature Cabbages at a glance. Men with carts follow them, gather up the heads and haul them to the shipping sheds, where they are trimmed and packed into crates by women."[27] It is a matter of interest that the garden calendars make clear that nineteenth-century kitchen gardeners preferred the sugar-loaf, Savoy, and Battersea for local consumption.[28]

Shifts in public taste influenced what was grown in the coastal truck farms. The growing craze for salads, fueled by cookbook writers and the cooking schools at the end of the nineteenth century, led to an intense demand for lettuce, radishes, and cucumbers. For decades, forced lettuce had been grown in the glass-house farms ringing the country's major cities. The vulnerability of lettuce to pests and animal depredation militated against unprotected field cultivation. All of the Lowcountry cities—Wilmington, Charleston, Savannah, Brunswick, and Jacksonville—undertook lettuce farming, growing two crops, one to mature around Christmas time, the other in April.[29] "In the vicinity of Charleston, lettuce and cucumbers are used in succession under muslins or muslin-covered frames. . . . The production of lettuce under muslin involves certain difficulties which cannot be dealt with as economically and as satisfactorily as in forcing houses. Yet because of the small expense involved in the erection and maintenance of cloth-covered frames, a grower can afford to take chances which would not be justified under glass."[30] The growers in Wilmington, Charleston, and Savannah produced substantial crops but did not organize, preferring to sell directly at the shipping point or shipping on consignment.[31] The year 1900 marked the first intensive year of cultivation in South Carolina. Within a decade, Conway, Charleston Neck, and James Island produced the bulk of South Carolina's commercial crop. North Carolina followed South Carolina's lead with Wilmington and New Bern emerging as the center of cloth-cultured greens. The chief varieties cultivated were the big Boston (a heading lettuce), the Hanson (for the April picking), and romaine (or cos). The muslin protection remained erect to cover a following crop of dwarf, quick-growing cauliflower, such as the early snowball or the dwarf Erfurt.[32]

Beaufort, South Carolina, became a center of production for another salad vegetable, the radish, when brothers Frederic and Harry Whipple, two enterprising Rhode Islanders, moved to the ancient port town shortly after the turn of the century and began growing thirty-six acres of white olive-shaped radish, the French breakfast radish, and the Convent Garden radish. Because radishes are quick growing, they devised an annual cycle of rotations that planted two radish crops in succession, followed by beets, then cucumbers, then corn—five crops in a twelve-month period. The two radish crops alone brought them a profit of $10,000. Then the Whipples collaborated with two other growers to install an overhead irrigation system for lettuce on Port Royal Island. They accrued total sales of $27,500 off of six acres.[33] Creative and scientific, the brothers constantly experimented with fertilizers and became known as advocates for the use of swamp muck as a soil replenishment.

The cucumber enjoyed steady demand throughout the nineteenth and twentieth century, for pickling as well as for use in salads. It was among those needful plants included in the Trustee's Garden in Savannah to support the infant Georgia colony in the 1730s and remained a fixture of garden cultivation thereafter. When Savannah entered the supply system for the northern markets in 1872, its watermelons and cucumbers (in that order) proved the favorite commodities in the city markets. The quality of the soil skirting the Savannah River proved particularly nourishing to the white spine cucumber, the chief market variety, and agricultural reports spoke of five hundred bushels coming from a single acre.[34]

Savannah—like Charleston, Jacksonville, and Wilmington—benefited from its status as a port. The ports became the foci of an elaborate shipping system as rail lines from 1830 onward connected inland towns with the ports. Before the Civil War, the markets in the port cities became the destination of inland grains, fruits, and vegetables cultivated in market gardens along the transport lines. During Reconstruction, the network of railroads extended mightily, until "not only in the neighborhood of cities and towns, but near even little railroad stations along all the great lines of transportation that traverse all sections of our State, market gardens have multiplied and truck has reached those proportions, which entitle it to rank among the leading industries of Georgia."[35]

There were liabilities to this connectedness. When prices for produce in the northern markets far exceeded that of the southern cities, produce was sucked northward so efficiently that there might be shortages in Savannah or Charleston of things that grew in abundance a mile outside the city limits. A Massachusetts traveler reported:

> At Fernandina they expected to find bananas, but they all went to New York and Boston. On board the steamer, on their way to Savannah, there were over three hundred cases of cucumbers, and large quantities of cabbages, but not one was landed at Savannah; all went to New York, and they had none at their hotel in Savannah. At Baltimore they got some Southern fruit, and at New York plenty.[36]

Conversely, when prices in New York sank for Lowcountry produce, as would happen annually when the produce from Norfolk began to appear, localities would experience a glut of cheap vegetables and fruits.

A second liability arose from the enormous expansion of concentrated planting of certain vegetables. The dense populations and contact between growing centers by transport lines led to sudden scourges of insect pests and plant disease. Fusarium wilt in watermelons, anthracnose, downy mildew, asparagus rust, cucumber wilt, and cucumber mosaic spread through southern fields with aggravating regularity. Vegetable and fruit breeding became, as a result, obsessed with disease resistance rather than taste.

Finally, the handling, crating, and processing of truck vegetables forced breeders to create tougher produce that would withstand the rigors of the rails and seas. Watermelon growers thickened rinds—the Kolb's gem watermelon with its rhino hide being the model of train-travel produce—tomato farmers increasingly cultivated hard-fleshed fruit; strawberries were less juicy; lettuce was less buttery. A kitchen garden resistance to market vegetables emerged in the final quarter of the nineteenth century, served by seedsmen who offered tastier home alternatives to market varieties. The market garden thus diverged substantially from the kitchen garden.

PART THREE
Planting in the Lowcountry

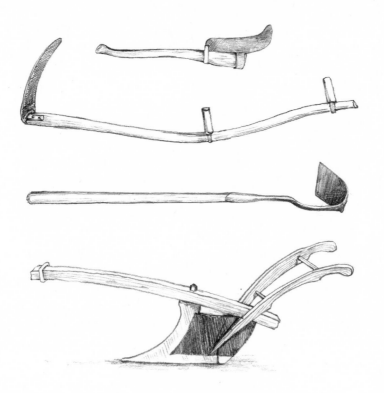

TWELVE *Carolina Gold Rice*

The famous Gold Seed rice of the Carolinas ranks among the best rices
in the world for size, richness of kernel, and large yield.
— Liberty Hyde Bailey (1910)[1]

There are several varieties of lowland rice, the most appreciated being
the gold seed, so called from the golden yellow colors of its husk when
ripe.
— *USDA Bulletin* 1 (1880)

It is perfectly white in colour, and when dressed for food is of good taste.
In quality it is equal, if not superior, to Peshanam paddy grown in the
neighbourhood of Nellore, and which is considered to be the best paddy
in this district.
— "Memorandum on the Introduction of
Gold Seed Rice to India" (1880)

FROM MYTH TO REALITY

When I moved to Charleston from the Hudson Valley in 1984, I felt sure
that I would fit readily into South Carolina's foodways. Charlestonians re-
putedly were a rice-loving people, and I, having learned to eat as a boy in

Tokyo in the early 1950s, cherished rice. Sure enough, when I visited the Harris-Teeter grocery store on East Bay Street, there was Carolina Brand long-grain white rice in abundance on the shelves. Purchasing bag after bag, I worked through the rice dishes in the local culinary Bible, the Junior League's famous collection, *Charleston Receipts*. A decade would pass before I learned that Carolina Brand rice was *not* grown in the Carolinas, that it was *not* the famous staple rice, Carolina Gold, and that its taste was *not* the storied taste celebrated in the paeans of memoirists and novelists when they described nineteenth-century southern breakfasts and dinners.

Riviana Foods marketed "Carolina" Brand rice, which vied with its sister brand, Mahatma, as the most popular long-grained rice in American groceries. The Carolina Brand rice I tasted grew either in Texas or Arkansas. When first sampled early in the 1980s, the chief white long-grain field rices planted by food corporations were New Bonnet and Lemont. A decade late, Drew, Bengal, and Cypress had supplanted them. While all of these varieties shared a lucent whiteness when milled and polished (an important concern given the clear packaging that Riviana used), they also shared a taste neutrality that had become the default in palatability tests during the late twentieth century. The varieties had been bred for growth yield, resistance to lodging, resistance to blast and sheath blight, and brevity of growth period.[2]

Founded in 1911, the year when gold rice ceased to be a commercial crop in South Carolina, Riviana Foods rose to eminence in the United States through innovative packaging and processing. In the 1930s, it pioneered see-through containers, so the buyer might inspect the pearly polish of its rice through the cellophane. Since the mid-twentieth century, the company succeeded because it invented and sold a succession of convenience rices—grains that could be prepared almost instantly. Minute Rice appeared in the 1940s, responding to the need to supply precooked, dehydrated rice that could be immediately reconstituted with hot water by service personnel during wartime. The 1970s saw the launch of Success, a boil-in-a-pouch rice, and in 2006, microwavable rice. Convenience came at the expense of texture and flavor.

Taste became associated in the eyes of Riviana and other major rice producers with specialty rices—Akitakomachi, Baldo, Della, Dellmont,

Dellrose, Jasmine-85, and Koshihikari—a taste for which emerged in some population segments, particularly immigrant communities, during the 1970s and 1980s. Non-aromatic long-grain white rice became a backstop for food, not a grain to be savored in itself. Riviana's genius was expended on convenience and marketing.

I suppose no one finds it odd that a food-processing company banks on old associations of rice with South Carolina when selling its wares, despite the non-productivity of Carolina's fields for a century. Myth sells more than truth in advertising, and imaginary verity has been favored over mere factuality since the days of P. T. Barnum. Hoppin' John Taylor spoke the words of disenchantment to me sometime in the early 1990s: "Only Dr. Richard Schulze grows Carolina Gold now; he brought it back in its duck ponds off the Savannah River. Carolina rice is no more, and hasn't been for most of the twentieth century." I wanted to taste that lost variety, whose reputation remained so potent that it sold millions of dollars of anonymous white rice in the nation's groceries.

In 2003 a friend shipped me a pound of Carolina Gold grown in Texas. Following the instructions for steaming rice found in antebellum newspapers, I prepared a bowl adorned only with salt and pepper. First, I noted that the grains were not so long as the store-bought brands. It had no pronounced aroma, yet the rice possessed a mild hazelnut flavor, and the pearly white grains produced a wholesome mouth feel, lusciously farinaceous. The grains separated nicely when cooked according to the classic method. Yet I had a hard time envisioning the contents of the bowl giving rise to a global market reputation or funding the vast plantations of the Lowcountry. There was a softness of focus to the taste—an imprecision. When I asked Glenn Roberts about it, he grumbled, "Conventional growing—the growers had doused the soil with the contents of their chemistry set, and so you are not getting any depth of flavor. We have to learn how the rice planters grew it." In 2006 I saw the repatriated crop growing in the field for the first time at Prospect Hill plantation. Witnessed three weeks before harvest, the field was a revelation.

Possessing the luster of an antique wedding ring rather than the yellow glare of the sun, the hulls of Carolina's staple rice distinguished it from the dozens of other varieties introduced into the Lowcountry before 1800.

Rippling in the breeze on a bright September afternoon, a cloud of rice-birds hovering in the air above the restless ripening panicles, gold seed rice (as it was called until the 1910s) afforded the most splendid sight visible in the agrarian South, as aureate and vivid as fields of Kansas wheat or the bright yellow froth of mustard in spring bloom. When it thrived—from the American Revolution until 1911—planters and buyers called it "Gold Seed" because, besides the edible grain, the region produce the purest and most valuable seed rice for those who planted the variety in Louisiana, Hawaii, India, West Africa, and South Asia. The rice assumed the name "Carolina Gold" just as commercial production died in South Carolina, killed in the global market by cheaper, more productive rice grown in other locales by the destruction of rice fields by hurricanes and by difficulty securing cheap steady labor.

Patch grown for home use in the Lowcountry and cultivated in pockets of Texas and Hawaii, Carolina Gold grew increasingly *un*commercial with each passing decade of the twentieth century. Rice breeders paid homage to the strain, particularly its superlatively wholesome mouth feel, by making it a parent strain of the new higher-yield and shorter-stalk varieties created for industrial-scale production. Supplanted by its offspring, Carolina Gold could scarcely be found in cultivation by the 1940s. Yet because it was such a legendary rice, and because it had been central to the cuisine of the southern Atlantic coast, it never evaporated from cultural memory. Writers' rhapsodies over the taste of wild rice–fed ducks in old Carolina, the family cookbooks filled with pilaus, perloos, chicken bogs, and other dishes that specified "Carolina Rice," made residents of the region wonder what had gone missing. Dr. Richard Schulze, a Georgian optometrist, dreamed of rice-fed ducks. Securing his seed from USDA agronomist Richard Bollock (a scientist intrigued by the storied place of Carolina Gold in American agriculture), Schulze planted his ponds with Carolina Gold in the 1980s, beginning two decades of private crop restoration.[3] Since 2005, it has been in commercial production, thanks in large measure to the efforts of Glenn Roberts, Anna McClung, the Carolina Gold Rice Foundation (CGR), and a new generation of rice planters led by Campbell Coxe.

What is Carolina Gold? The planter-naturalists who perfected it during the antebellum period described it thusly:

Gold Seed Rice: The ordinary crop rice most highly esteemed and therefore universally cultivated, an oblong grain 3/8ths of an inch in length,
slightly flattened on two sides, of a deep yellow or golden color, awn
short; when the husk and inner coat are removed, the grain presents a
beautiful pearly-white appearance—an ellipsoid in figure, and somewhat
translucent.[4]

This is precisely the medium-grain rice preserved by the USDA seed banks
and restored to the fields of the Lowcountry during the past decade. Yet
there was another form of Carolina Gold—"Long Gold"—that has perished entirely. It possessed even more mystique than the original.

In 1838 the overseer of Joshua John Ward's Brookgreen Plantation—a
Mr. Thompson—discovered a panicle of gold rice, a genetic sport, with
larger grains, five-twelfths of an inch in length. Ward had the seeds carefully cultivated and from 1838 to 1843 consolidated the seed stock of a new
type of "Gold Seed Rice."[5] This variant "is highly esteemed by foreign
consumers, when it is produced in perfection, commanding the highest
prices in the market. It is called 'long grain' rice."[6] From 1843 until 1861,
Carolina Gold came in two varieties: standard grain and long grain. The
latter stood as the benchmark white rice in the Western world for a generation, commanding extraordinary prices on the Parisian market, until
the Civil War disrupted the rigorous seed regimens required to maintain
it. It was extinct by 1863.

While we know a great deal about the "perfection" of Carolina Gold
as "Long Gold" in the early 1840s, we know surprisingly little about the
provenance of the first gold seed to appear in the Carolinas. Genetic analysis reveals that its ultimate source was South Asia. But did it come straight
from Indonesia? From Madagascar or West Africa? From Europe? The
antebellum historians of agriculture knew roughly when it came into cultivation in South Carolina: "Some time before the Revolutionary War,
the 'Gold Seed' rice was introduced (from what precise quarter, and how,
has not been accurately ascertained) which, owing to its superiority, soon
entirely superceded the white."[7] When commentators supplied names of
the first persons to grow Carolina Gold, both persons—Henry Laurens
and Hezekiah Mayham—were said to have begun the work with gold seed
rice in the wake of the American Revolution. John D. Legare, in an 1823

report of the South Carolina Agricultural Society on the importation of foreign seeds, noted that "the late Col. Henry Laurens imported a small quantity of what is called the Gold-seed Rice, soon after the revolutionary war, which was found to be so far superior to the white-hulled Rice before cultivated, that the latter is now scarcely to be met with."[8] No corroboration from Laurens's planting records has been found for this assertion. Robert F. W. Allston, the best informed student of rice culture in the antebellum South, observed in 1847 that gold seed rice "has been introduced into the Winyaw and Waccamaw region, since the revolution. It was planted by Col. Mayham, on Santee, in 1785."[9] All antebellum sources roughly concur that Carolina Gold appeared first in the Lowcountry in the period from 1770 to 1785, that its place of origin is unknown, that its qualities were immediately recognized, and that it supplanted "white rice," the staple crop in the region since the "seed from Madagascar" was introduced into the Carolinas at the end of the seventeenth century. The more precise commentators pinpoint its introduction to the period after the cessation of hostilities between the United States and Great Britain, circa 1783–85.

That Carolinians came to plant a new variety of seed in the wake of the Revolution makes sense. Carolina's Revolution was a civil war, disrupting agriculture and the maintenance of rice seed stocks. The mid-1780s was a time when enterprising planters were forced to look beyond customary sources of seed and supply to rebuild their fields. Mayham had been actively engaged in the conflict. Leaving his plantation in St. Stephen's Parish (Berkeley County, abutting Pineville), Mayham joined the partisan troop of the Swamp Fox, Francis Marion, as a captain of the cavalry. He would later head his own company as colonel. Fiery tempered, heroic, and ingenious, he engineered the patriot conquest of the loyalist haven Fort Watson by erecting a tower of logs and shooting over the protecting walls from a platform on the apex. Mayham towers became favorite devices for taking fortifications during the remainder of the war. Malaria contracted in the Lowcountry swamps disabled him in 1781, forcing his retirement from the field. He spent the following years striving to consolidate his holdings. His labors were legendary,[10] eventually inspiring William Gilmore Simms's comic novel *The Sword and the Distaff*. Simms figured Mayham in the person of the bumptious, stocky hero, Captain

Porgy, a hale fellow who fought Tories and debt collectors with equal ferocity.[11] Because of credit instability in the 1780s, all of the major rice planters experienced debt problems. Mayham became the hero of his class by forcing a deputy sheriff who served him a warrant for debt to eat the document before bodily expelling him from the grounds.[12] Convention did not much constrain Mayham when he was rebuilding his world in the wake of the Revolution. Consequently, he seems entirely likely as a candidate for trying out new rice seed to replenish his fields. Did he get his seed from Laurens? From some ship captain? It is a matter of more than academic interest. Mayham was the maternal grandfather of Joshua John Ward, who perfected Carolina Long Gold rice. Ward's rice and certain of his rice fields had been inherited from Mayham.

Genetics offers the most probable path to determining the provenance of Carolina Gold. When botanists ask, "What is Carolina Gold?," they seek features in the morphology and genetic composition of the variety that mark it clearly distinguishable from the multitude of world rice varieties. Anna McClung, of the US Department of Agriculture, and Gurdev Khush, the famed rice geneticist, reported that banked examples of Carolina Gold did indeed have a distinctive genetic marker, the RM 190 allele, lacking in over 99 percent of known rice landraces. Carolina Gold also possessed 43 percent other molecular characteristics that supply a signature of the grain.

Shortly after having ascertained the genetic character of Carolina Gold, McClung and Robert Fjellstrom searched the world germplasm banks for rice accessions bearing its traits, locating possible ancestors or close relations. At the November 2007 meeting of the American Society of Agronomy, McClung announced that she and Fjellstrom had identified a genetic match for Carolina Gold rice in a sample of seed rice collected in 1972 in Ghana. The African variety, called Bankoram, shared the key genetic marker, the RM 190 allele, that distinguishes Carolina Gold. The presence of this genetic component, controlling starchiness, prompted McClung and Fjellstrom to seek Carolina Gold's forty-three other molecular characteristics in the Bankoram sample. It possessed forty-two. When planted and grown, the rice greatly resembled Carolina Gold.[13] Since Carolina Gold had been distributed globally in the nineteenth century for breeding purposes, what remains to be determined is whether Bankoram is a result of that global distribution or descended from an African landrace shipped to Carolina in the 1780s.

If Carolina Gold does prove to have an African genesis, then geographer Judith Carney's arguments about the central importance of African practices and seed stocks to the consolidation of Carolina rice culture will receive vindication. In *Black Rice*,[14] Carney questions the early twentieth-century story, formed by A. S. Salley and popularized by Duncan Heyward in *Seed from Madagascar* (1937),[15] of the Asian origin of Carolina rices and cultivation practices. Both authors surmised that in 1685 James Thurber brought the ancestor of Carolina Gold into the Lowcountry from Madagascar, and Carolina White rice from the Dutch East Indies.

Salley's and Heyward's surmises ignored the several positive testimonies of antebellum agricultural historians that gold seed rice first appeared from places unknown in the Revolutionary era.[16] Whether the white rice grown in the Lowcountry during the eighteenth century gave rise to Carolina White—the closely related medium-grain rice, identical in configuration yet lacking the gold hull—is doubtful. No doubt exists, however, that the white rice that dominated the fields from 1700 to 1785 and made the Lowcountry a presence on the Atlantic grain markets during the colonial period had its origins in the East Indies.

The English botanist Peter Collinson in 1766 noted that Carolina merchant Thomas Marsh conveyed a "money bag" full of East Indian rice given by Charles Dubois, treasurer of the East India Company, in 1696. By 1698 this seed rice had "succeeded very well" in cultivation. Collinson noted that several importations of rice took place before 1713, and that it only became a "great article of commerce" in 1726.[17] From 300 tons exported in 1700, the Carolina rice crop expanded to 40,000 barrels in the 1726/27 seasons. It would eventually rise to 150,000 barrels in 1762. According to Fayrer Hall in the 1731 pamphlet *The Importance of the British Plantations*, the rice exported to England was of two sorts: "one called Red Rice in Contradistinction to the White, from the Redness of the inner Husk or Rind of this Sort, tho' they both clean and become white alike."[18] In time, the red rice, because of its invasive character, became the bane of rice planters in North America. The white rice was the variety that became vendible on the world market.

In 1705 Parliament added rice to the list of enumerated commodities in the Acts of Trade and Navigation, requiring all colonial American rice exported to Europe to pass through English ports. Most of Carolina's rice landed at Cowes on the Isle of Wight in 600-pound barrels. Until the American Revolution, English brokers transshipped the majority of the export crop to the German states, the Netherlands, and Portugal.[19] The English demand remained modest, for the grain could never supplant wheat in the people's imagination as hearty nourishment. Rice's muted flavor suggested that it was best served as an aliment for sickly persons lacking the stomach for bread, beer, and porridge. Hence its invariable place in English cookery books as a base for white puddings or in the section devoted to invalid cookery. Independence enabled American merchants to ship rice directly to those who desired it most avidly without the British middleman. In 1789 Thomas Jefferson concretized the commercial ties with French merchants that enabled the direct trade.

Jefferson's embassy revealed the reason for the suddenness of the switch from Madagascar White to Gold seed rice from 1785 to 1795. When trying to convince French merchants to buy American rough white rice, he met resistance. French buyers, a group more judicious on matters of grain aesthetics than their Dutch and German counterparts, preferred rice produced from the Italian Piedmont. Merchants suggested that the problem lay in the tendency of the colonies' white rice to break up while milling. Hearing this, Jefferson traveled to Italy and inspected the mills, which differed in no way from those of Carolina, England, or France. But he did notice that the rice was a distinctly different variety. He secured a quantity of the protected seed by clandestine means, and in 1787 shipped it to Ralph Izard in South Carolina, whose trials left him unimpressed with the product.[20] Since some Carolinians were already growing Mayham's rice, the Italian Patna did not appear the wise alternative to the old standard white. Gold seed yielded more per acre than the Piedmontese rice, exceeded it for pearly translucence, and surpassed it in lustrous mouth feel and wholesome taste. When the new Carolina Gold shipped to Europeans in the late 1790s, the planters' judgments were vindicated.

Robert W. Allston stated that gold seed largely supplanted the original white rice in Carolina's fields. Yet post-Revolutionary records speak of white rice being sent to market. We do not know when Carolina White, the sibling of gold seed that lost the pigment in its hull, became widely established. With the introduction of gold seed rice into the agricultural economy, planters became particularly conscious of the improvement of crop and cultivation practices. The formation of the Agricultural Society of South Carolina in 1785 attested to a consciousness among the planters of a communal interest in improvement. Before the end of the eighteenth century, the society had devoted significant attention to rice experimentation, including putting into trial cultivation the one hundred varieties of rice that Vice President Thomas Jefferson had procured from the Philippines.[21] Throughout the early nineteenth century, numbers of rice types were cultivated besides gold seed, most on an extremely short-term basis, then suspended to minimize the possibility of crossing with gold seed. Some rices that enjoyed a more-than-a-season grow-out included guinea rice, a fat grain shorter than most rice grown in the South, rarely cultivated as a crop, but used as a feed grain; "Common White Rice," with a cream-colored hull and a size similar to the shorter variety of gold seed, but cloudy white rather than pearly when cleaned; bearded white rice, introduced into Carolina from Pensacola, Florida, by William Genald in 1827, who indicated that it "came from South-America, where it grew wild."[22] Extensively grown in the 1830s because of its productivity and ease of milling, bearded white never established a presence in the market but was cultivated "more or less extensively for their negroes."[23] By 1850 the crop rice of Carolina consisted of the two types of gold seed rice and various forms of white rice, which were either "an improvement of the grain chiefly cultivated, arising from a long-continued, careful selection of seed," or a "commingling of the grain," in which gold seed and white planted in adjoining fields, fructify one another, producing a hybrid form.[24]

Another rice grew in the Lowcountry, one that inspired dread in planters. Weedy red rice appeared to sprout spontaneously in Carolina's fields, manifesting itself in five different forms. While edible, red produced little grain, grew quickly, and spread seed before cultivated crops, supplanting white rice in fields with startling rapidity. Planters resisted the invasion with rigorous and organized campaigns of weeding and seed purification.[25] As early as 1831, a group of planters in the Pee Dee region held yearly exhibitions of seed rice samples to determine whose lands produced rice with the least red rice contamination. A wineglass full of grains was taken from six locations in each plantation, spread out, with the red separated out. Out of 5,178 grains, the winning planter had only eight grains of red among the gold.[26] Winners' seed stock was avidly sought by planters, so the profit motive amplified the communal urge for improvement. Inspection and culling of seed rice was and is an extraordinarily laborious and painstaking activity. In the antebellum South, under the slave labor regime, only the most trusted hands were put to this task.

Weedy red rice remains a problem to this day. In twenty-first-century rice farming, the intensive labor of culling is bypassed, and the early sprouting red is attacked with herbicides that minimally effect later sprouting plants. Organic farmers must either resort to the rigorous disciplines of antebellum seed management, or do what rice farmers in the undeveloped world do and what the South did in the early twentieth century—pull up the plants by hand (easily spotted because of their loose drooping panicle bearing relative few grains) before they shatter.

A semi-aquatic plant, *Oryza sativa L.*, thrives in waterlogged soils, growing where no other grains and most weeds, with the dire exception of weedy red, cannot prosper.[27] While its root system permits it to grow in dry soils, the large-scale cultivation of rice has traditionally been most successfully managed in wetlands. Early colonial rice culture had taken place in cleared inland swamplands.[28] During the 1750s, rice planter Archibald Johnstone of the Estherville[29] plantation on Winyah Bay, devised the first tidal flow impoundment fields in the New World. Building levees along the riverside, he devised a system of locks, or water gates, that would open with the inrush of the tide and shut when it receded, trapping water within banked perimeters. The fields could later be drained by opening a set of trunks onto deep ditches. A system of trunks between fields regulated water flow. This relocated rice culture to the banks of the Lowcountry rivers. When Carolina Gold rice was introduced in cultivation during the 1780s, the water-based fields system was in place.[30]

Planters experimented with various water regimes of growing. In the mid-1820s, The Agricultural Society of South Carolina sought to regularize practices, publishing a list of queries composed by William Washington about rice planting methods.[31] The replies, published in the *Southern Agriculturist*, revealed that two schools of planting had emerged, each suited to the peculiar conditions of terroir: dry and wet culture.[32]

In dry culture, field hands plowed rice straw under shortly before Christmas and kept the field underwater until the frosts came. Then they drained the field. In March, laborers leveled the fields, cleared the drainage ditches, and trenched the areas within the embankments transverse to the ditches. Each shallow trench extended a hoe's width, about four inches, distanced a foot and a quarter apart. From mid-April until mid-May, slaves, including youths and "half-hands," sowed the trenches, "2-¼ bushels of seed to the acre."[33] Using a board attached to a hoe handle, a field hand dragged across the trenches covering the seed with a light coating of soil. Then the foreman opened the trunks, inundating the field up to six days to "swell the grain." He then drained the fields until sprouts could be seen, and when they stood as tall as a needle, he flooded the fields again to staunch weeds and worms. After six days, fields were again drained and the rice permitted to grow.

Ambitious planters took the time to discover cultivation schemes that either maintained or increased productivity. Since the rise of the water system of planting, they depended upon the nutriments carried in the water during the wet cycles in rice growing—"the natural deposit . . . of sediment when the rivers overflow their banks, or silt from seaward, when the turbid waters, admitted into the fields, are held there, undisturbed for days."[34] Yet it became evident in the mid-1830s that yield was declining. Planters in Waccamaw and Santee then began manuring fields with rice straw, chaff, and flour, and letting fields lie fallow. The result: "they produce[d] now rice of better quality than formerly."[35] Rotations were introduced in the late 1830s and '40s by the largest experimental planters on the Georgia Sea Islands, Thomas Spalding and James Hamilton Couper. Usual rotations of the 1850s were cotton, rice, benne, corn, and sweet potatoes, though a significant portion of planters in coastal areas retained their dependence on silt drenching for field nutrition. Every scheme attempted required extraordinary labor.

The human costs of creating the world of rice have occupied persons of conscience ever since. Attempts have been made to ascertain what contributions were made by African slaves to the organization of the early cultivation schemes as well. This history, however, concerns the period after this extraordinary effort—my concern is the period between 1820 and 1900. Consequently, we've relied particularly on the scholarship of historian Daniel Littlefied on the effort of African American slaves to maintain Carolina Gold as a viable staple, recounting how field hands crawled over rice fields on their knees with spoons weeding the new seedlings. Littlefield supplies a circumspect understanding of the whole experience of work—from the exercise of practical wisdom in growing, to the challenges and opportunities of the task system, to the drudgery of prolonged and repeated action, to the dangers inherent in laboring in this environment—exposure to insect-borne diseases and declines in fertility, for example.

What exactly was the nature of field work during the antebellum heyday of Carolina Gold, and what were those tasks? While the southern agricultural press of the period discussed labor schemes with great frequency, it did so without the circumspection found in accounts by visitors to the region. Perhaps the most informative contemporary account about antebellum plantation labor came from the pen of a *New York Times* correspondent in 1853. First, he explained that all slaves were categorized according to ability and work capacity as either quarter hands, half hands, three-quarters hands, and full hands. Then he described the method of work:

> The field hands . . . were nearly always worked in gangs, the number of a gang varying according to the work that engages it; but usually it numbers twenty or more, and is directed by a driver. As on most large plantations, whether of rice or cotton, in Eastern Georgia and South Carolina, nearly all ordinary and regular work is performed by "tasks": that is to say, each hand has his quota for the day marked out before him, and can take his own time to do it in. In making drains, in light, clean meadow land, for instance, each man or woman of the full hands is required to dig 1,000 cubic feet; in swamp-land that is being prepared for rice culture, where there are many stumps, the task for a ditcher is 500 feet; while in a very strong cypress swamp, only 200 feet is required; in hoeing rice, a certain number of rows, equal to one-half or two-thirds of an acre, according to the condition of the land; in sowing rice (strewing in drills,) two acres; in reaping rice (if it stands well,) three-quarters of an acre. . . . In plowing rice-land (light, clean, mellow soil,) with a yoke of oxen, one acre a day, including the ground lost in and near the drains, the oxen being changed at noon.

These tasks are lessed by one-quarter for three-quarters hands, and proportionately for the lighter classes. Also, in allotting the tasks, the drivers are expected to put the weaker hands where (if there is any choice in the appearance of the ground, such as where certain rows in hoeing corn would be less weedy than others) they will be favored.

These tasks certainly would not be considered excessively hard by a Northern laborer . . . and in point of fact, the more industrious and active hands finish them often by 2 o'clock.[36]

The reporter concluded his portrait by reflecting upon the sorts of punishments meted out by the overseer to insure that the regimen of work did not falter. "Punishment for light offences was administered with the whip, upon the back of a man or woman, with removing their clothes. The whip is a short stick, with a flat lash of leather. For graver offences, the negroes were placed in solitary confinement in a small dark house or jail kept for that purpose; and of this they had great dread, and much preferred being whipped. I asked how often punishment in any way was inflicted. 'Perhaps there will be none at all for three or four weeks; then it will seem as if the devil has got among them, and there is a good deal of it.'"[37]

The Civil War and the liberation of the workforce provoked a crisis in Carolina rice culture. A newspaper report of 1866 observed that because of "the general demoralization arising from the sudden change in the status of the negro, there has been almost an entire failure of the crop of the last season."[38] While rice culture during Reconstruction survived with free blacks working for wages or in tenant-farming arrangements, the business as a whole began an irreversible decline.[39] East Indian rice began making inroads on the American market, underselling Carolina Gold. As early as 1838, a prescient writer alerted southern rice planters that if shippers could clear $2.50 per 100 pounds, that would pay "all the expenses from the East Indies."[40] Planters did not then worry, because the quality of the rice was inferior to gold seed middlings. As the expense of planting rice rose under the wage system, the attractiveness of East Indian rice increased. So did that of rice from Louisiana and Texas, states that grew Carolina Gold with seed procured from Carolina. Lowcountry planters began losing market share.[41] Later in the century, Louisiana began growing cheaper Honduran rice in great quantities.

A second problem concerned the inability to command immediate labor forces, a necessity in maintaining Lowcountry rice dikes when breached by storms. Hurricanes in 1881, 1893, 1910, and 1911 put large tracts of rice wetlands out of commission, when the cost of field repair vastly exceed potential profit. Finally, there was a marked preference among black laborers for cotton farming over rice. It was easier, more remunerative, and healthier. As one postbellum observer noted, "There is no plant growing that has surrounding it a more trying atmosphere for the white man during the months of August and September, and even the negro suffers so much from pleurisy and pneumonia."[42]

In the United States, Louisiana became the first region outside the Lowcountry to embrace growing gold seed rice. Two local white bearded varieties of rice had been cultivated in the swamplands of the Gulf since 1718. In 1853, at the encouragement of the Southern Agricultural Society of Louisiana in New Orleans, planters began importing "thousands of bushels" of seed rice from Charleston. By 1856 the superiority of gold seed caused it to be generally "preferred for lowland culture."[43] Texas next embraced Carolina rice, as the diaspora of Lowcountry families, such as the Chisolms, brought coastal crops and tastes into the Southwest. From east Texas and Louisiana, it spread into Arkansas. But the most enthusiastic outpost of gold seed culture during the nineteenth century would be Hawaii. Upon its introduction in 1856, South Carolina seed produced enormous yields on volcanic soil. Local farmers ripped up their taro patches and planted paddy. In a short time, rice vied with sugarcane as Hawaii's cash crop, being intensively grown at Hanalei and Kauai until the degradation of seed stock by immigrant Chinese, who insisted on cultivating it according their traditional practices, diluting the variety in the 1880s and '90s.[44] The annual reports of the Hawaiian Agricultural Experimental research station resounded with complaints on the variety of rice types and qualities going under the name Hawaiian Gold seed. The degradation of rice quality led to a decline of the industry from the 1890s onward because of milling losses.[45]

Carolina rice's superlative qualities inspired an attempt to spread the variety globally. British Imperial officials imported tons of gold seed rice into India from the Carolinas annually from 1868 to 1875. While this effort did not supplant the local rices—Joomla, Barah, Bhúll, Mihi, Bansi, Amun, and Boro—it led to the crossing of gold seed with local varieties, improving both the taste and productivity of strains in various districts.[46] Carolina White rice would find a more welcoming reception in South America. Imported in substantial amounts in the antebellum period, it became a mainstay of agriculture in the Amazon basin when the Confederados, the population of defeated Confederates who refused to submit to the government of the Union, departed North America with their gold, seeds, and technological know-how, settling in Brazil.[47] There they attempted to re-create their plantation world in the tropical interior. While the Confederados planted Carolina Gold and Carolina White, the latter version proved easier to grow and more congenial to local tastes. Its culture and reputation spread until "Arroz Carolina" became the favorite rice of Hispanic Americans as well as Luso-Americans. Whether in São Paulo or Lima, the Sunday guest would be served lustrous white Arroz Carolina as a mark of favor. Brazilians, Peruvians, Columbians, and Ecuadorians did not, however, adopt the foodways that the Confederados brought with them, particularly the consumption of rice dishes for breakfast. One can find equivalents of the hoppin' Johns and red beans and rice served at dinners and suppers, but not the range of dishes that made breakfast the rice-most of meals in the Lowcountry.

Because of the researches of the late Karen Hess and her protégé, John Martin Taylor, the traditional rice cookery of the Lowcountry has been documented with some thoroughness. In her landmark *The Carolina Rice Kitchen: The African Connection*, Hess explored the pilaus, rice casseroles, rice and beans dishes, and rice breads that dominated Carolina's foodways as a marriage of several Old World cooking traditions in which the African rice stews dominated. Yet Hess did not elaborate the most peculiar dimension of the Carolina rice kitchen—its dominion over the first meal of the day.

BREAKFAST RICE

Before the Quaker Oats Company wheeled out its gun in 1904 and began puffing rice—before "Snap, Crackle, and Pop" excited the ears of sleepy children in 1928—hot rice dishes graced the breakfast table. Now they have disappeared from the family table and vanished from the breakfast bill of fare altogether. Here we will recall rice's place at the morning meal before the rise of cold cereal with milk as family fare in the early twentieth century.

Edmund Ruffin, the volatile Virginia-born agronomist whom many viewed as the savior of the South's cotton-starved soil, published a landmark survey of South Carolina's agriculture in 1844. It paid acute attention to rice, the state's staple grain. In appendix B of the survey, Ruffin provided four culinary and two household recipes for rice that were "common with us" yet "may not be found in all the manuals of house-keeping": instructions on how to boil plain rice, two recipes for breakfast rice bread, a related recipe for rice griddle cakes, and domestic directions for making glue and starch from rice.[48] Ruffin's brief foray into the kitchen is most interesting in its indication that the Carolina breakfast table was where one encountered rice in its baked and fried forms.

RICE BREAKFAST BREAD

Mix a spoonful of butter with some hot hominy, very thoroughly, and spread it to cool, then beat up an egg very light, add some milk, then mix in the hominy with rice flour until it is a thick batter, add salt, q.s., stir it well, then drop it from a spoon into an oven and bake quickly. (Vaux)

ANOTHER RICE BREAD

Have a buck for this special purpose—mix over nigh some hominy, or the eyes of the rice, boiled soft, with milk and rice flour, (having added salt q.s.) into a stiff batter, so that it will just pour—set it where it will not get warm, which injures it; in the morning stir it, pour it into the pan and set it to bake. (Gallivant)

GRIDDLES FOR BREAKFAST

Mix a thin batter with milk and rice-flour, adding salt, q.s. have your griddle-iron hot, grease it with lard, pour some batter on, spread it thin, turn it and brown it both sides.

Of the three recipes supplied, only the last retains some familiarity in the eyes of present-day breakfast eaters, because it is recognizably a form of pancake. In the nineteenth century, griddle cakes had already become a breakfast fixture throughout the United States. Best-selling cookbooks, such as *Miss Beecher's Domestic Receipt-Book* (1850),[49] supplied guidance for a whole range of "griddles"—buckwheat, corn, rye, wheat, and rice. The cooking surface was prepared similarly for every sort of griddle. The cook heated the griddle, put a piece of salt pork on a fork, and rubbed it evenly over the surface. This method prevented excess fat from being absorbed into the cakes. Beecher did offer one exception: "Fried Rice for Breakfast" uses day-old rice cut into slices and fried brown in sweet lard. When reading through Beecher's chapter of breakfast recipes, one learns that the breakfast breads that Ruffin had procured from Carolina cooks belong to a category of breakfast preparations called "drop cakes," thick batters spooned into tin rounds in Dutch ovens and baked until firm. The "Gallivant Rice Bread" departs from the norm by eschewing eggs, a usual ingredient in this sort of preparation.

Miss Beecher further expanded the repertoire by adding "Rice Waffles" to the breakfast table.

RICE WAFFLES

A quart of milk.

A tea-cup of solid boiled rice, soaked three hours in half the milk.

A pint and a half of what flour, or rice flour.

Three well-beaten eggs. Bake in waffle irons.

The rice must be salted enough when boiled. (96–97)

The rice waffle, particularly in its form employing rice flour, became a fixture in American breakfast fare in the nineteenth century. Light, crusty, and a touch sweet, it paired well with preserves and, when hot, with a dusting of confectioner's sugar. The lightness of the waffle, paradoxically, made it a favored component of hearty breakfasts, preceding a substantial meat: "Breakfast—Rice waffles, mutton croquettes, fried raw potatoes."[50]

One notices in the preparations encountered so far the absence of an ingredient that became increasingly prominent at breakfast—sugar. Because the natural starches in rice, when cooked, converted into sugars, there was, perhaps, a sense of redundancy in amplifying the sweetness. Nevertheless, the mid-nineteenth-century boom in cookie baking and sweet biscuit manufacture set cooks tinkering with formulas until a creditable sweet rice biscuit could be created. In 1854's *The Complete Biscuit and Gingerbread Baker's Assistant*, we encounter an early example:

> 3 lbs. of flour, 1 lb. of rice flour, 1 lb. 10 oz. of loaf sugar, 1 lb. of butter, ½ oz. of volatile salt, and ¾ pint of milk, or 4 eggs, and the remaining portion milk.
>
> Mix the two flours together, rub in the butter with it, make a bay, add the sugar, and make them into a dough . . . roll it out in a sheet the six[th] of an inch in thickness, cut them out with a plain round cutter of three inches in diameter, wash the tops with milk, and throw them on rice flour; place them on buttered tins so as not to touch, and bake them in a moderately brisk oven.[51]

While breakfast rice—whether boiled, griddled, or baked—dominated regional eating in the Lowcountry, it was reckoned so iconic a morning dish that it became part of the national meal as well. In novels of the 1850s, descriptions of breakfasts may be found with some frequency. Here is a political breakfast in Washington, DC, featuring dishes from all of the sections of the United States:

> We sauntered together into one of the largest, and longest, and handsomest breakfast rooms this side of Texas. A table of great length stretched across its centre, upon which was arranged in great profusion, Georgia potatoes, New Hampshire bacon, Virginia oysters and fried eels, South Carolina rice cakes, and Cape Cod fish balls—all strong incentives to the stomach of a hungry politician.[52]

The fame of Carolina Gold rice and its market spanned the continent, the hemisphere, and the Atlantic by 1855.

Students of breakfast will note that rice was frequently paired in recipes with hominy—meaning small hominy—or grits. Milled white corn existed in a mental zone of equivalency with rice in the minds of many cooks of that era. Mrs. Lincoln of the Boston Cooking School, in her *Boston Cook Book*, offered a version of griddles that announced complete substitutability: "Rice or Hominy Griddle-Cakes."[53] During the Civil War, the Union Commissary Department specified a daily allotment of "fifteen pounds of beans or peas, and ten pounds of rice or hominy" for every one hundred men.[54] There were, of course, regional inflections to this idea of gustatory proximity. A southern correspondent to the *New England Kitchen Magazine* observed:

> No Southerner in good health and in his right mind ever eats "hominy with milk and sugar" for breakfast. . . . Hominy in this part of the country is dressed with butter or a little of meat gravy, and is eaten with a chop, or a steak or bacon and eggs, or boiled ham, etc. Hominy thus served is a standard breakfast dish in the South and is fit for a king. It needs no sugar or cream or nutmeg, and to put either on it is to commit a crime against gastronomy. The same observations apply to rice, the standard dinner dish of the South, which the Northern menu-makers tell us to serve with cream and sugar.[55]

While this 1895 opinion informs us that boiled hominy had supplanted boiled rice as a southern breakfast dish, and that steamed rice had migrated to the dinner menu, the greatest point of interest is the resistance to sweetening grain porridges in general.

The objection voiced here was not universal. Hominy and molasses had been a staple dish of the laboring classes from the 1830s on. Yet the preference for gravy and butter certainly dominated middle-class tables and those of the gentry. The cookbook writers and arbiters of taste, too, frowned upon adding saccharine to boiled grits and boiled rice. This ban, however, did *not* extend to dishes prepared by other cooking techniques: frying or baking.

Many testimonies survive to the distinctive qualities of a traditional southern breakfast: the presence of both hominy and rice, the variety of cooking technique—boiling, baking, and frying—and the conjunction of grains and meats. William Gilmore Simms, the novelist and cultural critic, reflected on its character in *As Good as a Comedy*: "A Georgia, indeed a Southern, breakfast differs in sundry respects from ours at the North, chiefly, however, in the matter of breadstuffs. . . . *Hominy* itself is a bread-stuff; a dish that our mush but poorly represents. It is seldom eatable out of a Southern household. Then there are waffles, and rice cakes and fritters, and other things of like description, making a variety at once persuasive to the palate and not hurtful to health."[56] Simms noticed the familiar rice cakes yet added a new dish to the southern breakfast table: the rice fritter, or rice beignet. In this light concoction, rice, sugar, spice, and eggs are transmuted into something fine by boiling lard. In Louisiana, this was the famous calas, sold on the street as well as made in the home.

> Boil the rice in milk with some powder-sugar, orange-flower water, a pinch of cinnamon powder, and a little butter; when quite soft put to it a liaison of yolks of eggs, pour it into a pan to cool. Make your preparation into balls, about the size of an egg, dip them in egg, fry them, sprinkle them with sugar, and serve.[57]

Jules Harder, San Francisco's great celebrity chef of the 1880s, refined this basic croquette into its most splendid form.

> Wash one pound of Rice in cold water and drain it. Then put it in a sauce-pan. With two quarts of boiled milk, the peelings of one lemon and one stick of cinnamon. Cover the saucepan set it on a slow fire to cook gently, and when the Rice is nearly done add six ounces of powdered sugar and two ounces of butter and let it cook until thoroughly done. Should the Rice get too dry while cooking add a little more milk to it. Take if off of the fire, take out the lemon peelings and the stick of cinnamon, mix the Rice well together, and when it is somewhat cool, add to it the yolks of six raw eggs, a little essence of lemon or orange-flower water, (whichever may be desired). Mix it well together and put it into a buttered pan. Cover it with a buttered paper cover and let it get cold. Then roll the Rice in any croquette shapes desired, dip them in beaten eggs, then in fresh bread crumbs, arrange them in proper shape, fry them in hot lard, drain them, roll them in powdered sugar into which add a little ground cinnamon, and then dish them up on a napkin.[58]

His unsweetened version incorporated three ounces of grated parmesan cheese and six egg yolks, frying the fritters in butter rather than lard.

There is something inexplicably satisfying about the lightness, crispiness, sugariness, and mellowness of a beignet de riz, or the browned splendor of a rice waffle, or the filling rice griddle. Some pleasures that became passé are novel enough to become pleasurable again. Do "Snap, Crackle, and Pop" have to maintain their monopoly over breakfast, or may their reign be ending? Five years ago, Ari Weinzweig revived the Lowcountry rice waffle at Zingerman's Roadhouses using Carolina Gold and won fulsome praise in the *Atlantic*.[59] In 2011 Alex Young, Zingerman's chef, won the James Beard Foundation Award for Best Chef in the Upper Midwest.

Twenty-first-century chefs have embraced Carolina Gold for precisely those applications that originally won it reputation: for waffles, griddle cakes, and baked goods; for puddings (Mike Lata's rice pudding at FIG Restaurant in Charleston is the superlative version I've tasted); for one-pot stews and composite dishes such as hoppin' John, limping Susan, jambalaya; and as a bed for sauced seafood. It is for these uses that we have brought the storied grain back.

Time and taste, however, do not stand still. Recent changes in public taste favoring aromatic rices have relegated Carolina Gold to the side-lines at times, when a bowl of plain rice is called for at the table. Non-aromatic, Carolina Gold lacks the assertiveness of the aromatic jasmine varieties that have entranced Americans since the Thai restaurant boom of the 1980s, or the earthy aroma of the basmati varieties that have grown steadily in popularity since the health food renaissance of the late 1960s.

Dr. Merle Shepard, head of Clemson University's Research and Education Center in Charleston and one of the chief movers in the restoration of Carolina Gold, decided an aromatic variety of the classic Lowcountry grain was needed to suit the current preference for a side dish of plain aromatic rice. He did as the antebellum experimentalists did and began breeding a new version with the aid of his friend Gurdev S. Khush.[60] In 1998, using a form of pedigree breeding (the traditional controlled pollination of plants) rather than gene insertion, Shepard and Khush crossed landrace Carolina Gold with IR64, a long-grained short-stalked rice that had high productivity and resisted lodging (loss of crop by its blow-down in high winds). The offspring of this pairing was crossed with another short-statured strain (IR65610-24-3-6-3-2-3) that had aromatic qualities descended from landrace basmati. Dr. Anna McClung of the USDA-ARS Rice Research Unit in Beaumont, Texas, oversaw the refining process, using a rigorous regimen of plant selection over multiple generations to exclude tall, disease-vulnerable plants lacking golden seed hulls.

After twelve generations of cullings and plantings from 1999 to 2010, the qualities had stabilized: high productivity, short stature, disease resistance, gold hulls, traditional Carolina Gold mouth feel, and an appetizing earthy aroma. Certified early in 2011, the Carolina Gold Rice Foundation distributed seed for Charleston Gold, and Sean Brock, chef of McCrady's and Husk Restaurants in Charleston, began serving it to acclaim after the first commercial harvest in September 2011.[61] Jimmy Hagood grows the variety at Lavington Plantation in the ACE Basin, supplying Charleston's food hub GrowFood Carolina. Thirteen years from idea to plate, Dr. Shepard's dream of an aromatic version of Carolina's staple rice became the most savory of actualities.

Shortly after Charleston Gold became available, an older Charleston cook complained, "Why did you have to make a new rice? You went to all this effort to bring back Carolina Gold, and then you undercut it with this novelty." Since she was the kind of cook whose dinners were ceremonial reenactments of a gone golden age, I knew my answer would not quiet her misgivings. But I explained anyway: traditions bring the strongest elements of a community's tastes and practices into the future. A tradition thrives only if it does not foreclose creativity. The horticulturists who bred improved versions of garden vegetables for the market in the 1830s were always seeking plants that grew better, looked better, and, most of all, tasted better. Taste was a communal sense whose development registered in the market, advanced with the professional explorations of professional caterers, and periodically coalesced in a cultivar or a dish that became a benchmark of local food experience. One defied shifts in the communal sensibility at one's peril. If cultivated diners have developed a liking for fragrant rice, why not create a version of the beloved Carolina Gold, preserving its famous wholesome mouth feel but that also has a natural perfume. Carolina Gold remains available for use in all the classic composite dishes for which it was created. Charleston Gold exists for those who desire a bowl of unadorned aromatic rice.

The Carolina Gold Rice Foundation distributes seed for both Carolina Gold and Charleston Gold rices — gratis for those who will grow it organically. In the past several years, the demand for rice seed has expanded tremendously. Because Carolina Gold is a landrace developed for a pre-industrial growing regimen, the chemical fertilizers used in conventional farming would cause it to grow too rangy and suffer lodging (blow-down) with any windy thunderstorm. It is best grown organically. Charleston Gold—because of its short start, quick growth, and high productivity— is suitable for either traditional or conventional cultivation. Both varieties are widely available—indeed, standard fare at restaurants that create southern cuisine.

Since this restoration has been so successful, you may ask, "What next?" in terms of renovating the regional rice culture. The Carolina Gold Rice Foundation has determined that its next project is the re-creation of the fabled "Long Gold" rice of 1845 to 1860. This was the strain that most excited the Parisian rice market in the decade before the Civil War. As an encouragement to our efforts, we reprint this comic attestation to the splendor of Carolina Rice penned by the French father of gastronomy. Two obese diners are conversing in Brillat-Savarin's *Physiology of Taste* (1815). One round fellow objects to the other's consuming the broth, not the rice in a soup.

> *Another Fat Man*—What on earth are you doing there? You're eating the liquid from your soup, and leaving that wonderful Carolina rice!
> *Myself*—I am following a special diet I have prescribed for myself.
> *Fat Man*—What a dreadful one! I love rice as much as I do thickenings, Italian pastes, and all those things; there's nothing more nourishing, nor cheaper, nor easier to prepare.[62]

THIRTEEN *Sugar from the Sugarcane*

Sugars—those chemical nets of carbon, oxygen, and hydrogen making up the nutritive matter of plants as glucose, fructose, and sucrose—became sugar, the solid form of sucrose, when early chemists chanced upon a way to crystallize plant juices. Sucrose, the least soluble of the plant sugars, would precipitate out of the juice of grasses when boiled and exposed to chemical catalysts (lime and albumen were the earliest). The more a plant contained natural sugars, the more likely it could be rendered into sucrose. While many plants contained these compounds, several concentrated them particularly—sorghum, beets, and sugarcane. Of these, the sugarcane developed the most extraordinary mystique, the stuff of story and proverb: "Sugarcane is always sweet, people only sometimes so."

The plant came into Europe from the Middle East sometime before 1146 CE. Its need for heat restricted the areas in which it grew. In Europe, it prospered primarily in the kingdom of Sicily, and Sicily benefited from a near monopoly until Don Henry, the regent of Portugal, planted the island of Madeira with the cane in 1420. The demand for sugar became so intense among the European aristocracy that Portugal planted the Canary Islands and, in the sixteenth century, Brazil with sugar.[1] The Spanish planted cane in Hispaniola, the first center of their tropical American empire in 1507. According to Oviedo, the official historian of the West Indies, Spanish vessels began to ship African slaves to work the cane fields of Hispaniola in 1512. Planters first exported sugar to Spain in 1516. None of the West Indian plantations rivaled Brazil, which gushed sugar onto the Atlantic market during the final four decades of the sixteenth century.

Sugar inspired inexhaustible demand. The more produced, the lower the cost, so more could afford to sample it, desired it, then demanded it, prompting more planting. That the Catholic dominions exercised a monopoly on American sugar aggravated the Protestant Dutch and English. As soon as England consolidated control of part of St. Kitts in 1643, the colonists began planting cane. When the English conquered Jamaica in 1655, the settlers organized three cane plantations. Yet Barbados became the first English colony whose prosperity waxed as sugar took over the island agriculture. Richard Ligon's memorable chronicle of the rise of sugar culture, *A True and Exact History of the Island of Barbadoes* (1657), remains the single most eloquent testimony to sugar's allure during the formative years of English empire.[2]

While certain of the northern British American colonies imported raw sugar and molasses from the West Indies to process into refined loaf sugar and to distill into rum, none of the semi-tropical mainland colonies on the Gulf succeeded in sugar planting and manufacturing during the colonial era.[3] The amount of capitalization needed to create a refining complex inhibited even the most ambitious of planters. The New Smyrna colony in east Florida, founded in 1767 to produce cane sugar and indigo, suffered so great an undercapitalization that recruited laborers revolted in 1769. So Florida's Spanish and English residents never managed more than fitful patch farming of cane and the manufacture of sludgy syrup.

Historians have argued about which sugar project in North America could be called the first successful enterprise. Charles Gayaré, the Louisiana historian, detailed with antiquarian fastidiousness the multiple failures of crystallizing sugar after the Jesuits planted cane brought from Hispaniola in 1751.[4] During the period of Spanish rule, Antonio Mendez, aided by an expatriate of Santo Domingo named Morin, publicly exhibited the first Louisiana-bred and -refined sugar. But the scale of the project was so modest that Jean-Étienne de Boré, a native of French Illinois, is now celebrated as the father of the industry, having produced the first sugar on a commercial scale in 1794–95. The $12,000 he made after refining white crystal from his initial cane crop riveted the attention of the Louisiana planters victimized by the bust of indigo culture.

In 1806 Georgian agriculturist Thomas Spalding laid out a cane plantation on Sapelo Island, using the "Oteheite" derived from Louisiana. He knew if his efforts faltered, he could furnish canes or juice or molasses to the Savage sugar fining and baking plant at the west end of Broad Street in Charleston. A "book farmer" of the most experimental sort, Spalding had read the extant literature on sugar production and consulted with experienced Caribbean cane growers before planting. He possessed the capital to build a sugar house and had a clear vision of a Lowcountry agriculture based on diverse staples—rice, sugar, cotton, corn—rather than a single cash crop.[5] Spalding's one essential contribution to the cultivation of cane was his treatise "On the Culture of the Sugar Cane," which proposed a calendar of planting that optimized the chance of the cane coming to maturity in the short growing seasons of the mainland. He laid out a three-year crop rotation to preserve soil nutrition.[6] But the efforts of Spalding and his circle in the Sea Islands and Boré and his followers in Louisiana were marginal at best; the vastly more productive West Indian sugar plantations, with their raw or refined conical loaf forms, dominated the wholesale and retail grocery markets.

One thing that kept mainland planters from securing a fatter share of these markets was the material being grown. The Creole and Otaheite varieties of cane had thin walls and suffered frequent dieback from frosts. Not until Georgian John McQueen secured a boatload of ribbon cane from Jamaica in 1814 did the fortunes of the industry advance.[7] This fast-growing, thick-walled cane withstood the cooler climates of the Lowcountry and Louisiana, producing regular crops of excellent-tasting sugar. In 1825 Roswell King of St. Simons Island, Georgia, shipped a load of purple-striped ribbon cane to John J. Coiron of Louisiana. It transformed the Louisiana countryside. Each cane-growing district erected a West Indian–style steam sugar plant. (John Couper built the great Georgia Sea Island manufactory at Hopeton Plantation.) When the likelihood of the passage of a tariff on exports brought about a gut-wrenching drop in the value of long staple Sea Island cotton in 1827, South Carolina joined the ranks of the cane-growing regions. Edward Barnwell of Beaufort planted experimental plots, reported success in the pages of the *Southern Agriculturist* in 1828, and occasioned a cane boom in South Carolina during the 1830s.[8] Nearly every cane planter, once they noted the tendency of cane to exhaust soil, adopted the Spalding rotation: first year, cane; second year, cane stubble; third year, intercropped corn and cowpeas.

No type of agriculture in the United States was more cosmopolitan. Every variety cultivated was imported, from the original Otaheite and Creole to the purple-striped ribbon cane, from the black Java, LaPice, and Palfrey to the purple elephant and Japanese canes introduced in mid-century.[9] In 1886 Norman Jay Coleman, the US Secretary of Agriculture, instructed US consuls and sugar countries to secure examples of every sort grown. These were shipped to the newly established Sugar Experimental Station in Louisiana, and the analyses performed there formed the foundation of scientific cane agriculture in the twentieth century. Whereas American sorghum and beet sugar manufacture led the world in innovation, cane sugar production, with the exception of soil replenishment methods, followed the best practices pioneered elsewhere, particularly the English-speaking islands of the West Indies. Domestic production of sugar in the nineteenth century never supplanted the imported supply filling grocery shelves with muscovado, demarara, white loaf, and brown crystal. American genius in the sugar industry lay primarily in its retailing—in forming refined sugar and molasses into marketable shape, distributing it through grocery stores, and responding to consumer demands. We have seen how fruits and vegetables flowed through the markets of southern cities. Processed foodstuffs—such as sugar, salt, flour, and candy—came to the consumer via another system: a network of stores that crisscrossed the United States.

A DIGRESSION ON GROCERIES

There were and are elements of cookery that are not local. This is particularly true of town cookery. The hallmark of a town was the presence of a grocer, a broker in sundries beyond what was offered in the town produce market. It included preparations not available or made locally. A central

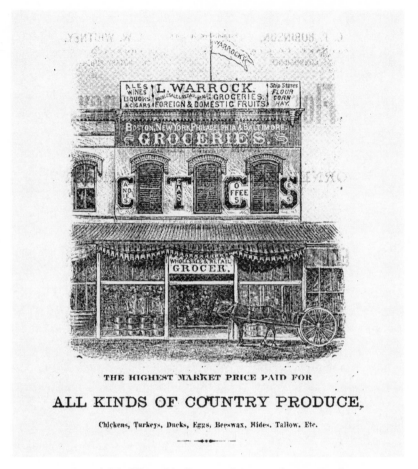

FIGURE 2. Ad for Warrock's. Courtesy American Antiquarian Society.

feature of a grocer's stock was sugar, for it—like salt, lard, butter, ginger, coffee, and tea—belonged to that broad category of commodities deemed necessary for a well-stocked household. An advertisement (fig. 2) from the 1870s of a grocer in the southernmost Lowcountry city, Jacksonville, Florida, suggests what these town purveyors offered, and consequently what they deemed desirable among the people. The top level of signs conveys the ultimate desiderata: alcohol, fresh fruit (foreign and domestic), and bread flour. Because of the dependence upon horses for mobility, hay, the primary equine food, was also advertised. Citrus-producing Jacksonville prospered to the extent that the taste for fruit—and not just the common apples, pears, peaches, pawpaws, and plums—activated popular fancy. That is why fruit stood at the center top. It would be in competing with produce markets by offering high-quality and exotic fruit that the grocers gradually impinged upon the business of fresh food selling.

Above everything blazoned on a flag flew a family name. In the nineteenth century, groceries were family businesses, and the reputation of a family guaranteed the quality of the goods. Families were connected by kinship, marriage, ethnic community, and sometimes religion, to other persons and places. Jacksonville's Warrock's declared their connection to Boston, New York, Philadelphia, and Baltimore—the chief importers of north Florida's produce—and the sources for many of the best prepared foods: Boston salt cod and pickled mackerel, New York beef, butter and cheese, Philadelphia flour and candy, and Baltimore oysters and terrapin.

The large "CTCS" dominating the façade called attention to four popular categories of product offered: candies, teas, coffees, and seeds. Prepared confections enjoyed increasing popularity in every settled portion of the country over the course of the century. The sugaring of America was under way. Caffeine, the favorite drug of commercial civilization, came via leaf or bean. Tea and coffee, important global commodities since the middle of the seventeenth century, stood front and center. And finally seeds: groceries served as outlets for the great seed brokers, Peter Henderson, Briggs Brothers, D. M. Ferry, Hiram Sibley & Co., James Vick, W. Atlee Burpee—an urban marketing alternative to their mail-order catalogs serving the rural districts. The early groceries incorporated the stock that we in the twenty-first century associate with country feed and grain stores.

Whether the grocery was located in Jacksonville, Chicago, New York, St. Louis, or San Francisco, it carried roughly the same retail stock. Warrock's, located in a port town important in the coastal shipping trade, sold ship provisions (cured meats and canned foods) and also functioned as a wholesale grocer. This means that they were commission merchants, supplying bulk goods to towns in Florida's interior. Their standard units of sale were barrel, box, tub, bag, bale, case, kit, and keg. Because wholesale grocers had to notify potential buyers (retail grocers, hotels, academies, etc.) in other locales what was currently in stock, they invariably resorted to print notification in newspapers. A purely retail establishment did not have to. Retail grocers serviced neighborhoods and used window signs and talk among the cook servants to excite trade. Few addressed the public in print. You could buy individual items, even portions of things, at a retail establishment.

How pervasive was the grocery in urban food supply? How cosmopolitan did it render a city's food? How were the groceries in a city organized spatially and commercially? City directories and newspaper advertisements give the raw ingredients for a portrait of Charleston's commercial landscape. (Similar profiles could be performed for every southern city.) In 1850 there were 215 groceries plying business. By mid-century, German grocers ran the great majority of these—161 in total. A handful of grocer dynasties—the Bredenbergs, the Bulwinkles, the Harbers, the Mehrtons, and the Meyers—owned outlets around the city. Charleston afforded a number of prime locations: King Street, Market Street, and the various intersections of downtown streets made up the desirable retail sites. East Bay and South Bay Streets on the Cooper River Waterfront, and Hasell Street, made up the wholesale district. Of the 20 grocers on King Street, the most fashionable shopping street in the city, 11 belonged to Germans, 7 to Anglo-Americans, and 2 to persons of other ethnicities. Of the 54 corners accommodating groceries, 45 were occupied by German grocers. On East Bay Street, the Atlantic waterfront of Charleston where ships' stores were restocked, 9 groceries were in the hands of Germans and 9 in the hands of Anglo-Americans. It was the least German street of the commercial landscape. The German community had three components: German Jewish families resident in the city since the 1700s; the descendants of Hessians who stayed in the city when the British withdrew at the end of the American Revolution; and immigrants who moved to Charleston in the wake of the 1848 political agitations in Europe. The first and last of these groups maintained the strongest transatlantic connections. Within Charleston, the German Friendly Society provided the principal social venue in which commercial rivalry could be put aside and the children of families might meet, court, and marry, thereby knitting family alliances.

The connections of and within the grocer community survived the Civil War. They enabled the rebooting of wholesale and retail trade in Charleston in late 1865 and early 1866. The January 1, 1866, issue of the *Charles-*

ton Daily News shows how the grocers' old northern suppliers and clients aided reconstruction. A page of the paper supplied New York advertisement for goods and hardware needed to rebuild the city. On the back page, three columns were devoted to produce and groceries. Charles L. Guilleaume advertised the longest list of offerings—it can suggest the makeup of typical retail stock while dramatizing the important place of sugar in the offerings. At his storehouse at 148 Meeting Street, Guilleaume offered (in order of listing):

> 500 Barrels B. Sugar, 100 Barrels AA Sugar, 100 Barrels A Sugar, 100 Barrels C Sugar, 50 Barrels C Coffee Sugar, 50 Barrels Crush Sugar, 500 Sacks Liverpool Salt, 250 Sacks Turks' Island Salt, 59 Cases Table Salt, 50 Sacks Rio Coffee, 25 Sacks Laguayra Coffee, 25 Sacks Old Government Java Coffee, 10 Sacks Ginger, 10 Sacks Pimento, 10 Sacks Spices, 100 Boxes Black Tea, 100 Boxes Green Tea, 250 Barrels Flour, 100 Half-Barrels Flour, 25 Barrels Sugar-house Molasses, 25 Barrels Syrup, 50 Half-Barrels Syrup, 50 Half-Barrels No. 1 and No. 2 Boston Mackerel, 100 Kits No. 1 and 2 Boston Mackerel, 500 Boxes No. 1 Herrings, 500 Boxes Seal Herrings, 250 Barrels Potatoes, 500 Kegs Nails, Spades, Shovels, Shot, H. S. Nails, Buckets, Brooms, Pails, Tubs, Blacking Brushes, Mason's Blacking, Matches, Willow and Oyster Baskets, Sieves, Pipes &c., 500 Boxes Spices, Mustard, Pepper, Ginger, Cassia, &c. Cream of Tartar, Soca, 100 Boxes Copperas, 100 Boxes Brimstone, 100 Boxes Alum, 50 Boxes Madder, 100 Cases Crackers, 500 Boxes Soap, 250 Boxes Fancy Soap, 1000 Boxes Candles, 500 Coils Rope, 250 Coils Manila Rope— various Sizes, 150 Bales Gunny Bagging, 20 Bales Sewing Twine.

Archibald Getty's, Guilleaume's chief rival, offered much the same, although Getty also offered "Superfine Flour," hams, bacon, ham shoulders, brown sugar, and powdered sugar. John King specialized in spices, pickles, oysters, lobsters, as well as mackerel and brown and crushed sugar. George Clark highlighted cheese and whiskey among his offerings. W. H. Chafe touted New York State butter, leaf lard, and English dairy cheese. Wagener, Heath, & Monsees, who did both wholesale and retail sales, offered Fulton Market beef, wines, Goshen butter, and the usual barrels of refined sugars, crushed sugar, and powdered sugar. Totaling the sugar announced in the wholesalers' advertisements, 12,800 pounds were available in dead midwinter in the city.

One might look at the newspapers from every port city from Portland, Maine, to St. Augustine, Florida, and find less dramatic versions of the same story. Sugar was ubiquitous. By 1865 it had become a traditional kitchen staple purveyed by the grocers who inhabited every town in the United States. To speak of a local sugar cuisine verges on nonsense, even in towns such as Jacksonville, Brunswick, or New Orleans, where cane grew locally.

No branch of kitchen art was and is more cosmopolitan than confectionery. The effort to uncover regional tweaks (e.g., pecans substituted for hazelnuts in the classic French praline recipe), while rewarding, gives rise to a minor sort of historical understanding. To grasp what the abundance of sugar created by the addition of American mainland supplies to West Indian and South American imports meant, we must turn attention to other culinary developments: the nineteenth-century explosion in homemade berry and vegetable wines, and the perfection of the use of sugar as a preservative. In both instances, sugar proved a remedy to the perishability of crops.

DRINKING THE HARVEST

Cultivators faced a number of problems in the nineteenth-century United States—a major aggravation was the lack of quality roads connecting towns with the rural countryside. The more abundant your crop, the greater the difficulty carting the quantity to a market where it might be converted to cash. Backcountry corn and grain farmers resorted to the ancient solution: they turned their wheat and barley into beer; their corn, wheat, and rye into whiskey. Acres condensed into portable barrels. With liquid grain, one need not worry about insect infestation of one's barns, or mildew, or handing over a portion of one's crop to the miller for payment. The same was true of apples and pears, which could be turned to cider and perry with only modest labor. Very few vegetables (sweet potatoes, sugar beets, parsnips) contained the carbohydrates that permitted them to be rendered into an alcoholic beverage. When sugar became plentiful, however, one could do this to almost any berry, fruit, or vegetable.

BLACKBERRY WINE

Squeeze fifty pounds of blackberries, strain them, and add 25 lbs. of New Orleans or clean white Havanna sugar; put all into a ten gallon Keg, and fill it with water. As it works add water, keeping the cask full. Add three pints of good brandy. The keg, if new, must be soaked with well distilled apple whiskey, or French Brandy.[10]

Published in 1824, this recipe recognizes the availability of American sugar. The general idea of the recipe—extract juice, add sugar, add water, and wait for natural processes of fermentation to occur—appeared in the earliest American cookbooks. Susannah Carter includes instructions for apricot wine, birch wine, gooseberry wine, quince wine, raspberry wine, and elderberry wine in her *Frugal Housewife* (1803); Lucy Emerson tells how to make currant wine and damson wine in *The New-England Cookery* (1808); "An Experienced Housekeeper" offers a recipe for ginger wine in *American Domestic Cookery* (1823). All have antecedents in late eighteenth-century English cooking manuals, for the British Isles underwent its sweetening at the end of the seventeenth century when Barbados and Jamaica sent its product to England. A circa 1700 recipe for cherry wine in a very English manuscript cookbook from Virginia called for three pounds of muscovado sugar for a gallon of cherry juice as the base for wine.[11]

If the template emerged in England during the late seventeenth century, certain of its applications in the nineteenth-century United States were ingenious. The *Southern Agriculturist* reported in 1837 the creation of dandelion wine by a woman in Concord, Massachusetts. She "discovered that a pleasant table beer may be made of the water in which dandelions have been boiled, by adding to each gallon a tea-cup full of yeast, and a pint of molasses. As dandelions are abundant and cheap, and their medicinal qualities well known, the experiment may be worth trying."[12] The report reminds us that sugar knew no region and that certain plants (dandelions, for instance) had so extensive a range that they verged on being universal as well. Another elegant creation was peach wine:

PEACH WINE

Take peaches, nectarines, &c., pare them, and take the stones out; then slice them thin, and pour over them from a gallon or two gallons of water, and a quart of white wine. Place the whole on a fire to simmer gently for a considerable time, till the sliced fruit becomes soft; pour off the liquid part into another vessel containing more peaches that have been sliced but not heated; let them stand for twelve hours, then pour out the liquid part, and press what remains through a fine hair bag. Let the whole be now put into a cask to ferment; add a loaf sugar a pound and a half to each gallon—boil well an ounce of beaten cloves in a quart of white wine, and add to it the above.[13]

One appreciates the more restrained hand in the administration of sugar in this preparation—only one and one-half pounds of loaf sugar to a gallon of peach liquid—half the proportion used in the early Virginia receipt for cherry wine. When American vignerons of the 1810s and '20s adopted the European practice of adding some sugar to the must in wine making in order to secure a robust alcohol content in a vintage, a problem arose when they used the three pounds to one gallon proportion used in early Anglo-American fruit and berry wine recipes. Viticulturist Nicholas Herbemont critiqued the syrupy quality of the wine of Major John Adlum, one of the patriarchs of American wine making.

> I cannot conceive the necessity or propriety of adding 3 pounds of sugar per gallon of must, be it ever so weak, as Major Adlum recommends. I know very well that when the grapes are not sufficiently ripe they do not contain a sufficient quantity of saccharine matter to give a due strength to the wine, and that young vines do not produce as rich grapes as old ones; and that, therefore, it is proper to add to them what they are deficient in. But it seems to me, that by adding 3 pounds of sugar to a gallon of juice that must already contain a considerable quantity of it, is to make a must richer in sugar, I should think, than any that can ever be made any where by merely extracting juice of very ripe grapes from old vines; unless the grapes have been, previous to pressing, partly dried in the sun, which is sometimes practiced to obtain rich *vins de liqueur*, which are only drank occasionally and in very small quantities, and are never used as an every-

day drink, being too sweet and too luscious for the taste of most people: nor are they considered as wholesome, at least for constant use.[14]

Herbemont's much more tempered employment of sugar in chaptalization would mark the way forward for Nicholas Longworth and subsequent American winemakers.

While using sugar in making wines led to generally palatable results, provided that a judicious sense of restraint was at work, the same cannot be said about the use of sugar in brewing. Mary Randolph's recipe for "Molasses Beer" in *The Virginia House-wife* has been re-created recently by a number of southern brewers.

> Put five quarts of hops, and five of wheat bran, into fifteen gallons of water; boil it three or four hours, strain it, and pour it into a cask with one head taken out; put in five quarts of molasses, stir it till well mixed, throw a cloth over the barrel; when moderately warm, add a quart of good yeast, which must be stirred in; then stop it closed with a cloth and board. When it has fermented and become quite clear, bottle.[15]

It invariably has an overly malty taste. Jane Randolph's 1743 recipe for spring beer had an even more outré taste. To a solution of brown sugar and molasses, Randolph added asparagus roots, horseradish, cinquefoil, spruce tops, watercress, wormwood, and sassafras bark. To this herbal decoction, she added muscovado sugar.[16] This beer tastes more pharmaceutical than gin.

The one sugar water/sassafras solution that would amount to something was "Sassafras Mead," the ancestor of root beer, found in recipe books of the 1840s. Mrs. E A. Howland wrote that this was a beverage that did not ferment and counted on the kick of snorting bubbles cast from the liquid by carbonate of soda.

Since the 1930s, the superiority of wine made from *Vitis vinifera* grapes has been maintained so insistently in culinary circles that the splendors of tomato wine,[17] rhubarb wine, and strawberry wine have been discounted. As a result we have lost not only the beverages, but a world of early pickles that employed vinegar made from fruit and berry wines rather than apple cider and European wine. Sean Brock is leading a recuperation of this last pantry of vinegars.

If the finest fruit, berry, and vegetable wines created in the eighteenth and nineteenth centuries have passed into the limbo of culinary neglect, the art of preserving with sugar by candying them or as conserves thrives. The commercial and home manufactures of preserves have given rise to some of the loveliest inventions of recent culinary history.

THE GLASSY GARDEN

Every fruit grown in the nation from the citron and the pawpaw found its way into a sugar suspension. The fig became particularly beloved of southern kitchen gardeners, and a short fichus tree became a fixture on farmscapes, often found in the vicinity of the bake house because of the natural yeast spores it supplied. In the Lowcountry, growers valued varieties for their eating qualities (celestial, white ischia, lemon, magnolia, ronde noire, pastelliere, and brown turkey), their cooking qualities (Adriatic white, Brunswick, magnolia, Marseilles white, and brown turkey), or their drying qualities (Smyrna, Angelique).[18] Because of the vulnerability of the fruit to bruising, spoilage, and infestation, no commercial crop of figs was produced in the United States outside of California. It was the home fruit par excellence. So when late summer's bounty arrived, the first impulse was not to take it to market, but to get a pot of syrup boiling. Lafcadio Hearn, the newspaperman and student of Louisiana culture, recorded the standard preparation in his landmark *La Cuisine Creole* (1885).

FIG PRESERVES

Let the figs be firm, not dead ripe or they will boil to a mass. They should be laid in alum the day before they are to be preserved, then taken out, washed, and put into the boiling syrup. Allow a pound of sugar to a pound of fruit, dissolve and boil the sugar and water (allowing half a pint of water to a pound). Boil the syrup until it is thin. Put in the figs and boil for three hours, or until transparent; then bottle as usual and seal up with wax.[19]

Alum—potassium aluminum sulfate—was a popular pickling used to keep cucumbers crisp, in this instance stabilizing the cells of the fig's rind, preventing it from dissolving to mush during the protracted sugar boil. Because this salt is toxic in large quantities, it passed out of favor as a cooking ingredient in the twentieth century. Hearn's recommendation that the figs be firm reveals that he desired solidity in the preserved product. Alum assisted in achieving this texture in the cooked fruit.

The popularity of fig preserves in the warmer regions of the United States can be gauged by the invention in 1840 of an imitation fig preserve using small yellow tomatoes. H. E. Elsworth of the US Patent Office thought so highly of the application of one E. Steiger of Washington, DC, that he communicated the recipe to the leading agricultural and horticultural journals of the day. Because of efforts by publicists in the late 1830s to present the tomato as a medical boon to humanity, it had come into an intense vogue shortly before submission of the patent application and sample.

TOMATO FIGS

Take six pounds of sugar to one peck (sixteen pounds) of the fruit: scald, and remove the skin of the fruit in the usual way: cook them over a fire, their own juice being sufficient, without the addition of water, until the sugar penetrates, and they are clarified. They are then taken out, spread on dishes, flattened, and dried in the sun. A small quantity of the syrup should be occasionally sprinkled over them whilst drying; after which, pack them down in boxes, treating each layer with powdered sugar. The syrup is afterwards concentrated, and bottled for use. They keep well from year to year, and retain surprisingly their flavor, which is nearly that of the best quality of fresh figs. The pear shaped or single tomatoes answer the purpose the best.[20]

The recipe became a fixture in nineteenth-century American cookbooks. It particularly excited the imagination of southern agricultural entrepreneurs trying to rebuild the rural economy after the Civil War. In 1870 a Georgian enthused to the editor of the *Southern Cultivator*:

Among the new articles capable of being utilized and converted into money on the farm, nothing to us looks more plausible than the making of tomato figs. The taste of tomato, whether a natural or acquired one, is universally popular—and there is hardly a vegetable which the public demand has required to be cooked and prepared for present and permanent use, in such a great variety of ways, as tomatoes, and which retains so readily its peculiar flavor. The time will probably come when large fields of them will be cultivated expressly for converting into figs, which we consider far preferable to common figs. They retain the tomato taste, keep as well as the others, and could as readily be exported or shipped long distances.[21]

Noteworthy here is that the selling point is no longer resembling figs in taste and look, for figs are less preferable; rather, sugaring preserves the basic taste of the tomato. One could use the preserved tomato for any of the multitude of tomato dishes one wished. Subsequent events would show that aspects of this analysis were correct: there *did* exist a broad demand for tomatoes that had been preserved somehow, and that the maintenance of the taste of the tomato in the preserved form would be a key to demand. Unfortunately, canned tomatoes would taste more like the fresh fruit than sugared. The tomato fig became passé with the turn of the century. Preserved figs have retained their homey charm.

One gets a sense of the place of preserves in the southern culinary firmament by noting the items for which instructions are given in cookbooks. Certain cookbooks, Lettice Bryan's *Kentucky Housewife*, for instance, incorporate preserves as a section with the old category of sweetmeats, any entity prepared with sugar—marmalades, jellies, jams, and fruit butters. Most, beginning with Mary Randolph's *Virginia House-wife*, acknowledge the importance of preserves as a class of preparation determined by function, granting it a separate heading in the cookbooks and subordinating marmalades and candied peels and rinds within it.

The Virginia House-wife (1824): Cling Stone Peaches, Soft Peaches, Peach Marmalade, Peach Chips, Pears, Pear Marmalade, Quinces, Quince Jelly, Currant Jelly, Quince Marmalade, Cherries, Morello Cherries, Raspberry Jam, Strawberries, Strawberry Jam, Gooseberries, Apricots in Brandy, Peaches in Brandy, Cherries in Brandy, Magnum Bonum Plums in Brandy.

The Kentucky Housewife (1839): Candied Citrons, Lemon Marmalade, Peaches, Pears, Quinces, Citron, Cherries, Lemon Rind, Limes, Oranges, Pine-Apples, Strawberries, Apricots, English Grapes, Fox Grapes, Green

Grapes, Tomatoes, Yellow Tomatoes, Tomato Marmalade, Plums, Damsons, Gooseberries, Cranberries, Green Crab Apples, Apples.

The Carolina Housewife (1847): Compote of Pears, Compote of Strawberries/Peaches, Compote of Apples, Peach Leather, Dry Peaches, Preserve Peaches, Marmalade, Shaddocks, Sour Orange Marmalade, Shaddocks, Oranges, Yellow Oranges, Candy Oranges, Figs, Tomatoes, Cherries, Pumpkin Chips, Quince Marmalade, Pine Apple Sweet Meat [four additional jellies and two brandied fruits].

The Southern Gardener and Receipt-Book (1860) [Under the rubric Preserves and Jellies; what follows eliminates Jellies]: Cucumbers, Orange, Orange Marmalade, Watermelon with the Pulp, Citron Watermelon, Golden Pippins, Peach Sweetmeats, Green Figs, Tomatoes, Tomato Figs, Quinces Whole, Strawberries, Raspberries, Grapes, Crab Apples, Cranberries, Pineapple.

Dixie Cookery (1867): Crab Apples, Pine-Apple Marmalade, Pine-Apples, Apples, Green-Gage Plums, Cherries, Apricots, Green Lemons, Green Peppers, Green Tomatoes, Water-Melon Rinds, Orange Marmalade, Peaches, Quinces, Pears, Strawberries, Cranberries. [The section concludes with Jams and Jellies.]

Mrs. Hill's New Cook Book (1867): Oranges Preserved Whole, Citrons, Glass Melon, Pineapple, Strawberries, Raspberries/Blackberries, Cherries, Grapes, Muscadines, Crab Apple, Figs, Peaches, Quinces, Pears.

Mrs. Elliott's Housewife (1870): Peaches, Cling-Stone Peaches, Water-Melon Rinds, Apple Marmalade, Apples Preserved like Ginger, Siberian Crab Apple, Apple Jelly, Dried Cherries or Damsons, Dried Peaches, Dried Apples, Dried Green Apples, Ripe Cantaloupes, Water-Melon Rind, Glass Melons and Citrons, Quinces, Pears, Pear Marmalade, Strawberries [section concludes with Jams and Jellies].

The Queen of the Kitchen (1874): Tomato Figs, Figs, Pineapple, Peaches, Apple Jelly, Apples, Hodge Podge (mixed preserved fruits), Citron

Melon, Citron, Watermelon Rind, Green Gage, Damson, Florida Oranges, Orange Marmalade, Lemon Marmalade, Limes, Pears, Pear Marmalade, Gooseberries, Currants, Green Tomato, Scarlet Cherries, Morello Cherries, Strawberry, Pumpkin, Crab Apple, Quince, Tomato, Green Rose Pepper, Blackberries.

The listings mix the expected and unexpected. The commonest fruits and berries appear frequently. The citrus being shipped from Jacksonville found ready employment, with orange, lemon, lime, and citron receiving multiple listings. Only the shaddock appears in a single recipe.[22] Watermelons, both pith and rind, appear, with the citron melon (a specialty melon bred for rind pickling and sugaring) receiving notice. Quinces—grown widely as stock for grafting and only edible when cooked with sugar— were broadly popular. Only the tomato, of produce generally categorized as a vegetable (it is a berry), appeared frequently, with green peppers and cucumbers the only other vegetables prepared. Only authors who lived in Tidewater or the Lowcountry included recipes for preserved figs. The imported pineapple appeared in every part of the South—a grocery luxury.

CODA

Antiquity supplied three vehicles for preserving fruits, berries, and vegetables: salt, alcohol, and vinegar. Since the sixteenth century, sugar, the modern preservative, supplied a fourth. It harmonized better with the natural sugars of plants than salt, and quickly became crucial to the work of prolonging the edibility of the harvest. Confectionery appears with the aura of luxury in early modern cookbooks, but nineteenth-century manuals make it evident that sugar-curing fruits and berries was more necessitous than luxurious.

A substantial scholarship over the past forty years, since the publication of Richard Dunn's classic *Sugar and Slaves* (1972), has made the connection between slave labor and sugar conspicuous in the historical memory. Many historians who have explored that connection have expressed sympathy for abolitionist attempts to boycott sugar because of the moral evils implicated in its production. In these pages, it should have become clear why these boycotts were foredoomed to failure. Anyone with an orchard or a berry patch in nineteenth-century America believed they had only three options for the bulk preservation of their food. By the nineteenth century, chemists had unraveled the process of fermentation sufficiently to know that both alcohol and vinegar were developments of fructose, glucose, or sucrose. Sugar joined salt as a necessity.

In the twenty-first century, sugar's place in culture has become more dominant. Whether in the form of cane sugar, beet sugar, corn sugar, or some manufactured entity, sucrose sweetens an ocean of soft drinks, a vast array of processed foods, morning cereals, and baked goods galore. Nutritionists excoriate sugar's spreading dominion, blaming it for childhood obesity, type 2 diabetes, and a host of behavioral disorders. No hygienic sermon, no legislative initiative, no maternal prohibition will countermand the desire for sugar's sweetness. The curious thing, given the potency of the desire for sweetness, is that cane has never been systematically bred for the quality of its dulcetness. It is not difficult to imagine what masterful confectioners could do with a sugar that possessed more finesse and distinctiveness of quality.

Yet sugarcane's dominion has spread beyond the kitchen and the bakery to the garage and factory. Brazil has pioneered its use as an effective fuel alternative to petroleum. Indeed, the country has been so successful in its substitution of cane-based ethanol for oil that it has become insulated from the economic damage of volatile petroleum markets. Inspired by the Brazilian example, the United States has granted millions of dollars to research laboratories to enable the perfecting of cane sugar as a biofuel. Yet the old liability of sugarcane—its intolerance for cold—imposes limits on the acreage that can be grown. This has caused attention to turn to the cold-tolerant cousin of sugarcane, sorghum, as the biofuel source of the future.

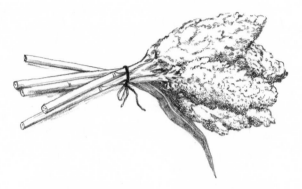

FOURTEEN *Sorghum*

While the Civil War caused staple scarcities that led to replacement crops—chicory root for coffee, field pea mash for wheat flour—only one substitute became a significant and enduring component of American agriculture and cookery: sorghum.[1] The disruption of the Louisiana and Georgia cane sugar production by the rebellion occasioned sorghum's widespread adoption in both the Union and the Confederacy. An experimental crop grown by progressive farmers in the late 1850s became a staple by 1862.

Sorghum's extraordinary transit from the margins to the center of American agriculture from 1855 to 1865 inspired Henry Clough to observe after the armistice:

> Sorghum is now a household word in all the great Middle and Western States of the Union. It came to us unannounced, was introduced into the country without parade or eclat, was treated at first with distrust and ridicule, was cultivated and worked without skill, and yet in the short space of ten years it has acquired a position among the permanent staples of the country, exhibiting a career of success without a parallel in the annals of husbandry.[2]

Clough, a Yankee editor and farmer who touted sorghum as a Union commodity, could have been speaking for southern farmers as well.

A traditional cereal grass grown throughout Asia and Africa, *Sorghum bicolor*, like most ancient staples, had given rise over the centuries to many employments: its leaves for cattle fodder; its seeds ground into flour for millet breads; its stalks crushed, boiled, and fermented for alcoholic beverages or used as building material. Though grown in colonial America on a small scale as a grain, sorghum seized the attention of agricultural experimentalists in the 1850s when French measurements of its saccharine content suggested that it might be used like sugar beets as a cheap alternative to cane sugar. What had been employed elsewhere in the world for centuries as cereal and fodder became a sweetener in the United States.[3]

Liquid sorghum tastes like the coppery evening sun: more mellow and malty than blackstrap molasses, less brilliant and wholesome than cane syrup, less piquant and poetic than maple. For half a century, from 1870 to 1920, the sorghum jug sat next to the biscuit basket on many southern and midwestern tables.

Sweet sorghum insinuated itself into American consciousness in the 1850s, when seed entered the United States from France and South Africa. In 1853 pomologist William Prince and D. J. Browne, agricultural agent for the US Patent Office, secured "Sorgho" seed in France, the "Chinese Sugar Cane." They distributed their stock through the northern states by members of Prince's seed network and via US congressmen. Leonard Wray—a British merchant-planter who became fascinated by the uses of imphee grass in Natal, South Africa[4]—experimented with methods of turning its sap to sugar and conveyed a substantial quantity of seed to southern planters, particularly ex-Governor Hammond of South Carolina.

James Henry Hammond (1807–1864; governor of South Carolina, 1842–44) began experimenting with Chinese sorghum at Redcliff Plantation, Beech Island, South Carolina, in 1856.[5] He had secured seed as part of the congressional distribution. His success that year with syrup boiling excited the agricultural press and attracted the notice of Wray. The Anglo-Indian planter proved so eloquent in arguing the superiority of South African imphee grasses as sorghum varieties that Hammond dug up fifty acres of just-sprouted Chinese sorghum in his fields and fifty acres of corn, replanting them both with South African cane.[6] After an abundant harvest, Hammond distributed seed to his network of agricultural and political connections. The favorable publicity of these experiments contributed greatly to the rehabilitation of his reputation, which had been soiled by the scandal of his sexual dalliances with his teenage nieces in the 1840s. He would be appointed US senator later in 1857, filling out the incomplete term of Andrew P. Butler. Politically rehabilitated, Hammond exploited his public station, famously proclaiming on the floor of the Senate, "Cotton is King."

Sorghum may not have attained regal status in Hammond's eyes, yet its qualities fascinated him and increasing numbers of farmers and planters as well, who read about the novelty in the agricultural press. Its morphology and botanical features became intense matters of discussion in print.

A decade of wrangling took place among botanists before they agreed that Chinese sugarcane and imphee were varieties of the same species, *Sorghum bicolor*. It took no time at all for the experimental community to realize that these tall, corn-like grasses promised to be a wonder plant. Agriculturalists adopted it from Minnesota to Georgia. By 1857, 20,000 acres were under cultivation—a noteworthy field allocation for an experimental crop. Sorghum engaged American imaginations for political as well as agricultural reasons. It tolerated cold better than sugarcane, so could grow well north of the coastal counties of South Carolina that marked the limit of sugarcane's cultivation. Northerners who bridled at tasting the sweat of African slaves in southern sugar and molasses saw sorghum as an ethical alternative that might enrich northern agriculture. The US Patent Office distributed free packets to anyone who made the effort to write for a sample. Hundreds of northern farmers did.

Events catapulted sorghum from a promising experimental crop to a staple in both the North and the South. The Civil War disrupted the flow of Louisiana and Florida sugar to the North in 1861 and, after the summer of 1863, to the South as well. Sorghum served in its stead.

> At home and abroad sorghum came to take the place of the vanished sugar. The children at home ate it in their ginger cakes, and the soldiers in camp drank it in their rye-coffee. The molasses and sugar of Louisiana were procurable in degree till the fall of Vicksburg; but the spirit of

independence was rife, and each State desired and determined to rely as much as possible on its own products. The theory of State sovereignty was extended even to sorghum; and its introduction was hailed everywhere as one of the greatest boons of a beneficent Providence. The juice of the cane, extracted in a primitive fashion by crushing the stalks between wooden rollers revolving upon wooden cogs and impelled by horse-and-little-darky power, was caught in an ordinary trough, boiled down into proper consistency in preserving kettles, kitchen pots, or whatever might be utilized for the purpose, and barreled for use as sorghum molasses. The syrup thus produced was quite a palatable one, with a slightly acidulous and not disagreeable flavor, but with an unpleasant tendency to make the mouth sore. It was known as "long-sweetening," in contradistinction to its predecessor, "short-sweetening," the sugar that was scarce.

From its use in the place of sugar sorghum soon leaped into high repute as an almost universal food staple.[7]

While this report from the *Century* stresses the continental embrace of sorghum during the war, other magazine commentators stressed the particular fascination with sorghum in the Confederacy.

Sugar, after the fall of Vicksburg, was almost as scarce as coffee. But in sorghum the people found a substitute which came perhaps nearer a success than any of the numberless makeshifts of the period. . . . It was about the sole thing of which there was no stint in the Confederacy. Verily the land was "submerged in sorghum." It sweetened the coffee, tea, and all the desserts of the time; sorghum candy was the national confection, sorghum "stews" the national festival. The strange creaking hum of the cane-mills pervaded the land. Every place was redolent of it; everything was sticking with it.[8]

Because it was an entire novelty, errors in growing and processing sorghum deviled its early adopters. Preparing syrup proved particularly fraught, with some undercooking it, others scorching it. "As the sorghum was in most cases unavoidably boiled in iron vessels, the habitual users of it were easily to be distinguished by their abnormally black teeth."[9] So it was in no way an unproblematic ambrosia, whose quality and salubriousness were granted universally. For every admirer of its dulcet taste, there existed a consumer with fouled teeth, sore mouth, or complaints about its flavor.

Sorghum bread, made from the brownish-pink flour of ground imphee seeds (many likened the appearance and texture to buckwheat) proved a rustic loaf lacking homely associations or high table refinement. Lacking gluten, it did not rise with leavening. So it was often admixed to wheat flour to make brown loaves that some said tasted like rye. When prepared from pure sorghum flour without a chemical rising agent, it came from the oven dense and black, particularly if made with black seed sorghum. In South Africa, the bread was traditionally thin and crusty without crumb. In the United States, all-sorghum bread usually combined sorghum meal, sorghum molasses, baking soda, lard, salt, hot water, and, when available, a spice such as ginger.[10] It was, perhaps, unfortunate that the most systematic institutional promoters of sorghum bread were the Union and Confederate prisons. When wheat supplies grew scarce, the prisons resorted to sorghum. "This was as black as a stove-pipe and sour when it came from the oven."[11]

Sorghum bread's associations with the time of privation and the experience of captivity had consequences once peace and commerce returned. Just as rye coffee (or okra seed coffee for that matter) vanished from the pantries of all but the poorest when roasting beans became available from South America, so sorghum bread vanished from the table when wheat began pouring into the South from Pennsylvania and California in the 1860s. The brief heyday of sorghum beer also ceased, not be taken up again until the Volstead Act of 1919 made the cheap illegal production of alcohol a very profitable enterprise.[12] The manufacture of spirits from sorghum — sucrat — was almost invariably illegal wherever it occurred, so no reliable statistics on its production or sale exist, though anecdotal reportage in newspapers indicates that this form of moonshine had a following.

Privation sometimes soured public perception of sorghum in another way. During the war some believed the claims that sorghum was a universal food, and during the periods of general scarcity grew and consumed sorghum as their chief staple. Sorghum "sore mouth" resulted. Ulceration of the cheeks is a symptom of pellagra, a dietary disease caused by the high concentrations of leucine in sorghum, preventing the conversion of tryptophan into niacin.[13] Sore mouth indicated a niacin deficiency in the diet. After the war, pellagra troubled those portions of the South where niacin-poor corn became the basis of the diet. Eating sorghum with corn exacerbated the pellagra problem. Where sorghum operated simply as a sweetener in a varied diet, sore mouth did not occur. One population that suffered sorghum-related pellagra disproportionately during the war were prisoners of war. Union captives held in Columbia, South Carolina, languished in "Camp Sorghum," so named for its prison diet: sorghum and corn bread.[14]

Sorghum remained important during the Reconstruction era for two purposes: as cattle fodder and as a sweetener. Its most pronounced benefit, its ability to be grown in areas north of the semi-tropical southern coast, remained in force. If one wished a locally sourced and processed sweetener that could *also* serve as livestock feed, one had to answer two simple questions: Would sorghum or sugar beets give you more of what you needed at less cost? And did you like the flavor of sorghum more than sugar beet sugar?

The question of flavor was complicated by the problem of "green taste." H. W. Wiley of Indiana discussed this fault's role in the abandonment of sorghum culture in parts of the Midwest after the Civil War. "The Sorghum syrup made at that time contained an unpleasant flavor, known as the sorghum taste or green taste, which was very unpleasant to many persons. This led to the gradual exclusion of sorghum syrup from our markets."[15] If midwestern farmers had read agricultural journals from other sections of the country, they could have avoided the problem. In a report on midwestern sorghum culture in an 1860 issue of the *Southern Cultivator*, H. Hinkley noted that green taste arose from the processing of immature canes. "Well matured cane has not this taste, nor has its syrup."[16] The widespread harvesting of immature cane can only be attributed to a lack of experience, a problem not uncommon with new introductions.

Those who correctly grew sorghum developed decided taste preferences among varieties. In northern states, numbers insisted that the Chinese sugarcane had a richer taste. (They also esteemed its great cold tolerance in the field.) Certain of the imphee canes developed enthusiasts in the South. Yet the descriptions of the samples of processed sorghum tested by the Illinois State Agricultural Society in 1859 make plain that extraordinarily variable boiling and fining gave rise to syrup and sugar that ranged from "very dark, exceedingly bitter and unpleasant" to "taste almost equal to honey."[17] Singularly unfortunate things happened to those who attempted to crystallize sugar by subjecting the juice to more and more heat. Mistakes in processing ruined the taste of perfectly good sorghum as frequently as using immature cane. Knowledge of how to process syrup without scorching and without impurities arose in the Union in late 1863 and early 1864. In parts of the South, this knowledge did not come until Reconstruction. The creation of fine sorghum sugar took place only after breeding refinements of Omseaana imphee cane produced plants with enough natural sugar to crystallize. This was largely a development of the 1880s.

ANTEBELLUM VARIETIES

A hallmark of the age of experiment in American agriculture (roughly 1820 to 1885) was the widespread tweaking of vegetable and grain varieties — seed selection, hybridization by cross-breeding varieties, and the careful development of natural mutations (sports) led to the quick proliferation of varieties. Seed companies attempted to secure the best of these improved varieties as proprietary cultivars. Each new variation bore a new name. Yet truth be known, the most significant crosses were made by multiple people with similar results in different locales, so a multiplicity of names designated a rather limited number of plant types.

Chinese sugarcane, a black seed sorghum imported from India, and Wray's sixteen imphee grasses from Natal constituted the basic breeding stock from which all the marketable varieties of sorghum originated. Only ten of Wray's imphee grasses mattered greatly in the development of America sorghum. Because of the time differentials for growing to maturation, the grasses were immediately categorized into northern short season and southern long season varieties, although all of the northern types could be grown in the South. The northern varieties: Nee-a-za-na, Oom-se-a-na, Boom-vwa-na, Shla-goo-va. The southern varieties: Shla-goon-dee, Zim-moo-ma-na, E-a-na-moo-de, Vim-bis-chu-a-pa, Zim-ba-za-na, E-both-la, E-thlo-sa, Boo-es-a-na, En-ya-ma, Koom-ba-na, See-en-gla-na, and E-engha.[18] Widespread notice of these varieties came through publication of Henry S. Olcott's 1857 treatise *Sorgho and Imphee: Chinese and African Sugar Canes* by the country's leading agricultural book publisher, A. O. Moore of New York. The book contained Wray's introduction to the South African varieties and translations of the French experiments at extracting sugar from the Chinese sugarcane. The volume prompted such interest that a separate appendix was issued within a year of publication, detailing aspects of sorghum's cultivation and surmising best practices for syrup and "wet sugar" manufacture.

Because landrace grains and oil seeds inherently possess a fair amount of genetic variability, numbers of the nominal varieties of the 1870s through 1890s were recognized by university field testers as rebranded versions of one of the original strains. Below I have supplied the predominant market name, probable parent strain, and a description of its salient features.

Honduras Cane: Seedsman Peter Henderson promoted this sorghum actively in the 1870s and '80s. According to Henderson, "Its seed-top is reddish-brown and spreading; hence the synonym 'Sprangle Top.' It is also called 'Mastodon' and 'Honey Cane.'" Collier identified "Honduras Cane" as a development of Wray's E-engha, of which he wrote, "This is a fine, tall kind, being from ten to twelve feet high when full grown, but it is more slender than either of the foregoing, and exceedingly graceful in appearance. It begins flowering in ninety days, and is fully ripe three weeks after. . . . The seed head of the E-engha is large and very pretty, the seed being upon long slender foot stalks, which are bent down by the weight of the seed, forming a graceful drooping. The seeds, which are of a dull, yellow color, are rather long and flat than round and plump." Wray himself thought that the Honduras cane was his Vim-bis-chu-a-pa.

Chinese sugarcane retained its name throughout the nineteenth century and collected "Sorgho" as an additional designation. Its cold tolerance recommended it in the more northern states and Canada. Its productivity never approached the imphee varieties, but the flavor of its syrup attracted strong adherents. Seedsmen employed it in hybridizing schemes, crossing the cane with imphee varieties. The French, who had supplied the original seeds, abandoned cultivation of the variety in the 1870s. In his 1884 *Report on Sorghum and Sugar Beet Culture*, Collier noted that Chinese sugarcane "is characterized by a rachia or central spindle, with a loose, spreading panicle; the branches are slender, drooping, bearing brownish colored seeds, enclosed in blackish, shining glumes."[19]

Early Amber Sorghum: This most popular of the nineteenth-century sorghum varieties also went by the names "Early Golden" and "Golden Syrup." By the 1870s, it had become farmers' favorite variety because of its high sugar content and the flavor of its syrup. It was a form of Wray's imphee Boom-vwa-na (literally "small red" in Kaffir). Wray commended the cane, writing, "I have eaten single pieces, containing certainly two or three per cent more sugar than the average juice obtained from large bundles of stalks, taken as they come. . . . [T]here is a clearness, a brightness, and a genuine sugarcane sweetness in the juice of this variety, and of the Oom-see-a-na, that I very much admire. In its growth and general appearance, it is very much like the E-engha [Honduras cane] but its stalks are brighter and more slender: its leaves are not so broad, and its seed vessels are upon shorter and stiffer foot stalks."[20]

White Liberian Cane: Known also as "White Imphee," "Early Orange," "Orange," "Wolf Tail," and "Gray Top," it had an easily recognizable short panicle, with branches that bent to one side. A small plant, its seeds were nearly white. First introduced into the United States by Wray as Nee-a-za-na, it had the reputation among Zulu-Kaffir farmers of being the sweetest of the imphee grasses. It could ripen in as early as seventy-five days, a great recommendation in the eyes of cultivators from regions with short growing seasons.

Liberian Sorghum: Was also named "Imphee" and "Sumac" by seed dealers of the nineteenth century. Admired for its vitality and robust tolerance of extreme weather, Liberian was the latest ripening of the imphee canes. It was characterized by its short, very stout, close-jointed stem, its small, compact panicle and diminutive reddish-yellow seeds. This was a development from Wray's Koom-ba-na, which he characterized as "one of the very sweetest and best I had."[21]

White Mammoth (White African Cane): One of the tallest of the imphee canes, it produced seeds as white as rice in black glumes. It had an erect habit, a long growing season, and a high sugar content in the stalks that commended it to early growers for distilling. This was Wray's En-ya-ma imphee. He noted in particular its height and its quality as a millet. Baker's Heirloom Seeds currently sells this original imphee variety as one of its heritage sorghums.

Purple Imphee: In the 1870s, a commentator wrote, "This tall, reed-like cane, with its trim, spear-shaped head, is the most remarkable of its race in being in some of its modified forms almost the only sort from which any sugar has heretofore been made." This was Wray's Oom-see-a-na.[22]

E-a-na-moodee Imphee: One of the tallest of the imphee grasses, topping ten feet, this was a greatly valuable forage plant. Wray reckoned it a soft and juicy cane, with 14 percent sugar. The seed heads grew large, erectly stiff, bearing round plump seeds "of a clear yellow color."[23]

Red Imphee: Tall, long-jointed, early ripening, and noted especially for its highly acidulous juice and its beautiful, wide-spreading, rust-colored panicle when the seeds are ripe. An evolution of Wray's Shla-goo-va.

Black Imphee: An early, not very productive variety, with a short stem and rather small and close panicle of a brilliant glossy black color—that of the glumes—which entirely enclose the seed. The juice of this sort possesses very strongly the peculiar flavor generally characterizing more or less all the imphee race.

All of these varieties were stripped of leaves twice during the growing season for fodder. The seed heads were picked and milled for flour upon maturation. The stalks were cut, carted to a mill, and processed for syrup.

MAKING SORGHUM MOLASSES

The demand for sweeteners during the Civil War accelerated the development of commercial-scale processing of cane for sorghum syrup. By the end of the war, every step had generated machines suited for the most efficient handling of the material. In 1865 the commissioner of agriculture of the United States summarized the accumulated knowledge in "Sorghum, or Northern Sugar Cane," in the USDA's annual report.[24] A paraphrase of the method follows.

After the leaves had been stripped for fodder for the final time, and the field had (1) come to maturity or (2) been subjected to a killing frost, workers cut the stalks with a corn knife. If no frost has occurred, the stalks should be left on the ground for up to two weeks to cure. If a sharp frost has taken place, the stalks were immediately put into shocks. Horse-driven carts outfitted with a long blade saved man-hours of labor of large plantings. Cane would be gathered in large piles, covered with straw. Cane that freezes and returns to warmth risks undergoing acetous fermentation, so insulating the piles was paramount.

At a convenient time, farmers carted the cured canes to a mill for crushing. Mills tended be comprised of three metal rollers arranged either vertically, for animal-powered operations, or horizontally, for water- or steam-powered mills. Numbers of iron foundries marketed patent cane mills in both configurations. Flanges on the sides kept stalks from spreading beyond the sides of the rollers. A juice-collecting pan sat beneath the rollers.

Because a substantial amount of vegetable matter gets mashed into the juice, the green sorghum sap had to be filtered before further processing. If this was not undertaken, the syrup would look dirty and contain a constellation of particles. So quality-conscious producers ran the juice through fine mesh screens or casks filled with straw.

Cane juice must be subjected to a process of evaporation to produce syrup. Since fuel costs could be exorbitant, much anguish attended the design of boilers to heat the raw sorghum juice. Experimenters invented steam evaporators, steam coil evaporators, and chimney systems to limit the fuel requirements. Several rules of thumb governed the cook-down of the juice: (a) "prolonged exposure of cane juice to intense heat is injurious" and (b) the time of exposure to heat must be proportional to the amount of juice in a batch. The southern tendency to subject juice to protracted boiling over open fires resulted in "a dark, tarry, offensive mass."[25] A short, rapid boil in shallow tilted pans in small batches became the standard, with the green juice being poured in the higher end of the pan and syrup running out the lower in a constant stream.

Having witnessed Joe Trapp, the most senior sorghum maker in South

Carolina, produce sorghum, I would supplement this general account with specific observations. Trapp's sorghum is noteworthy for its bronze translucency and fineness. He evaporates it at three different heats, informing me that the starches scum out at different temperatures. Only the three-temperature method produces clarity in the syrup.

Once the juice commenced boiling, certain starches and acid in the sap began separating out. First a green scum appeared on the surface of the liquid that had to be skimmed off. Next an amorphous white or yellow gum formed that also had to be separated out. A chemical admixture of slaked lime was added to aid in this segregation of the sugars from other components, but this process of "defecation" had mixed results. The chemical separation of pure saccharine liquid from the other chemical components of the sap proved the most troublesome problem facing sorghum processors in the nineteenth century. The lime had the additional benefit of counteracting the acidity of some sorghum batches.

The syrup had to cool to 175 degrees Fahrenheit before it could be bottled. This proved difficult with large batches, since the hot sugar retained heat. Sometimes bottlers ran a stream of syrup down a long open sluice to a funnel into the mouth of a gallon jug to cool the liquid. For producers desiring further refining, a second boiling run and bag filtering or heating it with bone coal removed all extraneous odors and matter.

Finished syrup had to possess several qualities: purity, clarity of color, hardy viscosity, a subdued odor, and mellow taste with perhaps a touch of acidic sharpness, depending on local preferences. During the Reconstruction era, a method existed for producing attractive syrup on a home or commercial scale. Quality begot demand. Table 2 charting the expansion of sorghum syrup production by decade tells the tale.[26] While most states experienced an expansion of syrup production from 1860 to 1870 to 1880, several decreased output from 1870 to 1880 (see New Jersey, for instance). Invariably, this demand tied to a local decline in the price for syrup and cane sugar to the point where it was more remunerative to plant other crops. Yet the overall production story was robust expansion.

Cost issues greatly complicated efforts to create a loaf-quality white sorghum sugar. During the war, producers met with little success perfecting the crystallization of saccharine in sorghum syrup. The best product was a sticky brown "muscovado" sorghum that did little to drive the visions

TABLE 2. Production of Sorghum Syrup According
to the Census of 1860–70–80 (adapted)

STATES AND TERRITORIES	Number of Gallons		
	1860	1870	1880
Massachusetts	0	0	18
Rhode Island	20	20	0
Connecticut	395	6,832	1,163
New York	516	7,832	1,134
New Jersey	396	17,424	1,261
Pennsylvania	22,219	213,373	69,767
Delaware	1,613	65,968	25,136
Maryland	907	28,563	19,837
Virginia	221,270	329,155	564,558
North Carolina	263,475	621,855	964,662
South Carolina	51,041	183,585	281,212
Georgia	103,490	374,027	981,152
Florida	0	0	10,199
Alabama	55,653	267,260	1,163,451
Mississippi	1,427	67,500	1,062,110
Louisiana	0	180	33,777
Texas	112,412	174,369	432,059
Arkansas	115,604	147,293	1,118,364
Tennessee	706,663	1,254,701	3,776,212
West Virginia	0	780,829	817,168
Kentucky	356,705	1,740,453	2,962,963
Ohio	779,076	2,023,427	1,229,852
Michigan	86,958	94,686	102,500
Indiana	881,049	2,026,212	1,741,853
Illinois	806,589	1,960,473	2,265,993
Wisconsin	19,854	74,478	314,150
Minnesota	14,178	38,725	543,869
Iowa	1,211,512	1,218,636	2,051,920
Missouri	796,111	1,730,171	4,129,595
Kansas	87,656	449,409	1,429,176
Nebraska	23,497	77,598	246,047
California	552	333	2,459
Oregon	815	0	2,283
Nevada	0	3,651	350
Colorado	0	0	3,227
Arizona	0	0	5,771
Dakota	20	1,230	17,012
Idaho	0	0	36
New Mexico	1,050	1,755	251
Utah	25,475	67,446	58,221
Washington	0	612	1,472

of pure granulated Louisiana purple-striped sugarcane sugar from one's imagination. By 1868 the Louisiana cane fields were producing again in quantity. So when, in the late 1870s, scientists and factories refined marketable sorghum sugar, the energy costs to do so inflated the sale price to a level where it was more expensive than the finer Louisiana cane sugar.

Sorghum never would become a significant alternative to sugarcane or sugar beets as a source for granulated sugar. As a sweetener, it prospered as a syrup, competing with maple syrup and corn-derived Karo syrup. In the twenty-first century, artisanal mills such as Muddy Pond, Briar Tree Sorghum Farm, Hubert Farms, Country Rock Sorghum, Sandhill Farm, Rolling Mills Sorghum, and Old School Sorghum keep the craft of syrup making vital. Production standards are set and maintained by the National Sweet Sorghum Producers and Processors Association. The year 2011 saw numbers of southern chefs rediscover sorghum: Linton Hopkins of Restaurant Eugene in Atlanta glazed pork belly with sorghum molasses; Mike Lata of FIG featured it in his desserts; and Sean Brock made sorghum grits with sorghum seed. Despite this new culinary interest, sorghum's value as an America crop will derive more from its use as a source of alcohol, animal feed, and biofuel.

With the dawn of the twenty-first century, sorghum found new champions of an old idea: the conversion of sorghum sugars to alcohol and ethanol. Sorghum's lack of gluten attracted brewers desiring to serve the large population of sufferers of celiac disease (gluten intolerance). Microbrewers such as Bard's Tale Beer, New Grist, and St. Peter's produced flavorful sorghum beers, prompting industrial brewer Anheuser-Busch in 2006 to launch Redbridge, its own sorghum product. Unfortunately, Busch decided it would gain greater acceptance if it produced a beer without pronounced taste.

The second group interested in sorghum as alcohol has been alternative fuel developers. Brazil's sugar-based fuel system has inspired the present generation of biofuel experts to turn attention to America's old sugar substitute. In August 2008, the USDA-sponsored International Workshop on Sorghum for Biofuels inaugurated a development push to employ the plant for making ethanol. Two approaches dominate: for sweet sorghum varieties, fermentation of plant sugars into ethanol—a process that retains all of the traditional costs of juice extraction and processing—prevails.

Gasification—the burning by fast pyrolysis of sorghum plants to form syngas and bio-oil for fuel—and charcoal for fertilizer is the method for creating cellulosic ethanol. While many of the biofuel initiatives have been tied to university research projects, the commercial exploitation of sorghum has begun in the United States with corporations such as Advanta US leading the way. The country that possesses the greatest confidence in and experience with biofuel systems—Brazil—has plunged into large-scale production of sorghum-based ethanol, in part as a hedge against spikes in the price of ethanol resulting from volatilities in the world sugar demand. Dedini SA is the major player in this effort. In the United States, sorghum's cold tolerance remains a powerful recommendation over sugarcane for growers, since the bulk of American farmland lies north of Climate Zone 8. Only southern Texas is one of the areas now growing biofuel sorghum that falls in this zone. The other major producing states—Oklahoma, Kansas, Nebraska, and Iowa—all lie in Zones 7 or 6. The race is on to breed varieties with the greatest disease resistance, cold stress, drought tolerance, and biomass yield. Because much of the sorghum is being grown in the grain belt where corn is sucking the aquifer dry, the creation of less thirsty forms of sorghum has scientists looking again at the old landraces first imported in the 1850s. The varieties created in the dry climate of Natal were suited to the most efficient use of available water. The oldest cultivated varieties hold the genetic key to the future of sorghum as a crop in the United States.

FIFTEEN *Prospecting for Oil*

Of all the quests that early American farmers and horticulturists pursued, none was more enduring and consequential than that for culinary oils or fats less expensive and more suitable for salad dressing than melted lard. From Thomas Jefferson's failed attempts to grow olive trees in Albemarle County, Virginia, to David Wesson's labors in the laboratory to free cottonseed oil of its natural stink, the history of experiments is a fascinating chronicle of popular taste, economic ambition, and food chemistry. It begins in the attempt to acclimatize the best-tasting oil-producing plants of the Old World onto the North American landscape, and ends with the industrial synthesis of wholly new entities—Crisco and margarine—devised to be inoffensive to taste, even tasteless. These developments played out in little over a century, from 1773 to 1890, largely in the American South and greatly influenced by African American dietary needs.

Phillip Mazzei settled in the hill country of Virginia in 1773 to establish an American Tuscany of vineyards and olive groves. But the scant three years between the planting of his fields and the outbreak of the American Revolution thwarted both projects. Ten years of growth at minimum must occur for an olive tree to set fruit; five for muscat vines to supply sufficient grapes for a crush. Living next to the governor of Virginia, Thomas

Jefferson, insured that Mazzei's lands would suffer spoilage at the hands of British invaders. Truth be known, Mazzei knew that the olive groves would not flourish well before the British came to Charlottesville. He had seen most of the saplings die when the winter temperature dipped below 15 degrees Fahrenheit in 1774. When Mazzei departed America for Europe on a secret mission to secure arms for Virginia in 1779, he left without having fulfilled any of the major ambitions that had brought him to America. Even the vineyard that Mazzei's workers had planted at Monticello for Jefferson would never produce a single vintage, falling victim to Virginia's rapacious raccoons, insects, and black rot.

One seed that Mazzei planted did bear fruit—the idea of diversified planting in the fertile soil of Jefferson's imagination. Mazzei's example had turned Jefferson, a rather traditional Virginia staple farmer with an interest in fruit trees, into a horticultural experimentalist.[1] That imagination in the following years would incandesce upon confronting a new plant or animal. In 1787, during his journey into northern Italy, Jefferson awoke to the virtues of Mazzei's cherished olive tree. Jefferson witnessed how fruit and oil grounded the diet of the Italian peasantry. His careful notation in his travel diary of the locales and elevations at which various cultivars flourished caused him to realize that the winter temperatures in most of the United States precluded its cultivation. Yet in the Lowcountry of South Carolina and Georgia, and in the territory of Florida (if and when it came under American control), conditions were roughly comparable to those in Italy. Jefferson contacted the one institution in this area that might oversee the establishment of olive, the Agricultural Society of South Carolina, which had organized in 1785. His letter commended olive oil particularly:

A pound of oil which can be bought for 3d. or 4d. sterling, is equivalent to many pounds of flesh by the quantity of vegetables, it will prepare and render fit and comfortable food. Notwithstanding the great quantity of oil made in France, they have not enough for their own consumption; and, therefore, import from other countries. This is an article, of consumption of which, will always keep pace with the production. Raise it, and it begets its own demand. Little is carried to America, because Europe has it not to spare; we, therefore, have not learnt the use of it. But cover the Southern States with it, and every man will become a consumer of it, within whose reach it can be brought, in point of price.[2]

Parts of Jefferson's letter must be explained—for instance, the claim that a pound of oil equaled many pounds of flesh in the preparation of vegetables. He spoke to his countrymen's propensity to fry vegetables in lard or bacon fat. The expense of raising a hog in terms of feed and time of growth, butchering and processing, far exceeded that of collecting and pressing a crop of olives.[3] Jefferson also confronted the question that hovered in the back of every reader's mind—since most Americans did not use olive oil, where would the demand come from that would make the olive a profitable crop? He reassured planters that European demand, particularly that of Revolutionary ally and trading partner France, exceeded supply; furthermore, he suggested that Americans, once familiar with a cheap and available frying medium, would do as southern Europeans have traditionally done, embrace it as the economical and most convenient culinary fat.

Many of the historically minded planters who read Jefferson's letter would have known that the idea that the Lowcountry could be the home of the olive dated from the time of Carolina's founding. John Locke, the secretary to the Lords Proprietors of Carolina, had composed a prospectus envisioning the colony as a quasi-Mediterranean haven of wine, olive oil, and silk.[4] Olive cuttings from Portugal and Bermuda had been planted along the Ashley and Cooper Rivers early in the 1670s, so that Richard Blom in 1678 reported flourishing groves. Mitchell King, the antebellum historian of Carolina olive culture, recounted the legend of John Colleton sticking a wand of olive wood into the sandy loam of Charleston and having it sprout.[5] Yet the colonial reports spoke of planting and growing, never of harvesting and pressing oil. Even Dr. Milligan's 1763 letter (quoted by King) remarking on olive trees in the city gardens suggests that they were novelties—specimens and conversation pieces. In 1747 Governor Glen did report the winter ice destroying one productive olive tree of a foot and half girth. But olive oil never appeared on the customs list as an export commodity, and the local crop of olives appears entirely to have been brined for home consumption.

The Agricultural Society never explained why these early experiments with the olive had such desultory results. Perhaps the members knew that the obsessive concern with rice, corn, and indigo made the olive beside the point, particularly since the populace loved pork fat when it came to frying. This preference had at times a cultic extremity. In 1822 "Virginian-sis Philoporcus" wrote the *American Farmer*, proclaiming bacon fat ("that precious essence which titillates so exquisitely the papillae of the tongue") was "far superior to all the oils that ever were discovered."[6]

Disruption of Carolina agriculture wrought by the American Revolution and the need to establish new commodities for the postwar free trade with all nations made Carolina's elite planters willing to consider new ideas. Indeed, Henry Laurens, who spent part of the Revolution languishing in the Tower of London, secured an English horticulturist and a shipload of olive cuttings to plant at Mepkin and Charleston upon his return, and according to John Adams harvested from fifty to a hundred bushels of fruit a year.[7] Jefferson's shipments to the society did not arrive until 1791. These were allotted to interested members and planted at several locations in the Lowcountry.

Jefferson's olives did not transform the Lowcountry. Nor did Laurens's. Isolated trees (two in Beaufort, six in Charleston)[8] grew to productive maturity and local renown, but Jefferson complained in a letter to James Ronaldson dated January 12, 1813, "It is now twenty-five years since I sent them two shipments (about 500 plants) of the Olive tree of Aix, the finest Olives in the world. If any of them still exist, it is merely as a curiosity in their gardens; not a single orchard of them has been planted."[9] Cold snaps decimated the inland plantings; humidity and the moisture of the Lowcountry soil caused most of the trees to fail. Like the colonial plantings, the post-Revolutionary olive experiment resulted in a scatter of hardy trees whose fruits were consumed locally. What was true in Carolina was true in Georgia and Florida. In 1827 a reviewer in the *American Quarterly* of Grant Forbes's utopian *Sketches, Historical and Topographical, of the Floridas* responded to the author's vision of an olive-rich east Florida, by observing, "Two olive trees, of very large size, and supposed to be of very great age, did grow near St. Augustine, and a few more were raised at New-Smyrna, but from what cause, none of them were fruitful."[10] Not a single cruet of oil came from the South's olive trees until 1831, when John Couper of Cannon's Point, St. Simons Island, Georgia, made some from his plantings.

Couper stood foremost among the generation of southern experimentalists who turned to olive trees as a possible way out of the soil exhaustion crisis of the 1820s. His letters on olive culture appeared in the first volume of the *Southern Agriculturist*, the journal founded by the South Carolina Agricultural Society to foster exchange among experimentalists in the face of political crisis over the US tariff on cotton and the degradation of the region's topsoil. His name appeared first on the list of endorsers of the "Report of the Union Agricultural Society of Georgia," proposing the olive as one "substitute for the rapidly depreciating staple, cotton."[11] Couper— along with Robert Chisolm of Beaufort, South Carolina; W. L. Crawford of Darien, Georgia; Mitchell King of Charleston; Thomas Spalding of Sepalo Island, Georgia; J. H. Mey; and Judge Johnson—engaged in large-scale plantings in Beaufort and the Georgia Sea Islands. The most successful olive planter was Louisa Shaw, of Dungeness on Cumberland Island, Georgia, whose grove of six hundred trees produced throughout the nineteenth century and became a tourist venue.

If Jefferson had known of Shaw's activities, it would have warmed his heart. The youngest daughter of General Nathanael Greene, the Revolutionary War hero, she planted the olives forwarded to Greene by the Agricultural Society of South Carolina. Under her vigilant care, they flourished and expanded. Their existence was known, via reports in papers like the *Darien Gazette*, throughout the literate South. The *American Farmer* in 1828 reprinted one such bulletin: "We are now informed on good authority, that 'olives of a very excellent quality, have for several years been quite abundant on Cumberland Island, in the vicinity of Port St. Mary's, Geo. And that during the month of August last, many bushels of them were sold at the latter place, at seventy-five cents the bushel.'"[12] Shaw's grove inspired hope in Couper, Spalding, and Chisolm that the olive could be made a merchantable commodity. Couper secured his two hundred trees from Provence and planted the three-and-half-foot-long branchless stems at Cannon's Point, St. Simons Island, immediately upon receipt in May 1825.[13] Eighteen of the plantings died. Surprised at the slow growth, and realizing there would be no return on his land for years to come, he intercropped sweet potatoes in the grove with good result. Couper attempted to expand his grove by cuttings but found that they failed. His experiments with planting from seed, after a false start, succeeded. J. H.

Mey also had success growing olives from seed.[14] Thomas Spalding, who secured his olive trees from the Leghorn in Italy, complained about the cost of such importations, saying that at $2.50 to purchase and transport, importation of olives on a large scale was "too much for us to afford." He requested that the state "establish nursery grounds for the Olive tree."[15] Georgia declined to undertake this public work.

The experiments in olive culture nearly came to naught in 1835 when brutal winter cold and ice destroyed most of the trees north of Cumberland Island on February 6–8. Couper was forced to cut his grove to the roots. Old Charleston trees, including a patriarch planted by Laurens on Lamboll Street, died. Yet Couper's roots sprouted shoots, and the grove renewed, with the trees bearing fruit in 1844. Once again planters were reminded that olives were a long-term project, with no expectation of quick returns. James Hamilton Couper, John Couper's son, wrote Charleston olive grower Mitchell King a letter reflecting upon the course of his family's efforts. He did not doubt that the olive could grow in the Lowcountry, regardless of the occasional freezes. Nor did he doubt that pickled olives would enjoy a ready reception.

> The question may be asked by those who have usually regarded olive oil as merely an article of household economy, of very limited use in North America, whether a ready sale of the oil can be depended on? They may believe with the late Abbe Correa, that our countrymen have "bacon stomachs," and that it will be very difficult, so far to conquer the obstinacy of established habit, as to induce them to substitute pure oil for rancid bacon. If the only use of this oil were for food, it would undoubtedly require time to introduce it into general consumption; but that still will effect it, there can be no doubt, from the intrinsic value of the commodity.[16]

In 1845, according to the *Report of the Secretary of the Treasury*, 82,655 gallons of olive oil were imported into the United States. Some of this was used in soap manufacture and for machine oil.

Despite the efforts of Mitchell King and J. Hamilton Couper, olive oil would not be produced in the South in more than experimental batches. Robert Chisolm of Beaufort, who exhibited sample vials of olive oil at the

South Carolina Institute Fair on two occasions in the early 1850s,[17] wrote botanist Francis Peyre Porcher with his view of the profitability of olive oil. Chisolm had planted his grove in 1833 using two types of Leghorn olives, a small round oil olive and an oval-fruited one. Chisolm observed, "I do not think that the making of oil from the olive will be likely to prove sufficiently profitable to be pursued in this country for many years, and other crops will necessarily take the lead unless the price of labor or soil in Europe should be increased, when there will, consequently, become a greater demand."[18] Porcher thought poppy seed oil would supply whatever culinary service olive oil might give. But another common southern plant would provide more economical and better suited to become a widely used culinary oil—benne, or sesame seed.

In 1808, when Thomas Jefferson despaired over the adoption of olive trees in the South, Governor John Milledge of Georgia sent the president a bottle of benne oil.[19] Served on a salad, Jefferson found it the equal of olive oil in delicacy and resolved to begin its production. It became one of the president's important agricultural experiments of the early 1810s. There was an irony in this. Jefferson had imagined that the olive tree would be, first and foremost, a boon for African slaves in the South, providing them a fat that could be produced with less expense and greater volume that lard or bacon grease. (John Couper would echo this sentiment in a letter of 1830, when he remarked, "I am not of the opinion the Olive will be an object of great profit, but if we could introduce oil amongst our slaves, it would add much to their comforts."[20]) Yet the slaves had brought with them the source of oil they needed in their diet, *Sesamum indicum*, or what the Mende called "benne."

Benne's wealth of oil (almost 50 percent of a seed's makeup) had been noted by agricultural writers repeatedly during the eighteenth century. As early as 1735, a "Mr. Garcia" announced in the *South Carolina Gazette* the establishment of a sesame oil press in Charleston. This press operated until the proprietor's death three years later. In 1769 John Morel of Savannah reported to the American Philosophical Society that "this seed makes oil equal in quality to Florence [olive oil], and some say preferable."[21] On February 5, 1774, Henry Laurens of South Carolina requested of his brother James that he "procure me as much Sesamum or Bene Seed as you possibly can, & encourage the planting [of] it by all the Negroes at each plantation."[22] Throughout the 1790s, the Agricultural Society of South Carolina offered premiums to planters who could produce superior oil from sesame, olives, castor beans, sunflowers, cottonseed, or groundnuts (peanuts). Governor John Milledge of Georgia and his circle of neighbors began field cultivation of sesame about 1800, hoping to supply a native substitute for olive oil. His friend and colleague Colonel Few moved to New York City and began selling sesame oil pressed in New Jersey commercially in 1804. Pressing the sesame in a manner similar to that used to extract flaxseed oil, Milledge enthusiastically reported extracting three quarts of oil from a gallon of seed. Contemporaries observed that this yield was wishful, and that two quarts of oil could be expected in most cases. Thomas Marsh Forman of Maryland tasted the Georgia oil in 1812: "At the house of my valued friend John McQueen, Esq. of Oatlands, the Bene plant was first made known to me. It was about the last of February, that dining with him, he requested my opinion of a bowl of fine Cabbage Lettuce; it deserved all the praise which I gave to the vegetable, as well as to the dressing, when Mr. McQueen smiling informed me, that the oil was of his own produce, from what made, and the value of the crop."[23]

The West African method of extracting oil was designed for a household level of production and consumption. The seed was pounded by mortar and pestle. After "bruising the seed, and immersing them in boiling water . . . the oil rises on the top and is easily skimmed off. Good casks filled, or bottles filled, and well bunged, or corked are proper to preserve this oil which, doubtless, will become rancid by heat, time, impurities, and air."[24] Twenty-first-century chemical and nutritional analysis finds that of the culinary oils high in polyunsaturated omega-6, sesame oil is least prone to turn rancid among those with high smoke points. This makes it the most stable of healthy frying media.[25]

Benne oil kept as well as olive oil, could be produced annually and abundantly without a ten-year wait for productivity, could be grown as far north as Maryland without much difficulty, and could be pressed and extracted with less labor and mechanism than olive oil. A simple iron press could do the job.

Many southern farmers grew benne. Indeed, the amount of benne grown cannot be calculated with any certainty, because substantial slave

patch plantings went unnoted in plantation record books. Judging by surviving record books, planters rarely attempted benne production on a scale
to create more than a modest, largely local market for oil (the maximum
plantings tended to be fifty acres), yet numbers of plantations engaged
in artisanal production, using sesame in crop rotations with corn, sweet
potatoes, and cowpeas, or with rice and sweet potatoes. A window on
the small-scale world of sesame oil production and benne cake livestock
feeding is found in the pages of the *Thomas Walter Peyre Plantation Journal
(1834-1859)* at the South Carolina Historical Society. On Peyre's estate,
the benne press, like the brew house, was first a plantation resource and
secondarily a production facility for market goods.

African American farming of benne can only be imputed by anecdotal
reports. Yet numerous records attest to benne's importance in the slave
diet. Indeed, a complex benne cookery adapted from African practices
was recorded. In 1820 John S. Skinner—editor of the United States' most
important agricultural journal, *American Farmer*—observed, "The Bene
vine or bush, has been produced for some time, in small quantities, in the
southern states, from seed imported directly from Africa, and from Asia—
It abounds in the former, and in Bengal. Many of the blacks of the Mississippi, have continued the propagation of the seed of the Bene, and make
soup of it after parching. The seed may be procured from them and from
the blacks in the Carolinas and Georgia."[26] Skinner's note revealed several things: the African genesis of the plant, the broad geographic range,
yet relatively low acreage of its cultivation, and the black oversight of seed
stock for benne. Skinner also provided a glimpse of its most notable culinary use—as the basis of benne soup.

Rich in oil and nutty in taste, benne can be eaten raw. Because it is
highly nutritious (25 percent protein), it could provide sustenance with
minimal preparation. But the African American population preferred to
intensify the flavorful nuttiness of the seed by browning it in a skillet. It
did not matter whether seeds had been hulled or unhulled, they could be
tossed onto the bottom of an ungreased Dutch oven or iron skillet, and
stirred until lightly toasted—not scorched in any part. Parched benne had
a host of uses. It could be eaten straight from the skillet, used as a condiment flavoring a pot of stew or greens, or pounded into a mortar and

pestle and used as a thickening agent or the basis of a pottage. Every surviving notice of benne mash's use in cookery indicates that it was mixed with something else. The two basic partnering elements were wheat flour and cornmeal. These were cooked in water with salt or stock.

BENNE SOUP

Robert M. Goodwin of Skidaway Island, George, observed in 1824, that for "negroes in this part of the country . . . it [benne] is thought . . . to be much better in soup than okra, and it is used by them in the same manner. I am told it is very good, but I have never tasted it."[27] In 1821 Calvin Jones noted the extensive use of benne in African American cookery in the east part of North Carolina, observing that "among negroes who get little flesh meat, it is a valuable article."[28] Meat rations on plantations tended to be restricted to three and a half pounds of cured pork per week maximum. On small-scale farms, there might be no ration, so that a slave had to hunt and trap during the off hours of labor to supply meat — often a problem.[29] Consequently, sesame would serve as a dietary protein supplement. The sole surviving recipe for benne soup appeared in Sarah Rutledge's *The Carolina Housewife* (1847), as a variation of groundnut soup. Though attentive to local vernacular cookery, Rutledge's collection was intended for a white readership with meat and seafood at its disposal. Oysters are added to benne and flour to make a dish that survives in Lowcountry cuisine as "Brown Oyster and Benne Stew." Sean Brock has made it a regular item in the autumn menus at Husk in Charleston.

GROUND NUT SOUP

To half a pint of shelled ground nuts, well beaten up, add two spoonsful of flour, and mix well. Put to them a pint of oysters, and a pint and a half of water. While boiling, throw a seed-pepper or two, if small.

BENNIE SOUP

This is made exactly in the same manner except that instead of a half a pint of ground-nuts, a pint and a gill of bennie is mixed with the flour and the oysters.[30]

Rutledge's soup can be considered an evolution of the basic benne soup cooked in the plantation quarters. That more basic soup had all its ingredients listed in Rutledge's recipe, but the mode of preparation was somewhat different, since she was concerned with preserving the quality of the oysters incorporated into the mix. The foundation soup was this:

1 cup benne seed,
Enough sesame oil to cover the bottom of a cooking vessel,
A handful of wheat flour,
Salt & Pepper, onions,
A quart of water.

Toast benne seed in a dry skillet stirring constantly 2 minutes until browned, but not burnt. Empty contents of the skillet into a mortar and mash the seed into powder. In the same skillet cover the bottom with sesame oil and mix in flour. Stir and cook this until you form a brown roux. Fry one large roughly chopped onion. Add finely crushed benne, and then hot water, steadily, stirring constantly. Cook at a constant medium until it is rich and thick and salt to taste. This is a hearty and flavorful soup.

Note: after making benne soups for half a year, some observations. The flavor and texture of the soup is enhanced by grinding it almost to the consistency of flour in a spice mill, rather than pounding it in a mortar and pestle. Having to cook it for vegans made me experiment with using tahini rather than roux as the soup starter, on the analogy of the soul food cooks who use peanut butter for peanut soup. It worked fine, as long as one had a flavorful vegetable (mushroom or otherwise) stock. Onions added to the flavor and a hot pepper pod (like Rutledge suggests) is essential. All of the eaters preferred it fou-fou style over rice or grits.

Because benne could be kept for winter use at a time when vegetables, aside from root vegetables, can be scarce. Commentators repeatedly remarked on the love of African Americans for onions, whether globe, spring, or wild leek.[31] A chopped onion might be incorporated into the soup, being added to the roux and allowed to become translucent before adding benne. This gives a sweet note to the soup and welcome texture. A seed pod of hot pepper was also a welcome addition. West Africans also add cooked meats to benne soup when available. The foundation soup operated as a canvas for improvisation.

BENNE AND HOMINY

"The Negroes in Georgia boil a handful of the seeds with their allowance of Indian Corn."[32] Three years earlier, a North Carolinian noted, "Mixed in due proportion with their hominy, it heightens its relish, and adds to its nutriment."[33] Whole seed, because of its different cooking time than cornmeal, does not amalgamate well in hominy and can stick in one's teeth. The handful of benne cast into the hominy pot most likely was parched and pounded.

"Hominy" designated three things: small hominy was ground cornmeal; large hominy was dried whole kernels of corn; it also meant *posole*, a kind of dried whole kernel corn soaked in lye to remove the outer envelope of the kernel. This recipe uses small hominy. Native Americans throughout the Southeast boiled cornmeal. English settlers substituted cornmeal for the familiar oat and wheat pottages of their homeland. Africans ate millet stews and so found the substitution of corn acceptable as well. Experiment suggests that the "due proportion" went something like this:

> 1 cup of rough ground white corn meals
> ½ cup of parched & mashed benne seed
> salt
> water or milk
> oil or butter

In a large vessel put 7 cups of water and bring to a boil. Stir in corn meal and benne gradually and moderate heat. Stir for 30 minutes making sure the substance doesn't stick. When think and bubbling add oil or butter & salt. Grits are given an extraordinary dimension by the addition of benne.

BENNE AND HOMINY 2

Another approach to mixing benne and hominy derives from the traditional West African practice of serving a groundnut or benne soup over a thick pudding of cassava. Hominy operates in the place of cassava. It would be prepared separately, placed into the bottom of a bowl, and benne soup ladled over it. Usually pieces of precooked meat or greens are added to the liquid prior to serving.

BENNE AND GREENS

In the 1770s Thomas Jefferson wrote that sesame "was brought to S. Carolina from Africa by the negroes. . . . They bake it in their bread, boil it with greens, enrich their broth" with it. His observation that they boiled benne with greens accords with long-standing practice among a number of West African peoples. While casting a palm full of whole seed into a cooking pot of collards (the premier cold-weather green), turnip greens, beet greens, or mustard was convenient, it did not release all of the fat from the seed, so did not render the dish as luscious as if seeds were mashed. In the second decade of the nineteenth century, when oil mills appeared on numbers of plantations, the mash cake left after pressing the sesame became a cooking condiment. "The oil cake is very pleasant at table, is eaten freely by horned cattle, swine, &c., and it is often used when fresh to boil with other vegetables, rendering butter unnecessary."[34] The employment of benne mash as an oleo in boiling greens and root vegetables resembled North African practices of using tahini (sesame paste) as a condiment in vegetable cookery as well as the West African habit of adding mashed benne to one-pot preparations. It remained a feature of plantation cookery through the antebellum period.

Oily pressed seed cake might fit into traditional (i.e., African) cooking practices, yet the demand for sesame oil in the white world of the marketplace was driven by a culinary innovation that had nurtured a new taste — a hankering for uncooked greens, vegetables, and fruits. In the 1790s, old ideas about the function of cooking as a necessary supplement to digestion began to dissolve, as did fears of the dire consequences of dyspepsia, that gastric distress brought on by eating raw fruits and vegetables. In Europe and, afterward, the young United States, the table fashion for salads composed of uncooked greens and vegetables spread. Celery rocketed into garden vogue. Lettuces became popular. Uncooked cabbage was shredded into slaws. These salads tasted best when lubricated by an acid (vinegar or lemon juice) and an oil. Melted lard would not do nor melted butter. It is no anomaly that the story of Jefferson's discovery of the virtues of benne oil have him eating it on a fresh salad. Jefferson was embracing two novelties simultaneously.

Over the course of the nineteenth century, the salad would grow in increasing popularity, until the 1880s, when Thomas J. Murrey supported himself with the sales of cookbooks specifically treating salads and sauces. Murrey belonged to that sect of Gilded Age gourmands who believed that since the genesis of salad was European, it should be dressed with the favorite European oil, that of the olive. "Cottonseed-oil, Gangilee oil, peanut-oil, bene-plant oil, poppy oil, and oil from seeds of the radish and mustard, and, in fact, a hundred other oils which are recommended from time to time for salads by over-enthusiastic writers, are a delusion, and should not be used in salads. They are excellent for frying purposes, and will one day take the place of lard; but never use them on a dainty salad."[35] He would be prophetic in his pronouncement of doom on lard. Though Americans would plant olive groves in California and Arizona, it would not be olive oil that filled the fryer vats of restaurants, or displaced lard, or even lubricated the greens of late nineteenth- and twentieth-century Americans. Crisco—the shortening that supplanted lard—Wesson oil, and most "vegetable oil" and "salad oil" used in most American salad dressings in the first three-quarters of the twentieth century were created from the first named of Murrey's demoted oils: cottonseed oil. The mills of the South pressed only a trickle of olive oil, only a modest stream of sesame oil. They would loose a river of cottonseed oil.

Centuries of culinary practice around the Mediterranean and in West Africa stood behind the attempts to incorporate olive oil and benne oil into the North American larder. No human consumed cottonseed oil until the age of experiments. During the eighteenth century, pharmacists had extracted oil from cottonseed in Europe and America as part of the Enlightenment investigation of the medicinal properties of all seed and nut oils. A patent for the extraction of oil from cottonseed was issued by the United States as early as 1793. C. Whiting's design mill for the extraction of the oil from the seed's hull earned a patent on March 2, 1799.[36] Yet the notion that humans might ingest the stuff as an element of common nutrition only arose after (1) the explosive growth of the cotton industry in the southern states after 1800; (2) the rise of a general concern with what to do with the surplus seed after planting stock had been reserved: (3) the observation that livestock had a taste for waste seed, particularly when ground in a mill; and (4) the development of a method for refining the raw oil into something odorless and palatable. It took almost the entire nineteenth century to meet these four conditions.

Early extractors of oil from cottonseed noted several things. First, the seed was four-fifths hull and one-fifth oil-bearing kernel. Second, the seed was only 17 to 21 percent oil, less than half that of benne seed and most nuts. Third, the hull had to be stripped off to get at the oil. (Follett & Smith first marketed the most popular commercial huller in 1829.) Processing cottonseed oil required milling the ripe seed on edged stones, cooking the seed meal, and then pressing the meal in an oil press of some sort. Captain Benjamin Waring, the pioneer agricultural experimentalist of the South Carolina midlands, had constructed an oil press in Columbia by 1800. The oil extruded from Waring's press flowed cloudy and dark brown and gave off a nutty odor that grew more pronounced and funky as the oil aged. Waring judged that it could not be used for human consumption, and because food concerned him more than producing livestock feed or the ingredients for soap, Waring turned his press to benne oil, which he produced in marketable quantities until his death.[37]

Eli Whitney's cotton gin, perfected in 1793, separated seeds from the bolls of short staple cotton efficiently. When the War of 1812 drove cotton prices skyward, a production boom began that led to vast planting. Despite this extensive planting, enough surplus seed came from the fields to become a nuisance. Governor David Rogerson Williams of Society Hill, South Carolina, determined to make the waste seed profitable. Already widely known for introducing the mule into southern agriculture, Williams in the late 1820s built a commercial oil mill with the intention of

manufacturing seed cake for cattle and hog feed, lamp oil for home illumi-
nation, and cotton fat for soap and lubrication.[38] Throughout the South,
enterprisers began constructing mills in some number, convinced that processing cotton by-products into salable commodities would bring a wave
of cash. James Hamilton Couper, of the olive-growing Coupers, invested
in plants in Natchez, Mississippi, and Alabama. They bankrupted him in
1836.[39]

Mills sprang up like mushrooms and failed in substantial numbers.[40]
The economies of scale did not work, particularly since no human culinary
demand drove sales of the product. Whale oil made better soap, linseed oil
a better paint base. Still the ubiquity of cottonseed encouraged regional
processors to appear until the consolidation of the processors under one
administration, the American Cottonseed Oil Trust, in 1880. Yet monopoly industrialization of itself did not fuel the rise of cottonseed oil;
chemistry did. Because of the expense of raising hogs, lard proved rather
costly as a kitchen staple fat. Chemists managed to refine cottonseed oil,
hydrogenate it, and mix it with lard into what became known as "compound" lard. At first this was done without notification, so when the presence of cottonseed oil in lard was revealed, it seemed to the public an
adulterant.

Compound lard differed from pure lard in several respects, including
a retention of cottonseed oil's distinctive smell. The elimination of that
smell became the next focus of research by chemists. In 1884 David Wesson of the N.K. Fairbanks Company of Chicago, a producer of animal-
based compound fats, began experimenting with compound lard. His success in creating compound lard with the texture of pure lard led to the
Oil Trust's absorption of the Fairbanks Company and Wesson's transfer
to another subsidiary that explored the chemistry of cottonseed oil exclusively. By 1899 Wesson had developed a process of fining, heating, and vac-
uum processing cottonseed oil in such a way that the odor and brown tint
of raw cottonseed oil were entirely removed. (Before 1899 a mitigation of
the odor had been achieved by blowing live steam through the oil at atmo-
spheric pressure.) Bankrolled by the trust, Wesson formed a manufacturing company and from a plant in Savannah, Georgia, began selling "Wesson Oil."[41] In 1903 chemists succeeded in the hydrogenation of oils into

solids, and the Wesson Company marketed Snowdrift, a lard substitute composed entirely of cottonseed oil. Yet it would be Procter & Gamble's chemist Edwin C. Kayser who in 1911 created a shortening of cottonseed oil that did not degrade at room temperature.[42] Crisco would eventually eclipse Snowdrift in the marketplace, fulfilling Murrey's prophecy that lard would be superseded as a frying medium and baking ingredient.

Cottonseed oil products did not come to dominate the market for culinary oil and shortening because of taste or because of need, but because of economy. Cottonseed, as a by-product of staple production, was waste turned to profit. To triumph in the marketplace of food, it had to lose its objectionable appearance and smell, and approximate a palatable blandness on the tongue. It had to be sold under names that did not announce its origin plainly. (An attempt to sell shortening as "Cottonlene" failed.) It had to be cheap at the point of purchase. Its virtues lay in the functions it performed, not its aesthetic quality; indeed, its aesthetics were those of innocuousness. It did possess an ethical advantage in the eyes of vegetarians by providing a frying medium and a baking fat that did not derive from animals. Crisco embraced this constituency warmly. *The Story of Crisco* (1913) in its section on "Vegetarian Dishes" declares proudly, "Crisco is entirely vegetable." When the author asked rhetorically why customers bought Crisco with such enthusiasm, abandoning traditional cooking fats, such as butter and lard, she answered, "This was because four classes of people—housewives, chefs, doctors, and dietitians—were glad to be shown a product which at once would make for more digestible, more economical foods, and better tasting foods."[43] Economical? Granted. Digestible? According to whom? Better tasting than butter? Who decided this?

What is instructive in the above quotation is who, besides the economy-minded female consumer, matters as authorities in regards to food: chefs, doctors, and dietitians. Only the first member of this trio has a professional interest in taste. At the dawn of the twentieth century, the experts on digestion, the nutritionist and the physician, had become the arbiters of good food.

We should not lose sight of the fact that housewives, physicians, dietitians, and chefs had nothing to do with the design, taste profile, or manufacture of Crisco. Food chemists, like David Wesson and Edwin Kayser, had created the product and were the new aestheticians of food. If the antebellum agricultural experimentalists created varieties mainly pursuing the next new salable taste, the food chemists at the dawn of the twentieth century made taste subordinate to matters of economy and functionality in the invention of their products.

SIXTEEN *Peanuts and Peanut Oil*

In 1904 George Washington Carver instructed the farmers of Alabama to grow less cotton and more peanuts. His was not a message the owners of the several newly constructed cottonseed oil mills wished to hear. Yet Carver's prophecies came true. The boll weevil marched through the South, decimating the cotton field. Soon the mills stood idle, awaiting another southern commodity that could be rendered to oil. In a decade— from 1905 to 1915—the peanut went from a city snack and regional food to a national staple. In 1917 the frying pans of the United States sizzled with peanut oil; an African slave food had transformed into an industrial commodity.

No one has determined definitively how and when the peanut entered the Northern Hemisphere of America. Native to South America, it was a second-phase article of "Columbian Exchange," taken to West Africa by Portuguese slave traders in the 1560s, and there naturalized and broadly cultivated within sixty years. When botanical writers began noticing it very early in the eighteenth century, it was identified particularly as African slave food. Hans Sloan in *The Natural History of Jamaica* (1707) reported, on the basis of mariners' testimonies, that the nuts "are brought from Guinea in the Negroes Ships, to feed the Negroes withal in their Voyage from Guinea To Jamaica."[1] He further indicated that the Portuguese employed it similarly when transshipping African slaves from St. Thomas to Lisbon. One can appreciate the rationale at work: the peanut was portable, protected by a hull, and resistant to spoilage. It could be eaten with minimal preparation, raw, straight from the shell.

The Gardner's Dictionary of 1754 observed that "all the settlements in America abound with it; but many persons who reside in that Country affirm, they were originally brought by the Slaves from Africa there." The *Dictionary* suggests that the plant became a secret source of nourishment, knowledge of which was withheld from masters: "Unless the ground is opened they never appear. The Negroes kept this a secret among themselves, therefore could supply themselves with these Nuts unknown to their masters."[2] Dimwitted masters may have been duped by the subterranean food source. Sharp-eyed European naturalists were not. Sloan and Griffith Hughes of Barbados noted its ubiquity and uses, including peanut paste poultices for snakebite and as an oil source. Edward Long's account in *The History of Jamaica* (1774) observes nothing novel about cultivation or uses, but gives us the English impression of African names. He stated that the "Pindal" "was first brought from Africa. . . . They are nourishing, and often given as food to Negroes on voyages from Guiney, where they pass under the name of gubagubs."[3]

Students of Creole language have not hesitated to see Long's "gubagubs" as a repeated form of Kokonga "nguba" and the antecedent of "goober," the southern English short form of "goober pea." What is curious is that for some southern users "goober" has designated another African subterranean legume, the Bambara groundnut, not the peanut. W.B., a Floridian correspondent of the *Rural Carolinian* in 1872, provided a clarification:

> An article in your December number confounds the pindar (pea nut) with the goober. The former has two kernels; the latter, only one; and they differ widely in foliage and habit of growth. Some of our planters cultivate patches of it for their hogs. These eat it readily, but prefer the pea nut. The goober can be cultivated much closer together than the pea nut, and the yield per acre is larger. Last year, I planted twenty hills, one

goober to a hill. The yield varied from 43 to 128 in a hill. Goobers may be drilled, or they may be planted in hills sixteen inches apart.[4]

The confusion that W.B. corrects may be found in Edward Long's account a century earlier. "Pindal" (pindar) is presented as a synonym for "guba-gubs." Astute observers of African American usage, however, noted a discrimination. Botanist H. W. Ravenel of Aiken, South Carolina, wrote in 1885:

> Among the negroes in the coastal region of South Carolina, the name "Goober" or "Goober Pea" is applied exclusively to the Voandzea, whilst "Pindar" or "Pindah" is always given to the well-known Pea nut, Arachis. . . .
>
> These two plants have the similar habits of blooming above ground, but ripening their fruit beneath the surface. The former is an oval, one-sided legume. The seed is hard and requires boiling before it can be eaten, and it is not used parched like the Pea nut. It is not as rich nor as palatable as the Pea nut. The Goober Pea, or Voandzea, was cultivated very commonly by them 50 or 60 years ago, but it is now very rarely seen. Other and better varieties of Beans and Peas have taken its place.[5]

Ravenel's remarks upon the different modes of preparation suggest something about the early history of the peanut's reception in Africa. In South America the peanut was consumed raw or roasted (parched). In West Africa, where boiling Bambara groundnuts had been customary, when the peanut appeared in the sixteenth century, it was prepared in the same manner. Boiling groundnuts remained the signature mode of African preparation. In 1806, when Francis B. Spilsbury wrote of his experiences at Fort Thornton in West Africa, he observed that "the pleasantest and most common nut here, and which is found in great quantities, is the ground nut, a pound of which is worth about twopence: they boil and dry them before they expose them for sale."[6] Since "ground nut" comprehends both pindar and goober, the 1854 testimony of Thomas Croxon Archer shows that both receive the same treatment: "The seeds of both these plants are boiled by negroes and eaten as peas."[7]

In the United States, boiling peanuts in shells in brine was a preparation practiced exclusively in the South. Periodic instructions for boiling appeared throughout the nineteenth century, in cookbooks, agricultural journals, and state yearbooks. Mrs. Washington's *Unrivaled Cookbook* provides brief guidance: "Choose fresh well-filled peanuts. Careful selecting them, as nearly as possible, the same size. Boil them in salt water, drain and serve. This is generally served before the soup."[8] A correspondent for the *Florida Agriculturist* provided ampler information about salting and length of cooking: "One of the neighbors sent in some Spanish peanuts, fresh dug, the other day, with instructions to boil two or three hours in water with about a double portion of salt, that the shell's would absorb a portion of salt."[9]

Peanuts and boiling water figure in a second preparation with an African genesis. John Lunan in *Hortus Jamaicensis* (1814) writes that a common beverage in which peanuts are "roasted, ground, and boiled" as a "good substitute for chocolate."[10] The *Encyclopaedia Londinensis* (1810) notes that the inhabitants of South Carolina similarly roast the nuts "and make use of them as chocolate."[11] There was, of course, more to the preparation than simply parching, grinding, and boiling, since such a decoction tastes nothing like chocolate. But other sources indicate what more was needed. Anthony F. M. Willich's *Domestic Encyclopedia* (1802) points out that "a preparation of these kernels, combined principally with the dry bark of sassafras pulverised, is an excellent substitute for chocolate."[12] After loaf sugar became readily available in the South, the recipe expanded. "Peanut chocolate is made in some Southern families by beating the properly roasted nuts in a mortar with sugar, and flavoring with cinnamon or vanilla as may be desired."[13]

The roasting of peanuts in their shells became the favorite way of consuming them in North America outside of the South. The roasting of beans for beverages had the precedents of coffee and chocolate. But the roasting of nuts for direct consumption was a traditional method of preparing chestnuts and almonds and, later, cashews and pistachios. While African Americans in the Carolinas and the West Indies throughout the nineteenth century grew fresh peanuts for local markets; the roasting and shipping of peanuts became commonplace in the early Republic when stores in major cities began featuring the peanut as a commodity. In 1832

R. M. Williams exemplified a new figure on the scene, a white supplier of peanuts servicing city demand: "I have shipped and sold them to the confectioners and fruiterers of Philadelphia, New York, and Boston. . . . To prepare them for eating, they are usually parched with the husk on."[14] The peanut in short order became a favorite city treat, indeed one of the emblems of the Bowery boys who filled the galleries of the theaters in that district. If a performer did not meet with the approval of the "gallery gods," he or she would receive a "tribute" raining upon them.[15] The peanut became so much the rage of New York that quantities were imported from West Africa and Spain, because domestic production from the South nowhere near met demand. The peanut supplanted the roasted chestnut as street food by midcentury. Located on the pavement near major intersections, the peanut stand became a city institution, selling pint bags of nuts. Peanut vendors were also located at railway stations, with agents often peddling product on the railway cars. To foreign visitors, the peanut stands became an emblem of distinctly American urban foodways, since they did not exist in other countries.

The expanding sale of roasted peanuts in the cities swelled demand. Southern growers registered the growing popularity and gradually expanded acreage. But southern planters did not seriously engage in growing crops of peanuts until the 1810s. The area around Wilmington, North Carolina, became for seven decades the prime peanut-growing country in America, cultivating a thin-shelled, high-oil, regularly shaped, oval-kerneled smallish nut on a plant with a running habit called the Carolina peanut or the African peanut. There were usually two kernels per pod. A sport variant, the Wilmington, had a thicker shell and sometimes three kernels per pod. The price of imported peanuts in the major cities was sufficiently low to give pause to those considering it as a cash crop. (Remember, they were cheap enough for apprentices to throw them in quantity at lame performers.) Only persons with unremunerative chalky lands, or who sought cheap fodder with which to fatten swine, began growing it on a large scale. Those around Wilmington had extensive tracts of land more suitable for growing peanuts than corn or cotton. Furthermore, they harbored a hope that had long animated experimenters in that region of a more rewarding possible use of peanut—as a source for culinary oil.

In 1769 George Brownrigg of Edenton, North Carolina, had communicated a flask of oil expressed from local peanuts to the Royal Society in London. Its freshness after enduring a several-month Atlantic crossing in hot weather impressed the natural philosophers of the Royal Society. "Neither the seeds nor oil are apt to become rancid by keeping; and as a proof of this, the oil before you, which was sent from Carolina in April last, and, without any particular care, has undergone the heats of last summer, is yet perfectly sweet and good. These seeds furnish a pure, clear, well-tasted oil; and, as far as appears to me, may be used for the same purposes, both in food and physic, as the oils of olives and almonds."[16] Olive oil had become the standard against which to measure any culinary lipid. Brownrigg noted that the cost of manufacturing peanut oil, by his calculation, was a quarter of that of olive oil. Then he noted the intensity of demand in Europe and America in the 1760s, reporting that New England annually consumed 20,000 gallons of imported olive oil. If this were not enough incentive, he noted that the peanut cake remaining after oil extraction was "excellent food for swine."

Though the reporter from the Royal Society chided Brownrigg for his presumption that the experiment in extracting peanut oil was a first, Brownrigg had been perfectly aware of Hans Sloan's experiments with oil in Jamaica several decades earlier. Sloan was a regular correspondent of George's brother, Dr. William Brownrigg, FRA, and William instructed George in projects. Indeed, William Brownrigg's scheme for extracting salt from seawater came into operation at the mouth of the Cape Fear River under the initiative of George and several partners. The salt used in seasoning roasted peanuts or for the brine used in boiling peanuts derived from Brownrigg's initiative.

Because of the rise of the benne oil manufactory in the South during the antebellum period, and successful production of sunflower oil in Bethlehem, Pennsylvania, the pressure to produce peanut oil never reached a critical level until the Civil War. In 1862 T. C. and B. G. Worth built an oil mill in Wilmington, most of the product being used as a lubricant in cotton mills.[17] When peace was restored, the unexpected boom in demand for roasted peanuts put an end to the manufactory. The high cost of manufacturing oil in the face of immense immediate demand for limitless quantities of inexpensive raw and roasted peanuts prevented the consolidation of the industry. It is difficult now to understand the intensity of the craving for peanuts that broke during Reconstruction. Seven years after the armistice, H. E. Colton declared in the pages of *Scientific American*:

> There is hardly an article of American production, of apparently so little note, that has grown so rapidly in importance as the peanut. Instead of 1,000 there are fully 550,000 bushels sold annually in the city of New York City alone. Previous to 1860, the total product of the United States did not amount to more than 100,000 bushels, and of this total, fully five-sixths were from North Carolina. Now North Carolina produces 125,000 bushels; Virginia, 300,000 bushels; Tennessee, 50,000 bushels; Georgia and South Carolina, each 25,000 bushels; while from Africa come about 100,000 bushels a year.[18]

Of the several mythological explanations for the peanut boom of the late 1860s and '70s, one favored by Virginians circulated most widely. It told how the major armies of both North and South crisscrossed Tidewater and Southside Virginia repeatedly during the war. Since the 1840s every farmer in that region had planted peanut patches, either to feed hogs or to provide jumbo peanuts to the market. The enlisted men helped themselves to the contents of the local gardens and fields, developing a taste for the peanut. Since the combatants hailed from every part of the continent, they returned home wishing to be supplied with their favorite campfire treat. So a demand that had been limited to New York City, Philadelphia, Boston, and the South spread to all parts of the United States.

The emergence of Virginia as the chief producer can be attributed largely to that state's cultivation beginning in the mid-1840s of a Bolivian variety of great size, what we now know as the jumbo Virginia peanut. On the street these impressive peanuts seized the eyes of passersby, eclipsing the Carolina peanut as street food. The oilier, small Carolina peanuts, though they may have tasted better, lacked the marketability of the Virginia. The Virginia peanut was embraced by the northeastern cities, while the Carolina peanut serviced the Deep South and Northwest. In the 1870s, however, the Wilmington production came to the notice of the French, and by 1877 many Wilmington peanuts were shipped to France, "where they are used in the manufacture of oil."[19] French confectioners used peanut oil as a substitute for cocoa butter as the binding fat in chocolate. (The price for cocoa butter was so great, that it was taken from the bean and put to other uses, with peanut oil operating in its stead in candy making.) There was more than a little debate as to whether peanut oil constituted an adulterant or a constitutive ingredient of commercial chocolate. "Peanuts are largely used to adulterate chocolate, and so far as wholesomeness is concerned, are not objectionable. In containing a great deal of starch and oil, peanuts resembling the cocoa-bean, though without the nitrogenous principle, theobromine (which closely resembles caffeine), to which its nutritive qualities are largely due."[20]

Because the peanut contains from 39 to 46 percent fat (along with 26 percent protein), a bushel of Carolina peanuts could produce one gallon of oil when compacted by a hydraulic press. Heating while pressing produced more oil, but with degraded taste quality; so, cold pressing became the standard method of rendering culinary peanut oil. Freshly pressed it is colorless, or a faint straw color, mild tasting, and agreeably and faintly fragrant. Second-press oil tended to be employed as lamp oil. The peanut mash would be heated, and the third pressing would be employed in soap manufacturing.[21] The French imported more peanut oil for soap making than for confections in the final quarter of the nineteenth century. It became the basis for the famous "castile soap" of Marseille.

In the 1890s, during a scare concerning tubercular milk and amid a burgeoning campaign against butter conducted by the vegetarian wing of the physical culture movement in the United States, several persons (John Kellogg among them) began manufacturing nut butters as butter substitutes. In 1897 the Lane Brothers of Kokomo, Indiana, erected a factory to produce peanut butter on an industrial scale.[22] The peanut exceeded almost all other nuts in its ability to resist chemical degradation and rancidness. The tendency for oil and peanut matter to separate, however, remained an issue. Sanitariums and health resorts snapped up Lane's "Health Food Company" peanut butter. At the same time George Washington Carver published instructions for "Peanut Butter Candy" and other products from his experiment station in Tuskegee, Alabama. As with the cottonseed oil products—Crisco, oleomargarine, and Wesson oil—touted by the hygienic food movement, the adoption of peanut butter and peanut oil by the American population took time, substantial advertising, periodic food scares, and the development of an industrial infrastructure to accomplish. Peanut butter benefited from a general interest in nuts as a nutrition source during the 1890s . . . and the general inability of the population to distinguish legumes from nuts in the case of "ground nuts." Peanut oil benefited from the excess capacity of cottonseed oil factories erected in Virginia, North Carolina, South Carolina, and Georgia.

At the beginning of the twentieth century, a handful of industrial peanut towns had emerged, characterized by multistory fireproof brick warehouses abutting railroad lines: Suffolk and Petersburg, Virginia; Wilmington, North Carolina; Cordele, Georgia; Gainesville, Florida. Of these cities, Suffolk boasted the most extraordinary array of buildings—huge cleaning and hulling factories for the Suffolk Peanut Company, Lummis & Company, Martin & Sons, the Bain Peanut Company, Old Dominion Storage, Pond Brothers Peanut Company, John King Peanut Company, Holland & Lee Company, Birdsong Storage Company. All of these substantial buildings served the roasted peanut and confection trades. Only one establishment, the Suffolk Oil Mill—a branch of the Sea Island Cotton Oil Company of Charleston—pressed oil, taking the submarket-quality crop to press for oil. Farther south, the situation altered dramatically. In the decades before World War 1, the boll weevil had spread his devastation throughout the cotton states, leaving the huge cotton oil factories built in the late 1880s and 1890s undersupplied. Conversion of the mills to peanut oil plants and the substitution of peanut oil for cottonseed oil in a host of products took place in direct proportion to the weevil's destruction. By 1918 the southern landscape was dotted with dozens of converted mills: the Southern Cotton Oil Company plants in Dawson, Cordele, and Columbus, Georgia, pressed peanuts, while their Atlanta plant extruded peanut butter. The Empire Cotton Oil Co. of Atlanta produced Empire Brand Peanut Oil and Empire Brand Nut Meal. The International Vegetable Oil Company (formerly the International Cotton Oil Co.) in Arlington, Georgia, produced peanut butter and oil, while its branch plants in Raleigh, North Carolina, Savannah, Augusta, Houston, and Dallas produced oil. Cottonseed Products Company in Atlanta became Law & Company Peanut Products Laboratory. "During 1914–15 the boll weevil proved so disastrous to the cotton crop" in Donalsonville, Georgia, that its huge oil mill was converted to peanut oil manufacture.[23]

A similar fate befell the oil mill in Prattville, Alabama. In sum, peanut oil emerged in the second decade of the twentieth century as an industrially produced frying medium and salad oil to replace the diminishing supply of cottonseed oil. The mass production of peanut butter in the 1910s was a by-product of the redirection of industrial capacity from cotton to peanuts.

GROWING GROUNDNUTS

Every early account of the cultivation of peanuts first notices it in the garden plots of African slaves. As David Ramsay indicated in 1809, "They are planted in small patches chiefly by the negroes for market. They thrive best in light sandy soils. They produce 80 bushels to the acre."[24] Yet George Brownrigg had observed that as early as the 1760s, white planters had begun adapting the plant to their own uses: "Besides what the negroes cultivate for their own use, some planters raise a considerable quantity of it for the feeding of swine and poultry, which are very fond of the ground pease, and, when they are permitted to eat freely of them, soon become fat."[25] The novelty of the peanut's operation, flowering above-ground yet forming the ovapods beneath the soil surface, early on drew the attention of horticulturists and agricultural experimentalists. Andrew Parmentier, proprietor of Brooklyn's most famous horticultural garden, attempted hothouse cultivation in the North and supplied seed to North Carolina planters. Agricola (Robert L. Withers) of Clarke County, Alabama, employed peanuts in his field plantings as an intercrop, "grown with corn, rice, sweet potatoes, and cowpeas!"[26] Yet the characteristic most frequently noted by agricultural observers about peanuts was their capacity to grow in poor soils—an English consular official noted of the peanut lands around Wilmington, "corn, cotton, or any other crop usually grown in this section would likely not produce in value one-half the amount" as peanuts. The sandy loam with an admixture of lime proved suitable for the crop.

Peanuts were sufficiently robust a crop to grow in almost any soil. After the roasted peanut became widely vended in public, market preferences dictated the soil chosen for cultivation: "For the color of [peanuts] . . . is the effect of the soils in which they were raised. A dark soil colors the outside 'shuck' or shell."[27] Lighter peanuts were most desired. Red or chocolaty clays stained the shells so dark that no amount of cleaning in the warehouse could lighten them. So light gray, friable soils became the optimum since they nourished light-colored peanuts. Hog breeders who cultivated peanuts for feed on the farm, of course, did not worry about shell staining.

In Virginia and North Carolina, peanuts were grown in rotation, not as a specialty crop in the same field repeatedly. A peanut planting frequently followed corn, tobacco, or cotton, but never sweet potatoes. After the peanut harvest, the optimal benefit to the soil would come if rye was planted as a winter pasture cover; this would be plowed under. Cowpeas would then be planted in the spring for use as autumn forage for hogs. Corn or cotton would be planted the following year, the cycle repeating. Some farmers interposed a year of potatoes or sweet potatoes after the rye plow-in. But this expanded rotation required application of commercial fertilizer.[28]

The field underwent shallow plowing—not more than six inches of soil turnover. Peanuts thrive on limed soil, so if there is a deficiency of calcareous matter, an application of marl or wood ashes would improve yield markedly. The seed nuts were deposited in ridges three and a half to four feet apart early in May. Large podded varieties germinated better if the seeds were hulled. Spanish peanuts (introduced into the Deep South in the mid-nineteenth century) were planted in the shell and could be planted as late as mid-June. The only attention the plants required was weeding. Indeed, of cash crops, peanuts demanded the least oversight while growing of any field plantings for Tidewater and Lowcountry farmers. If one's fields remained untroubled by frost for most of the year, had abundant sunshine, fair drainage, and a modicum of organic matter intermixed, the crop would respond. Even low rainfall did not much diminish the yield.

Because farmers generally wished to use peanut vines as "hay" with which to feed stock, the crop would be harvested before frost caused their decay. In Deep South areas where frost did not come until late, the yellowing of the vine usually betokened the ripening of the nuts. Traditionally the plants were lifted from their beds by a one-horse turning plow, then freed from the soil by hand. The plants are spread on the ground to lie in the sun several hours, then gathered and arranged in stacks around a seven-foot stake to field cure. Strips of lath were laid at the base to prevent the curing peanuts from making contact with the soil. Stackers placed vines out, nuts toward the center. If the farmer properly sloped the vines, the stacks shed water. A wad of vine topped the stack. In dry weather, the peanuts cured in three weeks; in wet, four or more. Workers picked the pods from the vines only after they have dried. If local populations of mice or birds threatened the crop with their depredations, it would be picked earlier. Handpicking prevailed in the South until World War I, when mechanical picking machines became popular. Farmers carted their crop to factories for grading, cleaning, and sometimes hulling. Farmers then bundled peanut hay and stored it in barns for winter feed.

In the antebellum period, two peanut varieties vied for preeminence: the Carolina (African, Wilmington) and the Virginia. The former was a "running" plant, spreading its massive dark green foliage over the ground. It is the ancestor of that category termed "runner" peanuts, many of the modern offspring retaining the taste characteristics of the ancestor. The medium-size pods held two, sometimes three nuts. The latter was a small, bunched plant with lighter foliage and large pods clustered at the base of the plant. After the introduction of the Virginia into cultivation in the 1840s, farmers crossed the two varieties, forming the Virginia runner, which had foliage and a growing habit like the Carolina, with the large pods of the Virginia. After the Civil War, the Spanish peanut became established in the Deep South. This robust plant had an upright habit, abundant foliage (producing lots of peanut hay), small pods containing two brown nuts sheathed in red skins. It became the favorite peanut for the manufacture of peanut butter until the introduction of the Valencia peanut early in the twentieth century. The Valencia, like the Spanish, had a high oil content but produced greater yields, with more nuts in a pod. For plentitude of nuts in a pod, no nineteenth-century variety rivaled the Tennessee red, which bore as many as five or six. Like the Spanish, the nuts were small, but their coloration tended toward red rather than brown. The length of the pods and the color of the nuts proved a drag on the street roasted peanut market, so the Tennessee red became a favorite cultivar for hog breeders, who grew peanuts for feed.

The original culinary uses of the peanut had employed the Carolina peanut. We have discussed boiled peanuts, roasted peanuts, peanut "chocolate," and peanut oil. Yet like benne, African Americans had employed groundnuts in a complex array of dishes, which was captured occasionally over the course of the nineteenth century. White women recorded and published most of these. Sarah Rutledge in *The Carolina Housewife* supplied a recipe for "Ground Nut Soup": "To half a pint shelled ground-nuts, well beaten up, add two spoonsful of flour, and mix well. Put to them a pint of oysters, and a pint and half of water. While boiling, throw on a seed-pepper or two, if small."[29] May Fornay of Philadelphia, a collector of peanut recipes, printed a simpler recipe, closer to West African peanut soups:

PEANUT SOUP

Shell and hull carefully three pounds of roasted nuts; pound them to a smooth paste in a mortar. Put the paste into a saucepan, set it over a fire, and stir into it slowly two quarts of boiling water; season well with salt and cayenne pepper, and let it simmer gently until it thickens, stirring occasionally to prevent burning. Serve very hot.[30]

Fornay also recalled the specialty of black women street vendors, the confection known as "ground nut cakes" that we would recognize as peanut brittle:

PHILADELPHIA GROUNDNUT CAKES

Boil two pounds of light-brown sugar in a preserving-kettle, with just enough water to thoroughly wet it, and when this sirup begins to boil throw in the white of an egg to clear it. Let it boil until a few drops of the sirup put into cold water become brittle; it is then sufficiently done, and must be taken from the fire and strained. Have ready a quarter of a peck of groundnuts, roasted in the shell and then shelled and hulled. Mix the nuts thoroughly through the sirup while it is yet hot. Dampen with a brush a pasteboard or marble slab, free from all grease, and drop the hot mixture upon it in little lumps, which must be flattened with a spoon into thin cakes the size of a tumbler-top. When cold take them off of the board with a knife.[31]

A simpler confectionery treatment of peanuts is recorded in Dr. Francis P. Porcher's compendium of useful South Carolina plants, *Resources of the Southern Fields and Forests* (1863). He noted that they were "often parched, and beaten up with sugar, and served as a condiment or dissert."[32] Sugared roasted nuts became a staple of fruiterers' shops in northern cities in the 1850s. The uses of molasses as a sweetener in peanut candy is found in any number of recipes from the last half of the century. *Ballou's* printed a typical version in 1888:

PEANUT CANDY

Remove the shells and brown skins from the nuts; then boil two cups of molasses, one cup of brown sugar, a piece of butter the size of a small egg, and a tablespoonful of vinegar; boil until nearly brittle; then place the peanuts in a buttered pan, pour the candy over them, and cut into squares or bars.[33]

The African penchant for frying and converting food into the form of fritters gave rise to a family of peanut-based dishes. In Philadelphia, Fornay came across one that she rebranded "Peanut Croquettes."

PEANUT CROQUETTES

To make these, remove the shells and bulls from three pounds of roasted nuts; simmer them gently in good broth or gravy until they are soft enough to rub through a sieve with a potato masher. To each pint of this mixture add one ounce of butter and a palatable seasoning of salt and pepper, and stir these ingredients over the fire until they are scalding hot, then place the saucepan where the contents will keep hot without boiling; stir into them the yolks of six raw eggs, stirring the mixture constantly until the yolks thicken, taking care it does not boil, in which case the eggs will curdle. Cool the puree. Now wet the hands slightly with cold water and mold tablespoonfuls of the cold mixture into little pyramids. Boll them in cracker or bread-crumbs, dip them in beaten egg and then a second time in the crumbs, and drop them in boiling lard sufficient to cover them. When brown, take them out of the fat with a skimmer, lay them for a moment on coarse brown paper which will absorb the grease, sprinkle a little salt over them, and serve at once in a folded napkin.[34]

Finally, one encounters a peanut recipe that is an exact analogue of an antebellum recipe for benne and hominy. Almeda Lambert, a physical culturist, included what appears to be a traditional recipe in her 1899 culinary handbook, *Guide for Nut Cookery*:

PEANUTS AND HOMINY

Soak together equal quantities of hominy and blanched peanuts in water overnight. Put on the stove early in the morning in the same water, and when they have boiled an hour or two, or until the water begins to thicken, put them in a double boiler, and let them cook eight or nine hours.[35]

These dozen preparations constitute the sum of traditional peanut cookery. From the 1890s on, the hygienic food advocates with their peanut butter, peanut salads, peanut roasts, and a host of invented fare would flood the pages of housekeeping magazines and cookbooks with their novel inventions. Peanut oil would grow increasingly important, particularly as a frying medium, throughout the twentieth century. Roasted nuts and peanut candies would maintain their time-honored appeal. Few, however, would have predicted at the end of the twentieth century the return to the atavistic return of the most ancient preparations: peanut soup and boiled peanuts. Only the peanut fritter of the ancient dishes suffers neglect.

When I began writing *Southern Provisions*, I believed that the ancestral southern peanut, the Carolina African peanut, had gone extinct. Peanut breeding, responding to the spread of blights and viruses and the effects of root knot nematodes, had retired the old varieties, creating new crop peanuts designed for extensive planting and conventional handling. In 2013 even the most reputable of the resistant strains of runner peanuts, the Florunner, was considered an old variety, having been created in 1969. Yet I could never credit that the ancestral peanut of the South had disappeared entirely from the face of the earth. (I knew the black-skinned peanut circulating through the seed-savers exchanges were not the original Carolina African peanut for which photographs and illustrations exist in some number.) For several years I called peanut growers in North and South Carolina seeking leads. In April 2013, I contacted the staff of Poplar Grove Plantation, the great peanut plantation near Wilmington, inquiring if they grew Carolina African peanuts there at the historical site. They did not, but informed me that Dr. Tom Isleib of North

Carolina State University had a bank of historic peanuts in his laboratory. He did indeed—a collection begun in the early 1930s when researchers at North Carolina State canvassed peanut farmers for the varieties then being grown to establish a seed pool for a breeding program. When I inquired whether he had the Carolina peanut variety, he asked me to hold while he consulted a database. (Two minute pause.) "Yes, I do. Carolina number four and Carolina number eight."

I explained to Dr. Isleib that we wanted to preserve the peanut on the Slow Food Ark of Taste as an endangered agricultural resource. He quite understood and forwarded seed to the Clemson Coastal Research and Education Center south of Charleston, where Dr. Brian Ward took charge of the grow-out of the seeds. So as this manuscript goes to press, another of the linchpins of southern cookery has been restored—the original boiling peanut, oil peanut, soup peanut, and fritter peanut—one of the central items of the African food diaspora would be put into the hands again of farmers and chefs at about the time this volume issues from the press. When the two varieties were harvested in November 2013, Brian Ward and I determined that Carolina #4 was the Carolina-African, the South's ancestral peanut.

SEVENTEEN *Citrus*

Citrus exoticized the Lowcountry markets in the eyes of visitors, but its tang became a home feature of Lowcountry food, the acid vitalizing fish, the sour balancing the sweet in marmalades, syrups, and icings. Fresh fruit adorned the breakfast table. Candied fruit supplied the final taste of an evening's repast. Lime, lemon, and orange juices became standard health tonics and the sine qua non of plantation punches. In other regions of the country, oranges, lemons, limes, and grapefruit were treats or hallmarks of hotel gastronomy. In the Lowcountry, citrus played an integral role in taste construction of the cuisine.

Unlike rice or benne or the tanya, citrus fruit has never ceased to be locally grown or consumed. Its cultivation and improvement, interestingly, has remained in the hands of the growers as much as the university experimental stations. While land-grant university agricultural laboratories generate much of the research on flavor chemistry, entomology, and nematology, twentieth- and twenty-first-century growers have spearheaded the creation of new varieties with their experiments in hybridizing or their discovery of sports and promising open-pollinated new seedling varieties such as the pixie tangerine or the honeybell tangelo. Certain of these creations are splendid fruit—novel in flavor and versatile in employment. Others respond to the least refined elements of mass taste, such as the noxiously sweet honey tangerine, or the various "convenient" seedless grapefruits and oranges, or the faddishly small "cutie" mandarin oranges. Despite the vagaries of citrus fashion, history shows that citrus in the twenty-first century largely conforms in its aesthetics and culinary roles to the original Lowcountry conception of the fruit as a breakfast staple, a beverage, a component of sweet-sour confectionary, an acidic substitute for vinegar, and a health tonic.

Traditional Lowcountry meals celebrated the tang of citrus in season. Because the fruit only ripens on the tree and has a short shelf life, timeliness of harvest and quick transport from orchard to market to table mattered. In antebellum St. Augustine, Savannah, Charleston, and Wilmington, the destination table that mattered most was the breakfast table. On the eve of the Civil War, Mrs. Schoolcraft included a portrait of an urbane Charleston breakfast in her novel *Black Gauntlet*. A southern matron, Schoolcraft indulged in no invention in her depiction.

> Fruit-baskets . . . on either side of the table, contained the yellow, brown, and blue fig, the sugar pear, and pomegranate, and luscious oranges, growing to full perfection, and turning a rich yellow, on the trees in her own garden (not plucked half-green in the West Indies and merchandised here, where the color is produced from the "sere and yellow leaf" of decay, as is always the case in the Northern market where this splendid fruit is brought so unripe as to give no idea of its natural taste where it grows to perfection), a large covered dish of small hominy (for this bolted corn grits is the standard breakfast of South Carolina), piling plates of rice waffles, and johnny cakes, and sweet potato fritters, and corn flannel cakes, and fried young drum fish, and whiting, and mullet, completed this family breakfast.[1]

Schoolcraft's claim that the oranges were home produce is entirely plausible despite the city's location well north of the USDA Plant Hardiness Zone 9 recommended for citrus culture. Charleston gardens, beginning with the great show gardens of the 1750s, nearly always featured one or more varieties of citrus tree. Garden historian James R. Cothran notes that Charlestonian James Kerr sold handpicked oranges in the city as early as

1737.[2] Elinor Laurens's four-acre garden in Ansonborough maintained by English nurseryman John Watson specialized in limes.[3] A visiting botanist chronicled the bounty of Laurens's garden: "Among a variety of other curious productions, he introduced olives, capers, limes, ginger, Guinea grass, the Alpine strawberry, bearing nine months in the year; red raspberries, blue grapes; and also directly from the south of France, apples, pears, and plumbs of find kinds, and vines which bore abundantly of the choicest white eating grape, called the Chasselat blance."[4] Thomas and Elizabeth Lamboll's garden on the corner of King and Lamboll Streets (where the chinaberry was introduced into southern landscaping) contained pomegranates, China oranges, and sour oranges. Martha Logan's garden did as well.[5] A grove of orange trees graced a green that stood at the location of Charleston's current Orange Street.

Early Carolinians and Georgians grew oranges because when they first settled they discovered a sour wild orange already growing on the coastal islands. They did not know that the wild oranges were not indigenous, but naturalized trees of the sour Seville orange planted by the Spanish around St. Augustine in the final quarter of the sixteenth century. These had been transported northward along the coast by Native peoples who traded the fruit. Only on the Sea Islands did the seeds produce substantial groves north of 30 degrees latitude. According to A. J. Harris, wild groves were "generally found along the margins of the lakes and rivers, but sometimes we see scattering trees growing in the high hammocks of the interior, away from either river or lake."[6]

During the nineteenth century, the "wild" sour orange proved popular among southerners for making marmalade, as the Seville orange had been to the planters' English and French Huguenot forebears. The bitter white pulp beneath the rind made it unpleasant to eat raw, unless care was taken to remove every fragment from around the fruit. In Florida and Georgia, settlers often pressed the juice from the fruit, adding substantial quantities of cane sugar to create orangeade. Yet the distinctive local beverage concocted from the fruit was orange wine. Harris provided the favorite recipe:

ORANGE WINE

Take one part orange juice, strain or filter well, to four parts of pure water (rain-water preferred), add three pounds of good, pure sugar to each gallon of the mixture, put the whole into a vessel, and let it undergo fermentation; in about three months rack it off several times, allowing it to settle after each racking; then bottle and set away in a dark, cool place for future use.[7]

Commercial planting of oranges by non-Spanish Floridians began early in the 1800s, primarily to service the Savannah and Charleston market with fresh fruit and foreign importers with aromatic oil. Perfumers desired the essence of wild orange blossoms because is proved more aromatic than the oil of cultivated varieties. Growers servicing the fresh fruit market more esteemed the wild orange as rootstock for grafted groves of sweet China orange. Hardy naturalized trees were recognized as possessing superior resistance to local pests and diseases than lately introduced varieties. Francis Holmes, a gardener who supplied the Charleston market during the 1840s, provided the first glimpse of Lowcountry tastes and uses of orange:

This fruit with us is well known as a dessert, and a grateful relish to the sick; it is also much used in confectionary, both ripe and when green. In perfumery, the orange is used to form various perfumes and pommades, and the flowers distilled, produce orange flower water, used in cooking, medicine, and as a perfume. The usual mode with us, is to put the flowers into bottles, filled with three fourths good old brandy. It is then called orange flower brandy, and is used for the same purposes that the orange flower water is—like wine, the older it gets the better it is. The varieties are very numerous, but the principal ones grown in the Southern States, are the sweet, or Chinese, and the Seville, or bitter sweet. The trees (north of Georgia,) when young, should be protected with matting during the winter months. The light sandy soils produce the best oranges, these have thin skins, crowded with juice, and are very luscious; the dividing integuments of the plugs are thin and tender, and when fully ripe, they partake of a slight, but fine musky flavour. The orange tree is so averse to much, and particularly fresh manure, that penning, or fattening cattle, or horses among them, the passage of foul gutters near them, or the frequent use of the wash tub under their shade, soon produces disease and death; consequently low rich soils, and abundant manuring, are not favourable to the growth or quality of the sweet orange. It is propagated generally from seeds, and by budding.[8]

Holmes's warnings concerning temperature merited strict attention. Subzero freezes killed trees. To minimize the effects of winter cold, citizens in Charleston and Savannah espaliered trees against sunny south-facing walls, providing good wind protection and drainage. The Lowcountry's first horticulturists paid close attention to citrus in Georgia. Georgia's founders included oranges among the plants grown in the Trustees Garden in Savannah during the 1730s. William Stephens, the colony secretary, reported in 1740 that these did not do well because of spring chills. Yet General Oglethorpe planted them on his farm in Frederica, where the St. Simons Island microclimate proved more favorable. The trees outlived the settlement, for William Bartram observed thriving oranges and pomegranates among the ruins of the abandoned town in 1777. These groves remained vital until the great freeze of 1835, which decimated trees from St. Simons to St. Augustine.[9]

One cannot overstate the destruction to the citrus groves of the Sea Islands and east Florida inflicted by the freeze of 1835. Prior to the decimation of the groves, harvesters picked 1.2 million oranges in the vicinity of St. Augustine from trees planted by the Spanish in 1700 and bearing as many as four thousand fruit each.[10] The town supplied about 5 percent of the country's annual national consumption — the rest being imported from the West Indies, South America, Spain, and Sicily. Orange and lemon trees above 28 degrees latitude were killed by the 7 degrees Fahrenheit cold. Small pockets of wild oranges survived south of New Smyrna and in a few protected areas along the St. Johns River and on Drayton Island. Orchardists seriously considered turning the land into cane fields, since one did not have to wait for eight years to get a return from sugar. The revival of the Florida groves depended upon the initiative of a very few individuals, chief among them the man elected mayor of St. Augustine in 1838 and the boldest of Florida's citrus growers of the nineteenth century, Francis L. Dancy.

THE COMMANDER OF THE GROVES

Colonel F. L. Dancy epitomized the omni-competent public man and planter experimentalist. An engineer trained at the US Military Academy, he graduated in the class of 1826 and immediately entered artillery school at Fort Monroe, Virginia, as a second lieutenant. A skilled cartographer and an ingenious architect, he alternated between tours of topographic duty and ordinance. When promoted to first lieutenant in 1832, he received assignment in the Second Artillery at Fort Moultrie, South Carolina, serving there briefly before being dispatched to Fort Marion, Florida. His extensive mapmaking and road building in east Florida equipped him with an unequaled knowledge of the countryside. When the Second Seminole War erupted in 1835 in Florida, he operated as commissary and quartermaster of the Florida forces engaging in combat at Oloklikaha on March 31, 1836.[11] On September 11, 1836, he resigned his commission and was immediately hired by the US government as a civil engineer to erect a seawall at St. Augustine. His skill won him popular admiration, contributing to his election as mayor of St. Augustine for two terms. When the Seminole War rekindled in 1840, he served as lieutenant colonel of the Florida Volunteers, the state militia. After the militia disbanded in 1841, Dancy won election as a member of the Florida House of Representatives. In 1842 Dancy removed from St. Augustine to an expanse of land on the St. Johns River, where he built Buena Vista, his plantation house in 1844.[12] His public career reactivated in the 1850s when he secured appointment as state engineer and geologist, and, afterward, US surveyor general for Florida from 1859 until the outbreak of the Civil War.[13] During the war, he laboured as adjutant general of the Confederacy, serving in Florida and northern Virginia. When the US Congress prohibited former Confederate officers from the franchise and ability to hold public office after the Confederacy's loss of the Civil War, Dancy devoted all his energies to the cultivation of citrus fruit and the guava. No one approached him for energy or earnestness of purpose in improving the cultivation of oranges, lemons, limes, and tangerines in his region.

Dancy's signal contributions to citrus culture began early in his public career. After the great freeze of 1835, he reckoned that cutting back trees to stumps would activate root growth. In the second year after the cold, this happened. His active part in reviving the groves also contributed to his election as St. Augustine's mayor in 1838. As mayor, he emphasized the extraordinary profit that came from oranges and realized that while east Florida could not easily compete with Louisiana as a sugar-producing territory, its advantages as an orange-growing country were marked. He used his political authority to move planters toward full restoration of the groves, rather than converting them to cane fields.

Having surveyed much of the St. Johns River basin, he noted locations where wild oranges thrived naturally. To would-be growers, he counseled the siting of orchards on these wild groves, grafting cultivars on wild rootstocks. In the 1840s, he codified the new orthodoxy concerning how to establish citrus orchards:

> Select a location with an open exposure to the Northwest (this being the point from which our coldest freezing winds come) with as broad a sheet of water as possible to the north-west of the site chosen. In passing over this sheet of water, ice winds lose a portion of their cold and are rendered less damaging to tender vegetation than where no water exists. This exposure also retards the flow of sap, rendering the trees less sensitive to the effect of sudden cold. The land should be sufficiently high to drain itself; if it does not, it must be drained artificially. It is by no means necessary that the soil should be very rich; a sandy loam that in this region will yield twelve to fifteen bushels of corn per acre, will do. It should be well prepared by deep plowing and harrowing. The holes should be dug three feet deep, and according to the size of the tree, two and a half to five feet in diameter; a bushel or two of swamp muck thrown into each hole and well mixed with the surrounding soil. The holes should not be less than twenty-five feet from center to center. Trees fifteen to twenty years old, will nearly or quite shade the whole space at twenty five feet. This distance gives a free growth and makes a more shapely tree, allowing it to expand equally in every direction.[14]

Dancy located his most productive grove at Orange Mills, twelve miles north of Palatka on the east side of the St. Johns. In 1876 he wrote, "From these trees, covering more than one-half acre of ground, I shipped for market 58,250 oranges. . . . My twenty-year-old trees had not what I call a full crop for trees of their age; some had as many as 2,500 to the tree."[15]

Inspired by the lemon groves of T. H. Shaw on Amelia Island, Dancy planted lemons in the late 1830s.[16] In 1842 the scale insect invaded. "These insects came in swarms, and were as thick as the hair on a man's head." He noticed that budded, rather than seedling trees, responded to the onslaught vigorously. He communicated to the circle of lemon growers that budded trees scrubbed with carbolic soap could withstand scale. "I turned my attention to the cultivation of the lemon, and in twelve years had 3,000 trees in profitable bearing. The product of one tree brought $130. So that you see the lemon is equally as profitable as the orange, if not more so. The trees are healthier, and the fruit keeps longer for market."[17] Dancy knew that diversification of orchard products hedged against financial ruin arising from a disease or pest wiping out one's plantings. He made the lemon a strong secondary crop. He also grew and promoted lime orchards, touting the health benefits of imbibing lime juice. He testified to Florida's fruit growers that "by making free use of lime, you can shut up the doctors' shops."[18]

Of all Dancy's many contributions to the consolidation of citrus culture in the United States, the greatest may have been the introduction in 1867 of the Dancy tangerine. Grown from the seed of a Mandarin orange planted on the property of N. H. Moragne at Palatka, Florida, Dancy's fruit, like many citrus trees grown from seed, produced fruit different in quality, configuration, and taste than that of its parent. Since the parent had been thought to have been procured from Morocco, it bore the name the Moragne "tangierine," alluding to Tangiers. Dancy recognized the superlative quality, distributed cuttings to his circle of fellow growers in 1872. It became one of the first Florida citrus varieties around which a breeding discipline was imposed. In 1890 the Rolleston Nursery in San Mateo began large-scale commercial propagation, making the variety universally available in the United States. For all intents and purposes, it can be said to have established the tangerine as a citrus brand. "Tangerine" has now come to denominate any kind of Mandarin orange.

What made the Dancy tangerine one of the great citrus novelties of the century? First, its thin leathery reddish-orange skin was easily peeled. Next, the flesh color was deeply orange. The number of seeds was moderate — from six to twelve. Most importantly, the flesh melted on the tongue, suffusing the mouth with richly flavored juice, with a bright ringing acid note. Dancy, at the end of his life, believed its sweetness harmonized with the sweetness of cane sugar better than any other orange, lemon, or lime.

Having by a happenstance of nature become the beneficiary of a fruit superior to any existing in its category, Dancy confronted the problem of how to replicate his find, preserving its qualities. In short, he had to confront the question how does one maintain a variety? M. S. Moreman, who became a grower in the early 1870s, immediately after the discovery of the Dancy tangerine, recalled in the twentieth century how this issue began to impinge on the consciousness of citrus planters. "Very little was known of varieties, and little thought given to it. An acquaintance had a seedling grove. Also in the town, which then was quite a tourist town, he had a store. In order to meet the demand for certain varieties, he provided a row of neat bins labeled with the names of the various varieties, but was careful to put into each bin certain sizes. The African Sweet was his favorite. It was a small russet of about 250. Now these different bins were frequently filled from the same tree. But they answered his purpose and his customers were satisfied."[19] In the antebellum period, when planters only grew the native sour orange and bittersweet orange, or the Portugal or China sweet orange, they planted a grove all of one kind, using seeds from the fruit, confident that since no other kinds were pollinating the orange blossoms, roughly the same tree would be produced. But as growers sought market distinction in the Reconstruction era, they began importing varieties from Asia and Europe. The Botelha was imported from England, the Creole from Louisiana, the Du Roi from Europe, the Dulcissima from Paris, the blood from Malta, the navel from Bahia, Brazil, the sustain from England, the St. Michael's from the Azores, the Tahiti from the South Seas. The atmosphere of the citrus-growing areas of Florida filled with foreign pollen. The crosses produced several seed-grown varieties that themselves became noteworthy. Dancy isolated two: the Buena Vista and the Old Vini. Mrs. Mary Richard on the Arlington River nurtured the Nonpareil. The popular Homosassa took its name from the Florida town where it was first discovered. The Magnum Bonum was thought to have been a seeding of a Homosassa. The Reverend William Hicks, like Dancy, developed two: the Arcadia and the very important sweet Seville. The peerless first appeared as a seedling in an old grove on Drayton Island.

By 1870 Dancy grasped the principle that apple growers had come to understand through a half century of experiment. Planting from seed introduced variation and variety instability. Grafting and budding on root-stocks produced uniformity: "A great diversity of opinion exists in regard to the orange. Some contend that the plant from the sweet orange seed will be a sour orange tree, and that a bud from the budded tree on the sour stock, will produce a sour orange. My experience is that, without exception, the seed from the sweet orange will produce a sweet orange; but that they may and do differ in flavor and sweetness from each other; and that the bud from a budded tree will produce its like—the product from the bud partaking of the nature of the parent bud and not of the stock budded."[20] To maintain a superior variety, a planter had to graft, not plant, seeds when propagating. Though Dancy considered himself a practical and experimental grower, rather than a scientific one, he had arrived at the crucial insight of scientific pomology, and when he published his findings in 1870, articulated for his community for the first time the path forward. The major instruction guides to citrus growing composed in the next decade: T. W. Moore's *Treatise and Hand Book of Orange Culture* (1877) and E. A. and H. A. Manville's *New Guide to Orange Culture* (1879) elaborated the insights presented in Dancy's seminal article, "Orange Culture in Florida."

In the last decades before his death at Buena Vista on October 27, 1890, Dancy undertook one final campaign on behalf of a non-citrus fruit, the guava. "I esteem it of equal importance to either [the lemon or lime]." He repeatedly spoke on its behalf at public meetings, sent samples to fellow growers, and provided much of the information for Dr. M. B. Lazarus's seminal article, "The Guava (*Psidium sp.*) in Florida," in the *Rural Carolinian* of 1872.[21] It would take a half century for Florida's growers to come to Dancy's opinion.

Fruit growers, like grain farmers or livestock raisers, constitute a community, a society in which rivalry and common purpose jostle, and custom confronts innovation. Colonel Dancy was not nearly the scientific grower that Reverend William Hicks at Arcadia was. He did not grasp the importance of container design and railroads in the promotion of product as

A. E. Manville did. He did not possess the eloquence and fluency with the pen that his friend Dr. Lazarus had. Yet no one mattered more in the reconsolidation of citrus agriculture after the ruin of the Spanish plantings in 1835. His training in engineering and geology made him systematic in his approach to problems. His experience as a military officer and elected official gave him an acquaintance with people and a habit of leadership. His cartographic work made him as familiar with the geography of Florida as any person of his generation. His perseverance, curiosity, and refined taste made him an ideal experimental cultivator. His sociability made him an ideal participation in the institutional world of agriculture in the age of association and corporation. He made the groves at Orange Mills a tourist destination, inviting the public, and particularly fellow growers, to walk the groves. In sum, Dancy nearly single-handedly saved lemon culture in the 1840s, created the variety that popularized the tangerine in the 1860s, codified the modern method of orange propagation to maintain varietal character in the 1870s, and championed the guava when few thought the fruit worth cultivating. The key to his importance was his effectiveness in convincing his fellow growers to do what he had done.

While the bounty of Florida's citrus groves delighted the cooks and consumers of the Southeast, a substantial portion of the crop found its way to the great cities of the North by rail and steamer packet. So the efflorescence of recipes employing lemons, limes, oranges, and tangerines was not restricted to the Lowcountry or the South. Indeed, Miss Parloa and the students at the Boston Cooking School proved particularly adept at inventing novel citrus dishes. Yet a particular fascination resides in what the culture of the growers did with the ever-expanding assortment of fruit being grown. How did Lowcountry cuisine deploy the bright acids?

SWEET AND SOUR

During the nineteenth century, lemons, oranges, and citrons circulated about the Atlantic, their acidic tartness treasured as an alternative to vinegar. All became incorporated into the cosmopolitan cooking of the coastal cities. Of these, the lemon enjoyed the greatest popularity. Indeed, only with the greatest difficulty can one assign a purely local character to a lemon recipe. Everyone used it to brighten the taste of fish, give a pungent counternote to sugar, or to marry with cream and eggs in custard. Lemon sauce (white sauce with juice added) appeared in every London cookbook of note. Lemon soufflé became a signature dish of American high-end hotel cookery. The northeastern cooking schools taught students how to make lemon candies and ices.

The orange, however, received far less ubiquitous coverage in culinary letters. And it gave rise to preparations distinctive to the regions of its cultivation. Annabella Hill, for instance, in her discussion of the orange as a fruit, instructed her Lowcountry readers to present it in a way that made its local nativity evident.

> A pretty style of preparing oranges for the table is to cut the rind through with a sharp penknife into quarters, leaving the pulp whole. Peel off the rind, leaving it attached to the orange at the stem end, and turn in the separated points, so as to form a cup-like receptacle for the fruits. Heap this in stands, and ornament with orange leaves.[22]

Hill included two popular lemon custard recipes in her *New Cook Book* and two orange custards, the second of which evinced Savannah's predilection for adding wine and brandy to desserts:

> Cream half a pound of sugar with half a pound of butter; add the grated rind and juice of two oranges, and one wineglass of mixed wine and brandy. Beat six eggs light, and pour on gradually. Line the plate with puff paste; pour in the custard, and bake.[23]

While using the fresh juice and grated peel of lemon or orange was the conventional way of imparting citrus tang into a dish, other liquid forms of citrus flavor developed in the Lowcountry, particularly using the blossoms of the "wild" sour orange. Orange blossom water and orange flower syrup appeared in numbers of recipes included in Sarah Rutledge's *Carolina Housewife*.

ORANGE FLOWER SYRUP

To a quarter of a pound of dried blossoms, add two pounds of sugar, and four pints of water; boil to a rich syrup. N.B. The orange-blossoms should be gathered as soon as they fall from the tree, however few in number;

keep them in a cool shady place till a sufficient quantity be procured for boiling.[24]

Rutledge's liquid decoctions of orange blossoms found their way into a host of recipes: into sweet potato pone to deepen flavor, into almond ice, almond pudding, and the batter of almond biscuits to work a counterpoint to the bland unroasted nut meat, into orange cake to make the orange taste emphatic, and into coconut puffs to complicate the sweetness.

Because two broad varieties of orange—sour and sweet—grew in the Lowcountry, Rutledge took care to indicate in recipes which was to be used. Dishes requiring a marked aromatic dimension or a play of sour and sweet called for the "wild" sour orange. Those that needed only a note of citric flavor called for the sweet. The most traditional Anglo-American sour orange preparation, orange marmalade, appeared in a particularly forceful version. Sour orange juice supplied an edge to two other traditional English items: calf's foot jelly and mincemeat. But the sour orange preparations that most attract attention are orange pie (the first American instance of a dessert that would become a fixture in nineteenth-century American cookbooks), orange wafers (a fruit and sugar confection), and candied orange peel.

ORANGE PIE

Chip half a dozen oranges very fine; take half a dozen more, and cut a small hole in the top of each; scoop out all the pulp; boil the skins till they are tender, changing the water several times, to extract the bitterness. Then take six or eight apples, pare and slice them; put to them part of the pulp of your oranges, from which the strings and seeds must first be picked; then add half a pound of fine sugar, and boil till quite soft, over a slow fire; then fill your oranges with it, and put them into a deep dish, without paste, have first placed in the dish three-fourths of a pound of sugar, and as much water as will wet it. Be care to place the oranges with holes uppermost; lay over them a light paste, and bake an hour and a half in a slow oven.[25]

While folk wisdom suggests that apples and oranges are fruits so distinct as to have nothing in common, their marriage in a bath of sugar can be a splendid melding of their different qualities. Rutledge's is the most texturally interesting version of a pie that underwent simplification with the passing decades until reaching its minimal form in "Orange and Apple Pie" in Mrs. J. L. Lane's *365 Orange Recipes* (1909).[26] Mrs. Lane paired the two fruits in three other dishes in her calendar: "Orange and Apple Marmalade," "Orange and Apple Pudding," and "Orange and Apple Salad." Interestingly, a version of Rutledge's recipe alternating sliced oranges and apples became "a much esteemed delicacy" in the country districts of England over the century.[27] Though Rutledge did not specify the variety of apple to be used in the pie, only six types grew well in the Lowcountry. The early summer varieties were the Astrachan red, early harvest, red June (or Carolina), and striped June (or Margaret) apples. The chief summer apple was the Family. The chief winter apple was the Etowah, also called Cooper's red.

ORANGE WAFERS

Take the best oranges, cut them in half, and take out the seeds and juice: boil them in three or four waters till they are tender, then beat them to a pulp in a marble mortar, and rub them through a hair sieve; to one pound of this pulp, allow a pound and a half of loaf sugar; take half of your sugar, and boil it with the oranges till it becomes ropy; then take it from the fire, and when cold, make it up in paste with the other half of your sugar; make but a little at a time, for it will dry fast; then with a rolling pin, roll them out as thin as tiffany, upon paper. Cut them round with a wine-glass, let them dry, and they will look clear.[28]

While it may not be entirely clear from the above, Rutledge intended that the peel of the orange be boiled with the de-juiced flesh. These are quite magical items when made properly, with the appearance of orange isinglass. In his 1807 classic, *The Complete Confectioner*, Frederick Nutt provided the idea for this sugary treat, yet Rutledge's half-cooked/half-uncooked sugar combination produces a much finer end result.[29]

TO CANDY ORANGE PEEL

Leave your oranges on the tree until the rind is thick—any time in January will do. Weight the fruit, and allow an equal weight of sugar; cut the oranges in half, and take out the pulp; boil the peels until quite tender, changing the water (Which should be hot,) frequently; cover the kettle close while the peels are boiling; moisten your sugar, put in the peels, and boil them until thoroughly impregnated with the syrup; then take out the peels, lay them on tin sheets, and put them in a cool oven. When quite dry, lay them again in the syrup until they become saturated, return them to the oven, and continue the process until the syrup is exhausted.[30]

All three of Rutledge's recipes here make use of the peel of the sour orange, rendered palatable by multiple boilings and cooking it with sugar.

Rutledge's employments of the sweet orange were more conventional. Its grated peel went into cake and cookie batters, its juice (mixed with the juice of lemons) went into orange jelly, and it was the preferred orange consumed cut and chilled for dessert. The rind of the sweet orange would, after the Civil War, provide an alternative flavoring source to the sour orange blossom in creating syrup. The New Orleans Christian Woman's Exchange offered a recipe for "Orange Peel Syrup" in *The Creole Cookery Book* (1885): "The peel of 3 sweet oranges in 3 pints of cold water, to be boiled down to 1 quart, ½ lb. of loaf sugar added, and boiled together. Very nice."[31]

It was generally believed that citrus syrups (orange, lemon, and citron—the grapefruit was still rather a novelty) like citrus juices had healthful properties. Colonel Dancy swore by their salubrious influence and dosed his fifteen children with lime juice and orangeade. Since vitamin theory had not yet been broached, the general conviction that citric acid conduced to well-being formed inductively out of a multitude of observations of persons who ingested it regularly. By the late 1850s, it became a culinary article of faith, and the fruits appeared in manuals of invalid cookery, alongside arrowroot, beef broth, and rice gruel.

In the first decade of the nineteenth century, Campbell Wylly and John Couper began growing arrowroot (*Maranta arundinacea*) on the Georgia Sea Islands. The fine-grained starch made from the roots, the delicate flavor of puddings and jellies made from arrowroot, and the refined mouth feel of arrowroot gravies brought it to wide culinary attention. It became one of the favorite experimental kitchen ingredients of midcentury. Because the orange and the arrowroot grew in close proximity, it was perhaps inevitable that the ingredients would be combined to create ultra-healthy food. Alexis Soyer, the international face of French cooking, contributed the first of these concoctions in *The Modern Housewife* (1850):

ORANGEADE

Proceed as for lemonade, but using the whole of the orange, a little of the peel included, sweetening with sugar candy, and adding a teaspoonful of arrow-root mixed with a little cold water, which pour into the boiling liquid at the same time you put in the orange. The arrowroot makes it very delicate.[32]

Southerners tended to prefer their orangeade without the arrowroot fillip, but they did adopt the tastiest of the dishes that combined the two healthful ingredients,

ORANGE ARROWROOT JELLY

Bring to a boil 3 pints of orange juice, 3 pints of water, 1 pound of sugar and ½ ounce of stick cinnamon tied in cheesecloth. Skim and remove the cinnamon; then add to the boiling syrup 1½ pounds of arrowroot, stirring constantly. Boil fifteen minutes, then turn into small moulds. When cold and firm serve with whipped cream or with custard flavored with orange-flower water.[33]

While citrus growers diversified their groves in Florida — adding limes, grapefruit, citrons, and shaddocks to the inventory of fruit — Lowcountry cooks developed their own preferences. The grapefruit never found a substantial following during the nineteenth century. The rind of the citron found its way into a panoply of puddings. The shaddock was rendered into preserves and little else. Lime juice gradually insinuated its ways into icings, puddings, simple syrup, and, in the 1890s, salad dressings. Throughout the century, the orange and the lemon exercised dual dominion in the kitchen as they did in the marketplace, the gardens, and the groves of the Lowcountry.

The single most salient difference between the popular uses of citrus in the nineteenth century and its employments in the twentieth was the vast increase in the percentage of crop devoted to juice production. There existed from the beginnings of the American Republic that modest percentage of the population who, like Dancy, believed in the antiscorbutic power of citrus. The success of the English navy in fighting scurvy on shipboard with a ration of limes from the 1790s onward had alerted the intelligent public about the importance of this class of food for human wellbeing. While many planters entertained the notion that their lime punch, lemonade, and orangeade were somehow healthy, few shared Dancy's conviction that only the pure juice—unadulterated with water, sugar, or other fruit juices—was conducive to health. The antiscorbutic qualities of citrus made it attractive to the naturist wing of the physical culture movement at the end of the nineteenth century. Health spas and health gurus touted the value of orange juice particularly, with magazine publisher Bernarr Macfadden an enthusiastic cheerleader for its "body building" qualities. The articulation of vitamin theory in 1912 took place immediately before the great expansion of juice production in the second and third decades of the new century.

The determination that citrus abounded in vitamin C would not occur in 1928, and the physiological mechanisms by which vitamin C became absorbed into the body awaited the explanations of Albert Szent-Györgyi in 1931. These discoveries made orange juice a nutritional darling. Fortuitously in happened at a time when farmers had expanded acreage and output of their groves to the level of glut. New paths are only blazed in food when necessity demands. The glut of fruit from the expanding Floridian and Californian plantings had growers desperate for a new product or a new market. The pasteurization of the juice and its packaging in cans overcame long-standing problems of spoilage. By 1930 the tall glass of OJ had become the invariable companion of the glass of milk and the cup of coffee. Orange juice's success led almost immediately to imitation and adulteration. Orange-colored beverages, charged with sugar and scant of citrus, began to appear on grocers' shelves. From that day to this, the war between nutritionists and those who would pander to the nation's sweet tooth has continued unabated.

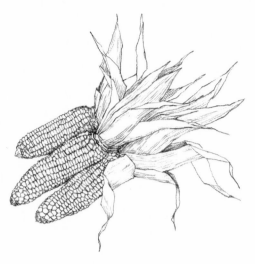

EIGHTEEN   *The Return of the Tastes*

Three years ago I ran across an attestation by a writer in the *U.S. Census Report for 1880*: "The finest, as food for man, of all the known varieties of corn is the white flint corn, peculiar to the sea islands."[1] Flint corn on the Sea Islands? This seemed improbable. After all in the great story of corn origins told by botanical etiologists, the round, starch-packed flint corns descended from the Central American Chapalote corn and became, because of their quick-growing habit, the staple of northern Native peoples. The southern Native Nations grew dent corns descended from the Mexican Palomero Toluqueño variety. Called gourdseed corn by American settlers, dent corn had a thin, wrinkled top to the kernel, particularly pronounced when the grain dried. It was said to resemble in shape the seed of a dipper gourd or the crown of a molar. They are softer and more easily milled than flint corn, and some claimed that they were easier to digest than flint varieties. Why were farmers growing a northern corn variety on the Sea Islands in the 1870s? Why were they growing so traditional a cultivar in the 1870s when the seed catalogs contained dozens of new high-yield varieties?

My first impulse was to attribute the Sea Island white flint to that binge of seed distribution undertaken by the US Patent Office during the

1850s. In 1854 the US secretary of agriculture had declared that "the varieties best adapted for the Middle and Southern States are the large white and yellow Gourd-seeds; the yellow 'Shoe-peg,' or 'Oregon'; and the New Mexican and North Carolinian 'White-flints.'"[2] The government began issuing seed for the recommended varieties. There were two white flints listed amid the expected dents (shoepeg, like gourdseed, was a dent). But I quickly found evidence that white flint had been established in island agriculture well before the Patent Office distribution. In his sketch of Edisto Island in *Statistics of South Carolina* (1826), Robert Mills observed, "Standing provisions consist chiefly of that variety of the maize which is distinguished by the name of flint corn. An acre produces from 15 to 25 bushels. The quantity grown is not very considerable. In ordinary years it is barely adequate to the consumption of the island. It rarely happens that a superfluity is made to send to market; but such is the provident disposition of some of the planters that they often keep on hand a supply of corn sufficient for the consumption of two years. The corn blades are carefully cured, and preserved as a substitute for hay."[3] So white flint corn was being used for provision, not market, on the Sea Islands in the 1820s.

John Lorain of Pennsylvania and Virginia—the first great corn experimentalist of the experimental era—described the Native-nurtured landraces of corn in field culture in the middle and southern states during the first decades of the 1800s. In 1825 four kinds of flint corn predominated: the large white and yellow and the small white and yellow—and one kind of dent corn—white Virginia gourdseed. He described them thusly:

> The cobs of the two first-mentioned are thick and long, the grains are
> much wider than deep, and where the rows of grains meet and unite with
> each other, their sides fall off almost to nothing. This gives the outside
> of the grain a circular form; and communicates to the ear an appearance
> something like a fluted column. This formation greatly diminishes the
> size of the ends and sides of the grains, and is the cause of the hard flinty
> corns being less productive, in proportion to the length and thickness of
> their cobs, than the gourdseed corn. As the little white and yellow are
> formed much in the same way, and the cobs are considerably smaller, they
> are still less productive than the big white and yellow, but ripen earlier.
> The grain of these four flinty kinds are very firm, and without indenture

in the outside ends. The two smaller kinds seem to be still more hard and solid than the larger; and the color of the little yellow, deeper than that of the big. The ears of the Virginia gourdseed are not very long, neither is the cob so thick as that of the big white and yellow; but the formation of the grain makes the ear very thick. They frequently produce from thirty to thirty-two, and sometimes thirty-six rows of very long narrow grains, of a soft, open texture. These grains are almost flat at the outside end, are also compactly united from the cob to the surface of the ear, without any of that fluted appearance, between the rows of grain, which causes the flinty corn to be much less productive in proportion to the size of the ears. The gourdseed ripens later than any other, but is by far the most productive. It is invariably white, unless it has been mixed with the yellow flinty corns: then it is called the yellow gourdseed, and too many farmers consider it and most other mixtures original corns.[4]

Lorain leaves little doubt that flints of several sorts had been established in the eighteenth century in the South. Indeed, when a visiting agriculturist toured Beaufort, South Carolina, on the eve of the Civil War, the white flint corn seemed so suited to the locale that he believed it native: "A species of Indian Corn, called 'white flint corn,' and which when cooked is very nutritious and white as snow, seems indigenous to these islands. It is much superior to the common varieties."[5]

Had the Creek farmers of the coast cultivated white flint when the Creek farmers of the interior planted gourdseed? It is doubtful that ethnobotanical archaeology can make a definitive determination about whether it was the first corn of the region or a later introduction. What we can determine was why it was embraced during the period when rice culture made the islands and the coast the locus of extensive plantation culture with large slave labor forces. From Robert Mills's testimony, we know that the corn was planted on the islands at a level for provision, not market supply, at the beginning of the nineteenth century. Acreage in the islands went to the cash crops—cotton or rice. But the labor force had to be fed. Both cotton and rice planting were strenuous activities requiring solid nutrition to maintain the strength of slaves. Anglo-Americans possessed an ancient conviction that grains—in the forms of porridge or bread—formed the basis of health and strength.[6] Wheat could not readily be grown in much of the Lowcountry. So the grains that could—rice and corn—supplied the grain ration.

Why did planters not grow the more prolific gourdseed variety? The obsessive notation of the nutriment of white flint corn suggests one reason. At the outset of the nineteenth century, the old Galenic model of nutrition had collapsed and a new chemical understanding of nutrition was organizing. Starches and sugars were known to be the most nutritive elements in food, more so than oil. So white starched corns with the greatest density were deemed the most nutritive. Yellow, oily corns, less so. When the Monticello Agricultural Society of inland Fairfield County, South Carolina, debated between the planting of white gourdseed and white flint in 1838, the question turned on these matters.

> It must be admitted, that the flint is the heaviest, according to measure, and contains more nutritive matter; but it is equally certain that the gourd-seed will measure most from the acre, with equal advantages otherwise, and sufficient too to make up more than the loss of weight. Admitting, however, as an hypothesis, that this should not be realized, your committee, on other grounds, would give the gourd-seed a decided superiority. It is more easily ground into meal: in a horse-mill, thirty bushels of this corn would be ground with as much ease as twenty-five of the flint. It is more digestible; horses and hogs masticate it with less difficulty.[7]

For the Fairfield farmers, the ease of mastication of the softer gourdseed for horses and hogs, combined with the high yield of the dent corn, won the nod. Human nutrition or palatability was a secondary consideration.

The equation played out differently on the coast. Planters placed the premium on human nutrition. For the feeding of livestock, they had rejected the Pennsylvania scheme of grain feeding and opted for a food source with substantially higher output of sugar and starch per acre than corn—sweet potatoes. As Mills had noted of Edisto Island in 1826, "The yam, or sweet potato, is more extensively cultivated on Edisto island than perhaps in any other part of the state. They are a most valuable root, and deserve more of the attention of the planter, as an article of provision, than is commonly paid them. An acre manured as a cow-pen, or otherwise, has produced, and may be made at any time to produce 300 bushels of 60 weight each, or 24,000 weight to the acre, in the crude or raw state."[8] The sweet potato, like the white flint corn, and like the pork that fed on the sweet potatoes, went into the slave food ration on the Lowcountry plantations.

Yet a final consideration argued in favor of having white flint be the corn of the Sea Islands—the destructions of the corn weevil (*Sitophilus zeamais Motsch*), the scourge of southern corn farmers, particularly those who let the ripe corn stand on the stalks to dry out. In his 1857 *Cotton Planter's Manual*, J. A. Turner said of white flint corn, "No other [variety] will stand the depredations of the weevil."[9]

In the 1870s, experiments in Georgia proved that yield of white flint could be boosted by a liberal application of cottonseed manure. Ironically, the cultivation of cotton on the Sea Islands decreased precipitously during the Reconstruction era, giving way to truck farming of watermelons, sweet potatoes, vegetables, and more corn. The liberation of the slave labor force and the resultant suspension of any need for a plantation to grow provision crops on a large scape changed the local growing dynamic. African American tenant farmers and white planting families grew corn for the market. They grew the corn that knew and esteemed. By Reconstruction, the singular quality of white flint as human food was fixed in public opinion, a truism for producers and consumers.

In contrast, the gourdseed corns by the 1870s became particularly noted for the quality of their meal and for distilling. Meal from white flint "is not so pleasant to the taste of those unaccustomed to its use, as that made from the soft farinaceous varieties of the South and West."[10] When John Lorain began breeding crosses of the flint and dent corns in the 1820s, his hybrids had the floury qualities of gourdseed, with the quick growing season of the flints. Later nineteenth-century breeders, however, could not instill in Tuscarora or the other crosses the taste quality of white flint or the floral aromatics of the original white gourdseed. Upcountry distillers of corn liquor would not abandon gourdseed for the larger, more prolific, and quicker-growing hybrid varieties.

In 1997 Glenn Roberts, while driving the back roads of upcountry South Carolina searching for antique corn, found the classic white gourdseed in a bootlegger's field near Dillon. He identified the strain as "John Haulk," which had been bred to its form in the 1850s in the Appalachians. From this seed stock, he began the first of his restorations of landrace grains.[11]

In 1905 USDA collectors came to the Sea Islands and collected strains of white flint for the national collection. Roberts secured sample seed corn from the USDA germplasm bank and began growing it out in 2011. Both of the pillar corn varieties employed in Lowcountry cuisine should be available for the use of chefs and cooks in autumn of 2013.

The stories of the Sea Island white flint and white gourdseed corn follow the form of so many stories in this book: plants developed out of ancient landraces—cherished for qualities of nutrition, animal edibility, and palatability—eclipsed by later varieties that had the advantage of greater productivity, insect resistance, and processability, yet preserved over the twentieth century by persons to wishing to keep their tastes alive. In the twenty-first century, white flint corn returns to the table because its qualities of taste and texture are so distinctive.

In 2012 corn bread, hominy, grits, and spoon bread are perceived as southern dishes. But corn, like every staple grain, gave rise to a range of dishes of generic cast—a porridge, a pudding, a biscuit, a bread, a fritter. Consider cornmeal porridge—the dish made by pouring a measure of meal into boiling water and cooking it for half an hour. "Called Mush, by the Pennsylvanians; Suppon, in the state of New York; Stir-a-bout, in Ireland; Polenta, in Italy; and Api, by the ancient Peruvians" and "Hasty Pudding" in New England, its local character was almost entirely dependent upon the type of corn being grown in the region.[12] Hasty pudding was traditionally made by Rhode Island white-cap flint or King Philip corn, polenta with red flint, mush with large yellow flint, and grits with Sea Island white flint, Api with Morocho white corn. Corn bread had a similar geographical ubiquity and a commensurability of preparation. In the mid-nineteenth century, it appeared nearly universally on hotel menus. Judson's Hotel, on Broadway in New York, had a recipe for "Superior Corn Bread,"[13] that if one were to judge by appearances in print, was a more famous version than that of the Planter's Hotel in Charleston. The preparations were much the same; the salient difference would have been the Tuscarora corn used for New York meal and the white gourdseed used in Charleston.

Many people think of region as operating at the level of the dish. But

I've taken some pains to suggest that in terms of grain preparations the recipe may be the same from region to region with different names and different varieties of the specified ingredients. Even dishes held up as signature preparations of places, such as Louisiana's traditional sweet rice beignet, the calas, have exact parallels in the Lowcountry's rice fritter, as Karen Hess and Damon Lee Fowler have indicated,[14] or Jules Harder's "Rice Croquette." The rice fritter of Savannah in 1880 used Carolina Gold rice; that of New Orleans, Honduran white rice.

Now that I have insisted that regional resides in ingredients most of all, I must remind myself of the definitions of cuisine that began this inquiry. Yes, it lives in ingredients; yes, it resounds with the taste of terroir, the soil of the places where ingredients were grown. But it is also about perceptions and consciousness. The calas matter more to New Orleans than the rice fritter in the Lowcountry, where the rice waffle prevailed at breakfast. Because the white flint corn tasted so splendidly to Carolinians and Georgians, they paired shrimp with it as often as with rice, while in Louisiana, shrimp Creole insisted on rice and no other grain. Terrapin has for nearly a century and a half been more numerous in the waters of the Carolinas then in the Chesapeake, yet terrapin was a fixture on the Maryland menu and only a visitant on the Charleston hotel menu.

So it is not enough to know the ingredients or to restore them. Nor is it enough to renovate the chemically saturated soils of the coastal plain and explore the rehabilitation of the soil through historical methods. Nor is it enough to know the kitchen preparations in the big house and the cabin, the city hotel and the town house. Cuisines thrive with the development of a consciousness. The stories connected with farming, plant breeding, fishing, transporting, selling in the market, cooking, eating, and drinking have to be recovered and restored. I've tried to do this in a way that was not schematic or pro forma. Somewhere here you will encounter breakfast, supper, and dinner. You will visit the fields and orchards from the Cape Fear to the St. Johns Rivers. I've tried not to retell tales that others have told about labor in the fields, or the origins of dishes and cultivars, or the way a tradition should look. I know there are more stories worth telling— about peaches, or the arrowroot boom on the Georgia Sea Islands, or invalid cooking in the Lowcountry. But with a great cuisine and strong tradition, there is always more to say and do.

THE RETURN OF THE TASTES

Taste is never a purely physiological phenomenon. As Brillat-Savarin indicated, a kind of intelligence about what one eats colors one's appreciation or disgust with what is on the plate. That we speak of refining taste or educating the palate attests to our consciousness that the tongue and the imagination combine in the experience of the meal. For this reason, some developments among the flavor sciences community have a comical reductiveness. The Toyo taste meter that certain Asian rice experimentalists subject new strains to may rank the ratio of amylose and amylopectin at certain protein levels in the grain, but it will never measure in any phenomenological sense the experience of rice quality that a human has.[15] The look of the rice matters. These days, the aroma. The wholesomeness of the mouth feel. And if one knows something of the rice's background—that it is a koshihikari rice grown watered from spring-fed impoundments in a valley in Japan noted for soft water, scrupulous handling, and milling that nicks the bran to retain its flavor—then one's attention becomes particularly focused on the taste.

For producers, the pursuit of superlative taste imposes a discipline. When a grower becomes conscious of how many factors—quality of seed, character of soil, purity of water, timing of harvest, insect management, disease resistance, weather, care in handling—influence taste, he or she must adhere to a regimen of action to achieve a good result.[16] This is how aesthetics drives an agricultural ethic.

One of my colleagues in the Arnold School of Public Health at the University of South Carolina asked why nutrition did not serve as the ideal driving our efforts. While I was tempted to reply that eating anything free of pesticide residue and the traces of the chemical supplements used in industrial agriculture would be more nutritious than standard produce, I did not. Rather, I said that nutrition has always been one kind of intelligence that has influenced the appreciation of food. Yet a problem with this sort of intelligence has been the changeability of Western culture's convictions about what is nourishing. From the time of the founding of the United States, there have been different schemes for adducing the nutritive content of food, with different units of determinative value—humors, calories, chemicals, vitamins, amino acids—emerging with each generation. In terms of agriculture, what changed was not what was grown, but accounts of what constituted nutritive worth. A cayenne pepper planted in the 1780s might have been considered a hot dry substance, valuable for counteracting phlegmatic dispositions. Decades later, its 21 calories per pod would have been seen as significant. Still later the chemical effects of its capsaicin (8-methyl-N-vanillyl-6-nonenamide) would have been cited. Or maybe its high concentration of vitamin A would have been celebrated. This changing body of information does matter, particularly in case in which plants once thought to be tonic and healthful are learned to be harmful. Sassafras (filé gumbo) was thought by early herbalists to be a panacea promising relief from most human ills; now the safrole it contains is known to be carcinogenic. Yet how much it matters and how much attention is granted, nutritive information is an open question. (Who greatly cares about the several carcinogenic potentials of black pepper?) As labels on food become more elaborate, longer, and more scientific in nomenclature, the more they risk becoming unintelligible to the broader public.

Another issue with predicating our work on nutrition science is the present provisional status of knowledge derived from real-life ingestion scenarios. So much of the analysis until recently has concentrated on measuring the somatic effects of an ingredient in isolation. Yet much food is consumed in meals, in which many ingredients are intermixed and interact chemically. Only recently has analysis turned away from single ingredient–based analysis to meal-ingestion scenarios. There has not been a sufficient body of findings to construct a new description of real-life ingestion.

Anthropologists have indicated that traditional cultures over time ascertain what is necessary for the sustenance of their populations. Then they improve the quality of those foodstuffs. The development of squashes by Native Americans in North America was a case in point. At first the seeds of the squash supplied the nutrition; but Native cultivators refined the flesh of the plant from a woody gourd-like texture to the soft meat we know today. The edible material of the squash has been both refined and amplified. The various landraces of grains and garden vegetables underwent this long process of improvement, predicated on a multi-generational observation of the nutritive effects of food.

You can understand, perhaps, now the values guiding Glenn Roberts,

Gary Nabhan, David Bradshaw, Merle Shepard, Poppy Tooker, Bill Best, and John Coykendall in their labor to preserve the most ancient components of cuisine for the future—to insure that the landraces of corn, rice, wheat, barley, rye, sorghum, and sugarcane remain available so that we can understand the primordial and enduring flavors of bread, beer, and candy is to retain the fullness of human experience. To retrieve the best of the neglected creations of the age of agricultural experiment is to wrest some kind of control over the unthinking operation of fashion and market forces in the annihilation of the old by the new. Let there be a culinary heritage, just as there is a musical heritage, an architectural heritage, a literary heritage, a museum of artistic masterpieces.

Aesthetical initiatives lead to ethical insights: let there be an agricultural heritage as well, a retention of that which was best about the practices that gave rise to regional cornucopia. The care for the soil; the sense of comity of animals, plants, and human beings in a farming scheme; the experimental curiosity by the grower about the tastes of fruit, grain, vegetables, and meat; the conviction of the meaningfulness of the work of growing, herding, and breeding; the desire to associate and help fellow farmers to meet the challenges of weather, disease, infestation, and accident—are all honorable.

What spiritual richness or emotional reward accrues from regarding oneself as a minor component of the international corn and soybean market?

However much the restoration of the best farm practices (the most effective crop rotations, stock feeding, or manuring) might promise a sustainable, organic way of producing food, we realize that replicating the fields, gardens, and markets of the antebellum period, or the even richer Reconstruction era Lowcountry, is not a possibility. No one moment or one model plantation constituted a perfect system sufficient to be replicated in its totality. A complex of economic, agronomic, market, and political forces caused farm practices to change. Furthermore, the experimental disposition of the most expert planters prompted them to alter aspects of the growing schemes continually. Even those plantations that were conceived as "model plantations"—Thomas Spalding's South End on Sapelo Island; James Hamilton Couper's Hopeton Plantation in Glynn County, Georgia; R. F. W. Allston's Chicora Wood, Joshua John Ward's

Brook Green, William Summer's Ravenscroft—that is, comprehensive and self-sustaining agricultural enterprises worthy of emulation—never achieved auto-dynamic stability. External forces—the Civil War; the collapse of the Sea Island cotton culture; the liberation of the slave labor force; the rise of large-scale truck farming; hurricanes, freezes, and the tides of disease and infestation—disrupted field planting programs. So we have always looked slantwise at the planting journals and published reports, searching for the most durable practices to try experimentally in the field. The advances of the past century in the understanding of plant disease, entomology, nematology, and soil chemistry have alerted us to adapt those field and garden rotations that best manage the problems that the agricultural sciences have described so incisively, without resorting to the conventional pesticide regimens and chemical fertilization that intoxicate the soil.

To resuscitate a cuisine, one must first revivify the soil. But even when we convert fields into vital organic systems again, simply replicating what once was grown does not recognize other changes wrought by history. Sometimes the general perception of how produce functions shifts over the decades. Studying Creighton Leigh Calhoun's *Old Southern Apples*, one reads of breeding rationales for pre-1920s apples that stand at odds with those operating in 2012. We no longer seek single-purpose apples for drying, cider making, saucing, or baking. Versatility is the byword of the marketplace, and so a baker's dozen of multi-purpose sorts eclipse the multitude of varieties that have been bred and planted in the country: red delicious, golden delicious, gala, Fuji, granny Smith, Braeburn, honeycrisp, cameo, Cortland, McIntosh, empire, Jonagold, and Stayman. Regardless of their reign, once you taste a flavorful slice from an old drying apple, you wonder why you should remain content with a leathery cross-section of a red delicious.

One of the projects of the current generation of adventurous chefs is to renovate the most flavorsome of historic foods and repurpose old functions. Sean Brock's experimentation with vinegars, including the nineteenth-century fruit-wine vinegars, has revivified southern pickling. Bill Smith of Crook's Corners in Chapel Hill has used sorbet as a medium to transmit flavors such as yaupon holly and persimmon on new vectors. A hallmark of the age of consumption: the chef has eclipsed the horticulturist as the pioneering experimenter in the reformation of cuisine. Indeed, the great contest of the age for preeminence in determining the taste of food takes place not between grower and chef, but between the chef and the flavor scientist. Before he became the champion of landrace grains, Glenn Roberts was a cook. Sometime in the late 1980s, he realized that the path to superlative taste might run through historic landscapes rather than the laboratory test kitchen. In the 1990s he transitioned from chef to grower and processor. He knew what chefs desired. And it meant entering into another community that had oddly restricted relations with restaurateurs: the heritage gardeners.

While Alice Waters consolidated the lines of communication between historically minded growers and culinary professionals on the West Coast in the 1980s, a separation remained between chefs and the seed savers keeping southern garden heritage alive. When one reflects on the careers of the important southern seed savers—Jeff McCormack of the University of Virginia and his partner Patty Wallens, who founded Southern Exposure Seed Exchange, or David Bradshaw of Clemson University, or John Coykendall of Tennessee—their efforts were directed toward the community of gardeners. Coykendall, alone of these figures, engaged in the culinary presentation of his cultivars, as part of the farm-to-table concept of Blackberry Farm.

Roberts was a pragmatist. He realized to make an effective intervention in America's food supply system, he had to avoid direct competition with the industrial food production and seed production companies. He had to scale his operation to the demands of that sector of the restaurant world fixed on superlative ingredient quality. He had to price his products to cover costs (an issue since landrace cultivars tend to be less productive), and grow them with such care that their quality fully warranted the higher price. He trusted in the taste of his brothers and sisters of the kitchen to gravitate to the fundamental flavors of his landrace grains. He located what was rare—Virginia white gourdseed corn secured from a bootlegger's field, naturalized Sea Island red peas from the wilds of Kiawah Island—and grew it so as to maximize its innate flavor. He established an artisanal growing and milling enterprise. The splendor of his corn made his fortune. Once he had established his business, he expanded cultivars, growers, fields, rotations. Since the institution of the

Carolina Gold Rice Foundation to do the research into historic agriculture, the plan of expansion and restoration has become increasingly systematic, and with the formalization of a research program, Roberts felt the liberty to expand his preservation efforts to landrace grains from other regions, collaborating with Gary Nabhan in Arizona and Native Nations in the American Southwest.

There are advantages to having a concrete perspective rooted in the real-world conditions of agriculture when pondering the aesthetics and ethics of food production. If you grow landrace corn in a way that maximizes its taste and field resilience, you know beyond a doubt that it is too expensive to use as livestock feed. So when one thinks of renovating feeding schemes to make hogs, cattle, and goats benefit from terroir, from the replenished soil, you immediately turn to growing schemes not using corn that have a historical track record, a visible cost advantage, and efficiency. Not maize, but grass, cowpeas, peanut hay, rye, sorghum, and sweet potatoes. This is how the greatest stock breeder in South Carolina, William Summer, fed his cows and hogs and Ravenscroft in the 1850s. This is how the Chinese feed their livestock today. The sweet potato produces substantially more nutrition per acre than corn while being more digestible for ruminants.

Growing out a cuisine with the guidance of the historical record gives you the most convenient grounds for experimentation with making ingredients as fine as they can be given the time, place, economy, and environmental conditions. Only by maintaining an experimental openness to the possibility of improving soil, cultivar, taste, and cost does a heritage condition itself for the future.

When tangible success comes your way—when you taste for the first time the nuances of rice grown on different waterways; when you see a mineralized field turn into a grassland nurtured by earthworms; when ricebirds return to the skies above rice fields for the first time in eighty years; when a spoonful of benne ice cream slides down your throat; or your marsh boils with terrapin—you become impatient with the intangible dictates made by various entities concerning agricultural policy. Your notion of natural vitality and sustainability departs from the carbon-metric (more reductive and autarkical than Liebigian chemistry was for nutrition in the 1800s), and your sense of the right practice of farming becomes less rhetorical and more precise than the term *organic*. Would the population at large benefit from eating more of the sorts of things that we and other artisanal producers grow in the South? I confess this is a question that recedes in interest from me with every initiative we undertake. In its place, the experience of repeatedly seeing people who have been exposed to the best ingredients makes me increasingly certain that those who partake will thereafter prefer. I don't feel compelled by righteousness to rip the bag of Cheetos from someone's fist and replace it with a Dancy tangerine. Those who seek a finer taste will be gratified; those who don't suffer an unwitting purgatory of the commonplace. I no longer worry that people will remain in ignorance of what is going on. The media has become fascinated with those who work at the restoration of American regional cuisines. The chefs of the Southern Foodways Alliance have championed the cause in every of the many arenas that they operate within.

In the past six years, we have brought back Carolina Gold rice, benne, the Carolina sieva bean, the Sea Island red pea, Sea Island white flint corn, and the Herbemont grape. The rice pea, Carolina African peanut, white imphee sorghum, the purple-ribbon sugarcane, the Hayman sweet potato, the Bradford watermelon, the Palmetto asparagus, and several southern peppers are on the horizon. Though we have focused on repatriating pretwentieth-century varieties because we considered them most at risk, we in no way believe that plant breeding since 1900 has failed to produce superb cultivars. Quite the contrary. The Charleston gray watermelon and the Clemson spineless okra have rightly won devotees, and the Florunner peanut is a splendid thing to grow and taste. Some of these newer creations are imperiled too or verging on rarity. Yet when reconsolidating a historic cuisine, one hews to the essentials. Those essentials were in place by 1870 and remained fixed until 1910. This book describes that accomplishment and documents the effort to bring back the storied tastes a century after they began to vanish.

NOTES

CHAPTER ONE

1 See the "Call for Papers" published on August 22, 2002: http://www.h-net.org /announce/show.cgi?ID=131069.

2 See http://www.ansonmills.com/.

3 Published as a souvenir for the South Carolina Interstate and West Indian Exposition of 1901, Mrs. Samuel G. Stoney's *Carolina Rice Cook Book* (Charleston: Carolina Rice Kitchen Association, 1901) is the focus of Karen Hess's famously opinionated study, *The Carolina Rice Kitchen: The African Connection* (Columbia: University of South Carolina Press, 1992).

4 John Martin Taylor, *Hoppin' John's Lowcountry Cooking* (New York: Houghton Mifflin, 1992).

5 While terroir, the culturally recognized influence of soil and environment on the taste of a locality's products, has long been a concept employed in the connoisseurship of wine, it entered into mainstream thinking about food with the launch of Arlin Wasserman's food consultancy business, Changing Tastes, in 2004. Amy R. Trubek's *A Taste of Place: A Cultural Journey into Terroir* (Berkeley: University of California Press, 2008) critiques the practice of industrial agriculture in light of a sensibility informed by terroir. Bernard L. Herman's "Drum Head Stew: The Power and Poetry of Terroir," *Southern Cultures* 15, no. 4 (Winter 2009), explores how cultural consciousness operates in the sense of terroir. By the second decade of the nineteenth century, Lowcountry planters had developed a rough mental map of produce, soil type, and locale for the coastal region. Without using the term, they understood its consequence for farming.

6 My books—*Oracles of Empire: Poetry, Politics, and Commerce in British America, 1690–1750* (Chicago: University of Chicago Press, 1990), *Civil Tongues and Polite Letters in British America* (Chapel Hill: University of North Carolina Press, 1997), and *Still: American Silent Motion Picture Photography* (Chicago: University of Chicago Press, 2013)—have all been histories that supply the first summary views of their subject matters.

7 Jean-François Revel, *Culture and Cuisine: A Journey through the History of Food* (New York: Doubleday, 1982).

8 Sidney Mintz, "Cuisine: High, Low, and Not at All," in *Tasting Food, Tasting Freedom* (Boston: Beacon Press, 1996), 96–97.

9 The concerns of the Carolina Gold Rice Foundation are laid out here: http://www.carolinagoldricefoundation.org/page5/page5.html.

10 John Taylor, *Arator: Being a Series of Agricultural Essays, Practical & Political*, 2nd expanded ed. (Georgetown, WA: Carter, 1814); Agricola [George W. Jeffreys], *A Series of Essays on Agriculture and Rural Affairs* (Raleigh: Joseph Gales, 1819); [Nicholas Herbemont], *Observations suggested by the late Occurrences in Charleston* (Columbia: State Gazette Office, 1822).

11 See the introduction to the special issue I edited, "American Food in the Age of Experiment: Farming, Cooking, and Eating by the Book," *Commonplace* 11, no. 3 (April 2011), http://www.common-place.org/vol-11/no-03/.

12 The manifold uses of the sweet potato plant, its culture and employments, received extensive treatment in print in the nineteenth century in the *Southern Agriculturist*: vol. 1, nos. 4, 8, 9 (1828); vol. 2, nos. 3, 4, 7, 9 (1829); vol. 3, nos. 2, 3, 6, 8, 9 (1830); vol. 4, nos. 4, 6, 11 (1831); vol. 5, nos. 1, 3, 5 (1832); and vol. 6, no. 4 (1833).

13 Adapted from J. V. Jones, Burke Co., GA, *American Farmer* 11, no. 11 (May 1856): 347.

14 Essex Committee, "Vegetables," *17th Annual Report of the Secretary of the Massachusetts Board of Agriculture for 1869* (Boston: Wright & Potter, State Printers, 1870), 140. For a splendid history of the autumnal marrow squash, see T. W. Harris, "Pumpkins and Squashes," *Farm Journal* 5 (1850): 158–60.

15 F. L. Gilette, "Pumpkin Pie #1," in *White House Cook Book* (1887), 272.

16 Gary Nabhan, *Enduring Seeds: Native American Agriculture and Wild Plant Conservation* (Tucson: University of Arizona Press, 2002).

17 Jessica Harris, *Iron Pots and Wooden Spoons: Africa's Gifts to New World Cooking* (New York: Simon & Schuster, 1999).

18 Indeed, the effect of Carver's recovery is to call into question the "soul food" paradigm of black food as making do with leftover and marginal ingredients. Doesn't Carver's panoply of dishes suggest that African American food, like West African, had an articulated and diversified handling of a body of staple ingredients?

19 Joyce E. Chaplin, *An Anxious Pursuit: Agricultural Innovation and Modernity in the Lower South* (Chapel Hill: University of North Carolina Press, 1996); S. Max Edelson, *Plantation Enterprise in Colonial South Carolina* (Cambridge, MA: Harvard University Press, 2006).

20 Charles G. Steffen, "In Search of the Good Overseer: The Failure of the Agricultural Reform Movement in Lowcountry South Carolina, 1821–1834," *Journal of Southern History* 63, no. 4 (November 1997): 753–802; William M. Mathew, *Edmund Ruffin and the Crisis of Slavery in the Old South: The Failure of Agricultural Reform* (Athens: University of Georgia Press, 1988).

21 Gary Paul Nabhan, *Renewing America's Food Traditions: Saving and Savoring the Continent's Most Endangered Foods* (New York: Chelsea Green Publishing, 2008).

22 Jedidiah Morse, *A New Universal Gazetteer or Geographical Dictionary* (New Haven, CT: Sherman Converse; Hartford, CT: Silas Andrus, 1821), 156.

23 Elisha Mitchell, "On the Character and Origin of the Low Country of North Carolina," *American Journal of Science* 13 (New Haven, CT, 1828): 336–44.

24 "Chester District, South Carolina 1850," *The Executive Documents, Thirty-First Congress, Second Session, Document 32* (Washington, DC: GPO, 1850), 358.

25 I have grown suspicious of the use of the term *sustainability*—a concept that emerged in the 1980s in macroeconomic projections of global development and that retains meaningfulness only in the largest-scale calculations of the use of resources—in connection with local initiatives.

CHAPTER TWO

1 "Southern cooking" appears in a number of places in 1860, perhaps most interestingly in a report from New York of the first anniversary meeting of a club of Virginians there called the Old Dominion: "All the other National Societies will turn out strong on the occasion to give the organization a good christening, and some genuine Southern cooking and drinking will add novel and enjoyable attractions to the occasion." *Charleston Courier*, May 16, 1860. "Southern food" gains currency in a widely reprinted article from the August 9, 1861, edition of the *New York News* entitled "What Is the North Fighting For?" discussing export trade: "The food exported, which embraces a good deal of Southern original and also of Northern, is supplanted at the North by Southern Food."

2 Peter S. Onuf, "The Political Economy of Sectionalism: Tariff Controversies and the Differing Conceptions of World Order," in *Congress and the Emergence of Sectionalism: From the Missouri Compromise to the Age of Jackson*, ed. Paul Finkelman and Donald R. Kennon (Columbus: Ohio University Press for the United States Capitol Historical Society, 2008), 47–74.

3 Edited by J. D. Legaree and published in Charleston, the *Southern Agriculturist* supplanted the *American Farmer* (first published in Baltimore in 1819) as the preferred periodical venue for the exchange of information about planting, farming, and gardening in the lower South.

4 John Lauritz Larson, *Internal Improvement: National Public Works and the Promise of Popular Government in the Early United States* (Chapel Hill: University of North Carolina Press, 2000).

5 The English-most elements—the beef recipes, certain of the puddings, and the porridges—appear in the sections on invalid cooking in *The Kentucky Housewife*.

6 *Baltimore Sun*, January 8, 1847.

7 *Baltimore Sun*, February 11, 1864.

8 *Annapolis Gazette*, January 30, 1868.

9 "Notice," *Washington Daily National Intelligencer* 19, 5669 (April 7, 1831), 1; "The subscriber particularly requests," *Washington Daily National Intelligencer* 24, 7349 (September 1, 1836), 3; "American and French Restaurant," *Washington Daily Intelligencer* 25, 7461 (January 10, 1837), 3; "American and French Restaurant," *Daily National Intelligencer* 25, 7490 (February 13, 1837), 2.

10 "L. Galabran," *Daily National Intelligencer* 25, 7763 (December 30, 1837), 1.

11 "John Prevaux, Restaurateur," *Daily National Intelligencer* 28, 8390 (January 6, 1840), 1.

12 "Gautier's Saloon," *Washington Evening Star*, November 12, 1855, 2.

13 Daniel Garrison Brinton, *A Guide-Book of Florida and the South, &c.* (Gainesville: University Press of Florida, 1978), 26.

14 *Augusta Chronicle*, November 10, 1858.

15 *Augusta Chronicle*, August 28, 1877.

16 Brinton, *A Guide-Book of Florida*, 62.

17 *Mobile Register*, August 16, 1858; February 8, 1862; April 8, 1862.

18 J. H. I., "Dots and Lines #1," *The Ladies Companion* 11 (New York: Snowden, 1839), 40–42.

19 *St. Louis Missouri Republican*, September 4, 1851.

20 *Scholes Memphis Directory* (Memphis, 1885), 125.

21 The information in this section is drawn from an examination of every extant issue of the following newspapers from post-Revolutionary and antebellum South Carolina: *Charleston Evening Gazette, Charleston Morning Post, South Carolina Gazette and Evening Advertiser, South Carolina State Gazette, City Gazette* (Charleston), *Charleston Courier, Southern Patriot,* and *The State.*

22 Mrs. A. P. Hill, *Mrs. Hill's New Cook Book* (New York: Carleston, 1872), 196.

23 Mrs. Mary Randolph, *The Virginia House-wife; or, Methodical Cook* (Baltimore: Plaskitt, Fite & Co., 1838); Mrs. Lettice Bryan, *The Kentucky Housewife* (Cincinnati: Shepard & Stearns, 1839); [Sarah Rutledge], *The Carolina Housewife; or, House and Home: By a Lady of Charleston* (Charleston, SC: W. R. Babcock & Co., 1847); Mrs. Barringer, *Dixie Cookery; or, How I Managed My Table for Twelve Years* (Boston: Floring, 1867); Mrs. Sarah A. Elliott, *Mrs. Elliott's Housewife* (New York: Hurd & Houghton, 1870); Miss Tyson, *The Queen of the Kitchen: A Collection of "Old Maryland" Family Receipts for Cooking* (Philadelphia: T. B. Peterson & Brothers, 1874); Marion Cabell Tyree, *Housekeeping in Old Virginia* (Louisville, KY: John P. Morton, 1879); Mrs. B. C. Howard, *Fifty Years in a Maryland Kitchen*, 4th ed. (Philadelphia: J. B. Lippincott & Co., 1881); Christian Woman's Exchange, *The Creole Cookery Book* (New Orleans: T. H. Thomason, 1885); Lafcadio Hearn, *La Cuisine Creole* (New Orleans: F. F. Hansell & Bro., 1885); [A. G. Wilcox], *The Dixie Cook-Book* (Atlanta: L. A. Clarkson, 1885); Mary Stuart Smith, *Virginia Cookery-Book* (New York: Harper & Brothers, 1885); Mrs. Washington, *The Unrivalled Cook-Book and Housekeeper's Guide* (New York: Harper & Brothers, 1885).

24 William N. White, *Gardening for the South; or, The Kitchen and Fruit Garden* (New York: C. M. Saxton & Co., 1857), 267–68.

25 Jules Arthur Harder, *Physiology of Taste: Harder's Book of Practical American Cookery in Six Volumes.* Vol. I: *Treating of American Vegetables and all Alimentary Plants, Roots and Seeds* (San Francisco: Jules Arthur Harder, 1855), vi. Subsequent quotations from Harder's book will be noted by page number.

26 "New York is the finest market place in the world." Jules Harder, "Good Livers," *Lancaster Intelligencer*, June 27, 1883; reprinted from the *N.Y. Express.*

27 "The Nadeau's New Cook," *Los Angeles Daily Herald*, December 12, 1886. Because of inheritance issues arising from the death of Remy Nadeau, Harder moved to the Hotel Del Monte in Monterey in 1888, where he presided for a decade until lured by the Macfarlane family in 1898 to become chef of the Hawaiian Hotel in Honolulu, a post he held for four years until his children convinced him to return to San Francisco. He died in 1912.

28 "A Saratoga Cuisine," *Oneida Circular* 12 (September 6, 1875), 36; "Faits Divers," *Courrier de Etats-Unis* 70 (March 11, 1879), 2; "The Art of Dining," *Evening Star*, June 26, 1883, 3; "Three Famous Banquets," *Los Angeles Herald*, February 26, 1902, 3; "The Palace Hotel," *Newport Daily News*, August 5, 1875, 1; Obituary for J. A. Theodore Harder, *Courrier des Etats-Unis* 22 (January 27, 1873), 3; "The Nadeau's New Cook," *Los Angeles Daily Herald*, December 2, 1886, 5; *Hawaiian Star*, November 22, 1898, 1.

29 Paula Forbes, "Sean Brock on His Southern Cookbook Collection and What Blows His Mind," *Eater*, December 9, 2011, http://eater.com/archives/2011/12/09 /sean-brock-cookbook-shelf.php (accessed January 6, 2012).

30 *Los Angeles Daily Herald*, December 12, 1886.

31 Jane Eddington, *New Orleans Times-Picayune*, May 8, 1921.

CHAPTER THREE

1 Christian Woman's Exchange, *The Creole Cookery Book* (New Orleans: T. H. Thomason, 1885), title page.

2 See note on Creole cookery in *New Orleans Cookbook Bibliography*, ed. Susan Tucker, M. A. Johnson, Wendy Bruton, and Sharon Stallworth Nossiter (New Orleans: New Orleans Culinary History Group, 2011), 66. Hearn claimed to have included recipes by chefs, but none bear the names that mattered in the city's cuisine. See http://www.tulane.edu/~wclib/New%20Orleans%20Cookbook%20 Bibliography%202011.pdf (accessed February 14, 2012). Lylie O. Harris, born in August 1855 in Louisiana, was Hearn's friend. She published Creole recipes in national magazines as well as prose sketches from the 1880s through 1910. She worked intermittently for the *Times-Picayune*.

3 Judy Walker, "Local Historian Digs Up Long-Lost Info on the *Times-Picayune* Cookbook," http://www.nola.com/food/index.ssf/2011/10/local_historian_digs _up_long-l.html (accessed February 15, 2012). Rien Fertel's MA thesis, "Creole Cookbooks and the Formation of Creole Identity in New Orleans, 1885–1900" (New School for Social Research, New York, 2008), defines precisely the print-culture tradition against which I am counterposing the restaurant-food culture of the nineteenth century.

4 [Marie Louise Points], *The Picayune Creole Cook Book*, 6th ed. (New Orleans: Times-Picayune Publishing Company, 1922), iv.

5 Obituary "Laporte," *New Orleans Times-Picayune*, September 2, 1906, 8.

6 John Smith Kendall, "Hotel Life in New Orleans," *History of New Orleans* (Chicago: Lewis Publishing Company, 1922).

7 Advertisement, St. Charles Hotel, *New Orleans Times-Picayune*, October 5, 1879. Leon Lamothe, when he leased the right to run the St. Charles Bar and associated lunchroom in November 1882, was the first public caterer to have a name associated with the hotel.

8 Notice of who presided over the hotel kitchens only came into print when chefs departed to set up restaurants under their own direction in the city.

9 Walter H. Van Rensselaer (1817?–1849) was New York born and trained. "Walter" emerged as a name in New Orleans cooking as caterer of the Bishop's Hotel (the

City Hotel) in his teens circa 1836. Shortly after the opening of the St. Charles Hotel—perhaps as early as 1839—Walter was hired away from the Bishop to preside over the second-floor dining saloon, an immense hall accommodating three hundred seats arrayed along three lengthy tables. His was a difficult task, adjusting the cuisine to the tastes of the army of Mississippi Valley brokers, traders, and foreign merchants who occupied the hotel from October through May, and securing sufficient local diners to tide the hostelry over during the summer season. There were but few places where tastes coincided: the Creole beefsteak, roasted wildfowl, and oysters. On November 8, 1843, Walter took leave of the St. Charles to create a more intimate setting for fine dining. The Crescent Restaurant (sometimes Coffeehouse) at 46 St. Charles Street served breakfast, lunch, and dinner. Walter counted upon the "friends" he made during his time at the hotel to lunch on "turtle soup, red fish chowder, and other 'fixin's.'" At the Crescent Restaurant in 1846, Walter pioneered the adaptation to New Orleans of a culinary institution famous in Philadelphia, Baltimore, and Washington, DC: the oyster cellar. An ad for Walter's Grand Oyster Saloon read: "In the Oyster Saloon will always be found the fattest and finest Oysters from Cat Island, Brand Pass, Barataria, Biloxi and Mobile, which will be served up at all hours, day and night, in every variety of style. In the Restaurant, Game of all kinds of Fish, fresh from the Lake, of every variety—Beefsteaks—Mutton Chops—Poultry—Turtle Soups, etc. etc. will be found at all hours, and they will be served up on short notice in a style to suit all palates." In late 1848, Walter began to sicken. He returned to New York with his wife, Emeline L. Gladding, and died in May 1849. Oyster bars survived as a permanent fixture of cosmopolitan American dining in New Orleans into the twentieth century. (The above comes from notices in the *Daily Picayune*, September 8, 1846; December 2, 1846; December 5, 1846; and November 8, 1848.)

10 John Galpin was a versatile figure in food culture of New Orleans in the nineteenth century. A native of Bethlehem, Connecticut, he brought an expertise with meat to Louisiana nurtured in the most advanced locus of herding and livestock breeding in the United States. Occupying stalls 3 and 5 in the St. Mary's Market, and later stalls 1 and 3 in the Old French Market, Galpin sold prime cuts of meat from cattle and sheep sourced in Indiana and Kentucky. Galpin was "the only premium sausage-maker . . . in the South." In the early 1840s, he opened an eating house at 264 Tchoupitoulas, and in 1854 he became caterer of the Veranda Hotel. With O. J. Noyes as host and Mr. Ensign as manager, Galpin provisioned the kitchen and oversaw food operations at the hotel for five years. Upon severing his connection with the hotel, he launched a full-fledged restaurant at Exchange Place below Canal Street in October 1859. In December 1860, he established Galpin's Restaurant at 32 Royal Street, with Paul Viel as maître d' and E. Coutreau in the kitchen. After the war, Galpin experienced a psychological crisis. In 1866 he closed the restaurant, which was taken over by his friend and successor, Philippe Forget, then moved to New York. His large family, some of whom remained in New Orleans, attempted to salvage his various enterprises, even opening a produce stand at Terpsichore and Prytania Streets in 1868. Galpin died in May 1868, in New York, and McClure & Jonte took over his butcher stalls in the French Market shortly thereafter. As an artist of processing meat, his place was filled to some extent by Peter Forshee. (The above gleaned from the *Daily Pica-*

yune, October 15, 1848; February 12, 1851; January 25, 1852; December 31, 1852; June 1, 1854; October 20, 1858; September 3, 1859; December 2, 1860; February 8, 1864; October 12, 1865; October 15, 1865; December 17, 1865; December 23, 1866; and obit. May 22, 1868, and from the *Daily Delta*, December 31, 1852.)

11 *U.S. Census*, New Orleans, Ward 3, Municipality 1, p. 16. "Tromale" may be a mistranscription of the French name by the American census taker. A word on census designations: food persons were designated with the following titles: restaurant keeper, coffee house keeper, beer hall keeper (mostly Germans), cook, confectioner, pastry cook, and baker (mostly Germans).

12 *New Orleans Times-Picayune*, November 2, 1884.

13 *New Orleans Times-Picayune*, January 27, 1874.

14 Grace King, *New Orleans: The Place and the People* (London: Macmillan, 1917), 290.

15 Astredo's Lake restaurant was a branch of its main venue in the French Quarter, renowned as the home of the po'-boy. A *Times-Picayune* blurb advised, "Old man of bad habits, if you want peace at home go to Astredo's restaurant, 595 Magazine Street, and get a well fried oyster loaf for your lady" (November 9, 1880).

16 Retired ship captains for the most part ran these establishments. See the discussion of the Marin-Real Inn in Shannon Lee Dawdy, *Building the Devil's Empire: French Colonial New Orleans* (Chicago: University of Chicago Press, 2008), 132.

17 Rebecca L. Spang's *The Invention of the Restaurant: Paris and Modern Gastronomic Culture* (Cambridge, MA: Harvard University Press, 2000) has become the classic account of this development.

18 A. K. Sandoval Strausz, *Hotel: An American History* (New Haven, CT: Yale University Press, 2007), 20–25.

19 The coffeehouse with an abundance of alcohol was a fixture of antebellum New Orleans. For a comprehensive description of this hybrid institution, see "A Peep at a Café," *Daily Picayune*, January 18, 1847.

20 Advertisement, *Abeja*, December 10, 1830.

21 Advertisement, *Abeja*, November 9, 1830.

22 "Ice Creams & Sherberts," *Abeille*, August 29, 1829, 4.

23 "Café Tricolore," *Abeille*, April 12, 1831, 4.

24 "At a meeting of Coffeehouse Keepers held at Brintnall's Coffee House," *Abeja*, February 9, 1830.

25 The Arcade would continue for a period under the proprietorship of Martelle.

26 "Hewlitt's Exchange," *Daily Picayune*, November 15, 1843.

27 *U.S. Federal Census, 1850*, Third Representative District, Parish of Orleans, Louisiana, p. 10.

28 Victor Bero (1840–1904), a Belgian-born cook, shared his first name with one of the greatest chefs of the golden age of New Orleans restaurant cuisine, Victor Martin. Much of Bero's later career consisted in attempting to rewrite history by inscribing himself over Martin's identity and legacy. When Bero died in 1904, his memorialists represented him as the last of the members of the vieux regime—with Madame Eugène, Madame Bégué, John Bosio of the Four Seasons, and Antoine Alciatore—but he was a generation younger than any of the great names and did not reside in the city before the war (obit., *Times-Picayune*, June 12, 1904). He originally emigrated to New York with his brother and sister in 1855 at the age of fifteen and only arrived in New Orleans in 1864, during the federal occupation of the city, at age twenty-four. He had received his culinary training in New York hotels, not in New Orleans. He immediately sought employment and was hired as a cook by Jules Martin of Victor's Restaurant. Victor's devolved to Jules's nephew George Martin, who died in 1873. Bero became at this juncture the proprietor. When the restaurant burned in January 1874, the reporter noted the decline in the cuisine since George's death. Bero set about resurrecting the establishment in 1874, erecting the new version at 38 Bourbon Street and calling it Restaurant Victor. In 1875 he advertised that it was "the Cheapest Restaurant in the City" (*New Orleans Times*, September 1, 1875). In the 1880s Bero was absorbed in hotel ventures, becoming a partner in the Charpiot Hotel in Denver, opening the Hotel Chalmet on 100 St. Charles Street (with Xavier Faucon in charge of cuisine), and installing his son Victor Bero Jr. as manager of boardinghouses on Custom House Street in 1885. In 1891 the Ocean Club at Grand Isle contracted Bero to do cuisine at the resort. He died in 1904. The collection of Bero's recipes published in the 1937 edition of *Bégué's Recipes of Old New Orleans*, because of their ten-person banquet portions, appear not to be the à la carte preparations used at Victor's but rather the banquet portions used in the Ocean Club.

29 "Victor's Restaurant Burned," *New Orleans Times-Picayune*, January 11, 1877. The Mexican venture alluded to in this article was the Richelieu Hotel in Bagdad, Mexico, purchased by Jules Martin in 1865, no doubt as a hedge against possible financial chaos in the South in the event of the Confederacy's loss of the war. See *Times-Picayune*, April 13, 1864.

30 Baptiste Moreau (1815–1868) was born in France and was present in New Orleans by 1837. John Baptiste Moreau (though he preferred styling himself B. Moreau in public communications) founded his first restaurant on Custom House Street in 1837. In 1839 he moved the premises to Chartres Street and sold controlling interest to his assistant, F. Moulin. Circumstantial evidence suggests he spent the early 1840s as chef for the St. Charles Hotel. In 1847 he entered into partnership with L. Tournoi in establishing Restaurant du Cardinal at 41 Natchez, an eatery that boasted: "Meals are reserved at all hours in both American and French styles." The split personality did not lead to success. By 1849 the joint venture was abandoned, and Moreau was attempting to dispose of the empty premises. He would then move to Bayou St. John and with assistant cook Jean Chiffer opened one of the great temples of resort cuisine. Besides seafood, the house was famous for its signature dish, Gelatine Truffée à la Gelée, a dish he taught to Moulin & Rhodes (*Daily Picayune*, October 20, 1853). After the Civil War, he devoted great effort to improving the Resort at Spanish Fort, but his efforts were curtailed by illness and eventually his death in the spring of 1868.

31 "Canal Street Still the Battle Ground," *Times-Picayune*, June 22, 1899.

32 Claiborne T. Smith, *Smith of Scotland Neck: Planters on the Roanoke* (Baltimore: Gateway Press, 1976), 54. See also "Charles Rhodes: Death of a Famous New Orleans Restauranteur," *Times-Picayune*, March 22, 1894.

33 "Moreau's," *Daily City Item*, July 18, 1880, 1; "Moreau's," *Times-Picayune*, January 10, 1881.

34 A brief memoir of Miguel's early life was supplied in his obituary (*Times-Picayune*, October 6, 1889).

35 "Phoenix House," *Times-Picayune*, March 30, 1853, 4.

36 William Makepeace Thackeray, "A Mississippi Bubble," *Roundabout Papers*, in *The Works of William Makepeace Thackeray*, 24 vols. (London: Smith, Elder; Philadelphia: J. B. Lippincott, 1879), XXII, 147.

37 "Miguel's Restaurant," *Times-Picayune*, May 23, 1866.

38 "Death of Miguel," *Times-Picayune*, October 6, 1889.

39 "Phoenix House," *Times-Picayune*, April 30, 1879; see also "At the End of the Lake, a Restaurant on the Water," *Times-Picayune*, May 2, 1875.

40 "Pioneers Pass. John Tresconi, Once the Foremost Spirit of Milneburg," *Times-Picayune*, October 2, 1902. Tresconi was nationally known as a chef in his own right, winning particular renown for his artichoke patties.

41 "New Shell Road Hotel," *Times-Picayune*, August 23, 1843.

42 *Times-Picayune*, June 11, 1869.

43 "Boudro Is Dead!," *Times-Picayune*, October 18, 1867.

44 *Times-Picayune*, June 5, 1868.

45 *Times-Picayune*, May 13, 1869.

46 *Daily Picayune*, October 15, 1846.

47 "Victor's Restaurant, on Boulevard Street," *Baton Rouge Daily Advertiser*, October 25, 1860, 1.

48 This pattern is mirrored in other wards. A comprehensive statistical portrait is hindered by the number of illegible pages in the surviving 1850 census records. Yet an examination of over 60 percent of the 1850 and 1860 entries shows that restaurant keepers, confectioners, coffeehouse proprietors, and bakers were nearly completely non-native. Census takers designated race by putting *B* for black and *M* for mulatto, leaving white citizens blank. Another cell of the entry noted place of nativity. When the census taker came to a premises that served as a hotel, eating house, or café, every person in the household was noted; the proprietor and his or her family, the waiters, barkeeper, cooks, and servants. The numbers of African Americans listed in the eateries was minuscule.

49 *1900 U.S. Federal Census*, New Orleans, Sixth Ward, Fourth Precinct, Sheet #6.

50 "Madame Eugène's Restaurant over the Gem Saloon," *Baton Rouge Daily Advocate*, October 23, 1858, 1.

51 "A prophet is not without honor except in his own land." *New Orleans Crescent*, March 14, 1866, 2.

52 Ibid. "Auguste's curry is still as good as ever, and if he is 'touched in the wind' he does not 'blow' when he says that in the preparation of a first-class dinner he never had his equal, nor perhaps ever will in America."

53 Giulio Adamoli, "Letters from America: 1867, III," *The Living Age* 313 (1922): 37. The Cosmopolitan Restaurant, located at 11–13 Royal Street, operated under the proprietorship of Louis Chaplain beginning in 1866.

54 Walter Hale, "The Passing of Old New Orleans," *Uncle Remus Magazine* 1, no. 10 (March 1908): 43.

55 "Gabriel Julien, Confiseur Distillateur," *Abeja*, December 13, 1830.

56 "Vincent's New Confectionary Store," *Daily Picayune*, March 5, 1854.

57 "J. [*sic*] Lefevre," *Daily Picayune*, March 14, 1856.

58 Madame Eugène's identification with this crème—a creation for the Empress Eugènie of France—is an interesting instance of the convergence of great reputations and the confusions inspired by fame.

59 S. Frederick Starr, "Introduction," *Inventing New Orleans: The Writings of Lafcadio Hearn* (Oxford: University Press of Mississippi, 2001), xi–xxvi.

60 See the landmark study, Jennifer Rae Greeson, *Our South: Geographic Fantasy and the Rise of National Literature* (Cambridge, MA: Harvard University Press, 2010).

61 William Head Coleman, *Historical Sketch Book and Guide to New Orleans and Environs* (New York: William H. Coleman, 1885), 88.

62 Ibid., 89.

63 The Creole Exchange dining room, organized by the sponsors of *The Creole Cookery Book*, was the first public eatery that bore the name opening in 1885. The first commercial eatery, the Creole Restaurant, opened in the mid-1890s at 201 Bourbon Street.

64 Besides Victor's and Moreau's—Antoine Alciator, Restaurant, 85 St Peter; Thomas Appoloni, Restaurant, Orleans and Dauphine; Jules Blineau, Restaurant, 15 Bourbon; J. Bosio, Restaurant, 155 Chartres; Auguste Broue, Restaurant, 15 Madison; Mrs. Coutoula, Restaurant, 114 St. Charles; Marcel Douat, Restaurant, 175 Orleans; John Galpin, Restaurant, 32 Royal; B. Gastinel, Restaurant, St. Louis corner Dauphine; Hypolate's Restaurant, 85 Dauphine; Louis Peoge, Restaurant des Ames, 27 St. Philip; B. Solache, Restaurant, 17 St. Philip; John Strenna, Restaurant Mason Doree, 144 Canal; Evariste Sugasti, Restaurant, 17 St. Philip.

65 Leon Lamothe (1840?–1892), heir of the Camors culinary dynasty in New Orleans, was born in the Bas-Pyrenees in France, the second son of a physician. Leon's brothers Andre and Felix Camors had become active restaurant keepers in the 1850s. Andre supplied financial backing for Fritz Huppenbauer's management of the Commercial Restaurant, and when Felix decamped, Fritz Camors took over control. Andre next partnered with Philip Billman in taking over Boudro's at Milneburg. Concurrently Andre and Fritz assumed proprietorship of Pino's Restaurant at 23 St. Charles Street in 1869. This they renamed Camors Restaurant in 1870. The brothers, wishing a successor from their own family promised their French brother-in-law that his son, Leon, would enjoy a life of consequence and responsibility if he would consent to be trained as a caterer in New Orleans. Leon left his home and France at age nineteen and undertook training in both the front and back of the house at the Camors Restaurant. Partnering with Antonio Graffigna, who directed the wait staff at Camors, he began serving as proprietor in 1871. Leon renovated the restaurant at 23 St. Charles Street, renaming it Leon's Restaurant upon the retirement of Andre Camors in 1877. In 1882 he bought the lease for the St. Charles Bar Room on the ground floor of the hotel and made the bar the central node in the wagering world of city horse racing. His culminating act was acquiring Victor's Restaurant at 23 St. Charles Street. Upon his death after a decade of declining health in 1892, this array of enterprises was taken over by Graffigna and Leon's widow in partnership. The partnership lasted a year, when Widow Lamothe wrested control of the enterprises and appointed Leon's brother, Frank Lamothe, manager. From the *Daily True Delta*, November 27, 1859; and the *Times-Picayune*, September 1, 1877, April 14, 1892 (obit.), and June 2, 1892.

66 Thomas Cooper De Leon was born in 1839 into a Franco-Jewish family in Columbia, South Carolina, served in the Confederate army for the duration of the Civil War, and was stationed in New Orleans for a period early in the hostilities. After

Appomattox, he settled in Mobile, Alabama, during the Reconstruction, where he edited the city's major newspaper. He also organized Mobile's Mardi Gras. A versatile man of letters, he composed plays, memoirs, essays, and novels as well as journalism. He became blind shortly after the turn of the twentieth century and died in 1914.

67 T. C. De Leon, "In the South, Part II, of Creole and Puritan," *Lippincott's Magazine*, October 1889, 472.

68 George Augustus Sala, *America Revisited* (New York, 1882; reprint, Arno Press, 1974), 3, named Madame Venn's one of the four great New Orleans French restaurants, along with Moreau's, Victor's, and Flêche's.

69 "Frozine's Restaurant," *Time-Picayune*, November 24, 1867.

70 One reservation: it was Madame Bégué who would enjoy the enduring reputation for the late breakfast, not Madame Eugène.

71 M.A.B., "Three New Orleans Dishes," *Good Housekeeping* (1887), 191.

72 Ibid.

73 Antoine B. Beauvilliers, *L'Art du Cuisinier* (Paris: Chez Pilet, 1814), 27. Both Beauvillers and Louis Eustache Ude (1822) call for using egg yolk for thickening this potage rather than the more unctuous *crème de riz*.

74 The prospect of adding an additional revenue stream by publishing a restaurant cookbook would not have occurred to these caterers. The first cookbooks by European American restaurant chefs date from the Civil War era—William Volmer's *United States Cookbook* (1859) and Pierre Blot's *What to Eat* (1863). They were drubbed in the marketplace by instructional manuals by northern cooking school matrons, and various housekeeper/cook-authored books. The professional audience remained small until the 1880s compared to the housewife audience.

75 The status of Victor Bero's recipes printed in the 1937 edition of *Bégué's Recipes of Old New Orleans* (New Orleans: Harmanson, 1937) should be reiterated here. Because all of the recipes are designed for ten persons, the recipes are not the à la carte portions prepared for restaurant customers, but banquet preparations probably written down in 1891 as instructions for hired cooks when Bero contracted to be caterer for the Ocean Club at Grand Isle. While of interest, there is no indication that they reflect the tradition of Victor Martin's kitchen.

76 *Boston Cooking School Magazine* (1899), 73.

77 The identity of Mrs. Washington has puzzled numbers of cookbook scholars. Based in New York at the time of the book's publication, she indicates a life of extensive foreign travel; a knowledge of French, German, and Russian; a familiarity with parts of America east of the Mississippi; a connection with the culinary world; and an ability at letters.

78 Mrs. Washington, *The Unrivalled Cook-Book and Housekeeper's Guide* (New York: Harper & Brothers, 1885).

79 "A Pleasant Occasion," *Times-Picayune*, December 21, 1877.

CHAPTER FOUR

1 See http://www.msa.md.gov/msa/mdmanual/01glance/html/food.html (accessed August 23, 2011).

2 Lagroue's role as Maryland Club chef was revealed in an advertisement in Baltimore's *Sun*, April 28, 1862, 3: "Lagroue, late Chef of Maryland is prepared to receive Boarders, at his home, No. 77 St. Paul St., on very reasonable terms."

3 Thomas Jefferson Murrey, "Dinner à la Maryland," *Valuable Cooking Receipts* (New York: George W. Harlan, 1880), 118–19. "A patriotic son of Maryland has suggested as a perfect dinner, the choice of the amphitryon being restricted to the productions of the State." The minimal menu appeared in the following magazines from 1878 to 1885: *The Century* 15 (1878): 13; *Frank Leslie's Popular Monthly* 9 (1880): 747; and *Scribner's Monthly* 15 (1877): 13.

4 Blanchard Jerrold, "American Dinner in London," *The Epicure's Year Book and Table Companion* 1 (London: Bradbury and Evans, 1868), 90.

5 "Clubs, Club Life, Some New York Clubs," *The Galaxy* 22 (New York: Sheldon and Co., 1876), 230.

6 The club still exists and has published a history: Robert J. Brugger, *The Maryland Club: A History of Food and Friendship in Baltimore, 1857–1997* (Baltimore: Maryland Club, 1998), 3–48.

7 George Washington Howard, *The Monumental City* (Baltimore: J. D. Ehlers, 1873), 78.

8 "The New Baltimore," *Harper's New Monthly Magazine* 93 (February 1896): 345–46.

9 "Canvas-back and Terrapin," *Scribner's Monthly* 15, no. 1 (February 1877): 2.

10 John Stuart Skinner, *The Dog and the Sportsman* (Philadelphia: Lea and Blanchard, 1845), 41.

11 *The Living Age* 168 (1886): 509.

12 Jules Arthur Harder, *The Physiology of Taste: Harder's Book of Practical American Cookery* (San Francisco: by the author, 1885), 129.

13 G. M. Haramis, "Canvasback," in *Habitat Requirements for Chesapeake Bay Living Resources*, ed. S. L. Funderbunk, J. A. Milhursky, S. J. Jordan, and D. Riley (Annapolis, MD: Living Resources Subcomm., Chesapeake Bay Program, 1991), 1–10.

14 K. A. Moore and J. C. Jarvis, "Using Seeds to Propagate and Restore Vallisneria americana Michaux (wild celery) in the Chesapeake Bay," *SAV Technical Notes Collection* (ERDC/TN SAV-07-3) (Vicksburg, MS: U.S. Army Engineer Research and Development Center, 2007).

15 Ernest Ingersoll, *The Oyster-Industry* (Washington, DC: GPO, 1881).

16 Ibid.

17 *Statistics of the Fisheries of the Middle Atlantic States for 1904* (Washington, DC: US Bureau of Fisheries, 1905), 118.

18 Harrison W. Burton, *The History of Norfolk, Virginia: A Review of Important Events . . . 1736 to 1877* (Norfolk, 1877), 213.

19 Philip H. Mitchell and Raymond L. Barney, "The Occurrence in Virginia of Green Gilled Oysters Similar to Those of Marennes," in *The United States Bureau of Fisheries Yearbook* 35 (Washington, DC: GPO, 1918), 137–39.

20 "Fact No. 14," *Nature Lore* 4 (1936): 178.

21 K. K. Chew, "Wild Populations of American Oysters in the Chesapeake Bay," *Aquaculture Magazine* (2006): 32.

22 See http://www.lynnhavenoystercompany.com/content/about-us (accessed August 24, 2011).

23 Scott Harper, "Virginia Reopens Lynnhaven Oyster Grounds," *Virginia Pilot*, March 3, 2011.

24 M. L. Tyson, *Queen of the Kitchen: A Collection of "Old Maryland" Family Receipts for Cooking* (Philadelphia: T. B. Peterson & Brothers, 1874), 114.

25 Nevertheless, chemical runoff from lawns has led to odd problems in the population, such as the rise of undersize female breeding crabs.

26 Mrs. Washington, *The Unrivalled Cook-Book and Housekeeper's Guide* (New York: Harper & Brothers, 1885), 580.

27 *Annual Report of the Commissioner of Agriculture* (Washington, DC: GPO for the USDA, 1879), 80.

28 Mrs. B. C. Howard, "Dressing for Crabs," *Fifty Years in a Maryland Kitchen*, 4th ed. (Philadelphia: J. B. Lippincott & Co., 1881), 99.

29 See *Ballou's Monthly Magazine* 64 (1886): 345.

30 "Canvasback and Terrapin," *Scribner's Monthly* 15, no. 1 (February 1877): 11.

31 Ibid.

32 "Salmon, Ducks and Terrapin," *Forest and Stream* 46 (1896): 389.

33 Mrs. Washington, *Unrivalled Cook-Book*, 48.

34 Alexander Filippini, *100 Ways of Cooking Fish* (New York: H. M. Caldwell, 1892), 99.

35 "The Social Athens of America," *Harper's Magazine* 65 (1882): 32.

36 Ibid., 33.

37 South Carolina Department of Resources Bulletin, *Diamondback Terrapin*: http://www.dnr.sc.gov/cwcs/pdf/DiamondbackTerrapin.pdf (accessed August 25, 2011).

38 Ken James, *Escoffier: The King of Chefs* (Cambridge: Cambridge University Press, 2002), 211.

CHAPTER FIVE

1 Henry Jakes and his successor, B. F. Simms, were nationally famous black caterers in Baltimore, as was John R. Young. During the mid-nineteenth century, John Dabney and William H. Diggs enjoyed similar repute in Richmond.

2 A description of the inaugural banquet appears in "The New Hotel," *Charleston Courier*, March 28, 1838.

3 *Southern Patriot*, January 1, 1835.

4 "Planter's Hotel, by Chas. H. Miot," *Southern Patriot*, December 22, 1847.

5 "Moore," *Columbian Herald*, May 26, 1785.

6 "Adam Prior," *Charleston Morning Post*, June 3, 1786.

7 Sale notice, John Ward Estate, *South Carolina Gazette and General Advertiser*, February 3, 1874.

8 Larry Koger, *Black Slaveowners: Free Black Slave Masters in South Carolina, 1790–1860* (Columbia: University of South Carolina Press), 39.

9 "Society of the Cincinnati," *Charleston Courier*, January 1, 1833.

10 "Proceedings of Council," *Charleston Council*, July 26, 1838.

11 *Charleston Courier*, February 17, 1845; March 10, 1848; February 2, 1850; March 2, 1851.

12 Koger, *Black Slaveowners*, 150.

13 *City Gazette*, October 11, 1823.

14 "Cheap Confectionary Stores," *Charleston Courier*, April 8, 1829.

15 *Charleston Courier*, October 1, 1831.

16 *Charleston Courier*, April 19, 1832.

17 "United States Coffee House," *Charleston Courier*, January 14, 1837.

18 *Charleston Courier*, May 24, 1837.

19 *Charleston Courier*, February 12, 1838.

20 *Charleston Courier*, April 16, 1838.

21 "Look at This!" *Charleston Courier* 41, no. 12563 (December 19, 1843), 3.

22 "Concert at Hibernian Hall," *Southern Patriot*, February 16, 1848.

23 Matrimony notice, *Charleston Courier*, January 7, 1850.

24 *Charleston Courier*, April 8, 1850.

25 *Charleston Courier*, November 28, 1850.

26 *Charleston Courier*, May 3, 1851.

27 *Charleston Courier*, August 15, 1851.

28 *Charleston Courier*, October 6, 1851.

29 *Charleston Courier*, April 1, 1852. The idea of al fresco dining had been experimentally ventured by L. Eude and A. Antonion in 1833 at "Tivoli Garden," where "Breakfasts, Dinners, Suppers, and Goutes" were prepared to order while patrons enjoyed music and promenading. The experiment was short-lived.

30 *Charleston Courier*, June 8, 1854.

31 "New York Game," *Charleston Courier* 52, no. 17248 (January 28, 1856), 2.

32 From the surviving documents, it is difficult to determine whether the family suit and sale was a ruse to forestall a similar attempted takeover from another creditor. That is, the A. Mignot suit may have been a preemptive action.

33 *Charleston Courier*, November 22, 1858.

34 *Charleston Courier*, December 14, 1858.

35 *Charleston Mercury*, December 8, 1859.

36 *Charleston Mercury*, May 21, 1860.

37 Again, it is difficult to determine whether the disappearance from Charleston was truly because of disease or to forestall various legal actions against various of his creditors. Because the separation would last the duration of the war, and because the couple re-formed in its wake, the disease explanation may have some merit.

38 "Mount Vernon Restaurant," *Charleston Courier*, October 28, 1861.

39 "A First-Class Boarding House," *Charleston Mercury*, May 28, 1862.

40 The game market was part meat stall, part tavern, with a storage area and kitchen. Poet Henry Timrod loved to drink at Fuller's when it occupied King Street.

41 "Christmas! Christmas!," *Charleston Courier*, December 24, 1856; "Wild Game, etc.," *Charleston Courier*, April 11, 1854.

42 "Communication: What We Are to Eat," *Charleston Courier*, January 19, 1857.

43 "The Elmore Mutual Insurance Company," *Charleston Mercury*, July 20, 1860.

44 "Notice," *Charleston Courier*, October 10, 1860.

45 "Bachelor's Retreat," *Charleston Courier*, December 27, 1861.

46 "To Companies and Committees," *Charleston Mercury*, February 27, 1861.

47 "Estate Sale," *Charleston Mercury*, March 21, 1864.

48 *Charleston Courier*, November 25, 1862.

49 "Nat Fuller," *Charleston Courier*, December 23, 1863.

50 "Turtle Soup and Wild Turkey," *Charleston Mercury*, September 21, 1864.

51 "Our Fireman at Charleston," *Daily Constitutionalist*, May 1, 1866.

52 Benjamin Quarles, *The Negro in the Civil War* (Russell and Russell, 1868), 329.

53 *U.S. Federal Census for 1850, Parishes of St. Michaels and St. Philips* [Charleston], 128.

54 "Vanderhorst & Tully," *Charleston Courier*, September 16, 1859.

55 *Charleston Daily News*, April 20, 1866.

56 "One Hundred and Thirty-Seventh Anniversary of St. Andrew's Society," *Charleston Daily News*, December 1, 1866.

57 "Death of a Culinary Artist," *Macon Telegraph*, October 31, 1883, 1.

CHAPTER SIX

1 *The South Carolina Jockey Club* (Charleston: Russell & Jones, 1857), 152–53.

2 The Jockey Club staged two large-scale catered events: a ball, whose preparation was conducted by Nat Fuller; and the banquet, conducted by Eliza Seymour Lee. The expense records have not survived in the club archives in the Charleston Library Society, so it cannot be determined how much of the $1,000 was expended in the preparation.

3 George Vandenhoff, *Leaves from an Actor's Note-Book* (New York: D. Appleton, 1860), 183.

4 "Editorial Correspondence: The Return to Town and Dinner," *Spirit of the Times* 30, no. 1 (February 11, 1860): 6.

5 Pierre Blot, *What to Eat, and How to Cook It* (New York: D. Appleton, 1863), 241–43.

6 "The Return to Town and Dinner," 6.

7 Interestingly, northerner Mrs. H. W. Beecher published the most ample recipe for this dish: "Turtles," *Christian Union* 22, no. 15 (October 13, 1880): 308–9.

8 Kate Brew Vaughn, "Stewed Pigs' Feet," *Culinary Echoes from Dixie* (Cincinnati: McDonald Press, [1917]), 50.

9 "Fine Flocks of Sheep in the Vicinity of Columbia, South Carolina," *Southern Agriculturist, Horticulturist, and Register of Rural Affairs* 5, no. 7 (July 1845): 268.

10 "Boston Cooking School," *Massachusetts Ploughman and New England Journal of Agriculture* 56, no. 14 (January 3, 1897): 8.

11 "English Modes of Cooking Mutton," *Ohio Cultivator* 7, no. 24 (December 15, 1851): 380.

12 J.B., "Life in the State of Iowa," *Spirit of the Times* 15, no. 2 (March 8, 1845): 16.

13 Blanche L. MacDonell, "Game and Its Treatment," *New York Observer and Chronicle* 74, no. 37 (September 10, 1896): 409.

14 Eliza R. Parker, "Game—Variety in Cooking," *Ladies' Home Journal* 6, no. 11 (October 1889): 16.

15 An elaborated form of this recipe is contained in Lafcadio Hearn, *La Cuisine Creole* (New Orleans: F. F. Hansell & Bro., 1885), 253.

16 T.S.M., "The Mode of Hunting Wild Turkeys in the South," *American Turf Register and Sporting Magazine* 2, no. 8 (April 1831): 388.

17 Ibid.

18 "Receipts: Boiled Turkey," *Saturday Evening Post*, January 1, 1870, 8.

19 "Turkey-Dinde," *The Picayune's Creole Cook Book* (New Orleans: The Picayune, 1901), 111.

20 Mrs. Washington, *The Unrivalled Cook-Book and Housekeeper's Guide* (New York: Harper and Brothers, 1885), 154–55.

21 Thomas Spalding, "Dorking Fowls," *Southern Agriculturist, Horticulturist, and Register of Rural Affairs* 3, no. 6 (June 1844): 164.

22 *Bulletin of the South Carolina Experimental Station 62* (Columbia, SC: R. L. Bryan, 1908), 4–6.

23 "To Choose Poultry," *Poultry World* 120 (1890): 200.

24 "Jockey Club Madeira," *Charleston News and Courier*, July 8, 1900, 6.

25 *Southern Literary Messenger* 30, no. 6 (June 1, 1860): 469.

CHAPTER SEVEN

1 Johnson Jones Hooper, "The Colonel," *Simon Suggs' Adventures and Travels* (Philadelphia: T. B. Peterson, 1858), 168.

2 John MacLean, "Field Peas," *American Farmer* 2, no. 24 (November 15, 1822): 266–67.

3 St. John's, Colleton, "Account of the Mode of Culture Pursued in Cultivating Corn and Peas," *Southern Agriculturist* 4, no. 5 (May 1831): 235–37.

4 [Sarah Rutledge], *The Carolina Housewife; or, House and Home: By a Lady of Charleston* (Charleston, SC: W. R. Babcock & Co., 1847), 44.

5 Mrs. Lettice Bryan, *The Kentucky Housewife* (Cincinnati: Shepard & Stearns, 1839), 21.

6 J. V. Jones, Burke Co., Georgia, *American Farmer* 11, no. 11 (May 1856): 347.

7 I.M., "Some Dainty Southern Recipes," *Boston Cooking School Magazine* 19 (June–July 1914): 59.

8 G. W. Carver, *Tuskegee Agricultural Experiment Station Bulletin #5* (Tuskegee, AL, 1903), 8.

9 George Bagby, "How to Make a True Virginian," in John Garland James, *Southern Student's Hand-book of Selections for Reading and Oratory* (New York: A. S. Barnes & Co., 1879), 119–20.

10 William Russell Smith, *Reminiscences of a Long Life*, vol. 1 (Washington, DC: by the author, 1889), 273–74.

11 Marion Cabell Tyree, *Housekeeping in Old Virginia* (Louisville, KY: John P. Morton, 1879), 129.

12 Mrs. Grayson, "Our Early Vegetables," *Table Talk* 9 (1894): 114.

13 Bret Harte, "South-Western Slang," *Overland Monthly* 3 (San Francisco: A. Roman & Co., 1869), 130.

14 *Annual Report of the State Board of Health South Carolina*, no. 2 (Columbia: For the S.C. Board of Health, 1881), 288.

15 "Virginia Sports," *Chautauquan* 11 (1890): 570.

16 Napier Bartlett, *A Soldier's Story of the War* (1874), 108.

17 Jessup Whitehead, *The Steward's Handbook* (Chicago, 1889), 384.

18 Mrs. Sarah A. Elliott, *Mrs. Sarah Elliott's Housewife* (New York: Hurd & Houghton, 1870), 71.

19 Solomon Northup, *Twelve Years a Slave* (Auburn: Derby, 1853), 201. See Herbert C. Covey and Dwight Eisnach, *What the Slaves Ate: Recollections of African American Foods and Foodways from the Slave Narratives* (Santa Barbara, CA: ABC-CLIO, 2009), 121–23.

20 A Virginian, "Personal Recollections of the War," *Harper's Magazine* 33 (1866): 559.

21 *Atlanta Medical and Surgical Journal* 14 (1898): 787.

22 Frances E. Owens, *Mrs. Owens' New Cook Book and Complete Household Manual* (Chicago: Owens' Publishing Company, 1899), 143.

23 Elliott, "Barbecue Possum," in *Mrs. Sarah Elliott's Housewife*, 72.

24 R. A. Wilkenson, ["Carve Dat Possum"], *Current Literature* 1 (July 1888): 39.

25 Nineteenth-century antiquarians collecting traditional street cries recorded the traditional Scots vendor call in Glasgow, "Nouts' feet and cow painches!" John Strang, *Glasgow and Its Clubs* (London: Richard Griffin, 1856), 167.

26 [Christian Isobel Johnston], *The Cook and Housewife's Manual by Margaret Dods* (London: 1826), 16.

27 Sarah Josepha Hale, *Mrs. Hale's New Cook Book* (London, 1857), 141.

28 "Dublin Street Cries," *Ainsworth's Magazine* 26 (1854): 72.

29 Annabella P. Hill, *Mrs. Hill's New Cook Book* (Philadelphia, 1872), 60.

30 Hale, *Mrs. Hale's New Cook Book*, 141.

31 Margaret Dods [Christian Isobel Johnstone], "Indian Meal Fritters," *The Cook and Housewife's Manual* (Edinburgh: Oliver & Boyd, 1847), 497.

32 Eliza Leslie, *Miss Leslie's Lady's New Receipt Book* (Philadelphia, 1850), 137.

33 Johnson Jones Hooper, "Squire A and the Fritters: Sketches of *Flush Times in Alabama and Mississippi*," *Southern Literary Messenger* 19 (1845): 88.

34 James Troop and O. M. Hadley, "The American Persimmon," *Purdue University Agricultural Station Bulletin* 60, no. 7 (Lafayette, IN, 1896): 50.

35 "American Chestnuts," *Nut Culture in the United States* (Washington, DC: GPO for the US Division of Pomology, USDA, 1896), 78.

36 Jessup Whitehead includes two particularly fine recipes in *The American Pastry Cook* (Chicago: Jessup Whitehead & Co., 1894), 102.

37 The recipe for raisin wines of this sort appears in Maria Eliza Ketelby Rundell's early cookbook, *American Domestic Cookery* (New York: E. Duyckinck, 1823), 275.

CHAPTER EIGHT

1 "The coastwise trade of South Carolina is carried on by the following lines: From Charleston: New York and Charleston Steamship Company, Clyde Steamship Line, Charleston and Florida Steamship Line, Merchants' Packet Line, Charleston and Baltimore Packet Line, New York and Charleston Packet Line, Packet Line to New York and Philadelphia. From Georgetown: Jones's line sailing vessels, Hurlburt's line sailing vessels. From Beaufort: Steamer Seminole, Beaufort to Savannah; Schooner Bertha, Beaufort to Savannah. In addition to these, the Mallory line of steamers touch at Port Royal, 4 miles below Beaufort, and bring freights for Beaufort. The local traffic between the ports of South Carolina is done by the following: Beaufort and Edisto line (steamers Pilot Boy and Silver Star), Sea Island Steamboat Company, and between Georgetown and Beaufort by the Sea Island Steamboat Company." William F. Switzler, "South Carolina," *Report on the Internal Commerce of the United States* (Washington, DC: GPO, 1886), 283.

2 *Digest of the Ordinances of the City Council of Charleston from the Year 1783 to July 1818* (Charleston, SC: Archibald E. Miller, 1818), 147–69.

3 Jonathan H. Poston, *The Buildings of Charleston* (Columbia: University of South Carolina Press, 1997), 395.

4 William Jeronimus and C. J. Heronimus, eds. and trans., *Travels by His Highness Duke Bernhard of Saxe-Weimar-Eisenach through North America in the Years 1825 and 1826* (New York: University Press of America, 2001), 283.

5 Through the 1830s and '40s, New Orleans produce and meat were divided into several venues—the French Vegetable Market, St. Mary's and Washington Market, the Meat Market on the Levee between St. Anne and Main, and the Poydras Market. Whereas commerce shut down (with the exception of the fish market) in Charleston for the Sabbath, New Orleans's great market day was Sunday. Benjamin Moore Norman, *Norman's New Orleans and Environs* (New Orleans: B. M. Norman, 1845), 135–36.

6 G. M., "South Carolina," *New England Magazine* 1 (1831): 246.

7 Mrs. Anne Royall, *Mrs. Royall's Southern Tour*, 3 vols. (Washington, DC, 1831), 1:7–9.

8 James Stuart, *Three Years in North America*, 3 vols. (London, 1833), 2:91.

9 *The Gardener's Monthly & the Horticulturist* 25 (1883): 14. In the West Indies, the tanya (now *Colocasia esculenta*) is known as eddoes and remains a favorite breakfast food.

10 "Account of the May Exhibition of the Horticultural Society of Charleston," *Southern Agriculturist and Register of Rural Affairs* 6 (1833): 355–56.

11 "Horticultural Society of Charleston, SC," *Magazine of Horticulture, Botany, and All Useful Discoveries* 2 (1836): 358.

12 "Horticultural Society of Charleston, SC," *Magazine of Horticulture, Botany, and All Useful Discoveries* 5 (1839): 77.

13 "On the Trees, Shrubs and Plants, Valuable for Their Fruits or in the Arts, that Might Be Introduced and Cultivated to Advantage in Carolina," *Southern Agriculturist* 11, no. 11 (1834): 369–75.

14 "Mr. Michel's Garden, near Charleston," *American Gardener's Magazine* 1 (1835): 273–74.

15 S., "Description of the African Potato; Read Before the Barnwell Agricultural Society," *Farmer's Register* 9 (1841), 4.

16 *Southern Farmer's Register* (1841): 2.

17 "Mr. Michel's Garden, near Charleston," 273.

18 Ibid.

19 *Southern Agriculturist and Register of Rural Affairs* 9 (1836): 444–47.

20 *Southern Agriculturist* 5 (1832), 365.

21 *Magazine of Horticulture, Botany, and All Useful Discoveries* (1839): 77.

22 "Anniversary Proceedings of the Horticultural Society," *Southern Agriculturist* 7 (1834): 411.

23 *Southern Agriculturist* 12 (1838): 15.

24 Francis S. Holmes, *The Southern Farmer and Market Gardener: Being a Compilation of Useful Articles on These Subjects from the Most Approved Writers. Developing the Principles and Pointing Out the Method of Their Application to the Farming and Gardening of the South, and Particularly of the Low Country* (Charleston: Burges & James, 1842).

25 *Southern Agriculturist* 7 (1834): 572.

26 *New-England Magazine* 1 (1831): 246.

27 William Bingley, *Travels in North America* (London: Harvey & Darton, 1821), 129–30.

28 "Ice," *Century* 10 (1880): 464.

29 John Lambert, *Travels through Canada and the United States . . . in the years 1806, 1807, & 1808*, 2 vols. (London, 1816), 2:145.

30 Stuart, *Three Years in North America*, 2:66–70.

31 *Museum of Foreign Literature, Science, and Art* 21 (1833): 221.

32 Royall, *Mrs. Royall's Southern Tour*, 92.

33 "Voyaging on the Savannah," *McBride's Magazine* 33, 190.

34 George White, *Statistics of Georgia* (1848), 223.

35 *Report of the Secretary of Agriculture* (Georgia State Government, 1851), 321.

36 Not to be confused with the citron watermelon, a variety cultivated for its rind since it tasted best of any variety when pickled.

37 Daniel Jay Browne, *The Trees of America* (1846), 472.

38 "Market Gardening at the South," *Soil of the South* 3 (1853): 633.

39 Royall, *Mrs. Royall's Southern Tour*, 92.

40 Philip A. Strobel, *The Salzburgers, and Their Descendants* (1855), 296.

41 Alexander Harrison MacDonell, *The Code of the City of Savannah* (Savannah: Savannah Times Publishing Company, 1888), 121.

42 [William Tell Harris], *Remarks Made during a Tour throughout the United States of America . . .* (London, 1821), 69.

43 *Report of the Secretary of Agriculture for the Year 1851* (Washington, DC: GPO, 1852), 320.

44 Emily P. Burke, *Reminiscences of Georgia* (J. M. Fitch, 1850), 139.

45 Charles MacKay, *Life and Liberty in the United States* (New York, 1859), 210.

46 Ernest Ingersoll, *The Oyster-Industry* (Washington, DC: GPO, 1881), 191.

CHAPTER NINE

1 See Samuel Hollander's classic "Adam Smith and the Self-Interest Axiom," *Journal of Law and Economics* 20, no. 1 (April 1977): 133–52.

2 Thomas F. De Voe, *The Market Book, Containing a Historical Account of the Public Markets in the Cities of New York, Boston, Philadelphia, and Brooklyn*, 2 vols. (New York: by the author, 1862), 1:48, passim.

3 "The Prospects and Policy of the South," *Southern Quarterly Review* (1854): 443.

4 Karl Bernhard, Duke of Saxe-Weimar-Eisenach, *Travels through North America in the Years 1825 and 1826*, 2 vols. (Philadelphia: Carey, Lea & Cary, 1828), 2:6–10.

5 Daniel Blowe, *A Geographical, Historical, Commercial, and Agricultural View of the United States of America* (London: Edwards & Knibb, 1820), 492.

6 Mrs. Anne Royall, *Mrs. Royall's Southern Tour*, 3 vols. (Washington, DC, 1831), 2:7.

7 [Sarah Rutledge], *The Carolina Housewife; or, House and Home: By a Lady of Charleston* (Charleston, SC: W. R. Babcock & Co., 1847). One recipe is supplied for each fish in this central compendium of antebellum Lowcountry cuisine. Oysters were the predominant form of seafood; shrimp appeared next in frequency; crab, third.

8 George Brown Goode, *The Fishery and Fishery Industries of the United States; Section II: A Geographical Review of the Fisheries Industries . . . For the Year 1880* (Washington, DC: GPO, 1887), 506. The northern supply of saltwater fish dated from the 1810s. A report from 1821: "In winter, the markets of Charleston are well supplied with fish, which are brought from the northern parts of the United States, in vessels so constructed as to keep them in a continual supply of water, and alive. The ships, engaged in this traffic, load, in return, with rice and cotton." William Bingley, *Travels in North America* (London: Harvey & Darton, 1821), 130.

9 Task fishing is well documented in "Routine of Incidentals on a Sea-Island Plantation," *A Documentary History of American Industrial Society* (Washington, DC, 1919), 203–5.

10 Testimony of Mr. Middleton, *South Carolina Legislative Times* (Columbia, 1856): 82.

11 "The Prospects and Policy of the South," 443.

12 David S. Cecelski, *The Waterman's Song: Slavery and Freedom in Maritime North Carolina* (Chapel Hill: University of North Carolina Press, 2000).

13 Bernard E. Powers Jr., *Black Charlestonians: A Social History 1822–1885* (Fayetteville: University of Arkansas Press, 1994), 66.

14 William R. Ryan, *The World of Thomas Jeremiah: Charles Town on the Eve of the Revolution* (New York: Oxford University Press, 2010), 52–54, 67. Much was made during the war of Robert Smalls, the black pilot who smuggled a ship from the harbor into Union hands; but Smalls forfeited his future in his home city. Leslie did not.

15 Goode, *The Fishery and Fishery Industries*, 507.

16 "Everybody knows that oysters are splendid in all months with an R, but they don't know that Terry & Nolan, at the fish market, have Norfolk oysters for sale. Norfolk oysters are the biggest and best of the bivalves." *Charleston Daily News*, November 15, 1869.

17 *The Constitution of South Carolina . . . and the Acts and Joint Resolutions of General Assembly Passed at the Special Session of 1868* (Columbia, SC: J. W. Denny, 1868), 660. The Savannah River had anti-obstruction shad fishing laws regulating catch during the antebellum period.

18 "Piscatorial," *Charleston Daily News*, January 11, 1868.

19 "Meetings," *Charleston Daily News*, December 27, 1869.

20 *Charleston Daily News*, December 11, 1869, 1.

21 "Phosphate Diggers of South Carolina, Petition Asking for the Right to Dig Phosphate on the Coosaw River" (undated), Petition to the South Carolina Legislature, South Carolina Department of Archives and History, Item 05834, Ser S165015.

22 "From St. Mark's Church, Charleston, SC," *Journal of the Proceedings of the Bishops, Clergy and Laity of the Protestant Episcopal Church in 1886* (NY: printed for the convention, 1887), 848–52. Paradoxically, Leslie's most vexing encounters with white racism would be in connection with St. Mark's thwarted attempts to seek admission into the area episcopate and to secure an African American rector recognized by local Episcopal clergy during the 1880s.

23 George Brown Goode, *The Fisheries and Fishery Industries of the United States*, 2 vols. (Washington, DC: US Bureau of Fishers, 1888), 1:519.

24 Ibid., 509.

25 "A Proposed Radical Change," *Charleston Daily News*, December 14, 1869.

26 "South Carolina," *Index to the Miscellaneous Documents of the House of Representatives, 2nd Session, 47th Congress, 1882–83*, vol. 2127 (Washington, DC: GPO, 1983), 148–49.

27 When Thomas W. Carroll bought out Leslie's business upon his retirement in 1906, Carroll secured Leslie's famous map of the South Atlantic fishing grounds from Cape Hatteras to north Florida annotated with prime locales for fishing and seasonal patterns of movement. The map disappeared well before the Carroll family closed down their fish business in 1984.

28 Goode, *The Fisheries and Fishery Industries of the United States*, 2:xi–xii.

29 George Brown Goode, "A History of the Menhadden," Appendix A, in S. F. Baird, *Report of the Commissioner, United States Commission of Fish and Wildlife*, Pt. 5 (Washington, DC: GPO, 1879), 5:40.

30 George Brown Goode, *American Fishes* (New York: Houghton, 1888), 91.

31 J. Richard Dunn, "Charles H. Gilbert, Pioneer Ichthyologist and Fishery Biologist," *Marine Fisheries Review*, Winter–Spring 1996.

32 The 50 varieties of locally caught fish in the Charleston Market should be compared with the 139 varieties of fish secured from sources throughout the United States including Charleston documented as being the New York City market after the Civil War by Thomas F. De Voe in *The Market Assistant*, 2 vols. (New York: Hurd & Houghton, 1867). The minor role that freshwater fish had in the Charleston Market contrasts with the wealth found in New York.

33 *Proceedings of the U.S. National Museum* (Washington, DC: GPO, 1882–83), 580–620.

34 *Proceedings of the U.S. National Museum* (Washington, DC: GPO, 1887), 269–70.

35 Charles C. Leslie, "Scarcity of Blackfish in the South," *Bulletin of United States Fish Commission 2* (Washington, DC: GPO, 1883), 179.

36 *Bulletin of the United States Fish Commission 4*, no. 17 (Washington, DC: GPO, July 30, 1884).

37 Leslie ad, *The Watchman and Sothron* (Sumter, SC), October 3, 1888.

CHAPTER TEN

1 Thomas F. De Voe, *The Market Assistant* (New York: Hurd and Houghton, 1867), 20.

2 Fearing Burr Jr., *The Field and Garden Vegetables of America* (Boston: J. E. Tilton & Co., 1865), 183–87.

3 Introduced by US Navy officers from Japan by way of Hawaii, the apple-pie melon came into cultivation in Georgia and California in 1856. Its meat was boiled, then used as pie filling. "The Pie Melon," *American Cotton Planter* 1, no. 1 (January 1857): 25.

4 James John Howard Gregory, *Squashes: How to Grow Them* (New York: Orange Judd, 1867), 49.

5 The career of gardener Peter Henderson of Bergen, New Jersey, is instructive in this matter. Upon the cessation of the Civil War, he published *Gardening for Profit* (New York: Orange Judd, 1865), targeting the market gardener as the ideal consumer of his horticultural information. The public that wrote to him, however, tended to be amateurs tending personal flower beds and gardens, desiring information on flowers as much as vegetables. His *Practical Floriculture* (New York, 1869) envisioned a dual readership of market florists and amateurs. This publication stimulated a storm of correspondence, requesting plant material as well as information. In 1871 Henderson went into the seed business. Finally, *Gardening for Pleasure* (New York, 1875) directly addressed the community that had become his main customer base: the small-plot city grower and the country-kitchen gardener.

6 Noel Kingsbury, *Hybrid: The History and Science of Plant Breeding* (Chicago: University of Chicago Press, 2009), 107–9.

7 Thomas F. De Voe, *The Market Book, Containing a Historical Account of the Public Markets in the Cities of New York, Boston, Philadelphia, and Brooklyn*, 2 vols. (New York: printed for the author, 1862).

8 De Voe's equivocation may have stemmed from a sense that the meat industry was transforming away from its guild character into the corporate slaughterhouse. See Jared N. Day, "Butchers, Tanners, and Tallow Chandlers: The Geography of Slaughtering in Early-Nineteenth-Century New York City," in *Meat, Modernity, and the Rise of the Slaughterhouse*, ed. Paula Young Lee (Lebanon: University of New Hampshire Press, 2008), 178–98.

9 De Voe, *The Market Assistant*, 23.

10 Solon Robinson, "A Letter about Hogs," *The Western Farmer and Gardener* (Cincinnati: James, 1848), 509–11.

11 Eli Nichols, "Fattening Hogs on Apples," *Genesee Farmer and Gardener's Journal* 2, no. 40 (October 6, 1832): 317.

12 For my history of the role of ham in the nineteenth-century food system, see David S. Shields, "The Search for the Cure: The Quest for the Superlative American Ham," *Common-Place* 8, no. 1 (October 2007), http://www.common -place.org/vol-08/no-01/shields/ (accessed February 17, 2014).

13 De Voe, *The Market Assistant*, 151.

14 Ibid., 153.

15 Ibid., 172.

16 December 19, 1857.

CHAPTER ELEVEN

1 Frank Osborn Braynard, "Coastwise Steamship Lines," *History of American Steam Navigation* (New York: Samitz, 1908), 445.

2 Immediately after the Civil War, the trans-shipment of rattlesnake watermelons from Augusta contributed to these numbers, but with more direct rail routes from that city to northern markets, this component of the Charleston statistics disappeared by 1872.

3 USCA, Bureau of Statistics, Miscellaneous Series, *Bulletin*, Issues 15–23.

4 William Robinson, "Tomatoes," *The Garden: An Illustrated Weekly Journal* 3 (1873): 425.

5 *South Carolina Board of Agriculture Report* 6 (1885): 103.

6 "Asparagus Varieties," *Report of the Pennsylvania State College for the Year 1915–1916* (Harrisburg: J. L. L. Kuhn, 1918), 559.

7 "The Trucking Industry," *Year Book 1909, City of Charleston* (Charleston, SC: Walker, Evans & Cogswell, 1910), 10.

8 Miriam R. Pflug, "When Asparagus Was King," *Palmetto Farm Credit Leader* 2 (2003): 8–11.

9 The variety grown in the Lowcountry was the garnet chili introduced from South America in the 1850s and cultivated widely in the United States because of its resistance to blight.

10 "The Markets of New York," *Harper's Magazine* 35 (1867): 223.

11 "Truck Farming," *Fruit Recorder and Cottage Gardener* 3 (1871): 161.

12 Produce was packed as follows: apples—standard barrel, asparagus—24 bunches per crate (colossal) or 35 bunches per crate (standard), beans—1½ bushel box, beets—100 pounds in refrigerator chests, cabbage—100-pound lot crated, cantaloupes—bushel box or 1½ bushel box, cucumbers—bushel box, cymling—standard barrel, eggplant—standard barrel, kale—standard barrel, lettuce—standard barrel, onions—standard barrel, peas—bushel box or 1½ bushel box, potatoes—100-pound lot or standard barrel, squash—standard barrel, turnips—standard barrel.

13 *Report of the Commissioner of Agriculture of the United States* (Washington, DC: GPO, 1885), 610.

14 *South Carolina in 1884: A View of the Industrial Life of the State* (Charleston: News & Courier Press, 1884), 16.

15 Peter Henderson, "On Market Gardening," in *Profitable Farming in the Southern States*, by J. W. Fitz and Josiah Ryland (Richmond, VA: Franklin Publishing, 1890), 361.

16 Rev. E. T. Hooker, "Letter from Charleston," *American Missionary* 38 (1884): 111.

17 Stevenson Whitcomb Fletcher, *The Strawberry in North America: History, Origin, Botany and Breeding* (New York: Macmillan, 1917), 23–25.

18 "Nunan's Early Prolific Strawberry," *Charleston Daily News*, May 21, 1870, 3.

19 Stevenson Whitcomb Fletcher, *Strawberry Growing* (New York: Macmillan, 1917), 303.

20 "Vegetables," *American Garden* 9 (June 1888): 248.

21 "Strawberries," *South Carolina Department of Agriculture Report* 9 (Columbia: Charles A. Calvo, 1890), 20.

22 [D. H. Jacques], "Nunan's Prolific Strawberry," *Rural Carolinian* 4 (1873): 473.

23 Andrew Samuel Fuller, *The Illustrated Strawberry Culturist* (New York: Orange Judd, 1887), 22.

24 C. F. Myers, "Cabbages," *Market Growers Journal* 3 (1908): 30.

25 Walter Hines Page, *The World's Work* (New York, 1907), 9030.

26 Ebbie Julian Watson, *Handbook of South Carolina* (Columbia: South Carolina Department of Agriculture, 1907), 297.

27 "South Carolina Cabbage," *Market Growers Journal*, May 27, 1908, 9.

28 "Southern Garden Calendar," *Lady's Annual Register* (1837): 79.

29 Lee Cleveland Corbett, *Garden Farming* (Boston: Ginn & Company, 1913), 277.

30 Ibid., 282.

31 "Lettuce," *Report of the Maryland State Horticultural Society* 9 (College Park, MD, 1907), 45.

32 *Bulletin . . . of the North Carolina Department of Agriculture* 33, no. 1 (Raleigh, 1912), 14.

33 *South Carolina Department of Agriculture Annual Report 1906* (Columbia: Gonzales & Bryan, 1907), 20.

34 Obediah B. Stevens and Robert F. Wright, *Georgia, Historical and Industrial* 3 (Atlanta: George W. Harrison, 1901), 233.

35 Ibid.

36 *Transactions, Massachusetts Horticultural Society* (Boston: printed for the Society, 1881), 55.

CHAPTER TWELVE

1 *Cyclopaedia of American Agriculture* (New York: Macmillan, 1910), 535.

2 Nathan Slaton, Karen Moldenauer, and James Gibbons, "Rice Varieties and Seed Production," *Rice Production Handbook* (University of Arkansas Extension Online Publications), http://www.uaex.edu/Other_Areas/publications/PDF/MP192/MP-192.asp, 18–20.

3 The reintroduction is chronicled in Richard Schulze, *Carolina Gold Rice: The Ebb and Flow History of a Lowcountry Cash Crop* (New York: History Press, 2005), 65–78.

4 R. F. W. Allston, "Rice Culture," *Commercial Review of the South and West* (1846): 327.

5 Letter of Joshua John Ward, "Proceedings of the State Agricultural Society," *South Carolina Temperance Journal* (1843): 55–56.

6 Robert W. Allston, "Sea Coast Crops of the South," *DeBow's Review*, XVI, n.s., Vol. 2 (1854): 607.

7 Ibid.

8 John D. Legare, *American Farmer* 24 (1823): 187.

9 R. F. W. Allston, "Rice Culture," *Commercial Review of the South and West* (1846): 327.

10 See the stories contained in the brief biography in Joseph Johnson's *Traditions and Reminiscences, Chiefly of the American Revolution in the South* (Charleston, SC: Walker & James, 1851), 286–91.

11 William Gilmore Simms, *The Sword and Distaff; or, Fair, Fat, and Forty, a Story of the South at the Close of the Revolution* (Philadelphia: Lippincott, Grambo, & Co.,

1853). The book was so popular, it was reprinted the following year, entitled *Woodcraft*.

12 David P. Szatmary, *Shay's Rebellion: The Making of an Agrarian Revolution* (Boston: University of Massachusetts Press, 1984), 184.

13 Erik Stokstad, "American Rice out of Africa," *Science NOW Daily News*, November 16, 2007, http://news.sciencemag.org/2007/11/american-rice-out-africa. Since 2007, the number of genetic markers for the rice has multiplied.

14 Judith Carney, *Black Rice: The African Origins of Rice Cultivation* (Cambridge, MA: Harvard University Press, 2001). Yet it should be noted that Carolina Gold is *not* a form of *Oryza glaberrima*, the predominant West African rice variety.

15 A. S. Salley, *The Introduction of Rice Culture into South Carolina*, Bulletins of the Historical Commission of South Carolina 6 (Columbia: South Carolina Historical Commission, the State Publishers, 1919). See also Duncan Heyward, *Seed from Madagascar* (Chapel Hill: University of North Carolina Press, 1937).

16 Another critique of the rice origins stories has been advanced by historians Peter Coclanis, *The Shadow of a Dream: Economic Life and Death in the South Carolina Low Country, 1679–1920* (New York: Oxford University Press, 1989), 59–62, and S. Max Edelson, *Plantation Enterprise in Colonial South Carolina* (Cambridge, MA: Harvard University Press, 2006), 53–91.

17 Letter of Peter Collinson, *Gentleman's Magazine*, May 26, 1766.

18 F. Hall, *The Importance of the British Plantations* (London: J. Peele, 1731), 19.

19 R. C. Nash, "The Organization of Trade and Finance in the Atlantic Economy," in *Money, Trade, and Power: The Evolution of Colonial South Carolina's Plantation Society*, ed. Jack P. Greene, Rosemary Brana-Shute, and Randy Sparks (Columbia: University of South Carolina Press, 2001), 87–88.

20 Sri Owen, *The Rice Book* (New York: St. Martin's, 1996), 72.

21 "Domestic Occurrences, Charleston, April 29," *New York Magazine, or Literary Repository*, May 1797, 277.

22 William Mayrant, "On the Cultivation of Bearded Rice, by William Mayrant," *Southern Agriculturist* 2, no. 2 (February 1829): 75.

23 Allston, "Rice," 327.

24 Ibid., 328.

25 Edmund Ruffin listed four varieties of red weed rice and believed that cultivated strains reverted to a primitive form of rice when left in the soil over winter. "Volunteer Rice," *Report on the Commencement and Progress of the Agricultural Survey of South Carolina* (Columbia, SC: A. H. Pemberton, 1843), 110–11.

26 Davison McDowell and J. H. Allston, "Seed Rice," *Southern Agriculturists and Register of Rural Affairs* 4, no. 4 (April 1831): 221.

27 Frans R. Moormann, *Rice: Soil, Water, Land* (Luzon, Philippines: International Rice Research Institute, 1978), 8–19.

28 Edelson, *Plantation Enterprise in Colonial South Carolina*, 74–76. In the 1980s, the SRI cultivation method employing substantially less water enjoyed success in developing countries.

29 Many histories, following D. D. Wallace's *History of South Carolina* (New York: American Historical Association, 1934), incorrectly attribute the creation to McKewn Johnstone, who was not yet born in the 1750s.

30 The evolution of the cultivation systems for Lowcountry rice has been comprehensively laid out in the book by CGR Foundation board member Richard

Porcher and coauthor William Robert Judd in *The Market Preparation of Carolina Rice* (Columbia: University of South Carolina Press, 2014), chap. 4.

31 "Queries on the Culture of Rice; by William Washington, with Answers, by Hugh Rose of St. Thomas," *Southern Agriculturist* 1, no. 4 (April 1828): 166–67.

32 See, in particular, the replies of Charles E. Rowland of Charleston, *Southern Agriculturist* 1, no. 8 (August 1828): 352–58; William B. M. Myrick of Wilmington, North Carolina, *Southern Agriculturist* 4, no. 6 (January 1831): 287–92; Charles Munnerlyn of Georgetown, *Southern Agriculturist* 1, no. 5 (May 1828): 215–24; James C. Darby of North Santee, South Carolina, *Southern Agriculturist* 2, no. 6 (January 1829), 248–54; "Columella," *Southern Agriculturist* 6, no. 5 (May 1833): 225–29; J. Bryan from Camperre Plantation, Cooper River, South Carolina, *Southern Agriculturist* 5, no. 9 (September 1832), 457–62 and 5, no. 10, 528–34; T. F. Goddard from Georgetown, *Southern Agriculturist* 1, no. 11 (November 1827), 498–502; Roswell King of Hampton Plantation, South Carolina, *Southern Agriculturist* 1, no. 9 (September 1828), 409–14; and William Small of Camp North, Santee, South Carolina, *Southern Agriculturist* 1, no. 10 (October 1828): 456–59.

33 Allston, "Rice," 335.

34 Robert Francis Withers Allston, *An Essay on Sea Coast Crops* (Charleston, SC: Miller, 1854), 39.

35 "Rice and Rice Culture," *American Farmer's Magazine* 5 (1852): 49.

36 Yeoman, "Visit to a Rice Plantation," *New York Daily Times*, July 21, 1853, 2.

37 Ibid.

38 "The Rice Crop of South Carolina," *New York Times*, August 29, 1866, 2; reprinted from the *Charleston News*, August 23, 1866.

39 The causes of this decline are thoroughly documented in James Tuten's admirable *Lowcountry Time and Tide* (Columbia: University of South Carolina Press, 2009). Competition with the cheaper rice of the Southwest and East Indies impelled an erosion of the market for expensive gold seed rice.

40 "Importation of East Indian Rice," *Southern Agriculturist* 11, no. 1 (March 1938): 127.

41 Toward the end of the nineteenth century, the Gulf states began cultivating Honduran white rice, a cheap prolific grain, that did not require the scrupulous seed management of gold seed. Its low cost made it attractive to undiscriminating buyers, and it came to dominate the bulk rice trade.

42 "The Rice Crop of South Carolina," *New York Times*, August 29, 1866, 2; reprinted from the *Charleston News*, August 23, 1866.

43 "Rice Culture in Louisiana," *DeBow's Review* 1, no. 3 (September 1856): 290.

44 Arthur Grove Day, *Hawaii and Its People* (Honolulu: Meredith Press, 1968), 171.

45 "The ordinary Hawaiian rice, while largely of the Gold Seed types, is really a mixture of a great many different types, so in order to get the best results in harvesting, some of the rice will be so ripe that the grain shatters, while a portion of the plants in the field have perhaps barely attained a sufficient degree of ripeness to warrant their being cut." Jared G. Smith, *Annual Report of the Hawaii Agricultural Experiment Station for 1906* (US Department of Agriculture, 1907), 22.

46 L. Liotard, *Memorandum Regarding the Introduction of Carolina Rice to India* (Calcutta: Home, Revenue and Agricultural Department Press, 1880), 13.

47 Thomas Hargrove, "The Odyssey of Carolina Gold Rice," in *The Golden Seed*, ed. David S. Shields (Charleston, SC: Carolina Gold Rice Foundation, 2010).

48 Edmund Ruffin, *Report on the Commencement and Progress of the Agricultural Survey of South Carolina* (Charleston, SC, 1844), 29.

49 Catharine Beecher, *Miss Beecher's Domestic Receipt Book* (New York: Harper, 1850), 96–97.

50 Estelle Woods Wilcox and Ellen Clow, *Practical Housekeeping* (Minneapolis: Buckeye Publishing, 1883), 389.

51 George Read, *The Complete Biscuit and Gingerbread Baker's Assistant* (London: Dean & Son, 1854), 52.

52 Timothy Templeton, *Adventures of My Cousin Smooth* (Washington, DC, 1855), 50.

53 Mary Johnson Bailey Lincoln, *Mrs. Lincoln's Boston Cook Book* (Boston: Roberts Brothers, 1896), 100.

54 "An Army: Its Organization and Movements," *Continental Monthly* 4, no. 1 (July 1864): 5.

55 "The Southern Menu," *New England Kitchen Magazine* 3 (1895): x.

56 William Gilmore Simms, *As Good as a Comedy; or, The Tennessean's Story* (New York, 1852), 27.

57 A Boston Housekeep, *A Cook's Own Book* (Boston: Munroe & Francie, 1840), 175.

58 Jules Arthur Harder, *The Physiology of Taste: Harder's Book of Practical American Cookery* (San Francisco: by the author, 1885), 305.

59 "Grits Bits Waffle, Dixieland Delight," *Atlantic*, March 13, 2009, http://www.theatlantic.com/life/archive/2009/03/grits-bits-waffle-dixieland-delight/722/.

60 Gurdev S. Khush was head of Plant Breeding, Genetics and Biochemistry at the International Rice Research Institute in the Philippines.

61 Anna McClung, B. Merle Shepard, and Gurdev S. Khush, "Charleston Gold Rice," Submission document to the Texas Department of Agriculture, March 2011.

62 Jean Anthelme Brillat-Savarin, *The Physiology of Taste; or, Meditations on Transcendental Gastronomy*, trans. M. F. K. Fischer (New York: Vintage Classics, 2011), 242.

CHAPTER THIRTEEN

1 The standard general histories of the rise of Atlantic sugar culture are Elizabeth Abbott, *Sugar: A Bittersweet History* (London: Duckworth Overlook, 2009), and Sidney W. Mintz, *Sweetness and Power: The Place of Sugar in Modern History* (London: Penguin, 1985–86).

2 For the English sugar ambitions, see Karen Ordahl Kupperman's introduction to her edition of Richard Ligon, *A True and Exact History of the Island of Barbados* (1657; reprint, Indianapolis: Hackett, 2011), 16–19.

3 John J. McCusker and Kenneth Morgan, "The Business of Distilling," *The Early Modern Atlantic Economy* (Cambridge: Cambridge University Press, 2000), 206–16.

4 Charles Gayaré, *DeBow's Review* 19 (1855): 610–11.

5 Joyce E. Chaplin, *An Anxious Pursuit: Agricultural Innovation and Modernity in the Lower South* (Chapel Hill: University of North Carolina Press, 1996), 155–56; Ellis Merton Coulter, *Thomas Spalding of Sapelo* (Baton Rouge: Louisiana State University Press, 1940), 111–16.

6 Thomas Spalding, "On the Culture of the Sugar Cane," *Southern Agriculturist* 1, no. 12 (December 1828): 352–59.

7 Thomas Spalding, letter of September 1, 1830, to the US Congress regarding Sugar Manufacture, Document #62: Sugar Cane, etc. Letter from the Secretary of the Treasury, *Documents of the United States House of Representatives, 21st Congress, 2nd Session, Treasury Department* (Washington, DC: GPO, 1831), 37. See also James E. Bagwell, *Rice Gold: James Hamilton Couper and Plantation Life on the Georgia Coast* (Macon, GA: Mercer University Press, 2002), 64.

8 Edward Barnwell, "On the Culture of Sugar," *Southern Agriculturist* 1, no. 11 (November 1828), 483–88.

9 William Carter Stubbs and Daniel Gugel Purse, *The Cultivation of Sugar Cane* (Savannah, GA: Morning News Print, 1900), 56.

10 *American Farmer*, March 3, 1824, 398.

11 *Colonial Virginia's Cooking Dynasty*, ed. Katharine E. Harbury (Columbia: University of South Carolina Press, 2004), 178.

12 *Southern Agriculturist*, September 1837, 452.

13 *American Farmer* 7, no. 17 (July 15, 1825): 135.

14 Nicholas Herbemont, *American Farmer* 8, no. 26 (September 15, 1826): 202–3.

15 Mrs. Mary Randolph, *The Virginia House-wife; or, Methodical Cook* (Baltimore: Plaskitt, Fite & Co., 1838), 175.

16 "Jane Randolph's Cookery Book" (1743), in *Colonial Virginia's Cooking Dynasty*, 408.

17 Miss Tyson, *Queen of the Kitchen, a Collection of "Old Maryland" Family Receipts for Cooking* (Philadelphia: T. B. Peterson & Brothers, 1874), 349–50.

18 J. G. Woodroof and J. E. Baily, *Fig Varieties and Culture*, Georgia Experiment Station Circular 97 (December 1931), 31.

19 Lafcadio Hearn, *La Cuisine Creole* (New Orleans: F. F. Hansell & Bro., 1885), 214. The recipe combines instructions for creating the base syrup from "Preserved Huckleberries" with that for "Fig Preserves," which references the instructions.

20 Andrew F. Smith, *The Tomato in America* (Columbia: University of South Carolina Press, 1994), 186.

21 "Tomato Figs," *Southern Cultivator and Farming* 28 (1870): 315.

22 Nowadays called the pomelo, this citrus was native to Malaysia but was introduced into the West Indies, and from there to Florida, in the eighteenth century.

CHAPTER FOURTEEN

1 A survey of the substitutes is provided in Mary Elizabeth Massey, *Ersatz in the Confederacy* (Columbia: University of South Carolina, 1993).

2 Henry Clough, "Sorghum or Northern Sugar Cane," in *American Agricultural Annual* (New York: Orange Judd, 1867), 109.

3 The American 1840s and '50s were the pharmacological era in botanical experi-

ment, when traditional uses of cultivars might be ignored by analysts in favor of some chemical property. Inspired by Justus Leibig's chemical explorations, botanists and naturalists broke down plants into chemical components and sought their exploitation. For instance, the produce of Florida's orange groves were processed for the production of citric acid for industrial use as much as for human consumption.

4 English by birth, Leonard Wray began his career as a sugar planter in Jamaica but was ruined financially by the emancipation of the slave labor force. He moved to India and planted there for several years before transplanting a second time to Natal, South Africa, where he applied his sugar-making skills to the locally grown millet canes.

5 Located in Aiken Country, South Carolina, Beech Island became the home of singer James Brown during the final decades of the twentieth century.

6 Edmund Ruffin recorded his seeing the replanting in May 1857 in William Kaufman Scarborough, ed., *The Diary of Edmund Ruffin: Toward Independence October 1856 to April 1861* (Baton Rouge: Louisiana State University Press, 1972), 74.

7 *Century* 14, no. 36 (1888), 766.

8 David Dodge, "Domestic Economy in the Confederacy," *Atlantic Monthly* 58 (1886): 235.

9 Ibid.

10 A version of this recipe was employed in the 1920 USDA experiments on "The Digestibility of Grain Sorghums," *Bulletin of the U.S. Department of Agriculture* 451 (Washington, DC: GPO, 1920), 5.

11 David Henry Hanaburgh, "Salisbury Prison-Fare," in *History of the One Hundred and Twenty-Eighth Regiment: New York Volunteers* (Poughkeepsie, NY, 1894), 189.

12 Prohibition made sorghum-based intoxicating beverages popular again for a decade. After repeal, it underwent a second quiescence until 2006, when Anheuser-Busch rolled out Redbridge, a sorghum-based beer designed to serve the millions of adults in the United States suffering from celiac disease and who could not metabolize beer made from gluten grains (e.g., barley, wheat, oats, and rye).

13 Tom Sanders and Peter Emery, *Molecular Basis of Human Nutrition* (London: Taylor & Francis, 2003), 199.

14 Lynn Salsi and Margaret Sims, *Columbia: History of a Southern Capital* (Charleston: Arcadia, 2003), 70.

15 H. W. Wiley, "The Growth of Sorghum Cane and the Manufacture of Sugar and Syrup Therefrom," *Annual Report of the Indiana State Board of Agriculture* 23 (Indianapolis: State Board of Agriculture, 1882), 494.

16 H. Hinkley, "Sorghum at the West," *Southern Cultivator* 18 (1860): 83.

17 "Convention of Chinese Sugar Cane Growers," *Transactions of the Illinois State Agricultural Society* 3 (Springfield: Illinois State Agricultural Society, 1859), 308–9.

18 H. S. Olcott, "Sugar from the Sorgo," *Southern Cultivator* 15 (1857): 142–43.

19 *Report of Hon. John Stanton Gould on Sorghum and Sugar Beet Culture* (Albany, NY: Van Benthuysen's Steam Press Printing House, 1865), 14.

20 Lawrence Wray, "Imphee," in Henry S. Olcott, *Sorgho and Imphee: The Chinese and African Sugar Canes* (New York: A. O. Moore Agricultural Book Publisher, 1857), 223–24.

21 Letter from Wray to U.S. Commissioner of Agriculture, September 7, 1882, as

quoted in Peter Collier, *Sorghum: Its Culture and Manufacture Economically Considered as a Source of Sugar, Syrup, and Fodder* (Cincinnati: R. Clarke & Co., 1884), 67; Carleton R. Ball, "Saccharine Sorghums for Forage," *Biennial Report, Kansas State Board of Agriculture* 17 (Topeka: Kansas Department of Agriculture, 1911), 52–53.

22 F. L. Stewart, *Sugar Made from Maize and Sorghum* (Washington, DC: Republic Company, 1878), 26.

23 Wray, "Imphee," 206.

24 *Report of the Commissioner for Agriculture for the Year 1864* (Washington, DC: GPO, 1864), 60–87.

25 William Clough, "Sorghum, or Northern Sugar-Cane," *Executive Documents printed by the order of the House of Representatives during the Second Session of the Thirty-Eighth Congress, 1864–'65* (Washington, DC: Government Printing Office, 1865), 79.

26 Collier, *Sorghum*, 416.

CHAPTER FIFTEEN

1 The transformation of his crops can be seen under the 1774 listings in Thomas Jefferson's *Garden Book*, when a modest range of conventional colonial vegetables are suddenly supplemented by radicchio, Tuscan garlic, Salvastrella di Pisa, and other cultivars. Thomas Jefferson's *Garden Book* (ms.), Thomas Jefferson Papers, http://www.thomasjeffersonpapers.org/garden. My 2009 paper to the Adams/Jefferson Conference in Boston and Monticello, "Green Ink: Thomas Jefferson and the Print World of Transatlantic Agriculture" (2010), reflects on the evolution of Jefferson's agricultural philosophy: http://www.adamsjefferson.com/papers/GreenInk_Shields.pdf.

2 Thomas Jefferson, letter, *Southern Agriculturist* 1, no. 8 (August 1828): 366.

3 The cost of raising hogs varied greatly depending upon whether one penned the animals or let them range free. Because of the general destruction that hogs inflict on the landscape, reform-minded farmers were penning hogs with greater frequency during the final decades of the eighteenth century. In a 1792 experiment, George Washington raised shoats to maturity, keeping a record of the costs in an attempt to calculate the monetary expense of raising a pig in a compound.

4 Presented to Shaftesbury in manuscript in 1679, it was published as John Locke, *Observations upon the growth and culture of Vines and Olives* (London: W. Sandby, 1766). Two years later it appeared in the seventh edition of Locke's *Works*, the vehicle by which it become widely known in Anglo-America.

5 Mitchell King, *The History and Culture of the Olive: The Anniversary Address of the State Agricultural Society of South Carolina . . . November 26th, 1846* (Columbia, SC: I. C. Morgan, for the Society, 1846), 20.

6 "Virginiansis Philoporcus," "More Bacon," *American Farmer* 3, no. 45 (February 1, 1822): 360.

7 David Duncan Wallace, *The Life of Henry Laurens* (New York: G. P. Putnam's Sons, 1915), 64.

8 "One of your Readers," "The Olive," *American Farmer* 8, no. 24 (September 1, 1826): 189.

9 *The Writings of Thomas Jefferson*, ed. Albert Ellery Burgh (Washington, DC: Thomas Jefferson Memorial Foundation, 1905), 13:204.

10 "Review," *American Quarterly Review* (September 1827): 227.

11 "Report of the Union Agricultural Society," *American Farmer* 6, no. 7 (April 29, 1825): 41–42.

12 "Olives, from the Darien Gazette," *American Farmer* 10, no. 13 (June 27, 1828).

13 John Couper, [letter on olive culture], *Southern Agriculturist* 1, no. 7 (July 1828): 304.

14 "On Raising Olive Trees from Seed," *Southern Agriculturist* 6, no. 6 (June 1833): 309.

15 Thomas Spalding, "Olives," *Southern Agriculturist* 1, no. 3 (March 1828): 107–8.

16 King, *History and Culture of the Olive*, 20.

17 "South Carolina Institute Fair," *De Bow's Review of the Southern and Western States* 12 (July 1852): 113.

18 Francis Peyre Porcher, *Resources of the Southern Fields and Forests* (Charleston: Walker, Evans, & Cogswell, 1869), 568.

19 Thomas Jefferson, "Letters from Old Trunks," *Virginia Magazine of History & Biography* 48, 2 (April 1940), 97–103.

20 "Account of an Attempt to Cultivate the Olive—Letter 14th February 1830," *Southern Agriculturist* 4, no. 5 (May 1830): 214.

21 *Transactions*, I (Philadelphia, 1789), 309.

22 *Papers of Henry Laurens*, vol. 9 (Columbia: University of South Carolina Press), 268.

23 T. M. Forman, *American Farmer* 2, no. 38 (December 15, 1820): 400.

24 Ibid.

25 The American Diabetes Association findings are epitomized in Lee Ann Holzmeister's "Cooking Oils," http://www.diabetesselfmanagement.com/articles/nutrition_meal_planning/cooking_oils/print/, 2010.

26 John S. Skinner, *American Farmer* 2, no. 17 (July 21, 1820): 135.

27 Robert M. Goodwin, *American Farmer* 6 (January 9, 1824): 46.

28 Calvin Jones, *American Farmer* 3, no. 19 (August 3, 1821): 150.

29 The scholarly debate about the constitution of the slave diet has raged over two decades, troubled in part by the lack of documentary evidence and archaeological findings about slave nutrition from small-scale farms in the South. As Herbert C. Covey and Dwight Eisnach have argued, the widespread practice of pica signals some sort of dietary deficiency. *What the Slaves Ate: Recollections of African American Foods and Foodways from the Slave Narratives* (Santa Barbara, CA: ABC-CLIO, 2009), 10–38.

30 Sarah Rutledge, *The Carolina Housewife* (Columbia: University of South Carolina Press, 1979), 45–46.

31 "A considerable quantity of Scallions ought to be planted, for they are of easy culture, and to them the negroes are more partial than any other of the alliaceous tribe." *Southern Agriculturalist and Register of Rural Affairs* 3, no. 10 (October 1830): 522.

32 *American Farmer* 6 (1824): 36.

33 Raleigh, June 27, 1821, *American Farmer* 3, no. 19 (August 3, 1821): 150.

34 Skinner, *American Farmer* 2, no. 17 (July 21, 1820): 135.

35 Thomas J. Murrey, *Salads and Sauces* (New York: Frederick A. Stokes Co., 1884), 21.

36 Benjamin Franklin Taylor, *The Early History of the Cotton Oil Industry in America* (Columbia, SC: B. F. Taylor, 1936), 10.

37 Robert Mills, *Statistics of South Carolina* (Columbia, SC: Hurlbut and Lloyd, 1826), 212.

38 Harvey Tolliver Cook, *The Life and Legacy of David Rogerson Williams* (New York: Country Life Press, 1916), 199–204.

39 James E. Bagwell, *Rice Gold: James Hamilton Couper and Plantation Life on the Georgia Coast* (Macon, GA: Mercer University Press, 2002), 28–43.

40 For a brief chronicle of the stops and starts of the cottonseed industry in the antebellum period, see Leebert Lloyd Lamborn, *Cotton Seed Products* (New York: D. Van Nostrand, 1904), 18–20.

41 "American Contemporaries—David Wesson," *Industrial and Chemical Engineering* 21, no. 3 (1929): 290–91.

42 A useful summary of the development of hydrogenised oils is contained in the arguments of *Procter & Gamble v. Berlin Mills Company,* U.S. District Court (Southern District of New York 13-100), printed as an appendix in Carleton Ellis, *The Hydrogenation of Oils* (New York: D. Van Nostrand, 1919), 630–707.

43 Marion Harris Neil, *The Story of Crisco* (Procter & Gamble Co., 1913), 9.

CHAPTER SIXTEEN

1 Hans Sloan, *The Natural History of Jamaica* (London, 1707), 184.

2 Philip Miller, "Arachis," *The Gardener's Dictionary,* 3 vols. (London: John & James Rivington, 1754).

3 Edward Long, *The History of Jamaica; or, General Survey of the Antient and Modern State of That Island,* 3 vols. (London: T. Lowndes, 1774), 2:788.

4 W.B., Correspondence, *Rural Carolinian* (1872): 328.

5 H. W. Ravenel, *Gardener's Monthly and Horticulturist* 27 (1885): 281–82.

6 Francis B. Spilsbury, *A Voyage to the West Coast of Africa* (London, 1806), 29.

7 Thomas Croxon Archer, *Popular Economic Botany* (London, 1854), 68.

8 Mrs. Washington, *The Unrivalled Cook-Book and Housekeeper's Guide* (New York: Harper & Brothers, 1885), 304.

9 *Florida Agriculturist* 15 (1894): 596.

10 John Lunan, *Hortus Jamaicencis,* 2 vols. (Jamaica: Office of the St. Jago Gazette, 1814), 1:349.

11 John Wilkes, *Encyclopaedia londinensis; or, Universal Dictionary of Arts, Sciences, and Literature,* 22 vols. (London: John Adlard, 1810), 2:27.

12 A. F. M. Willich, *The Domestic Encyclopedia; or, A Dictionary of Facts, and Useful Knowledge,* 4 vols. (London: McMillan, 1802), 2:438.

13 B. W. Jones, *The Peanut Plant* (New York: Orange Judd, 1885), 59.

14 R. M. Williams, *Genesee Farmer* 2 (1832): 81.

15 "Humors of a Young Man about Town—The Opening of Spring in New York," *New-York Mirror* 9 (1831): 317.

16 William Watson, "Some Account of an Oil, Transmitted by Mr. George Brown-

rigg of North Carolina," *Philosophical Transactions of the Royal Society of London* 59 (October 1769): 379–80. See Andrew F. Smith, *Peanuts: The Illustrious History of the Goober Pea* (Champaign: University of Illinois Press, 2002), 12.

17 *Reports from Her Majesty's Consuls* 36 (1883): 1812.

18 H. E. Colton, *Rural Carolinian* 3, no. 31 (1872): 428.

19 "Peanuts and Peanut Oil," *Southern Cultivator* 35 (1877): 61.

20 Jones, *The Peanut Plant*, 59.

21 Henry Gathmann, *American Soaps* (Chicago: by the author, 1893), 59.

22 The role of C. H. Sumner, who sold peanut butter at the 1904 St. Louis Exposition, is entirely overstated in the history of the introduction of the product.

23 *Peanut Promoter* (1918): 95.

24 David Ramsay, *The History of South Carolina*, 2 vols. (Charleston, 1809), 2:564.

25 Watson, "Some Account of an Oil," 379.

26 "A New Mode of Cultivating Corn Mixed with Other Crops," *Farmer's Register* 2 (1835): 634–36.

27 C. T. Leonard, "Cultivation of Peanuts," *Fruit Recorder and Cottage Gardener* 9 (1873): 4–5.

28 W. R. Beattie, *The Peanut*, Farmers' Bulletin 431 (Washington: U.S. Dept. of Agriculture, 1911), 9–11.

29 [Sarah Rutledge], *The Carolina Housewife; or, House and Home: By a Lady of Charleston* (Charleston, SC: W. R. Babcock & Co., 1847), 45.

30 May Fornay, "The Peanut as an Article of Food," *Arthur's Home Magazine* 52 (1884): 594.

31 Ibid.

32 Francis Peyre Porcher, *Resources of the Southern Fields and Forests* (Charleston: Walker, Evans, & Cogswell, 1869), 228.

33 *Ballou's Monthly Magazine* 68 (1888): 504.

34 Fornay, "The Peanut as an Article of Food," 594.

35 Almeda Lambert, *Guide for Nut Cookery* (Battle Creek, MI: J. Lambert & Co., 1899), 153.

CHAPTER SEVENTEEN

1 Mrs. Henry Rowe Schoolcraft, *Black Gauntlet* (Philadelphia: J. P. Lippincott, 1860), 106.

2 James R. Cothran, *Gardens of Historic Charleston* (Columbia: University of South Carolina Press, 1995), 114.

3 Throughout the 1770s, John Watson maintained his own lime grove in a nursery on King Street.

4 John Shecut, *Medical and Philosophical Essays* (1819), 22.

5 William Darlington, *Memorials of John Bartram and Humphrey Marshall*, 3 vols. (Philadelphia: Lindsay & Blackiston, 1848), 3:436.

6 A. J. Harris, "The Wild Orange Groves of Florida," *Proceedings of the Florida Fruit-Growers' Association* (1875): 27.

7 Ibid., 28.

8 Francis Holmes, *The Southern Farmer and Market Gardener: Being a Compilation of*

Useful Articles on These Subjects from the Most Approved Writers. Developing the Principles and Pointing Out the Method of Their Application to the Farming and Gardening of the South, and Particularly of the Low Country (Charleston: Burges & James, 1842), 155–56.

9 George White, *Statistics of the State of Georgia* (Savannah: W. Thorne Williams, 1849), 139.

10 John Lee Williams, *The Territory of Florida* (New York: A. T. Goodrich, 1837), 166.

11 G. W. McCallem, *Biographical Register of the Officers and Graduates of the U.S. Military Academy* (New York, 1891), 369.

12 Letters of John Dancy, http://battleofolustee.org/letters/dancy.htm.

13 *Annual Reunion* (New York: U.S. Military Academy, Association of Graduates, 1890), 27.

14 Francis Dancy, "Orange Culture in Florida," *Southern Farm & Home* 2 (1870): 14–16.

15 *The Florida Settler; Sixth Annual Report of the Commissioner of Immigration* (Tallahassee: Florida Commissioners for Lands and Immigration, 1876), 153.

16 *Transactions of the Southern Central Agricultural Society* (Macon, GA, 1852), 139.

17 *Proceedings of the Annual Meeting of the Florida Fruitsellers Association* (Jacksonville, FL: Charles H. Walton, 1875), 43.

18 Ibid., 44.

19 M. S. Moreman, "Some History of the Pioneering Days of the Citrus Industry," Proceedings of Annual Meeting of the Florida State Horticultural Society, *Florida State Horticultural Society Quarterly* (1918): 183–84.

20 Dancy, "Orange Culture in Florida," 16.

21 "Let us conclude with due acknowledgments to Colonel Dancy and his lady, at whose suggestion we have penned this article, and whose approval supports its positions. May their Hesperides ever shower on them golden fruits, and sunset splendors light their patriarchal groves." M. B. Lazarus, "The Guava (*Psidium sp.*) in Florida," *Rural Carolinian* 2 (1872): 247.

22 Mrs. Joseph P. Hill, *Mrs. Hill's New Cook Book* (Philadelphia, 1873), 312.

23 Ibid., 274.

24 [Sarah Rutledge], *The Carolina Housewife; or, House and Home: By a Lady of Charleston* (Charleston, SC: W. R. Babcock & Co., 1847), 173.

25 Ibid., 115.

26 Mrs. J. L. Lane, "Orange and Apple Pie," *365 Orange Recipes* (Philadelphia: George W. Jacobs, 1909), 53.

27 Charles Martyn, *How to Make Money in a Country Hotel* (New York: Caterer Publishing Co., 1901), 148.

28 Rutledge, *The Carolina Housewife*, 164.

29 Frederick Nutt, *The Complete Confectioner* (New York: Richard Scott, 1807), 30. Nutt provided recipes for "Bergamot and Lemon Wafers" as well.

30 Rutledge, *The Carolina Housewife*, 163.

31 New Orleans Christian Woman's Exchange, "Orange Peel Syrup," *The Creole Cookery Book* (New Orleans: T. H. Thomason, 1885), 152.

32 Alexis Soyer, *The Modern Housewife* (New York: D. Appleton, 1850), 46. This translation of Soyer's *Ménagère* "edited by an American Housekeeper" made a

point of advertising on its title page that it featured meals prepared for "The Nursery and Sick Room."

33 Lane, *365 Orange Recipes*, 21.

CHAPTER EIGHTEEN

1 Harry Hammond, *South Carolina: Resources and Population, Institutions and Industries* (Columbia: S.C. Dept. of Agriculture, 1883), 12.

2 *Report of the Secretary of Agriculture* (Washington, DC: USDA, 1854), 98–99.

3 Robert Mills, *Statistics of South Carolina* (Columbia: Hurlbut and Lloyd, 1826), 480–81.

4 John Lorain, "Indian Corn," *United States Magazine of Science, Art, Manufactures* 2, no. 11 (1826): 244.

5 "Beaufort District—Past, Present, and Future," *Continental Monthly* 1 (1862): 384–85.

6 Trudy Eden, *The Early American Table: Food and Society in the New World* (DeKalb: Northern Illinois University Press, 2008), 23–44.

7 *Southern Agriculturist* (1838): 180–81.

8 Mills, *Statistics of South Carolina*, 481.

9 J. A. Turner, *The Cotton Planter's Manual* (New York: Orange Judd, 1857), 133.

10 *The Hasty Pudding: A Poem in Three Cantos by Joel Barlow with a Memoir on Maize or Indian Corn*, compiled by D. J. Browne (New York: W. H. Graham 1847), 51.

11 Glenn Roberts, http://www.ansonmills.com/biographies.

12 D. J. Browne, "Maize or Indian Corn," *Annual Report of the American Institute of the City of New York* (New York, 1847), 444.

13 Ibid., 446.

14 Damon Lee Fowler, *Classic Southern Cooking* (Layton, UT: Gibbs Smith, 2008), 329–30.

15 Ming-Mao Sun, Sailila E. Abdula, Hye-Jung Lee, Young-Chan Cho, Long-Zhi Han, Hee-Jong Koh, and Yong-Gu Cho, "Molecular Aspect of Good Eating Quality Formation in Japonica Rice," *PLoS ONE* 6, no. 4 (2011): e18385. doi: 10.1371/journal.pone.0018385.

16 I do not raise the additional issue that taste for animals matters in creating vegetables nearly as much as taste for humans. I have discussed the nineteenth-century measurement of saliva secretion in livestock to determine taste preferences in "The Roots of Taste," *Common-Place* 11, no. 3 (April 2011), http://www.common-place.org/vol-11/no-03/shields/.

INDEX